RULING BY TASK FORCE

RULING BY TASK FORCE

The Politico's Guide to Labour's new elite

by Anthony Barker

with Iain Byrne and Anjuli Veall

Politico's

In association with Democratic Audit

First Published in Great Britain
By Politico's Publishing
8 Artillery Row, London, SW1P 1RZ, England

Telephone: 0171 931 0090
Email politicos@artillery-row.demon.co.uk
Website http://www.politicos.co.uk

A catalogue record for this book is available from the British Library.

ISBN 1 90230 119 6

Typeset and designed by Tony Garrett
Printed and bound in Great Britain by St Edmundsbury Press
Cover design by Ad Vantage.

CONTENTS

The contributors

Anthony Barker has directed this research project on task forces as well as writing 'Invited to the Party', the analytical commentary. Anthony Barker has specialised in British government, Parliament and public policy-making at the Department of Government, University of Essex since 1967 and previously at the University of Bristol. His research work has included the rise of quasi-government (quangos) in Britain; the senior civil service; public inquiries into land-use planning disputes, major tragic accidents and policy issues at large; and committees, commissions or other groups advising government on future policy and practice ('decision advice processes'). The Labour government's 'outside' task forces and advisory groups, and internal policy reviews, forms one novel aspect of these processes. A book on this theme is in hand for publication next year.

Iain Byrne, formerly research officer with the Democratic Audit, is now research officer with the Human Rights Incorporation Project, King's College, London.

Anjuli Veall, formerly a researcher with the Audit, now works for Charter 88.

Professor Lord Smith of Clifton encouraged and commissioned this Democratic Audit study as chair of the Joseph Rowntree Reform Trust. Lord Smith, formerly Vice-Chancellor of the University of Ulster, is a political scientist and author of several books, including *Anti-Politics: consensus, protest and reform* and *The Politics of the Corporate Economy*

About Democratic Audit

The Democratic Audit is a specialist research organisation that inquires into the quality of democracy and political freedoms in the UK. The Audit monitors democracy and political freedom in Britain through a series of reports at regular intervals. It is an independent and non-partisan organisation, which is based at the Human Rights Centre, University of Essex.

Author's acknowledgements

The author acknowledges with warmest thanks the considerable assistance of many civil servants from junior to most senior and nominated 'outside' members of task forces, policy reviews and advisory groups. Whether giving information about particular groups, passing copies of minutes and other papers, or discussing their experiences and perceptions of being on a group, or of providing secretarial support, these sources have been invaluable in filling out this study. Some 12 Permanent and Deputy Secretaries at the head of departments also agreed to discuss the task force 'phenomenon' in more general terms, as part of the new Labour government's initial impact and working style. All civil servants and outsider members were promised anonymity to encourage frankness and the supply of information.

The author also acknowledges the support of the Economic and Social Research Council for his research into 'decision advice processes' in British government and public affairs at large, of which this research and analysis forms a part (grant R000235959). He also thanks the Joseph Rowntree Reform Trust for funding much of the detailed research into task forces and similar bodies through the Democratic Audit, at the University of Essex. Particular thanks are due to Iain Byrne and Anjuli Veall, former research officers with the Democratic Audit, for their work on the listings in this report and other research, and to Ruth Deyermond for her supplementary research support.

Stuart Weir, director of the Democratic Audit, commissioned, guided and edited this report. Both he and Professor David Beetham, of the Centre for Democratisation Studies, Leeds University, commented valuably on the author's commentary. Pam Short provided high-quality word-processing; Tony Garrett transformed a mass of data into a clear design; and John Berry, of Politico's, and Jacqui Buckley, took care of production. Thanks are due to all of them.

This is the first comprehensive study of an elaborate and uncertain novel aspect of British government and contains a mass of detail from a variety of sources. Even after months of listing and checking, some errors in people's names, affiliations or classification will have survived and apologies are offered in advance.

November 1999

PREFACE

The 'Task Force Revolution' is a dramatic event in British government because of its extensive scope and potential consequences. Being a constitutional watchdog is like painting the Forth Bridge: the work is never-ending. No sooner had the Nolan Committee on Standards in Public Life proposed reforms to minimise partisan appointments to quangos and other public bodies, than new creatures appeared in the *demi-monde* of Whitehall in the form of Task Forces, Advisory Groups and Policy Reviews. Patronage and nepotism had characterised appointments to the former, and had been an integral part of the sleaze that had become increasingly a feature of the Thatcher and Major governments.

Now, this new breed of bodies, invented by the Blair administration, needed to be subject to close scrutiny from the outset lest they, too, degenerated. Eternal vigilance is always necessary, which is why I proposed to Democratic Audit, which undertook the first full analysis of quangos, that it should carry out an early investigation of this new 'genetically modified' mutation in the body politic.

The outcome is this meticulous analysis by Anthony Barker, a specialist observer of government in Britain and one of the first to realise the significance of quangos (which he himself named). Thus this study of the new species of governing agencies follows on naturally from his earlier pioneering work. It is path-breaking, both in its detailed account of the bacterial growth of no less than 295 Task Forces to date – and still counting – and in the precautionary observations he makes to prevent them descending into a corrupt, cosy 'court politics' of favourites and hangers on. Indeed, one of the best antidotes to infection of any political sleaze is an early examination of their role, functions and behaviour, together with the promise of a watching brief being kept on their future evolution. So far, but it is early days, major problems have not arisen: they remain latent rather than blatant, but it is a potential sleaze minefield.

The 'Task Force Revolution' is an important development in the policy-making processes of British government. It is, however, but the latest in a series of suggestions and attempts to co-opt the expertise and experience of industrial, commercial and consumer groups into the formulation, scrutiny and even implementation of public policy that have littered British political history in the twentieth century. These range from the early proposal of the Webbs for an industrial and social chamber in Westminster (co-equal with the House of Commons) and Winston Churchill's suggestion for an industrial sub-parliament, to the creation of the National Economic Development Council and its 'little Neddy' offshoots that

waxed and waned throughout the governments of Macmillan, Wilson, Heath and Callaghan. The recommendations of the Fulton report on the civil service, the creation of a Central Policy Review Staff attached to 10 Downing Street, the appointment of ministerial special advisers, and Margaret Thatcher's recruitment of the two retailers – Derek Rayner and Roy Griffiths – to shake up Whitehall, are all part and parcel of attempts to modernise the state by successive governments.

It seems the leitmotif that runs throughout twentieth century government is a prime ministerial feeling of the need to import business expertise from outside Whitehall; to supplement the nineteenth century institutions of civil service, cabinet and Parliament with other more relevant, speedy and direct channels of advice and action, positioned in a more flexible set of arrangements. And who would gainsay such experiments, even though they create more problems?

It may well be, as Peter Mandelson has observed, that the era of representative democracy as developed over the last century and a half, is coming to a close. The 'Task Force Revolution' may be a symptom of this and also another nail in its coffin; certainly, other recent trends, such as the decline in the status of Parliament and cabinet, and government backing for a largely appointed second chamber, support the Mandelson view.

We must, therefore, be on our guard lest the wider principles of election and of accountability to the public are diminished or jettisoned. The 'elite participation' of some 2,500 people, mainly from private and public producer interests, in the task forces, however valuable their skills and opinions, can hardly be acceptable as a substitute for traditional forms of government accountability; and in any case, they themselves will need to be scrutinised, as Anthony Barker remarks. The age-old tension between efficiency and democracy, between collegium and hierarchy, remains and its proper mediation is one that is crucial for a democratic country whose constitution is still uncodified. At the very least, the task forces should be counted; astonishingly, this survey is the first to attempt to make a comprehensive count, something that government itself has not accomplished. Further, without impeding their efficiency, they should be tracked and monitored from both the standpoint of public accountability and management by government.

Most crucially they must not be allowed to proffer policy advice and influence policy and practice without wide political debate. They must not be allowed to coagulate into an hermetically sealed policy universe that effectively undermines due process and inhibits widespread open discussion. The danger of their functional role, on which Anthony Barker rightly lays such great emphasis, is that it tends to de-politicise many issues and problems which properly lie within the political sphere. At least, their deliberations, researches and processes should be rendered transparent to Parliament and the public.

Indeed, if they are part of a development to

modernise the activities of government, they should surely be put on the Internet in ways which not only render them transparent, but which also make possible much greater interactivity with citizens who are excluded from this elite form of inclusiveness. Successive governments have urged greater exploitation of the potentialities afforded by the revolution in information technology. More than 20 years ago, both Tony Benn and Jeremy Bray anticipated that the link-up between computers and government could as easily be made to serve democracy as ushering in the 'Big Brother' state. Very few of these new bodies have set up web-sites of their own. In the interests of open government this neglect of the public should be speedily remedied.

Information technology can go a long way in further developing democratic societies in the next century by making them more direct as well as more representative in character. The global polis is attainable, but that is another project for Democratic Audit. Meanwhile, this report offers the first extensive review of a new governing species that has largely avoided the public gaze. It will be an invaluable source for politicians, journalists, students of politics, and even Whitehall itself and, most importantly, for the concerned citizen.

Trevor Smith
(Professor Lord Smith of Clifton)
November 1999

PART ONE

ANALYSIS OF THE TASK FORCE PHENOMENON

SUMMARY

The purpose of this Democratic Audit report and the substantial listings in part 2 is to present and discuss a comprehensive review of the unprecedented wave of task forces, advisory groups, forums, and other advisory bodies on public policy issues set up by Labour ministers since 1997.

The Democratic Audit undertook the first full analysis of quangos in the early 1990s and, at the prompting of the Rowntree Reform Trust, asked Anthony Barker, Reader in Government at the University of Essex and a specialist in British government, to expand on his personal research on task forces[1] and examine the political and constitutional issues which these new creations raise. Anthony Barker's commentary, 'Invited to the Party', and brief descriptions by him of 25 task forces and other external bodies and their varied functions follow this summary.

Part 2 contains a list (List 1.1) of the 295 task forces and other bodies, and their sub-groups[2], which are largely, often wholly, composed of 'outsiders' (non-civil servants) which the government established in 1997-98. The list gives the known occupations or affiliations of the members of these 'external' advisory bodies. There is additionally a necessarily incomplete list of similar bodies set up in 1999; these amounted to 23 bodies by the shut-off date for this research exercise. A list (List 2.1) of internal Whitehall policy reviews (conducted by civil servants working to ministers) created in 1997-98 follows, and is supplemented by a similarly partial list of such reviews launched in 1999.

The lists for 1997-98 are as close to being comprehensive as is possible after intense research and media and website searches can make them. However, there is no ultimate 'correct' total for either 'external' task forces and bodies, or for 'internal' exercises. Central government has no across-the-board rules for establishing such bodies or co-ordinating their existence. Departments create and log them in often informal fashion and by varying practices. The definitions of such bodies are unformed, their titles vary considerably, official practices on consulting outsiders differ, and minor sub-groups proliferate but may meet only once or not at all (so any list-maker must use discretion on which of them to include). Departments sometimes fail to issue press releases, or to post details on their websites, and may even have no record of their existence.

As a result, even the Cabinet Office is unable to provide a full count; and some departments themselves cannot list all their own groups. Indeed, the Secretary of State's office at the Department of Trade and Industry proved to be ignorant of an advisory group specifically set up to give advice to his predecessor.

In all, government ministers and departments are known to have set up 318 task forces and 'external' advisory bodies since May 1997. This summary and report concentrate on the 295 task forces and other 'external' bodies created in 1997-98. A total of 2,459 'outsiders' served as chairs or members of these groups, occupying 3,103 places in all. Table 2 on page 27 in Anthony Barker's commentary shows their distribution between departments and sets out their occupations and the interest groups to which they may be said to belong. The additional outsider groups launched in 1999 are not likely to alter the broad analysis which emerges from our research, as the rate of new creations is very much slower and so far fewer people are engaged in giving advice. The net number of these bodies is also declining sharply, as they submit their final reports and usually shut down. About one dozen have become or led to the creation of standing bodies, adding to the number of new advisory and executive quangos which Labour has created. (Democratic Audit will analyse the government's use of quangos in spring 2000).

Anthony Barker's commentary places task forces and internal reviews in the context of traditional advice-giving and consultation processes in British government. He examines the Labour government's claims to have established a 'collaborative', or 'inclusive', style of government and explores why ministers wanted some 500 policy exercises in its early years. His analysis draws on interviews with civil servants and outside members of task forces. To illustrate the process in more detail, he describes and discusses the role and work of six of the more publicised 'task forces' – on better regulation, the Rogers review of urban planning, Eyre on the Royal Opera House, energy tax, the bruising Mellors football task force, and Bernard Crick's group on citizenship education. A functional analysis of the varied tasks which some 25 task forces have undertaken runs alongside the commentary.

Barker concludes that task forces do create a more inclusive and focused advice-gathering process than previous practice in consulting interested parties by government departments. He emphasises the functional nature of the process and the role of task forces in providing practitioner experience and advice, or in mobilising outside interests and professions in support of government objectives. He recommends the more open creation and operation of external advisory groups; better practice, he argues, would not limit ministers' rights to take in information and advice and to shape and manage the process to serve policy priorities. Constitutional and democratic issues would come into play if ministers seemed to cut out alternative sources while also arranging good access for their favoured sources. This unwelcome trend would stoke up charges of Labour 'cronyism', but he does not consider that such charges are justified by current practice. In the preface, Trevor Smith also argues strongly for more transparency in the operation of task forces, and warns that the drive for efficient government must not be at the cost of democratic and accountable government.

'INVITED TO THE PARTY'

Anthony Barker

1. Introduction

During the long pre-election period before his party's victory on 1st May 1997, Tony Blair was careful not to promise an initial period of '100 days of dynamic action', as Harold Wilson had done when preparing to launch his new Labour government in October 1964 (copying Jack Kennedy in 1960). The new Labour Government was just as committed as its two predecessors with ample Commons majorities (in 1945 and 1966) to redeem its leading pledges and many other lesser promises and hopes offered in its manifesto (177 pledges or 'action points' on Labour's own official figures).[1] Immediate steps were taken on the key pledges, notably the 'New Deal' transferring younger people from social security benefit into subsidised jobs, and on education and health.

But the Blair government's first three months were not remarkable or unprecedented, compared to the Attlee and Wilson debuts, because of these actions on flagship pledges. They were novel because of the snow storm of apparently countless 'task forces', 'advisory groups' and 'policy reviews' which ministers created to investigate and recommend new policies and practices or, in some cases, practical means of implementing policies on which Labour had already largely settled while still in Opposition. There were indeed, an initial '100 days of dynamic action' from Labour, but a good part of this dynamism was in launching a large number of what would become more than 300 'external' task forces, advisory or 'action' groups and about 200 internal departmental policy reviews. Table 1 offers an initial picture of this task force and review phenomenon, listed by Departments up to 31 December 1998.

The place of task forces in government advice-gathering

Since the initial flood of external policy groups and internal policy reviews during mid-1997, it has pleased some ministers or their Whitehall press officers (and fully satisfied the news media) to call almost any new inquiry exercise a 'new government task force'. A specialist research report must firstly distinguish this new term from more familiar ones in the policy inquiry field such as 'consultation' and 'review'. It should then offer some context for the new groups within established forms of external policy advice.

Whitehall Departments' **consultations** of 'interested parties' (and usually, also, the general public) are a routine part of civil service work. They normally rest on an official paper asking for opinions on various policy or administrative options and sometimes seeking reactions to probable or definite new official decisions. They are not policy inquiry exercises in the same sense as departmental policy reviews may claim to be. Consultations fall outside this Report's concerns with Labour's innovations since 1997 because it would be impossible to determine which of the many departmental consultations of May 1997 to December 1998 were directly stimulated by the change of government: the steady flow of these routine exercises irrespective of elections is too great to allow any clear comparison.

The **departmental policy review** is a broader (but not always open or announced) exercise in which current policy and practice is supposed to be

Portrait gallery

Task forces and similar bodies cover a multiplicity of issues and serve a variety of purposes. The following notes on 25 individual bodies in this column (from page 13 onwards) accompany the general analysis contained in the commentary to give a flavour of the diversity of functions they undertake. Task forces are not confined to giving ministers and Whitehall policy advice, nor are they necessarily about gaining privileged access or information, as some critics have assumed. Classifying the advisory bodies by their apparent purpose or function cannot be a strict or neat exercise. But this selection does show the various tasks or objectives that they are set, including providing information and advice *inputs* into Whitehall (Nos. 1 to 14) or promoting *outputs* from Whitehall in support of policy goals or the general public interest (Nos.15 to 25). The elaborate form this exercise takes is illustrated by the 25 bodies having 31 sub-groups to back them up, while the Social Exclusion Unit's Policy Action Teams (Note No. 5) – counted here as only one, for the sake of illustration – number 18, all being of equal status rather than sub-groups to a leading group. Page references are to Lists 1.1. and 1.2.

compared with new options. Again, not even the many senior officials who launched and oversaw the upsurge of these departmental ('internal') policy reviews after 1st May 1997 could say which arose directly from new Labour ministers and which were 'policy maintenance jobs' (as one Cabinet Office official describes them) which must often await a new minister or new government following some delay or even neglect. Table 1 (below) offers a total of 207 internal reviews in the 20 months covered: List 2.1 names them, with some Notes. These include mentions of informal groups of 'outsiders' (usually from representative 'interested parties' or experts) being invited in to discuss a policy review, possible also seeing internal papers or hearing about matters which officials and ministers might not wish to discuss in public. The relatively few outsiders associated (sometimes secretly) with departmental policy reviews as advisers or assessors are not included in this study: their role is traditional and their numbers are small compared with the 'task force phenomenon'.

Although it makes very little difference in substance whether an invited outside group forms part of an internal policy review or are members of a task force, the soft borderline between the two types of external advice-seeking certainly bedevils analysis – particularly trying to count 'internal' and 'external' exercises separately. Not many of the internal reviews in List 2.1 had an outside advisory group but relied instead on officials gathering written or oral information and offering ministers the usual type of conclusions and options. There are two broadly distinct classes of policy exercise – external and internal

Table 1: **Numbers of task forces and their sub-groups** (presented in List 1.1, below) and internal policy review (List 2.1, below) launched by each ministerial Government Department, 1 May 1997 – 31 December 1998. (Lists 1.2 and 2.2, below, list further groups and reviews of 1999)

		Task Forces (List 1.1) *see below*	Internal policy reviews (List 2.1) *see below*	Department totals
1	**Ministry of Agriculture**	6	13	19
2	**Attorney-General**	1	-	1
3	**Cabinet Office**	21	9	30
4	**Department of Culture, Media and Sport**	30	3	33
5	**Ministry of Defence**	4	3	7
	Department for Education and Employment			
	Education issues	(36)	(1)	(37)
	Employment and training issues	(15)	(2)	(17)
6	**DfEE TOTAL**	51	3	54
	Department of the Environment, Transport, Regions			
	Environment issues	(35)	(24)	(59)
	Transport issues	(4)	(13)	(17)
7	**DETR Total**	39	37	76
8	**Foreign and Commonwealth Office**	1	2	3
9	**Department of Health**	26	6	32
10	**Home Office**	17	30	47
11	**Department for International Development**	1	2	3
12	**Lord Chancellor's Department**	4	6	10
13	**Northern Ireland Office**	28	11	39
14	**Scottish Office**	15	28	43
15	**Department of Social Security**	6	5	11
16	**Department of Trade and Industry**	26	20	46
17	**H.M. Treasury**	12	22	34
18	**Welsh Office**	7	7	14
	Total	295	207	502

– but they overlap in their use of (often quite informal) outsiders' groups.

Coming next to this Report's principal topic – **the task force, advisory or action groups** launched in 1997-98 – there are 295 listed in List 1.1. Again, one cannot know which would have been born into a fifth Conservative administration: some are also 'policy maintenance jobs' which even a long-term government with (according to some of the senior civil servants interviewed for this study) little appetite to consult or review would have found to be necessary. A cautiously inclusive approach to making this list has deliberatively drawn in some marginal and arguable cases. Deliberate exclusions include the two **royal commissions** created by Labour (on long term care and the House of Lords); the **standing expert advisory committees** – notably at Health and Agriculture – offering medical and other scientific advice; and the **standing statutory advisory boards** which a few Departments are obliged by law to maintain. Otherwise, it is hoped that every group of 'outsiders' (not officials or ministers) recruited between 1st May 1997 and 31st December 1998 for some policy review or 'policy action' support – whether sitting on their own or alongside ministers and officials – appears in List 1.1. (A few of the listed groups did exist under the Conservatives but were re-launched, often with different terms or members, by Labour ministers.)[2]

With Labour's two royal commissions set aside, what of the more common traditional policy inquiry device of the **departmental committee of inquiry** (dci)? This has been, for more than a century, a less formal version of a royal commission and, latterly, had largely replaced the commission form. Since 1997 no new policy inquiry appears to have been formally called a 'dci' although several have been launched, for example the Department of Culture's 'Review Panel' on the BBC's finances and license fee (page 55) or its 'Review' of major sporting events on television (page 60). Despite their new names, both committees had only outsiders as members (no ministers or officials) and appear to have taken their evidence and produced and submitted their reports in the traditional arm's-length manner of a dci. Many others on the list could claim the same, particularly those with expert members providing a technical report. So, to a significant extent, Labour's 'rule by task force' has been an overlay of new methods on a continuation of traditional outside departmental committee of inquiry (dci) methods, with the new 'task force' and other labels applied at large. What ministers or their officials chose to call the many new groups which they launched in mid-1997 does not matter, even though incoherence in government operations is not admirable. There has been almost no hierarchy or reasoning behind calling some 295 external groups task forces, reviews, fundamental (or independent) reviews, advisory (or consultative) committees, working (or study, or expert, or management) groups, independent (or expert) panels, forums, quality council or 'scoping group' – and various other things. One or two ideas are conveyed by some of these labels, notably that a 'forum' or 'sounding board' (e.g., Tourism Forum (page 61) or Housing Sounding Board (page 96)) is for discussions rather than the definite work plan leading to a report or practical conclusions of a Working Group (such as Northern Ireland's Equality Commission Working Group (page 118) or Scotland's Working Group to Promote Biodiversity in Agriculture (page 122). These four examples also serve to show how the new-style external groups are often asked to consider how best to design and deliver an established Labour government policy rather than going off to consider what public policy should be and returning in due course with a report. The Tourism Forum and Housing Sounding Board have the responsible minister listed as their chairs while the biodiversity group was chaired by a Scottish Office official.

A further question worth asking about the task force initiative concerns the openness or secrecy of their working. An open method would entail not only the usual long list of potentially interested bodies being approached for any views but also meetings with such bodies for discussion – and then going beyond them to any member of the public, for either written or oral reactions, including at a public meeting. Although no systematic evidence on this point has been gathered, the impression gained while preparing this Report is that only some of

Providing Information and Advice to Whitehall

1. Fundamental Review of Transport Policy (DETR)

Labour's 1997 manifesto pledged 'an effective and integrated transport policy' and an 'overall strategic review of the roads programme'. The white paper presenting both took 14 months to emerge (July 1998). This small group of experts and practitioners (see page 100) had four research experts (including Professor David Begg, a transport management academic, as chair), two business, one trade union (TGWU) and one public transport practitioner as members. The remit was 'to provide integrated and expert advice on how best to define, implement, organise and fund' a new integrated policy. A successor standing body – the Commission for Integrated Transport – began work in 1999 with Begg in the chair and only one other review member, Stephen Joseph of Transport 2000. The purpose of this new advisory quango (non-departmental public body) is to monitor and report on the implementation of the July 1998 white paper – an unusual external spur for a department and ministers to create.

2. Youth Justice Task Force (Home Office)

The archetype 'action' rather than 'policy search' task force. Labour's 1997 manifesto promised to hasten, focus and co-ordinate youth justice (with young people responsible for seven million crimes a year). This 18-member task force (page 118) was not asked to reconsider the pledge, but to 'drive forward' government plans agreed by a ministerial review, offered for public consultation, confirmed in a white paper (No More Excuses, November 1997) and enacted in the Crime and Disorder Act. With the Home Secretary's Senior Policy Adviser, Norman Warner, as its chair, this mixed group of four senior officials (from three departments); four courts practitioners; three senior police officers; one county social services director; one head teacher; one Marks and Spencer executive; were joined by a recently retired chief probation officer and the director of a penal policy lobby group. There was no academic or research specialist. As intended, the task force's report mapped out ground for a new executive (monitoring and fund-allocating) quango: the Youth Justice Board. Norman (now Lord) Warner became its chair and one or two task force members applied for and were offered places on its board, following 'Nolan rules' requiring advertisement and formal selection methods.

Government seeks Expert Advice on Existing Scientific Knowledge and Current Research for Potential Policy Use

3. Review of the Latest Information Available on Inequalities in Health (Department of Health)

This small expert group (three epidemiologists, two health policy researchers and one public health director) reviewed the current scientific knowledge for policy-making to fulfil the manifesto pledge that 'Labour will set new goals for improving the overall health of the nation which recognise the impact that poverty, poor housing, unemployment and a polluted environment have on health'.) Sir Donald Acheson, the former Chief Medical Officer, Department of Health (and previously clinical epidemiologist) took the chair (see page 103).

4. Review of the Evidence Relating to Silicone Breast Implants (Health)

This entirely medical/expert practitioner group of six (page 105) assessed not only current scientific knowledge on risk from these implants but also best practice on advising patients requesting or considering this operation. This was not a manifesto issue but rather an example of technical issues which arise continually, demanding an authoritative review and recommendation as the basis for an official view and policy.

the 1997-99 task forces and internal reviews have reflected and carried forward the greater openness already noticeable before the general election. The Cabinet Office's new guide to Departments on conducting policy or practice consultations (which are outwith this Report) was already saying that arranging for written comments from the circulated 'interested parties' was no longer good enough: meetings were now necessary. But to advertise public meetings (or the taking of arranged evidence in public: 'hearings') is still unusual although no longer rare.

The major practical issue is to identify the relevant 'public', which very often does not exist beyond the range of interested bodies. Of the six internal groups featured in section 2, below, only the Urban and Football Task Forces held open meetings which approached being 'public'. The Football Task Force's were actually private: (meetings with directors, players and supporters of various football clubs to gain their views of the task force's list of issues). But to see four very senior Whitehall mandarins accompanying their distinguished business chair (Lord Marshall) to meetings with local interests affected by energy tax ideas (and, moreover, going outside London for the purpose) was progress indeed. The jobs to be done by some 300 outside groups have varied so much that a single framework of open or closed working methods is hard to conceive. A technical or management review of a problem (whether, say, the licensing of fishing vessels or the Royal Opera House) does not have a public opinion level to its actual working remit (as opposed to any wider issues of sea-fishing or opera and dance) in the way that a law reform or policy review exercise does. Thus the specialist or minority interest of the Review of the Law Relating to Surrogacy (page 105) as well as the much broader 'constituency' of the Disability Rights Task Force (page 81) – the latter reputed to have been particularly 'open' in operation – both included public meetings in various parts of the country. In practice, many advertised public meetings of task forces, a royal commission, the Nolan-Neill committee on public standards, etc., will attract few members of the general public who are not already supporters of one of the interested bodies in that field – and then probably only to listen to what these bodies have to say. But the principle is important and the marginal benefit, however modest, is real. As with the openness of public bodies (quangos) current and future task forces should be assessed on this measure using the test of much more openness being required unless clear harm to their work or the public interest can be shown.

The derivation of Labour's task force initiative from the party's election manifesto is an obvious feature to investigate and a full analysis has been made for this Report. It is made rather inconsequential, however, by the very large number of task forces and other external groups (at least 295, as presented in List 1.1) greatly outnumbering the Labour Party's own estimate of 177 manifesto pledges or 'action points' (mentioned above). With so many groups established, no special status attaches to either a manifesto pledge to establish a review on some issue or a pledge of action which has precipitated an external or internal policy review. The manifesto promised to establish or continue some 20 task forces or policy reviews (including internal departmental reviews) and ten of these were launched in the government's first year. Five more were also launched in other forms: a royal commission on long term care; the House of Commons modernisation committee and a review of EU legislation work; asking the Nolan-Neill committee on standards in public life to study party financing; and the independent commission on the voting system ('Jenkins'). Almost all major topics promised a review of some kind had been covered within 12 months. In the case of Lords reform, the promised joint select committee of MPs and peers will now await the intervening royal commission on reform options which is working closely to the government's elaborate white paper of early 1999: the joint committee will comment on the royal commission's work.

It may be prudent to conclude this outline of the new task forces with an elementary reminder that they are temporary inquiry groups which (normally) report and then disband. Only about one dozen have so far been turned into standing advisory bodies, included in the annual *Public Bodies* volumes as Non-Departmental Public Bodies and so properly to be called advisory quangos. Some others (Housing Sounding Board, Music Forum) were expected to be less formalised standing bodies, simply discussing problems with their Department, perhaps quarterly. Such standing discussion groups are not novel in Whitehall. But to call the entire task force set-up, as set out in a list such as List 1.1, 'Labour's new quangos' – as some hostile critics from right and left, as well as the Opposition, originally did – was merely to confuse temporary inquiry and advice with standing public bodies disposing of huge amounts of public money.[3]

Task forces and joined-up government

Having outlined the overlap of the task force labelling and style with traditional forms of departmental consultations and outside committees of inquiry, another context deserves to be noted. This is the wider language of public participation and mutual adjustment which Labour has (rather vaguely) claimed as its style of government. The task forces and policy review groups themselves have been offered as a major exercise in 'inclusiveness': Labour ministers reaching out to wider civil society – most notably and controversially to private business – inviting them to 'join the party' and help shape new public policy. Alongside 'inclusiveness', there has been some emphasis on 'partnership' with non-government interests to solve difficult problems. Academic observers have called this approach 'collaborative government'.[4]

The practical impetus is to tackle the most knotty and recalcitrant ('wicked') policy problems afresh and without conflict of aims or methods. As Labour has reiterated, 'joined-up' (that is, far reaching and inter-connected) policy problems require 'joined-up' government solutions. As to what exactly to do, the Prime Minister's phrase provides the key: 'what's best is what works'.

Armed with this question-begging agnosticism on methods, the government reckons to 'transform' public services – notably the NHS – over ten years. As a context for the task forces and policy reviews aspect of Labour's collaborative government, only two points need to be made. An administration with these ambitions must be kept well-informed on the problems and progress of the policy fields being reformed. That entails a strong and continuing task force and policy review style in close touch with actual practitioners as well as the usual interest groups. Secondly, there is a political difference between policy fields and issues where the government relies on these working interests for information on current trends and difficulties and those where Departments are not so dependent. If they truly depend on outside private interests for their own bearings on a problem, 'collaborative government' is unavoidable. If they do not, they may practise it from political choice — or, at least, claim to be doing so. Thus, for example, the Ministry of Defence's 'Smart Procurement Partnership' with its commercial contractors on page 66 is required by the Ministry's information dependency on these firms for their technical operating details and commercial returns. The finer points of Labour's new financial regime for local government ('Best Value') do not require a genuinely collaborative 'partnership' approach because the Department (DETR) does not depend on councils for equivalent information: it has the Audit Commission as its principal independent source. If DETR's ministers promised 'partnership' to local authorities (as they did in the summer of 1997) it was from political choice.

Labour's task force and policy review theme is, therefore, only one strand in Labour's claims to be developing a new type of collaborative government under which participation and inclusiveness will help to crack the wicked problems by applying joined-up solutions.

Why did Labour ministers want 500 policy reviews?

Why did Labour ministers commission such a vast number of ad hoc policy review groups, involving nearly 2500 'outsiders'? This author's interviews with

Government seeks Expert Advice on Pending Science-based Policy Issues

5. Review of Bovine TB in Cattle and Badgers (Ministry of Agriculture)

On the heated issue of whether badgers spread bovine TB among cattle, the new government inherited the MAFF research-based strategy of experimental, area-based, selective attempts to kill all badgers to permit comparison of resulting bovine TB figures. Three review members of this review group (page 41) were statistics/research design experts and three were animal disease experts (notably cattle and badger diseases). Their scientific 'objectivity' in overseeing and analysing this national experiment (previously proposed in the Krebs report on the badger/TB issues) remains heavily overlaid politically by the refusal of wildlife bodies to support any badger-killing and of some sections of the NFU to advise farmers ever to refrain from it, in the cause of the experiment. This further review group, following on from 'Krebs', was part of a typically difficult battle in which government tries to use 'best scientific advice' to get out of a policy impasse which lacks any agreed scientific or practical basis for policy.

6. Review of the Current Rules on Quarantine of Imported Pet Animals (Agriculture)

This medical/veterinary group (page 42), chaired by a lay academic medical ethicist, performed the classic experts' task of authenticating a potentially dangerous new anti-rabies policy: the 'pet passport, (rather than universal six-month quarantine) which would rely on medical tests and precautions. This was a plain example of a science-based policy change that no government would dare to make without this expert approval. This was a typical traditional departmental committee of inquiry on a technical issue, without the government policy embrace of other task forces and advisory groups since May 1997.

7. Review of the Law Relating to Surrogacy (Department of Health)

Only three experts (one legal ethicist; one medical ethicist and one family psychologist) comprised this review of social policy towards surrogate births (page 105). By no means only, or even mainly, a technical medical exercise, this expert inquiry recommended on easily accessible issues (e.g., paying surrogate mothers and their possibly refusing to give their baby away, as agreed). The group held consultation meetings and surveyed opinion (as described in its report). It was an example of new formal expertise (medical and legal ethics) being employed to obtain authoritative outcomes on morally contested but not technically obscure social issues.

Government seeks Expert and Practitioner Advice and Support in Reviewing or Developing Policy

8. Export Forum (Department of Trade and Industry, jointly with the Foreign Office)

The remit was to assess how well the UK's export programmes work, which includes government efforts (DTI, Foreign Office, British Council, etc.) as well as the private sector's own efforts and joint events such as overseas trade fairs. This broad, 22-member group (page 135) had eight Whitehall officials (two of them joint chairs) from eight departments, plus one official from each of the most relevant quangos (British Council and the British Overseas Trade and Project Boards). Balanced with these were 11 outsiders: six from business; three from leading trade associations: one business development adviser and a single, symbolic place for the TUC. With the DTI's Director-General of Expert Promotion as the main chair, the forum was mainly a listening exercise, with a possible developmental edge to encourage better exporting practice. The DTI's more executive Review of the Structure of Expert Promotion by government was a weightier exercise (page 135).

9. Quality Council on the Northern Ireland Strategy on Alcohol Misuse (and Project Team) (Northern Ireland Office)

This group (page 115) and its 'project team' was a similar review exercise on an established policy field (like export promotion) but with a less discursive, more executive, stance – hence the 21-member project team in its support. The 13-member council had seven NIO officials balancing five public service providers dealing with alcohol misuse and a medical official from the NI Health Promotion Agency (no academic/ research member). The project team was also half NIO officials and almost half alcoholism service providers, with one drinks industry representative and 'Joe Flynn: ex-service user', but no academic/research outsider. Four NIO policy analysis and review officials seem to have met that need. This very common approach to policy overhaul might be called intra-quasi-professional peer review.

more than one dozen Whitehall Permanent Secretaries, directors-general and directors (the former civil service grades 1-3) plus a number of less senior officials who were dealing directly with particular task forces, and also with task force chairs and members themselves, indicated several explanations. The senior officials all spoke about the new government's outward-looking, 'inclusive' style 'working with' the 'stakeholders' whom Whitehall saw as relevant and legitimate in any policy field. These interests and individuals had been (as several Permanent Secretaries put it) 'invited to the party'. (These terms in quotation marks had promptly become approved ministerial and civil service buzz-words by the summer of 1997). The new Labour ministers had brought in this 'policy group' style from Opposition, where it had been the best practical path by which they could have obtained broad-ranging policy knowledge from experts and practitioners in the field in question.

To recruit an outside policy advisory team of informed practitioners currently doing senior jobs in the field in question offered ministers direct practical knowledge; an alternative source of advice to add to the civil service's offerings; a public image of being open and 'inclusive'; and direct influence – even control – over what that outside group would (and would not) be asked to advise and comment upon. Compared with ministers' much more distant relationship with a traditional external departmental committee of inquiry or royal commission, the task force or similar external group offered ministers a more immediate and personal experience. The feedback of advice and opinion from this new type of group would also be much quicker and (in frequent dealings with the ministers' officials) more detailed.

The senior officials interviewed for this report were asked whether the new Labour ministers' wish for a surge of outside advice had reflected their feeling that civil service advice was either suspect (after 18 years of serving Conservative ministers) or under-powered (after serious staff cuts in recent years). The Permanent Secretaries were divided, some thinking that either or both of these considerations had somewhat influenced their own ministers. Government criticism of civil service support had been reported during Labour's first year, although whether it had run beyond the No. 10 Policy Unit into the Cabinet itself had not been quite clear. But several other Permanent Secretaries explained the working relationship derived from a new type of Labour minister who combined the Conservative ministers' common policy-active personal style with a more open and consultative political outlook. They all said that this greater openness to outside knowledge and current experience was welcomed by their Departments, some of them adding that it serves to supplement the hard-pressed policy work of a reduced senior civil service. Several also made the point that the study groups of experts and practitioners which had advised the Labour Opposition had often enjoyed the advantage of current practical experience in the field in question. But this meant they were part of sectional interests, or policy enthusiasts, or Labour supporters – or all three – and not as concerned as civil servants must always be with wider comparisons and national priorities. If that type of committed, sectional advice was carried wholesale into government itself, without being properly offset by what senior civil servants claim is their own objective advice (which, they insist, can come only from the civil service) then real dangers would arise. These senior officials said that they had 'hoped' that a civil service which needed to show new Labour ministers that it had not become conditioned to Conservative thinking would not do so by letting ministers receive outside advice of this kind without question, when its critical examination was essential. These senior officials claimed that their hopes had prevailed. Of course, as any government's principal professional advisers, senior civil servants have a distinctive interest of their own.

If a new government was recruiting outside task forces and advisory groups at the rate of more than two per average day for several months from early May 1997 – while also ordering many additional internal policy reviews to be conducted by civil servants themselves — then the question of the overall political control of these groups' collective pressure for new public expenditure came up promptly and dramatically. The basic control device was Labour's election pledge not to exceed Conservative spending limits for the first two years. With a general spending surge forbidden by a dominant Prime Minister and Chancellor, only those spending pledges which they would endorse could proceed. Other manifesto promises and all other policy topics involving any new spending had to wait – and then be assessed by the new triennial Comprehensive Spending Review (CSR) whose first decision cycle was launched soon after the election and published in July 1998 (Cm 4011).

The joint effect of the two-year spending limit and each Department's year of work on its sections of the overall Whitehall CSR was to suppress immediate new commitments and stimulate the number of task forces, departmental reviews and consultation exercises. Politically, to establish a review is at least better than doing nothing in the eyes of those pressing for action – particularly if the organised interest groups in question can be invited to join the reviewing group for genuinely inclusive (but, probably also, carefully managed) participation in shaping any new policy. So the managed postponement of spending commitments may have been another reason for launching so many studies and reviews.

For its own part, each Department was obliged by the CSR process to state and justify its financial priorities and this in turn required many reviews of existing departmental practices and established commitments. As a result, some of the task forces in List 1.1 – as also many of the internal reviews and consultation exercises, which have been run by officials themselves – had the CSR as their basis in whole or part. If Labour ministers had entered office in 1997 (as they did in 1945 or 1964/66) with no appetite at all for reviewing numerous current policies, there would still have been a marked upsurge of reviews in 1997-99 to meet the unprecedented demands of the first cycle of the new Comprehensive Spending Review. In practice, ministerial enthusiasm for reviews and the Treasury's virtual requirement of them under the new CSR regime combined their forces to produce this regiment of reviews of various types.

2. Task Forces at work: six sketches

Even the briefest glance at the multiplicity of task forces, policy reviews and other bodies (Lists 1.1 and 2.1 below) indicates the great variety of topics, tasks and contexts that they were established to tackle. The lists usually give the members of each body, their backgrounds and other affiliations. Most members are shown as practitioners of some kind within the group's particular area of work; but how the groups have worked or are still working – their constitution and methods, leading to their reporting to ministers – is not so readily listable. Six interesting cases are therefore sketched here, with outline points on their particular features or their relationship to other review groups in associated fields. This deliberately mixed bag comprises: the Better Regulation Task Force (Cabinet Office); the Urban Task Force (Department of the Environment, Transport and the Regions (DETR)); the Advisory Group on including the teaching of citizenship and democracy in the National Curriculum (Department for Education and Employment); the Task Force on taxing industrial energy use (Treasury); the Football Task Force (Department of Culture, Media and Sport) and the Independent Review of London opera (also DCMS).

The Cabinet Office's **Better Regulation Task Force** on page 43 is an unusually potent external review group because (exceptionally) it is supported by a Regulatory Impact Unit, which is part of the Cabinet Office, rather than the usual very small task force or review secretariat. It also carries extra weight because it is a revised version of the Conservatives' Deregulation Task Force which Labour ministers claim to have adjusted to a 'better' balance between dynamic enterprise and producer regulation. One member, Teresa Graham (a leading accountant for small firms) was also on the Conservative government's group. Its very broad but pointed formal remit is to advise on and ensure

Government seeks Practical Information and Advice (plus support and co-operation) to improve Whitehall's Own Working Methods

10. **Social Exclusion Unit: 18 Policy Action Teams (Cabinet Office)**

The 194 'outsider' places on these 18 teams (page 45) seem to be firmly at the 'support' or 'executive' end of the scale, rather than inquiring in a 'policy search' mode. They have been helping the SEU's officials to devise detailed policy and practice on 'cross-cutting' and 'wicked' (recalcitrant) aspects of social exclusion such as school pupil exclusions and truancy, rough sleeping, neighbourhood deprivation and teenage pregnancy (on all of which the Unit has issued reports in 1998-1999). Their expert and practitioner inputs are managed by extensive multiple memberships of the 18 groups held by SEU and other officials. Each PAT has its particular topic and 'champion minister'. These PATs are distinguishable in their purpose and operations from the other 'outsider' groups. More cross-cutting units (and, probably also, more PATs) are expected on the Whitehall scene, following the white paper on Modernising Government of Spring 1999. They form a new type of official advice-seeking, under the close 'policy embrace' of officials and ministers.

11. **Smart Procurement Partnerships Group and Procurement Consultation Group (Ministry of Defence)**

The senior outsider element here is the representation of a conventional trade association (the Defence Industry Council) on the MoD partnerships group set up to discuss this new defence equipment 'smart procurement' policy (or, perhaps, philosophy) of close collaboration with contractors (page 66). A junior defence minister takes the chair. Its support through the Procurement Consultation Group (page 67) has been highly unconventional, although quite small-scale, involving contractors' managers working alongside MoD Procurement Executive staff (not simply liaising or advising). List 1.1 (page 67) indicates this gratis service to MoD only notionally because it is being arranged informally and ad hoc.

12. **Review of the Structure of Export Promotion (DTI)**

This third example (page 135) of using outsiders to help improve Whitehall's own systems and methods was linked to the Expert Forum (see Note 8). As mentioned there, this senior review of Whitehall's export promotion efforts was the more applied side of this matter. With the Head of the Home Civil Service as chair, two very senior business figures and two others reviewed the subject with senior officials including a Foreign Office representative and the DTI's Director-General of Export Promotion (Tom Harris) (who also chaired the Export Forum). With so many firms affected by Whitehall's export promotions, it was odd that no 'peak' trade association, such as the CBI, was involved in this exercise.

Government establishes a 'Fire Brigade' Group for Urgent Information and Lobbying from Interested Parties on a Hot Political Issue

13. Oil and Gas Industry Task Force (DTI)

This 'fire brigade' group is perhaps the strongest example of 'bilateral corporatism' (business and government: no trade unions) among the government's outsider bodies. It was established (see page 136) because low oil prices have hit a previously highly profitable industry and declining UK production means that the UK will soon revert to being a net importer. Three officers of the off-shore trade association (all also leading industry executives) were joined by six further senior industry figures to press their case with energy ministers in London and Edinburgh (as chair and vice-chair of the task force) and four very senior officials (three at Director-General, former Grade 2, Deputy Secretary, level). It should not be assumed that the industry's lobbying of government has been the sole process at work: there is scope for official influence over the industry's leaders on how they might alleviate their problems.

14. Road Haulage Forum (Department of the Environment, Transport and the Regions)

This forum (page 145), created by the DETR in 1999, is both simpler and less significant than a high-powered task force such as the oil and gas industry task force (above). It was offered by the Minister of Transport as a 'civilised' alternative to the blockade of roads by trucking companies' lorries in protest at vehicle taxation, etc. The minimal nature of its conciliatory role was shown by the invitation to the first meeting of only the chief officer of the Road Haulage Association, although its representation was broadened after his protest. This 'fire brigade' or complaints session may develop into a mutually respected regular forum, despite its narrow and reactive original basis. It is a part of government advice-seeking activity and serves to confirm that listening to people complaining is a significant part of ministers' work.

'necessary' and 'affordable' government regulation of business, 'taking particular account of the needs of small businesses'.

It has an unusually actively engaged and politically well-placed chair: Chris Haskins (a leading food processing and retail businessman, veteran Labour supporter and financial donor, recently given a Labour peerage). This combination of executive capacity, within the powerful Cabinet Office; pre-1997 experience of advising along the anti-regulation line; wide ambit; and politically influential chair – is unique among all of Labour's task forces. At the outset, this task force comprised only two members with consumer affiliations (and one labour economics researcher) as against 13 with producer affiliations (whether business, public sector or trade union). Giving a roving commission to a group with such a plainly 'producer' profile was certain to provoke objections to its potential ideas for weakening the regulation of producers. Consumer and user representatives have little confidence in some producers of often costly and sensitive services. The task force's report questioning some of the regulation of old people's homes (May 1998) caused trouble – while also falling in a field which the government's first royal commission (on long-term care of the elderly and sick) was studying. Established specialist interests (including the sections of Whitehall Departments carrying statutory policy responsibility) may easily feel that an inexpert task force with a generalised brief is interfering, equipped with only a little knowledge but with a sectional approach. Chai Patel, the former head of the largest provider of residential, nursing and other long-term care in the country, is a task force member. The inter-departmental dimension of some policy reviews' reports was shown in the 'care homes' case: the Better Regulation Task Force (and the executive Unit) are in the Cabinet Office; responsible officials are in the Social Care Group of the Department of Health; and the junior minister for consumer affairs (who did not fully accept this report's recommendations) is in Trade and Industry. This group is one of the approximately one dozen task forces to have been designated a standing body (a non-departmental public body). It is also unusual in issuing annual reports and in having a two-year term arranged for its members. Being lodged in the Cabinet Office, all its potential studies and reports concern another Department's responsibilities (often statutory) so a continuing watch on its progress around Whitehall and the ultimate success of its various recommendations would help illuminate inter-departmental relations.

The **Urban Task Force** of the DETR (page 98) was a late arrival (May 1998) but launched one of most elaborate 'policy search' missions of all of the new government's many task forces. Its job was to identify and seek consent to changes in practical land-use planning and related policies which might result in as many as 60 per cent of all new-built houses and flats up to about the year 2008 being built on re-used sites, rather than new 'greenfield' sites. Nearly all re-useable sites are in already built-up areas so the main issue is their broad attractiveness to potential new residents (and therefore to the private housebuilding industry, which makes much easier profits from greenfield schemes). Possible policies making these built-up areas more attractive to newcomers (and ex-urban or truly rural sites relatively less attractive) soon spill over from direct land-use policies into issues about roads, public transport, public services and even tax questions such as council tax and mortgage tax relief. 'A broad framework for the future of urban areas in England' was the first requirement of the task force's formal terms of reference.

This most challenging brief would be best discharged by the combination of a technically heavyweight task force and a well-known and politically well-connected chair. The architect Richard Rogers is among the two or three most eminent British architects and a leading international practitioner. He differs from his most senior British professional colleagues in also being a long-standing prominent Labour figure who has helped produce party policy studies on urban design and planning problems. His attachment to the improvement of central London was well shown by his taking the title Lord Rogers of Riverside when Tony Blair made him a peer, to add to his knighthood awarded in 1991.

His work as chair and principal public champion of the Urban Task Force would plainly combine his worldwide reputation as an architect; his passionate conviction that an urban design 'renaissance' can be achieved in Britain; and his unquestioned direct access not only to his commissioning minister (the Environment Secretary and Deputy PM, John Prescott) but to the Prime Minister himself. Of course, the risk of appointing such a well-known figure to chair a potentially highly controversial task force would be that the mass media would absurdly personalise the whole affair as a one-man show. This effect did not arise in this case and the Task Force maintained its group identity well, even in the tabloid press.

The Urban Task Force was not, of course, a royal commission, although its published prospectus of July 1998 suggested enough policy review work to occupy at least two of those august institutions for a year or two. The set-up to tackle all this work was rather elaborate, however. The 14 task force members considered written studies and reports from their three working groups (composed of eleven members of the task force plus 29 further experts and practitioners) during 1998. Some of them then formed 'connector groups' with selected working group members to bring draft report text forward for the full task force's approval. An Interim Report in January 1999 was followed by a final one intended for May 1999 (although in fact published in July), prior to a trio of white papers due from the government later on urban, rural and housing policies. The working groups studied broad themes: the content and method of obtaining good urban design ('Defining the Product'); public and private sector land-use planning and investment ('Liberating the Process'); and stimulating investment in re-useable sites ('Providing the Finance'). Considerable consultations, British site visiting, overseas study tours and retreats ('awaydays') have been features of the Urban Task Force's work, in addition to some of its members joining in (and taking the chair) at meetings of its three working groups. One politically important consultation (three meetings) has been with an 'institutional sounding board' of representatives from the established professional, commercial, charitable and environmental bodies interested in land-use planning and the house-building and construction industries comprising very different approaches and opinions. They constantly watch the government (and each other) like hawks. This group was invited to comment orally and quite informally on the Task Force's progress from the opposed viewpoints of such bodies as the Housebuilders' Federation, Shelter, Friends of the Earth, the Civic Trust and the professional bodies of planners and architects (the RTPI and RIBA). In March 1999, its final meeting was comprehensively and confidentially briefed on the contents of the Task Force's draft final report, including various options not yet decided. The 'sounding board' members were clearly impressed and offered mainly supportive suggestions.[5]

Most of these features (except the 'sounding board' meetings) have been common to many other task forces and review groups. The Urban Task Force has been unusual in its relatively costly research and consultancy programmes and in having its secretariat partly seconded from a highly relevant public sector development quango (English Partnerships) and from the private sector (an urban renewal consultancy) rather than simply recruited from among DETR's civil servants.

Having created an exceptionally well-equipped exercise to work on an exceptionally demanding array of policy issues, DETR may naturally be expected to reflect the task force's analysis in its urban policy white paper (now due in December 1999, six months later than planned) and its rural policy and housing policy white papers (to follow). Urban Task Force members have been very conscious of their wider Whitehall audience: notably concerning the Treasury's control of any ideas for tax privileges, which could stimulate some commercially difficult urban development markets. Overall, this task force will probably be seen as a flagship for this style of active consultation and policy analysis, whereby one set of senior and expert figures reach out to the established interests through working groups and 'sounding boards', while

Government encourages New Professional Activities or Specialities to Strengthen Public Service Performance

15. Personal, Social and Health Education Advisory Group (and Panel of Expert Advisers) (Department for Education and Employment, jointly with the Department of Health)

The PSHE group (page 76), one of those task forces carrying promotional *outputs* from government in support of policy goals, is mentioned in the commentary alongside the Advisory Group on Education for Citizenship (page 68). Its remit includes sex and relationships education and overlaps with both citizenship education and the (already statutory) requirement that spiritual, moral, social and cultural (SMSC) development be taught in schools. The exploratory nature of this group may be indicated by its size : 25 members (22 of them outsiders) sitting with an education minister as their chair. It also has the support of an expert panel of 14 (see page 76). Among the more predictable topics represented, such as education on sex, health, drugs, parenting and even personal finance, it is interesting to see newly emerging specialities and their promotional groups. Two examples are a Development and Accreditation Network in this broad and loose field and (as a new would-be professional cadre) a National Standing Committee of Advisers, Inspectors and Consultants on Personal and Social Education. Government encouragement of new cohorts of practitioners, claiming expertise, is readily achieved by an active 'task force' approach to policy development in novel fields.

16. National Advisory Group on Special Educational Needs (and two Working Groups) (DfEE)

Although work on special educational needs (SEN) is much more firmly established than PSHE or SMSC work (above), Labour ministers clearly felt that it required review and development. Some 19 outsiders formed the main group (page 77), with a junior minister as chair, seeking to 'take forward the government's commitments on raising the standard of education' for SEN. Steven Crowne, the senior SEN official in DfEE, chaired one working group (on the role and training of educational psychologists: 16 further members) while a former education department official chaired the other (on speech and language therapy services: 13 further members). The use of the three groups (see page 77) to implement an existing policy by means of planned professional development is quite plain.

17. Northern Ireland Strategy for Education Technology: Strategic Management Group (and two Sub-Groups) (NIO)

This group (page 117) had to 'secure the implementation' of an already accepted 'education technology strategy' in Northern Ireland and to 'put in place' the UK policy of a National Grid for Learning within the province. It is an example of using a task force to help develop new specialities or expert cadres. It is interesting, however, that not one of 35 members or chairs of the main group and two sub-groups was recruited from the relevant information or education technology industries – all are public sector people (page 117).

18. Chronic Fatigue Syndrome Main Working Group (and two Sub-Groups) (Health)

The purpose of this group and its two sub-groups was simply 'to help promote better understanding of Chronic Fatigue Syndrome' (ME). The chosen route to this goal appears to be 'professional development'. All 51 members were already well-informed about ME as practitioners, charity supporters, sufferers or carers (page 102) and produced a valuable forum on the given task. No health journalist or other experienced publicist was included and no DoH officials or ministers are recorded as having attended their meetings, as members or observers. Strengthening the 'ME community' by creating a 'task force' seems to have been the department's main aim, with note to be taken of the group's conclusions. It seems not to have been organised for the public promotion and

possibly also approaching the public with polls or focus groups to gather consumer or other mass opinion data.

The Department for Education and Employment's **Advisory Group on Education for Citizenship and the Teaching of Democracy in Schools** (November 1997 – September 1998) (page 68) did not arise from one of Labour's 55 manifesto pledges or 'action points' in the education field. It did carry particular political weight, however. This was because those in charge of the public body responsible for planning the subjects to be taught in all state schools (the Qualifications and Curriculum Authority, or QCA) knew very well that the new Education Secretary, David Blunkett, was personally committed to making citizenship and democracy studies a part of the compulsory National Curriculum. They could also observe that his appointee as chair of this expert advisory group, Emeritus Professor Bernard Crick of London University, had long been the leading academic figure in the field of teaching about politics in schools and – more potent still – was Blunkett's former university tutor and prominent Labour co-partisan. Bernard Crick's job was to devise, with his group's agreement, a practical means of integrating this extra compulsory subject or topic into the notoriously limited time available within the National Curriculum. From the outset, Bernard Crick accepted that this new National Curriculum teaching subject might often be taught spliced in with existing school subjects such as historical, religious, moral or environmental studies. But mere optional status, with teachers or schools finding time for citizenship and democracy studies only if and when it suited other demands, was known to be unacceptable to the Secretary of State. To gain added political weight, Crick had welcomed the idea of appointing Lord (Kenneth) Baker – a prominent former Education Secretary – to the group. Baker would draw on his work for political education among school and college students with the Hansard Society for Parliamentary Government, just as Crick would on his work, which had led to his becoming president of the Politics Association (teachers and college lecturers in politics).

The Crick group on teaching citizenship and democracy had three or four 'sibling' post-election departmental reviews on new school subjects competing for the DfEE's priority. The QCA, the official organiser and adviser to ministers on the National Curriculum was already digesting an earlier national consultation exercise on its existing statutory duty to promote pupils' 'spiritual, moral, social and cultural' development (SMSC). Pilot teaching schemes were due to run during 1998-99 in 150 schools. A second task force – the Personal, Social and Health Education (PSHE) Advisory group (page 76) was launched jointly by DfEE and the Department of Health and had two junior ministers as its co-chairs. A third (joint DfEE/Department of Culture) group, chaired by Professor Ken Robinson, studied 'creativity and cultural education' (page 69) while, fourthly, Sir Geoffrey Holland (a former Permanent Secretary at Education) chaired a new Panel on Sustainable Development Education (joint DETR/DfEE) (page 97). Health ministers also wished to promote 'sex and relationship education', tying in with the PSHE theme. These fivefold new pressures on the National Curriculum added to established particular claims being made for ethics, religious and racial toleration to be taught more prominently in schools. The public inquiry into the investigation of Stephen Lawrence's murder stimulated the teaching in schools of racial toleration as an official priority, spliced in with teaching citizenship. SMSC (above) already had compulsory status; the Crick group's report recommended that 'no more than' a 5 per cent share of National Curriculum time (albeit to be partly lodged within various existing subjects' teaching) would meet their new subject's needs while the Sustainable Development Education group recommended merely that their interests be taken seriously when settling the Curriculum's details.

Not surprisingly, the Qualifications and Curriculum Authority has tried to assert its own control over what one major expert participant and multiple group member or consultant in this busy field has described in an interview as 'a nightmare of groups'. A further umbrella exercise (the Preparation for Adult

Life Group) has therefore brought together these various competing review groups' chairs, Ofsted (the inspectors of schools in England) and a group of head teachers as a QCA committee. This 'PAL' Group offers private advice to the QCA as part of its regular reviewing of the National Curriculum. The Crick group's public claim to compulsory Curriculum status for citizenship and democracy studies went on to the public record (it reported in September, 1998) and the Secretary of State's patronage of it was well understood by the QCA. This policy advisory (or, rather, policy development) group was typical of many others in its very simple form and process. It was rather unusual in having to fit in with a quite such an elaborate lattice of already established interests and rival claims in its field. It was very unusual in its strong political link to the responsible Cabinet minister who holds such a strong personal brief for its recommended objective. In view of this last point, the ultimate success of its bid for compulsory National Curriculum status for its particular subject of citizenship and democracy will deserve to be watched.

The results of the QCA's formal public consultation exercise on its final proposed version of a revised Curriculum for September 2000 were considered in the summer of 1999. The government was mainly concerned with its final position on aspects of English, history and geography but publicity was attracted to its renewed emphasis on teaching about the advantages of married family life within Personal, Social and Health Education. Citizenship education's 5 per cent share of teaching time appeared to be accepted when the decisions were announced in September 1999. But it was the social, moral and cultural aspects (including the priority to be given to both marriage and racial toleration and respect) which upheld the citizenship idea. Political citizenship and political system knowledge offered only a subsidiary theme. Further detail, due from the QCA in November 1999, may confirm this. But classroom priorities change with political winds and the principle of assured teaching of citizenship and democratic values seems secure.

The **'Marshall' Task Force on Economic Instruments for Industrial and Commercial Use of Energy** (page 139) was about possibly imposing a new national tax or licensing system on business and industry's use of energy. It is worth highlighting among these six selected task forces or reviews because of the great political and technical difficulty of this policy issue. Whitehall's chosen method for beginning to gnaw on one of the toughest of all political nuts was to keep this exercise well 'in-house', under very close senior official control; to keep it simple in operation; and (most important) to invite a leading captain of industry to broach this issue to his business peers on his own independent authority.

This exercise took the form of Sir Colin (now Lord) Marshall the current President of the Confederation of British Industries, Chairman of British Airways and of Inchcape, accepting the Chancellor's invitation of March 1998 'to examine whether economic instruments, such as an energy tax, have a role to play ... while maintaining the competitiveness of British industry' (to quote the Task Force's subsequent consultation paper). He had already agreed with the government that voluntary restraint on energy emissions would not be enough to meet the government's target that the UK's CO_2 emissions in 2010 should be 20 per cent below the 1990 level. He believed that some extra pricing burden on either energy use or emissions would be needed and sought the interested parties' views on these (or other) options. Lord Marshall was presented as an individual inquirer and adviser to the Chancellor. He was to chair and be 'supported by' a task force of four very senior (grade 2, director-general) officials, one each from relevant Departments: the Treasury (as the lead Department); DTI; DETR; and Customs and Excise. One of this official quartet, interviewed for this study, was clear that 'we are certainly not a committee'; the four-Department basis was, however, emphasised as crucial to the work. These comments may mean that it was not for the official quartet to form a group view on this highly sensitive and technically elaborate subject. The only conclusions and recommendations would be Lord Marshall's: the civil servants' job was to brief him and serve as either his sounding board or his closely attentive minders

awareness of ME, as its remit specified.

Government encourages Disparate Private or Public Sector Interests to become More Effective or Profitable

19. Review of Film Policy (Department for Culture, Media and Sport)

Labour's 1997 manifesto promised 'a strategic vision that matches the real power and energy of British arts, media and cultural industries'. This policy review group (page 55) was created by the DCMS to supply an action plan for the film industry within this strategy. The government's developmental purpose was clear in the composition of the group, consisting as it did of 11 private film business members (including an industry leader as chair), plus only a single official figure (from the Arts Council for England) and one independent expert. Despite its name, this was a policy planning group on the government's settled policies, with specific remits to double British films' share of the UK market, improve training, sustain investment, etc.

20. Film Policy Action Committee (and six Sub-Groups) (DCMS)

This action committee consisted of the review group (above), now trying to implement its own action plan, with 15 further members. The junior minister for film policy became joint chair with the review's senior business chair. Six sub-groups added nearly 50 further members, nearly all in the private film business (see page 56 for full listings). Each sub-group tackled a topic within the minister's strategy, as noted in the review group's action plan, such as broadening the cinema audience or inward investment. A new Film Council, with a films subsidy budget of £50 million, has since been created. It would seem that this business-dominated 'double group' was a detailed planning exercise for an established pre-election Labour policy to develop the British film industry with subsidies. But as four fifths of the exercise's members were drawn from the film business and a new quango is now dispensing a lot more public money, the impression of a successful lobby is bound to be given.

21. Tourism Forum (and 12 Sub-groups) (DCMS)

This has been the largest 'task force' exercise, with 201 outsider places on the main forum and its satellites (page 61) – and only few multiple memberships – and is a prime example of government encouragement for currently rather disparate interests to think and plan more consciously and coherently. Whether or not there is a single 'tourism/hospitality industry' or only separate sectors, the government will continue 'development' initiatives like this forum and the creation of new or replacement quangos, such as the new English Tourism Council. The main national policy is job creation, particularly at less skilled, lower-paying levels and in areas of depressed economies, like parts of the south-west, and with strong, but seasonal, tourism. At even half the scale of this particular 'forum' exercise, it must be questioned whether the department is able to absorb such a volume of information and discussion, however useful and sensible it may have been.

22. Market Development Group (for Recycled Goods and Materials) (DETR)

This group (page 96) was the plainest of development exercises to encourage a new industry for recycling, partly to relieve the policy and physical problems of landfill and incineration of waste. With the chair taken by the head of DETR's waste policy division, plus six further officials out of 19 members, the government's steering of the group's remit to 'propose to central and local government and industry' on possible waste taxes or levies was clear.

Government encourages (or pressurises) Industries and Trades to Improve their Performance in the Public Interest.

23. Cowboy Builders Working Group (and four Sub-Groups) (DETR)

The overall task set this improbably named but elaborate technical working group (page 92) has been to work out how building firms and their trade associations might be regulated by voluntary 'accreditation', supported by insurance cover against failures to complete jobs properly. With many thousands of small firms and individual operators comprising 'the industry', it is not surprising that some two thirds of the 63 places on the group and sub-groups were taken up by representative trade associations. Judging by duplicated memberships, the main group thought the sub-group on 'Approved Lists and Consumer Education' the most important. If the public would agree to hire only jobbing builders on a semi-official approved list government for house repairs and improvements (as has applied with house-builders for some 30 years, following effective threats by a previous Labour government), the cowboy builders problem would be solved. Until then, partial and voluntary customer protection schemes are the only option.

The absence from this exercise of the architects and surveyors as professional supervisors of builders is an interesting contrast to the original launch of voluntary housebuilding regulation and insurance (under government control) in 1936. At that time, the government made the professionals of central importance on house building standards.

24. Task Force on Banks' Assistance to Credit Unions (Treasury)

Another example of government using a task force to encourage or pressurise an industry or trade to improve its performance. This task force (page 138) is also interesting because it 'cross-cuts' with another and major policy action exercise: the Social Exclusion Unit (see page 45). Credit unions are mutual (member-owned) associations which can develop (as in the US, for example) into full-

on practical ways and means. The contrast was drawn with the role of the then managing director of Barclays, Martin Taylor, who had been advising the Chancellor on practical and policy links between the tax and social security benefits systems, also supported by a civil service team . He had been expected to provide an outside view on matters unconnected with Barclays affairs and on which the new government had major manifesto commitments to redeem. Lord Marshall was, by contrast, helping ministers to explore novel ground, of considerable significance for British Airways as his own principal company, on which no official policy existed beyond the UK's 2010 target and promoting the post-Rio global climate change Kyoto conference protocol (both of which had been specified in the Labour manifesto).

The Marshall exercise very largely turned on who he was: not only the current President of the CBI but Chairman of British Airways – a major energy-consuming and atmosphere-polluting company – in addition to other leading boardroom positions. If this leading businessman formally recommended the government to legislate either an extra tax on energy use by business and industry or some novel scheme to regulate and 'price' emissions permits, then, surely, British industry would accept it with less protest and evasion than if a minister simply announced it. If this business leader had consulted industry before submitting a report of obvious quality (albeit one written by civil servants) so much the better. 'Marshall' was all about legitimation by a prominent business peer leader. If he, as head of a major airline, could literally put his signature on proposed measures to tax CO_2 emissions, other industries must be impressed. The snag for ministers who need this key signature is that the eminent outsider will agree to only a minimal commitment to the controversial new policies, and probably call for more study and preparation. This is what Lord Marshall did in his report so that government policy seemed not much different in practical terms for having received his endorsement in principle: more consultation was announced. But this initial legitimation was important. The Chancellor moved ahead quite quickly, despite this generally cautious government stance, and introduced a new climate change levy (from 2001) in his 1999 budget. The protest from the CBI in general (and the Energy Intensive Users Group of companies in particular) showed little sign of having been converted or even just soothed by Lord Marshall's report. British Steel, for example, claimed that the climate change levy could cost them nearly £200-300 million per annum. The Commons select committee on Trade and Industry echoed this criticism in July 1999. Whereas the 'legitimation effect' of a review and recommendation such as Lord Marshall's can assist the government to place a hot new issue on to the practical policy-making agenda, new taxes of this order can be actually secured by the Chancellor only by determined resistance to industry's powerful lobbying in the different (and rival) relevant Whitehall Departments: Trade and Industry; Environment; Treasury; plus, without much doubt in a case such as this, the No. 10 Policy Unit and the Prime Minister's own Office.

The **Football Task Force** (page 58) has been the most dramatically flawed of all the many task forces, reviews or advisory groups. Its design and launching by the Sport and Recreation division of the Department for Culture, Media and Sport has been described by one of the principal participants as an 'almighty civil service cock-up' because it arranged the Task Force's membership before consulting its designated chair (the former Secretary of State for National Heritage, also responsible for sport policy, David Mellor). When David Mellor protested that the leading officials of the main football bodies ought not to be members of this review body, but its principal witnesses, there was a risk that this exercise would collapse at the outset. This risk was compounded by the football 'barons' due to represent such bodies as the Football Association, the Premier League and the Professional Footballers' Association finding David Mellor's chairing their task force just as illegitimate as he found their membership. In their view, this former Cabinet minister responsible for sport policy had become an irresponsible, populist journalist and broadcaster on football issues, playing to the gallery (that is, the terraces) for personal gain. It was not surprising that the Task Force did not meet for months. Taken on its own, it appeared during most of 1997 to be a dead letter, caught between David Mellor's (and some other participants') view that only a clearly independent task force could carry authority with the government and the public and the established football interests' insistence that only football's responsible bodies could identify and implement agreed changes.

Instead of publicly sinking, however, the exercise survived by David Mellor selecting (and the junior Sport minister, Tony Banks, endorsing) a parallel group of more independent individuals, with only one leading football official (the Chief Executive of the Premier League, Peter Leaver) sitting on both groups. This Working Group met fortnightly during the first few months and toured the country, offering talks and open hearings to football club directors, players and supporters. Some members of the Task Force joined in some of these Working Group visits but the main method was for the Working Group to draft reports (on racist conduct by some crowd members (March 1998) and on disabled supporters' access to good seats (July 1998)) which the Task Force would discuss, endorse and publish.

By the early autumn of 1998, relations between David Mellor and the leading football officials had improved somewhat, although partly only because the Task Force's most difficult job – the report required by the government on the increasing commercialisation of the game and the growing disparity between the few very wealthy clubs and the many poorer ones – was being postponed. The third draft report from the Working Group criticised clubs and players for neglecting their contractual agreements to undertake local community services to schools and youth organisations. When the Task Force accepted this for publication, its representative from the Professional Footballers' Association, Gordon Taylor, promptly withdrew himself and his organisation from the Task Force. David Mellor's initial view of July 1997 that a task force composed partly of 'barons' would either avoid the real issues about the new power of money in football or simply seize up, seemed correct.

In one participant's view, the position became less difficult after Gordon Taylor's departure and he was followed off the Task Force in the winter of 1998-99 by the chief executives of both the Football Association and the Premier League (Graham Kelly and Peter Leaver) when they lost their jobs; Peter Leaver also withdrew from his personal membership of the Working Group. Their respective Task Force replacements (David Davies and Mike Foster) are seen by one active member as much more likely to agree a worthwhile final report on football's commercial issues. The government's acceptance of the recommendation of the Monopolies and Mergers Commission that Manchester United may not be bought by the satellite television company, BSkyB, also cleared away a major issue before this report was to be drafted. A further reason for optimism was the growing together of the two groups: by March 1999, seven Working Group members were also on the Task Force.

Following a potentially fatal start, the combination of the improvised, pro-active Working Group and the official, reactive Task Force has worked out quite well. The Mellor view that more independent (but knowledgeable and experienced) people should inquire and report on the Task Force's officially requested agenda has been met. The football bodies' view that they must be fully involved if realistic changes are to be tackled has also been met: they have endorsed and helped to legitimate the Working Group's recommendations. David Mellor could probably have used his position as Tony Banks' personal choice as this task force's chair (as endorsed by 'No. 10' and probably by the Prime Minister himself) to insist that the Department's pre-arranged 'baronial' membership be cancelled and replaced by a different list of more independent names agreed between himself and Tony Banks. Instead, his own nominations to a 'Working Group' which was actually almost an alternative task force were endorsed by Tony Banks and administered in tandem by David Mellor and the Task Force secretariat. This initially pathological case has demonstrated the potential flexibility of the task force or review form. No such alternative group

range retail banks. On this task force representatives from six banks — one of them in the chair — have been required to explain to four mutual building society and credit union representatives and two independent experts why their own branches and retail services are shrinking in poorer areas and what they will agree to do to help credit unions to fill the gap. The Treasury is now the banking industry's regulatory authority although, strangely, neither their trade association (the British Bankers' Association) nor any Treasury officials had places on this group. The two Social Exclusion Unit teams which the Treasury has also been leading have each had one banker as members: but no banking trade association representation. The established key to better performance by firms or individuals is to encourage or pressurise their trade or professional associations to police them — using psychological leverage, at least. Good practice by more responsible firms usually leaves poorer people (or areas) being poorly treated by irresponsible firms.

25. Cleaner Vehicles Task Force (and six Sub-Groups) (DETR)

This exceptionally large exercise, with 75 outside members filling 99 places on the task force, a 'main working group' and five further subsidiaries (page 89), was designed 'to create a new partnership between government and the private sector to promote environmentally-friendly vehicles. The exercise covers not only car, truck and bus makers, but their users, garages, the fuel trade, and so on. The Minister of Transport and Ian McAllister, chair of Ford UK, jointly chaired the task force itself, and the energy and environment ministers were also members (as was Sir Robert May, the government's Chief Scientific Adviser). The two central bodies have been dominated by representatives of private businesses and trade associations, with a handful of civil servants and people from voluntary and environmental bodies, local authorities and consumer organisations. Two voluntary representatives on the 'main working group' from Energy Savings Trust and Friends of the Earth each chaired a specialist sub-group.. As with the Tourism Forum (see Note 21 above), it may be wondered whether such a large exercise can escape becoming more of a forum than a systematic analysis effort. Much valuable information may be generated and experience exchanged on the elaborate issues in hand – but when, for example, only three of the main working group's 33 members were officials, how much can actually be absorbed and used for policy-making? 'Consciousness-raising' is one of the purposes of all these bodies and is obviously linked to group size. This forum has certainly exposed a large and influential group of members of relevant industries to the issues surrounding cleaner vehicles – and given officials at least a sense of how they are likely to react to policy proposals.

could have grown up alongside a royal commission or departmental committee of inquiry: their format and public standing are too formal and familiar to permit such improvisation. The final report will be on finances: ticket prices, club merchandising, players' incomes and transfers, the role of players' agents, the floating of clubs on the stock exchange and huge media fees to a very few clubs. It is still awaited as this report goes to press (and described by the Department's 'minders' as undergoing fine tuning) having been planned to appear at least five months earlier. Avoiding a split majority/minority report remains a 'hope' rather than an expectation. If it is both robust and unanimous, the ground may prove fertile for a re-born Football Task Force in one or other form to be accepted as a standing monitoring, regulatory and standards body for football – perhaps linked at arm's length to the Football Association as the Press Complaints Commission or the British Board of Film Classification are to their industries.

On 30 June, 1998 the Culture Secretary, Chris Smith, received the report of the **Independent Review of the Future of the Royal Opera House and English National Opera**, which he had requested in November 1997 from Sir Richard Eyre, the former director of the Royal National Theatre at London's Southbank (page 59). This external review also offers special interest, partly because it concerned one of the world's finest opera houses and companies (the Royal Opera House) nearly ruined by a darker plot and with more blood on the stage than even the most extravagant opera librettist would dare to offer. This dramatic aspect guaranteed full media coverage of the Eyre review. But political interest also lies in this review's good fortune in having combined, in the end, the advantages of resting on a task force (officially called a 'working group' or 'review team') while being the individual work of an eminent national figure with an impeccable record of running the Royal National Theatre to a high artistic standard within a budget. It was this latter trick which had either spectacularly eluded those supposed to be in charge of the Royal Opera House or which had never seriously interested them.

The Eyre report nominally included the English National Opera at the London Coliseum but was in substance about the Royal Opera House (opera and ballet). The exercise was presented by the Department of Culture, both before and after the work was done, as an eminent practitioner's personal report: 'Sir Richard Eyre's review of the ROH and ENO'. In fact, it proved to be a subtle and effective combination of an individual report and a collective effort by quite a large group of practitioners, some of them independent of the events and issues under review and some fully responsible current managers of the two main bodies involved: the ROH itself and the grant-giving quango, the Arts Council of England. But this fortunate outcome does not seem to have been planned by the Department's Arts Division (which sponsors the Arts Council of England and so was concerned – to put it mildly – about the ROH as the major recipient of grant aid).

These officials copied their Sport colleagues' action four months earlier, when setting up the Football Task Force, by inviting the leading executives currently responsible for the bodies under review to be members of the review. Sir Richard Eyre in turn copied the Football Task Force's designated chair, David Mellor, in asserting that these persons should be his principal witnesses: the conflict of interest in their membership of his working group was obvious. The difference between the two cases was that Sir Richard Eyre had been invited to conduct a personal review; he therefore had the standing to separate the people whom he thought should be principal witnesses (who were to be called 'participants') from his supporting 'working group'. He experienced almost no friction when he made it clear to the working group, at the draft report stage, that it was to be his individual report, although he would canvass every point with them. Such personal standing was not available to David Mellor (or anyone else) when inquiring into the febrile and newly-moneyed world of professional football.

From January to April, 1998, Sir Richard Eyre's working group and its sub-committees studied such aspects as the practical problems of opera programme planning and touring; the quest for opera 'excellence'; the London arts context; public access to opera; and (crucially) opera's financing. Richard Eyre took the background, factual draft report prepared by his civil service secretariat and the sub-committees' written conclusions and recommendations to a weekend conference of his working group. He summarised each aspect orally and invited views, which he then summed up in prime ministerial Cabinet-meeting style to indicate his own conclusions.

It was well accepted by this stage that this would be his personal report, which partly explains the lack of conflict, both on this key occasion and during the subsequent final consultations with relevant parties, mainly on factual and technical points, which Sir Richard Eyre and his secretariat then pursued. But his conscious attempt to reflect the group's expert views, rather than appearing simply to use them as his scouts, is seen as a second explanation of this uncontested reporting process.

The 'Eyre review' of the ROH's opera and ballet operations had in common with the Football Task Force the need for Sir Richard Eyre and David Mellor to get around the unacceptable inquiry group memberships which Department of Culture officials had prematurely arranged. They adopted different ways of reaching the same goal of a more independent and authoritative form of inquiry. Sir Richard Eyre's personal role in legitimating a way forward from the ROH's horrendous financial problems and management record had much in common with Lord Marshall's personal role in putting energy taxes (or emissions levies) firmly onto British industry's practical agenda. Their names, drawing on their personal records of responsibility in their fields, were expected to carry weight and conviction with the relevant interested bodies and with political, press and public opinion at large.

These six sketches and the accompanying notes on 25 other task forces should be taken together in order to gain an idea of the variety of work and purposes served by the task force initiative as a whole.

3 Who has been 'Invited to the Party'?

For senior civil servants, the phrase 'invited to the party' indicates the novel and (they said) welcome openness and inclusiveness of the new Labour ministers' attitude towards policy advice. Telling their officials to establish numerous groups of outsiders to work with the Department on current problems and future policy ideas may (at a pinch) have seemed a little like throwing a large party for thousands of people, many of whom one does not know. This reference to party invitations is a useful reminder that these many outsiders were being seen by ministers and their mandarins as favoured guests allowed inside to help out, on a mainly informal and unruled basis. The section below on recruiting task forces, and part of the final comments of this Report, take up the selection methods and the unconsidered, *ad hoc*, basis of what turned out to be a major government initiative. All outsiders were recruited by the Whitehall Departments either directly or through an organisation which was asked to nominate one or more of its senior members or staff. (List 1.1 necessarily follows the Departments' own lists of some groups in naming only the nominating body, not the person nominated; the analysis in Table 2 (page 27) includes the estimated numbers of these 'representatives' of nominating bodies but the A-Z of outside advisers obviously cannot include their names).

The total number of outsiders on this basis comes to 2,459. If we ask, who has been invited?, we can answer fully only in terms of their affiliations – nearly always their employment or representative position in an organisation. In Table 2, the outside members are broken down for analysis into 14 classified affiliations, within two broad overall categories – private and public sector – and several smaller categories: a 'mixed' private-public category; representatives of trade unions and professional associations, who are classed as mixed producer-consumer and mixed producer members; voluntary or charitable consumer interests; academic and research members; and 'independents'. (See also page 40). As some outsiders serve on more that one group, the table records the affiliations of 3,103 place-holders. The table also breaks down the 3,103 place-holders and their affiliations by Department and shows how the places on bodies sponsored by the 18 ministerial Departments are divided between producer, consumer and other interests (as broadly defined).

As would be expected, the highly consultative traditions of the Education and Environment Departments have been confirmed in the task force initiatives, with 12 per cent and 14 per cent respectively, of memberships. With the Employment side of DfEE providing 7 per cent of the total (but the Transport side of DETR contributing almost nothing) the two Departments' totals are 19 per cent and 15 per cent of all outsider memberships. The new Department of Culture Media and Sport (until 1997, National Heritage) might also be expected to figure strongly. Like DfEE and DETR, it is a non-executive Department, surrounded by nearly 50 quangos whose work promoting the arts and sport it principally funds. But exactly half of its 401 outsider places (201) belong to one huge outside group, the Tourism Forum and its many sub-groups (see page 61).

The wide-ranging duties of the Northern Ireland Office (including most of the functions performed by elected local authorities in Great Britain) and a strong political will to involve people in public affairs, especially on a cross-community basis, helps the NIO share of these invited memberships into fourth place (9 per cent). The remaining 45 per cent of places is quite well spread, with a further six Departments accounting for between 4 per cent and 8 per cent (inclusive) of the total: (Cabinet Office 7 per cent; Health, Home Office and Scottish Office 5 per cent each; Trade and Industry 8 per cent and HM Treasury 4 per cent). Table 1 showed the different ratios of outside advisory groups to internal departmental reviews favoured by Departments. The Departments of Culture, Health, the Education and Employment wings of DfEE and also the Environment wing of DETR have either strongly or relatively favoured external groups while DETR's Transport side, Agriculture, Home Office, Scottish Office and the Treasury have maintained their traditional preference for internal policy reviews, with their greater resemblance to departmental consultations, rather than inviting large numbers of outside opinion-holders to party.

It is, of course, the provenance of the invited outsiders, rather than different departmental operating traditions within Whitehall, which deserves political attention. The combined total of 35 per cent of these 3,103 group memberships having been given to private (or privatised) business and their trade associations is striking. At more than one third of all places it is well ahead of other classes of membership. This 35 per cent which is the for-profit or commercial sector exceeds the 31 per cent of places held by not-for-profit public sector producer interests. The scale of the entire not-for-profit interest (producers plus the others) is striking, however. Their total comprises the public sector producer interest (31 per cent, as just noted); the voluntary/charity class (15 per cent); the trade unions (2 per cent); the academic/research class (nearly all university or public sector-based) (8 per cent); and the independents (4 per cent). Together, these non-commercial interests have taken up 60 per cent of all places, as against the commercial sector's 35 per cent – (only the mixed case of the professional associations (4 per cent) is excluded from this for-profit/not-for-profit bifurcation).

Beyond the 35 per cent private business share and the 60 per cent not-for-profit presence, the other striking profile is of producer interests as a whole (private and public sector) as against any consumer or user interest. If professional associations and trade union memberships (only 6 per cent combined) are set aside as mixed on this score (and if academic/research plus independent memberships are not relevant), then only the 15 per cent of places in the voluntary/charity sector stand against the combined private/public sector producer total of 66 per cent: a more than four fold difference. Of course, aggregate totals can be misleading and odd cases can skew overall figures. The Department of Culture's massive Tourism Forum exercises alone filled 114

Table 2: THE COMPOSITION OF THE TASK FORCE 'ELITE'

By interest group and occupation

Government Departments	Public producer interests — National public body	Judiciary	Health (NHS etc)	Local government body	Local public body	Education	Police	Private producer interests — Private business associations	Trade associations	Professional associations	Consumer interests — Voluntary/charity bodies	Producer/consumer — Trade Unions	Experts — Academics/research etc	Independents	TOTALS
Ministry of Agriculture, Fisheries and Food	4	–	–	1	–	–	–	13	12	–	5	–	21	3	59
Attorney-General	–	–	–	–	–	–	–	–	–	–	–	–	3	–	3
Cabinet Office	17	–	8	32	11	7	6	52	4	5	54	1	27	2	226
Department of Culture, Media and Sport	63	–	–	11	20	1	–	175	65	–	31	–	11	19	401
DETR	29	–	3	53	–	6	6	111	130	28	54	8	18	4	450
DfEE	63	–	4	57	42	132	–	78	25	21	94	–	39	26	581
Ministry of Defence	–	–	–	–	–	–	–	9	3	–	1	–	21	7	41
Department of Health	4	–	48	1	16	–	1	4	–	6	13	3	24	24	144
Foreign and Commonwealth Office	3	–	–	–	–	–	–	9	–	–	4	–	3	–	19
Home Office	10	5	–	19	7	1	9	16	3	19	49	4	6	6	154
Department of International Development	1	–	–	1	2	2	–	1	–	–	15	1	–	3	24
Lord Chancellor's Department	4	1	1	–	–	–	–	4	3	6	2	–	1	–	22
Northern Ireland Department	11	–	65	6	48	25	2	16	6	1	79	6	13	4	282
Scottish Office	15	2	9	20	5	15	1	29	5	2	24	7	16	9	159
Department of Social Security	5	–	–	2	–	–	–	6	12	1	22	2	8	1	68
Department of Trade and Industry	8	1	1	8	2	2	–	161	33	6	2	14	20	2	260
HM Treasury	3	–	–	–	–	–	–	49	40	7	3	–	4	2	108
Welsh Office	8	–	3	13	13	8	–	23	10	–	13	4	3	4	102
TOTALS:	**248**	**9**	**138**	**224**	**152**	**199**	**19**	**756**	**351**	**111**	**465**	**73**	**235**	**122**	**3103**
% of Grand Total	8%	0%	4%	7%	5%	6%	1%	24%	11%	4%	15%	2%	8%	4%	(100%)

This table shows the distribution of 3103 'outsider' places, occupied by 2459 individuals, on the government's first 259 task forces and other advisory bodies with external members, broken down by departments, interest groups and classified occupational affiliations (see p. 40). Government officials are excluded from the table. The full list of external members of these bodies is set out on pp.41-144.

Source: Research by Anthony Barker and Democratic Audit

private business (including trade association) memberships – with a few individuals being multiple members. It is no surprise to see the Department of Trade and Industry filling 194 group memberships with private sector business people and only two with voluntary sector people – or Health, on the other hand with only four commercial places as against 13 from the voluntary sector, 48 from the NHS and a further 12 from other public sector positions. Apart from these obvious institutional stances, it is interesting to see the new Cabinet Office section, the Social Exclusion Unit, having filled 43 memberships on its 18 Policy Action Teams with private sector producers as against 30 local authority and 43 other public sector producers (with 50 voluntary sector and 22 academic/research places). The share of private commerce overall in these 18 Action Teams is 28 per cent of outsider memberships.

There is another significant imbalance in the membership of task forces and other bodies with external members. Less than a third of the members seem to be women. Out of 2,306 individual members for whom Audit research has been able to establish a gender identity, just 699 (30 per cent) are women. These known women take 821 places on external bodies between them. Women are also unevenly distributed across departments. For example, 254 of the places for members we were able to identify as women, or 31 per cent, are on bodies established by the Department for Education and Employment By contrast, the Ministry of Defence could find places for only three people who were identified as women and Foreign and Commonwealth Office for just six known women. Such figures obviously reflect the unequal opportunities for women in the work force as a whole, but even so it is hard to justify the poor showing of the MoD, FCO and other departments, like the Treasury (11 known women), even after allowing for the fact that their total tally of women could be marginally higher.

4   'Rule by Task Force': issues for discussion

Policy search and policy implementation

There has been some interesting novelty in the precise forms and practices of these many task forces and their sub-groups. But it is their sheer numbers and the total effort which ministers and civil servants have put into creating and running them as sources of policy discussion and operational support which constitute a significant innovation in modern British government. Whether the record so far adds up to 'a whole new way of making policy' (as the not-normally-excitable Permanent Secretary of one, particularly review-laden, Whitehall Department described it in an interview) may be doubted. Generating this enormous amount of informed practitioners' experiences and comments, organised into this wide array of specialised task forces on so many public policy issues, is bound to have consequences for both interest group politics and the process of government. As most task forces have submitted, or will soon submit, their final reports and recommendations, ministers and senior civil servants must decide how far to incorporate them into official policy.

Once launched it would be hard for future ministers to withdraw from this task force and policy review method of exploring future issues with a reasonably representative group of practitioners and informed observers. Nearly 2,500 private citizens, mostly practitioners and experts discussing their own occupational field, have joined these many task forces and helped ministers either to see or appreciate a policy field or issue as they themselves see it or (in some cases) to hammer out practical ways of implementing the 1997 Labour manifesto, or otherwise advancing ministers' stated ideas. These two broad activities – policy search or description and practical policy design or implementation – have often given a particular group its character. To take a pair of extreme examples, the group of expert academics studying the possible future of the law relating to surrogacy in childbirth (page 105) has explored the boundaries of law and ethics in what was wholly an exercise in discovery and policy analysis. In complete contrast, the task forces in all four parts of the UK (pages 83, 143, 119 and 124) on 'welfare to work' policies have been engaged in policy implementation and the design of future executive processes. Looking at the huge array of all of these groups' policy interests, a broad spectrum can be seen, with some exercises apparently concentrating on policy-search and some, by contrast, very closely tied to the policy planning task such as senior civil servants have traditionally performed within the privacy of their Departments. Many task forces seem, not surprisingly, to have done work of both types – exploring the feasibility of new policy ideas or priorities with the established organised interests and more independent practitioners and experts who make up the memberships, while also using these members to clarify and assess both new and familiar proposals.

Recruiting task forces: 'party invitations' or public selection?

If a task force is designated a standing body (as about a dozen have been so far) the Cabinet Office tries to arrange for its listing in the next *Public Bodies* volume and for new members to be recruited on 'Nolan Rules', as required for standing public bodies (quangos) as opposed to temporary task forces or similar outsider groups. The rules require public advertisement and formal selection methods, rather than the private invitations received by temporary groups' potential members. The issue of requiring Whitehall to recruit task forces under Nolan rules has been raised. Such an idea would need to apply to all temporary committees, from royal commissions down to technical working parties, because there is no definition of 'task force' on which such a rule could rest. (If 'task forces' were required to follow Nolan rules but advisory groups or working parties were not, Departments would simply switch the labels.)

Putting the new task forces on a 'Nolan' basis was raised by one of the very few expressions of parliamentary interest in either the work or the procedural basis of the task force phenomenon – a Public Administration Committee report in early 1998. The then committee chair, Rhodri Morgan, and some members gave the impression of seeing this phenomenon as a second phalanx of quangos, just when actual quango appointments were adopting Nolan procedures, and so made the analogy.

An outside critic pressing for more open government may well reason that external appointees to all government policy review groups (whether 'task forces', royal commissions, departmental committees or technical and expert working parties, etc.) should have to answer an advertisement for members and be formally selected in competition. This would oblige the selectors to consider a wider range of opinions and backgrounds than secret, informal invitations from ministers or (much more often) their officials would achieve. A temporary committee to study and report is no different from a standing advisory body or, indeed, an executive body (the advisory or executive quangos). Representativeness and therefore democracy would be served and useful experience or expertise not previously known to the rather narrow channels of informal recruitment by senior civil servants or ministers' party contacts would at least be given a chance to impress with their application details.

All of this would be simply a part of the more generally open and systematic method of government which the country needs. Greater formality and attention to rule and published criteria are the necessary key to unlocking greater access to government for less favoured interests who cannot rely on the informality of the established Whitehall style to receive an 'invitation to a party'. On this view, ministers and their officials have the right to choose their advisory committees, task forces and so on but do not have a right to exclude legitimate potential recruits by either any deliberate bias or simply not taking the trouble to generate and consider a wider field. The Nolan rules for new members of quango would take some extra money and a lot more of ministers' and senior officials' time if they were extended to temporary advisory exercises.

But this would be right in principle and would also improve the pool of available talent and knowledge. Ministers could, of course, ignore this fact and approve lists of members still drawn only from familiar professional or partisan circles. But this practice would be much plainer than it now is and ministers would have to explain their choices against a public record of who had applied and been shortlisted. It is too late to apply these higher standards to the rush of new task forces of 1997-98 but it can be done for the far fewer new task forces now being launched. If the next election leads to a second wave of these exercises, the new rules would be well established if introduced now and would mark a valuable step towards fairer and better government.

The government rejected the select committee's suggestion in its response in the summer of 1998, simply declaring it to be 'disproportionate'. This means: too much trouble (including some cash costs but mostly ministerial and civil service time) for the likely benefit. This study's interviewees among both very senior and middle-rank officials (the latter actually 'running' some of the task force work described above) find the idea of 'Nolanising' temporary advisory appointments mainly impractical (on time grounds) but also undesirable (on quality grounds). If re-shuffled or promoted Labour ministers (not to mention an incoming Conservative government) find themselves in charge of even just some of Whitehall's Departments after the next election, there could be a second wave of task forces, albeit a smaller one. The pressure on policy-managing grades (the former grades 5 and 7 and HEOs) is always severe and, with a new manifesto to work on, their attention to how they should arrange for the advisory or review groups which ministers might demand would simply go under. Any rules taking up time and trouble would be evaded by ministers gathering sympathetic experts and contacts into informal circles without announcing anything. This device would probably damage the quality of advice available as well as offending the open government principle even more than current practice offends it.

Quality of advice, expertise or experience would certainly be damaged, on this view, by limiting advisory appointments to those who apply and undergo formal selection. The common experience is that the likely best appointees are usually too busy (whether or not formally retired) and take much persuading to 'allow their names to go forward': they would certainly not apply or be interviewed in competition. Vanity or snobbery may be at work in some cases, but the civil service's job of giving ministers a list of more-or-less-willing 'good' people without excessive delay must still be done.

A theoretical and obvious answer to such practical ('bureaucratic') objections is that open and systematic government will indeed cost more, so the extra staffing should be found – although whether it would make much final difference to either the lists of recruits to temporary advisory bodies or the advice tendered would probably be doubted by the officials. In their eyes, a great deal of arranged advice to government simply legitimates what sensible officials had already thought to do rather than bringing in new ideas which are both fresh and valuable ('sound').

Beyond these familiar bureaucrats' complaints and doubts, however, one might respond to the call for 'open due process' in recruiting all advisory groups with one further point. The call may assume that all advisory groups mainly give the government their opinions and recommendations (rather than nuts-and-bolts technical operational support on policies ministers have already adopted) – and, moreover, do so on interesting topics which are long on opinion and fairly short on technical difficulty, certainly of a kind which only trained experts can understand. If opinion is to dominate, representativeness is an obviously desirable feature and would suit a royal commission on foxhunting or abolishing pub licensed hours. It has been noted in this Report how many of the 295 task forces have had an 'action group' character, working out the detailed procedures for delivering accepted policies and practices. Outsider members of those groups are more like temporary officials than members of traditional commissions or committees: their opinions on policy merits (if they have any) must be set aside in favour of practical advice drawn from their expertise or experience. If they dislike the policy context they (unlike the officials themselves) can refuse to join in or can quit.

Of course, if it is believed that advertisement and selection procedures would increase the Departments' choice of good quality members of temporary advisory groups (as also of quangos and standing governmental advisory committees) then it would apply to these 'action' task forces as much as to the more familiar policy search groups. The ministers involved in the 18 Policy Action Teams (page 45), for example, would have selected from the formal applicants just as for, say, the Urban Task Force or the Scottish GPs' Out-of-Hours Service Working Group (page 123) – both of which were also charged with producing actual schemes of policy and administrative practice to fulfill stated government policies. The issues are: would this be a priority for extra civil service staffing and would public procedures broaden or narrow (strengthen or weaken) the actual likely selection of high quality members of groups – once 'quality' had been defined for the various types of policy, operational and technical jobs which task forces and other temporary commissions and committees are asked to do?

A pro-business bias?

Whether this partly novel set of task forces created within British government has been biased towards the producer interest in general and the commercial business sector in particular has had some outline debate already published. Two brief studies of this aspect of the new Labour government, based on some limited listings of groups and their members, were published in 1998. Although both were Labour-related, their approaches and conclusions were opposite. The Labour policy discussion group, Catalyst, published a hostile account by Steve Platt, suggesting that task forces are a centralist, manipulative scheme, pretending to produce consensus on political issues which actually require open and contested debate.[6] In contrast, a Cranfield University researcher, Lewis Macleod, produced a brief essay, with notes on some 52 task forces, which welcomed this 'task force revolution' (as he called his report) and quite heavily emphasised and endorsed the consultation between the Labour government and private business which it embodies. The promotion of this consultation has been the central objective of the Labour-supporting Industry Forum, which commissioned the Cranfield study.[7] With the one essay condemning the new government's alleged relationship with private business and the other celebrating it (and both possibly exaggerating it, at least as manifested through task forces) those observers seeking a conclusion on the point may take their pick.

The dominance of the 'producer interest' in this particular set of external groups created in 1997-98 by a new government must be seen in the context of organised interest groups in British (and other countries') public affairs. It is a traditional feature that associations of unofficial, private organisations and individuals operating at national or regional levels disproportionately represent producer interests, most of these being for-profit commercial producers – obviously so in the UK's case where the public trading sector (the nationalised industries) has almost disappeared. Broadly speaking and allowing for the invaluable work of the Consumers Association (publisher of the *Which?* magazines) it is mass representative politics, not specialised mass organisations, which represents the millions of parents, patients, pedestrians, shoppers or holders of savings accounts. Politically accountable ministers and local authority councillors listen to the organised voices of producers and judge how the unorganised publics affected will react politically to the action or consents they are being asked to approve.[8]

The task forces under discussion in this Report are very much 'mixed fruit', so that groups of differing importance or even purposes – working in varying policy fields and in contrasting official policy-making contexts – should not be seen as standardised items. Therefore memberships are also not to be standardised, at least without recognising that some groups' memberships have been potentially more important than others. Also, and more fundamentally, the

Footnotes

Summary (page 10)

1. Barker, A (1998), *The Labour Government's Policy 'Reviews' and 'Task Forces': an initial listing and analysis*, Essex Paper in Politics and Government No. 126, from the Department of Government, University of Essex, Colchester, Essex CO4 3SQ

2. Designated sub-groups (other than those composed solely of a main group's members) are counted as external advisory bodies in List 1.1 (page 40) on the functional ground that a sub-group in support of a main 'task force' has had at least as clear a job to do and as much working life of its own as its main group – often rather more. They contain external members in their own right whose experience of assisting the government in its task force initiative is broadly the same, whether a main group or a sub-group, within the wide variety of group tasks and rôles they undertake. Some task forces have delegated almost all their functional work to their sub-groups.

Commentary (page 11)

1. The government's first Annual Report (1998) offered this figure and its second (July 1999) repeated it (with the claim that only two promises had not yet been 'timetabled' for action: all others had been either fully met or put in hand).

2. Other exclusions are: quasi-judicial inquiries or tribunals conducted by senior judges, possibly under the Tribunals of Inquiry (Evidence) Act (the BSE inquiry and Bloody Sunday tribunal); statutory inquiries (planning inquiries, railway accident inquiries); the 'Patten' review of Northern Ireland policing (which resulted from international negotiations leading to the Good Friday Agreement, rather than a solely UK ministerial initiative); the Independent Commission on the Electoral System ('Jenkins') (whose fundamental constitutional topic set it apart from the issues of current government policy and administrative practices which have concerned 'task forces' at large); and any review or inquiry group launched by a statutory regulator or quango, rather than the responsible minister. As to involuntary gaps in List 1.1, departments were unable or unwilling to give membership details for 14 'task forces' within our research timetable. These were: Working Group on Chemical Contaminants and Joint Industry/ Department Working Group on Fixed Quota Fishing Allocations (Min. of Agriculture); Educational Development Plans Advisory Group (DfEE: Education) and Post-16 Partnership Advisory Group (DfEE: Employment and Training); Expert Scoping Group on Mental Health Policy, Sex and Relationships Task Group and Task Group on Vulnerable and Hard to Reach Groups (Department of Health); Retail Crime Reduction Team (Home Office); Northern Ireland Skills Task Force (Northern Ireland Office); Rural

familiar problem about assessing political influence naturally applies to individual memberships as to the groups themselves: it cannot be assumed that a particular policy outcome was the result of a task force – or a particular chair or member of it – having appeared to advocate it. Even when they submit published reports with findings, conclusions and recommendations – whose fortunes can be traced in subsequent policy outcomes – the logical problem remains. The government may have intended these outcomes from the start and set up the task force or other outside exercise to legitimate their intentions. The group has pushed at a door which was already open. For the 1997-98 task forces it is, in any case, too soon to attempt such an exercise: too many of them have either not yet seen a definitive policy laid down on their particular report, in a white paper or bill, while some have not yet even reported.

Any research effort to assess the various levels of influence enjoyed by even some of the 295 task forces would require case-by-case studies, aided by the passage of time to allow policy decisions and outcomes to unfold. As to lobbying the government by means of seeking and getting memberships or even chairs of task forces, of course not only the representative bodies (the trade associations, trade unions and many of the voluntary bodies) but also individual firms will have been looking to influence government's perceptions and policy priorities in standard pressure group style. But the main impression gained from repeated scrutiny of these 295 task forces and sub-groups and the interviewing of both task force members and their sponsoring departmental civil servants is less political and more technical. As the Summary opening Part 1 has suggested, the remarkable upsurge of outsider co-operation and consultation produced by the task force idea in mid-1997 has largely consisted of many of the 2,500 or so members discussing the substance, problems and potential opportunities of their own and their colleagues' jobs. Can it be assumed (and either damned or praised) that a more than 2:1 imbalance between private business and voluntary body members on a very large and hugely varied list of task forces must mean that business has been enjoying the same imbalance of influence with government? It would depend what those numerous business people have been doing and saying in these meetings. If thrashing out fine details of their particular industry's or sector's problems and opportunities for growth and improvement, they certainly have opportunities to influence officials and ministers, at least on what new ideas or practices they think are feasible. But the scope for them to receive as well as to exercise influence should not be discounted.

The sequence of Notes throughout this commentary offers a range of tasks and purposes which may explain the broad and varied nature of these numerous task forces. One principal distinction is between a government's traditional policy advice-seeking stance and the more novel use of formally advisory groups as promotional vehicles, allowing government to get a message into an industry or public sector field – preferably by recruiting practitioners and experts who will themselves take up that message and proselytise among their peers. Notes 19 and 22 offer some examples including the film and tourism industries, both of whose task forces organised by the Department of Culture brought in large proportions of managers and other senior figures from those industries, as also in the case of the Creative Industries Task Force (page 55). It was emphatically not the purpose of these groups to offer a platform for these industries' claims for public subsidy. In varying degrees they were developmental bodies, intended to make these industries more cohesive and effective through study and action on shared chronic commercial weaknesses. In the Tourism Forum's unique case, the Department's promotion of the tourism/hospitality industry as a self-conscious overall unity – from the Chief Executive of British Airways to the proprietor of an Isle of Wight hotel (both members) – was as bold as it was unconvincing. Even so, the 114 business memberships of the Forum and its 12 sub groups out of its 201 outsider members indicates the government trying to encourage an unformed proto-industry, mainly by self-development through study and discussion, rather than an opportunity for mass lobbying of the Department's Tourism Division.

Indeed, one of that Division's officials 'riding herd' on this, the largest of all the task forces, was quite philosophical when discussing the Department's need to keep on inventing new task forces (and even executive quangos) to keep up the pressure to improve the travel and hospitality industry's performance in the national economic interest. While tourism and other Department of Culture responsibilities offer clear examples of 'developmental' task force exercises, this character may be traced across many other fields, as the Box Notes suggest.

Although the research would be difficult, particularly after time has passed, the claim that Labour's task forces have largely represented major extra opportunities for commercial business lobbying as part of New Labour's political positioning does need some empirical study of actual cases. It may be that the numerical imbalance of business memberships has mainly been the result of ministers and their Departments wanting to know much more of how things work – whether well or ill – in many private sector fields while often wanting to bring managers together to develop their industry's identity and quality. Practicality may be more the cause of these business numbers than politics.[9] One aspect does require attention, however, and not only in the private business sector of these groups' members. Some simple form of declaring interests would add authority to the work of task forces in general, particularly where commercial matters are under review.

5 Conclusions and recommendations

The striking features of Labour's task force exercise as a whole have been its scale and novelty. It has represented a dramatic increase in invitations to outsiders to join in government (albeit usually to describe and discuss their own job or specialist knowledge of a working field). This inclusiveness and at least 2,500 'invitations to the party' represented by 295 task forces and their sub groups has helped to confirm Labour's general claims on 'collaborative government', outlined in section 1. But if this upsurge in outside participation in Whitehall's discussions was to be combined with excessive executive influence over the work done by outsiders, then the task force initiative would take on a much darker shade than the sunny talk of inclusiveness and openness to outside ideas would like to imply. It was suggested above that Labour ministers wanted so many task forces partly because they would bring the policy or operational discussions much closer to Departments, particularly if a minister or senior official served as the chair or an active member of the group. The group's remit can be closely defined (and changed – as with the Football Task Force, for example) much more readily than a royal commission or departmental commit-tee of inquiry could handle or even accept. A minister or senior official can get feedback from a task force (and certainly from any kind of subsidiary working or action group) more quickly and flexibly because the group will have been recruited on that basis. The process of benefiting from the group's knowledge and experience seems, at least, to be quicker if they are prepared to act as short-order cooks, even though the delay in receiving any final report from some of them has proved no less than with traditional commissions and committees.

The concept of ministerially managed outside advice is central to a democratic audit of the 'task force phenomenon'. Steve Platt's early essay in *Government by Task Force* was right to point out the dangers for genuinely plural and open public policy debate of ministers claiming to be open with invitations to sit on official advisory or collaborative committees while actually either limiting the range to politically acceptable people or then over-managing the committees' work to conform to their current ministerial priorities: things which ministers and their officials currently think they need to know about. By the same token, internal departmental reviews should not be presented in public as systematic and externally assessed when they remain inside jobs: there has been some criticism on this score, within and beyond Whitehall itself, of the principal departmental review of 1997-98 – the joint MoD/Foreign Office Strategic Defence Review (see pages 66 and 147).

Agenda Steering Group, National Transport Forum and Women's Advisory Group (Scottish Office); Welsh Advisory Group on Special Educational Needs and Welsh Advisory Task Force for Volunteers (Welsh Office). If all of these were genuine 'external' groups which had a working existence beyond an initial announcement or press mention (and this has sometimes been most uncertain) then the total of external groups might have been 309 rather than 295.

3. The Democratic Audit produced the first comprehensive study of UK quangos as it now has of the task force theme (Weir, S, and Hall, W (eds), (1994) *Ego Trip: Extra-Governmental Organisations in the UK and their Accountability*, Human Rights Centre, Essex/ (Charter 88 Trust) which was followed by Weir and Hall (1995), *Behind Closed Doors* (on advisory quangos) and Hall and Stuart (1996), *The Untouchables: Power and Accountability in the Quango State* (executive and advisory quangos) (both Human Rights Centre/Scarman Trust Enterprises). The review of quangos was updated in Weir, S, and Beetham, D (1998), *Political Power and Democratic Control in Britain*, chapters 8 and 9 (Routledge).

4. Several valuable initial articles on aspects of Labour's 'collaborative' claims appear in *Public Policy and Administration*, 14.2 (Summer 1999). Other papers presented at the Public Administration Committee's 1999 conference on this theme are listed at HYPERLINK http://www.york.ac.uk/depts/poli/pac/conf99.htm and http://www.york.ac.uk/depts/poli/pac/conf99.htm.

5. The author had consent to observe this meeting.

6. Platt, S (1998), *Government by Task Force: a review of the reviews*. Catalyst Paper 2, London, Catalyst Trust, Box 17729, London, N5 2WN.

7. MacLeod, L (1998), *The Task Force Revolution: a guide to task forces and advisory groups under the new Labour Government*, Cranfield Partnership Research Unit (Cranfield University) for the Industry Forum, Bedford.

8. Even so, the memberships of task forces offered to consumer and user bodies by Departments have been grossly inadequate. The designation in Table 2 of the entire voluntary/charity sector (15 per cent of the total) as being consumer/user in outlook is broadly reasonable and includes the handful of Consumer Association people. (The National Consumer Council's few memberships come within the 'national public body' column and so, as a very small anomaly, are counted as producers.) List 1.1 offers the details of each consumer body's places. Some, like Friends of the Earth, are fully consumer-oriented; other charities mainly produce services for members or clients (e.g. the National Trust). On government-interest group linkages, see chapter 10 in the Democratic Audit's major volume (Weir, S, and Beetham, D

(1998), *Political Power and Democratic Control in Britain*, Routledge.

9. Another major 'developmental' task force exercise — the Fundamental Review of the Economic Development Strategy in Northern Ireland (page 116) — helps to show how mere numbers of memberships may not reveal any profile of influence over ministers. The main review group, with six of its 12 members from private business, is included in the List 1.1 totals but the memberships of no fewer than 17 working groups were not supplied by the Department. If included, the overall business total would rise by perhaps 150 or more persons, yet the work done has been developmental rather than lobbying.

10. Barker, A (1998), *The Labour Government's Policy Reviews and Task Forces: an initial listing and analysis*, Essex Paper in Politics and Government No. 126, Department of Government, University of Essex, Colchester, CO4 3SQ. This initial study (spring, 1998) relied on the lists of 'task forces', 'reviews', etc., provided by ministers in Hansard in response to PQs put down haphazardly by a few MPs and peers. Counting, sorting, listing and classifying groups and their members over the past year has proved to be very slippery work. The strong departmental nature of Whitehall has been well-attested by some 18 Departments establishing some 500 groups and internal policy reviews with the Cabinet Office attempting no more than occasional ad hoc circulated enquiries of them to produce 'omnibus' lists in response to PQs. An announcement in July 1997 that only task forces approved by the centre should be added to the total launched since 1 May was either generously applied or ignored, by some Departments at least: the flow continued. In July 1999, the Cabinet Office abandoned the view that no overall review or analysis of these bodies and tried for the first time to collect an up-to-date list. The main idea was to get Departments formally to establish as non-departmental public bodies – that is, standing bodies which the Cabinet Office would include in the official volume, *Public Bodies*. The great bulk of task forces which would report and disband were plainly seen as Departments' own business, regarding both the way they were appointed and their procedures as well as the substance of their work.

It will be equally necessary that the traditional forms of royal commissions and departmental committees of inquiry should not wither away, leaving only the more manageable task force or working group type of exercise to serve the purpose of external inquiry into policy and operations; if inquiries such as the Urban Task Force or the Review Panel on the BBC's finance and licence fee (see page 55) are left alone to behave like a traditional commission or committee, it matters little that they carry other names. The great political strength of the traditional form is that an authoritative group of people go off and prepare a published report which must arise coherently from their published evidence if it is to carry weight with either the government itself or with informed public opinion. Transparency of process combines with demonstrably rational conclusions to produce what must, therefore, be at least reasonably arguable recommendations. Some of Labour's task forces since 1997 have displayed these qualities: as noted above, there has been significant overlap with traditional practice as the Urban and BBC finances groups attest.

The 'task force phenomenon' seems to be a new standing feature of British government, and may make the more arm's length policy inquiries by Whitehall-appointed committees or royal commissions fade away even further. In this event it should be Parliament's place to fill the gap by commissioning this work from expert and other suitable nominees, to report to the public through Parliament as an extension of the select committees' work. Parliamentary commissions would replace royal commissions.

The new types of advisory/action groups of outsiders working with ministers and Departments and loosely known as task forces appear to be a new political institution – or perhaps better, a new governmental custom and practice. That apparent fact stimulated the author's initial research in early 1998 and attracted the interest of Democratic Audit. A major criticism of the 'task force phenomenon' is that it has lacked a considered framework of rules and practice and now requires one. This would lift the curse of the usual mindless British constitutional 'ad hockery' which settled on it during the new government's hectic first three months. The senior civil service was then politically incapable of even seeming to question their new masters' preferences, for fear of being thought rigid or even irrelevant. Now, half way towards the next general election (and the prospect of a further, smaller crop of task forces being launched by at least some new ministers – whether Labour or Conservative) some systematic 'review of the reviews' is needed to put this generally useful reform on to a firmer and more authoritative base – known rules and customs controlling external groups, and more open recruitment and working methods are needed. In particular, some recognition of 'Nolan' values on recruitment might be possible without the administrative burden which 'Nolanised' appointments to standing public bodies (quangos) already – and quite justifiably – impose.

Overall, this commentary concludes that the vigorous extension of policy-making public participation which Labour's 500-odd review exercises (both task forces and internal departmental reviews) has represented is a welcome innovation: good for the interests involved; for the civil service; and for ministers themselves. Its public transparency and aspects of accountability (for example, possibly requiring declarations of members' interests and establishing useful lines to Parliament) could be improved while any tendency to entrenched bias or closed, corporatist, working lines which cut out other legitimate interests must, of course, be revealed and opposed. Having Parliament as a new and active alternative patron of informed policy reviews by outside parliamentary commissioners would be a healthy development: so would a robust adjustment of the broadly 66 per cent: 15 per cent producer/consumer ratio which Labour produced in 1997-98.

By all means let ministers expand and manage their information and advice sources. But excessive management would offend constitutional standards (and so may be at increasing risk from judicial reviews of the quality of any ensuing government decisions). The Democratic Audit drew attention several years ago to the true numbers and political importance of appointed public bodies (quangos) in British government. Although these 300 or so mainly temporary task forces are not public bodies, providing public services with public money, they have played a significant role (in addition to some important examples having been turned into advisory quangos). They seem likely to become a continuing feature of British public affairs and Democratic Audit's decision to add considerable further research to the author's earlier study has been justified.[10] 'Rule by task force' – in the sense of the task force becoming a normal stage or adjunct of British government policy-making – offers real advantages. But it must not become an exclusive device: the British political system has developed one of the richest relationships between the state and unofficial civil society to be found in the democratic world. The relatively closely politically managed government-appointed task force (including the policy action group) can enhance these existing channels of official consultation and public policy inquiry. They could not replace them, even in the exalted name of the 'new public management' of the government's responsibilities. No such attempt should be made.

Democratic Audit Overview

Democratic Audit was established in 1992 at the University of Essex to assess the quality of democratic arrangements and political freedom in the United Kingdom. Professor David Beetham, consultant to the Audit, and Stuart Weir have since been engaged in developing democratic criteria – the brainchild of Professor Beetham – to measure the quality of a country's democracy on a systematic basis. These criteria were employed in an exhaustive study of parliamentary democracy in this country, which was highly critical of the informal and unbalanced nature of government's processes of consultation with outside interests on policies and legislation[1]. The study concluded:

'Government consultation of interests and the general public is unsystematic and opaque. Much formative consultation takes place within policy communities of officials and interests which are generally closed to outside scrutiny . . . Overall, certain interests get preference over others, thus blocking political equality in government policy-making and, in some areas, seriously harming the public interest.[2]'

Democratic Audit is therefore sympathetic to the current government's attempt through task forces and similar bodies to make the consultative and advice-seeking process more open to the public, to broaden the base of policy advice and to make it more inclusive of different kinds of expertise from civil society. The task force phenomenon is a move towards more open and inclusive government which is far superior to the generally closed departmental links with interest groups and unsystematic and only partially open consultative trawls. We therefore welcome the government's attempt to be more inclusive in its approach to policy review and implementation. However, we are critical of three aspects of the task force approach which are important for democratic government in Britain:

1. *Procedural consistency.* Anthony Barker's scholarly analysis reveals once more the informality and ad-hockery that characterises central government in Britain. 'Making it up as you go along' has advantages for flexibility and fast response, but there is a worrying lack of common procedures, guidelines or rules governing how these external advisory bodies are constituted, how their existence and work are made public, how they should operate, and how their own processes of consultation should be arranged, and so on. This informality of approach was one of the main criticisms of the Democratic Audit study and is fully borne out by Barker's findings.

There is considerable variety in the nature and degree of consultation which has been undertaken by task forces, much of which has been confined to established organisations and interested parties (see for example ministers' answers to Parliamentary Questions from Dr Tony Wright MP, March 1999). The processes by which task forces and advisory bodies are established should be governed by sensible and systematic rules; procedures for giving public notice of their creation and operations should put in place; and the partial and uneven nature of their consultations needs to be raised to the level of existing 'best practice'.

2. *Openness.* There has been sufficient openness about task forces for Anthony Barker and Audit researcher workers to assemble all the information in your this report. But it has not been an easy task because the information is not available in a coherent way. Moreover, some departmental officials have refused or been reluctant to give even simple information about the composition of their task

forces. There is no reason at all, except the informal and even slipshod way in which the task force process has been organised, why the whole of this information has not been placed on a Cabinet Office web-site and regularly updated. Also, while task forces have consulted those whom they believe can provide useful responses, the general public has rarely been consulted or even informed of a task force's work, though some created informative web-sites, and few task forces gave useful information on the outcomes of their consultation. On the other hand, their exercises have at least brought the consideration of a range of policy issues out into the open and task forces do at least publish reports which generally enter the public domain. There is a need for improved co-ordination in Whitehall and guidelines to promote openness and wider consultation.

It is also important to assess the role of task forces within the perspective of a government which intends to give only restricted rights of access to official information in the forthcoming Freedom of Information legislation. Almost all the deliberative, information and research work of task forces could be encompassed within the broad exemption of policy formulation within central government, and so ministers and officials will be able to pick and choose what they choose to make public and what they conceal; and commercial confidentiality could also be often called in aid of secrecy rather than openness. In the view of the Audit, the whole paraphernalia of public executive and advisory bodies, national and local, ought to be subject to the rules of transparent conduct that obtain for such bodies in the United States and gain public access to their data, consultations and deliberations.[3]

3. *Representativeness*. The figures for members and the places they occupy on task forces reveals a producer dominance that gives real cause for concern, even when allowance is made for the task forces that clearly relate to producer interests and the functional nature of the exercise. Anthony Barker's painstaking analysis of the composition of the task force 'elite' in Table 2 divides members and places into 14 separate classifications and then groups them under four main heads. Private companies and their trade associations occupy over a third (35 per cent) of the 3,103 chairs and memberships. Public sector producer interests nearly take up another third (31 per cent). Altogether, then, producer interests swallow up two thirds of the task force places.

Voluntary and charitable bodies are broadly interpreted here as representing the interests of consumers or users of goods and services, both private and public. This 'consumer interest' has been allocated 15 per cent of the places. Academic experts (8 per cent) and 'independent' members (4 per cent), who may both be generally expected to fulfil a disinterested role on these bodies, obtain a combined presence of 357 out of the 3,103 places, or 12 per cent of the total. Trade unionists may be present either as worker and consumer representatives, or as producer interests, and they are shown as a 'mixed' category. But with only 73 places (2 per cent of the total), their role hardly disturbs the overall two-thirds to one sixth producer/consumer ratio, with a minority of academics and independents sharing an eighth of the places. Another ratio – that of men to women members – gives cause for concern, at two-thirds men to only one third women.

Task forces fall outside the Nolan rules for appointments to quangos (which have been duly observed in those cases where task forces have become quangos). Again in reply to PQs from Dr Tony Wright MP, ministers have explained that task force members have been chosen for 'specific experience and expertise', and that public advertising would be 'inappropriate and disproportionate', especially for bodies intended to be short-lived. This is persuasive reasoning. But short-lived or not, task forces are often involved at the formation stage of policy-making and so may have a long-lived influence. The selection processes could also be laid bare. It would be possible to release information on how far members are chosen by ministers and their officials, and how far they are nominated by organised interest groups, professional bodies and so on. The specific balance between the variety of experience and knowledge on tap could be made open for public scrutiny. Governing

Footnotes

1. See chapter 10, 'Networks in Power', in Weir, S, and Beetham, D (1998), *Political Power and Democratic Control in Britain*, Routledge.

2 Op cit, p.297

3 This experience is described in detail in the memorandum (no. 34) given in evidence to the Select Committee on Public Administration on behalf of the Audit by Stuart Weir and Greg Palast, *Freedom of Information Draft Bill*, CPA Third Report, Session 1998-99, HC 570- II, p. 138

4 The same point applies to the composition of advisory quangos (or non-departmental public bodies). See further Weir, S, and Hall, W (1995), *Behind Closed Doors*, Democratic Audit Paper No. 4, Human Rights Centre, University of Essex/ Channel 4 Television.

procedures for recruiting members need to be debated and installed; and the Commissioner for Public Appointments and select committees could be given a watching brief.

The producer dominance is understandable, up to a point. It reflects the well-known structure of interest group politics and at least brings it out into the open on a range of contested issues. Their dominant presence does not necessarily entail a dominant influence; indeed, in some cases, as Anthony Barker shows, their role is to transmit government influence back to their own constituencies or to prepare the ground there for new and perhaps unpopular policies. Further, the dominant *purpose* of the groups on which they serve is to provide functional advice, information and support from practitioners for shaping and sharpening government policies, many of them fixed in advance. Finally, it is government's job to represent the disorganised mass public and consumer interest.

Against all these considerations, Democratic Audit is bound first to make the simple point that absent voices remain unheard. It should be government's job to see that all relevant voices are represented when policies are being brought into practical being, so that they can be heard by one another as well as by government. Take for example the Treasury's Private Finance Initiative Task Force; a former banker presides over the deliberations of a dozen bankers, financiers and business professionals and five Treasury officials. True, its purpose is to advance the PFI initiative in line with established government policy. But surely it should balance its City representation with those at the sharp end of the PFI initiative in the NHS and public services? Surely, over all, the consumer interest and independent and expert academic voices should be added in greater numbers to the mix?

The goal of effective government is one of the driving forces of this government. It is an admirable goal, as Trevor Smith acknowledges. But the Prime Ministerial 'what works' test demands the question, 'works for whom?' The functional nature of the task force phenomenon cannot be gainsaid. But the argument that mostly experts and practitioners are giving mostly expert and practical, and therefore politically neutral, advice can and must be gainsaid – especially when their debates are generally conducted outside the public gaze. The idea of the neutral expert is no longer a valid one, if indeed it ever was. This is not merely a question of the particular interests an expert may represent, but of the whole framework of assumptions which condition the form of their expertise.[4]

The tendency of task forces is to de-politicise issues which are the stuff of representative politics – major divisions in views, moral dilemmas and scientific controversies; and the idea that they can be resolved rationally by chosen cadres of representatives of the private and public interests involved is grossly mistaken. A pluralist politics would recognise the diversity of goals which are likely to gather around significant policy issues, like, say, the PFI, cleaner vehicles or urban policy; would create an informed forum in which a variety of interests and approaches are openly acknowledged and debated on equal and informed terms; and presented for final decision to Parliament and government. There will often then be a role for task-oriented experts in bringing to fruition the policies which result.

Finally, the language of being 'invited to the party', as senior civil servants describe the process of recruiting task force members, is very revealing. While it may suggest a certain openness to outsiders, it also implies that government is an essentially private function; that to participate in it is within the personal gift of the 'party holders'; and that only a select group of potential party-goers will be chosen.

PART TWO

DATA: TASK FORCES AND POLICY REVIEWS

THE LABOUR GOVERNMENT'S TASK FORCES AND THEIR MEMBERS

Names, affiliations and classification of members
May 1997 to December 1998

CLASSIFICATION OF GROUP MEMBERS

1 Public Sector

1.1 Central Government
Ministers and officials in Government Departments and their Executive Agencies. (The seconded private sector-based Treasury staff in the Private Finance Initiative unit are classed as 'private business').

1.2 National public body
Non-departmental public bodies (quangos) and other (often statutory) national bodies created by Government.

1.3 Judiciary
Judges; any professional magistrates or court administrators.

1.4 Health
NHS and associated local health occupations.

1.5 Local government
Local authority members and officers and their associations and consortia.

1.6 Local public spending body
Local public or semi-public bodies relying on public funds.

1.7 Education
All levels, including university (except where an 'academic/research' role is indicated).

1.8 Police
Police officers or administrators.

2 Private Sector

2.1 Private business
Private commercial, for-profit, firms including professional or individual services such as lawyers and consultants.

2.2 Privatised business
Public sector undertakings sold into the private sector since 1979.

2.3 Trade association
All voluntary groupings, broadly defined, of private sector commercial companies.

3 Membership Organisations/Charities

3.1 Voluntary/charity
Voluntary membership, not-for-profit, associations (including political parties but excluding trade unions and professional associations) and registered charities.

3.2 Trade union
Registered trade unions.

3.3 Professional association
Voluntary membership, not-for-profit, associations whose members can claim professional status.

4 Expert or Experienced Independent Individuals

4.1 Academic/research
Experts in the field working in (or retired from) academic or research centre posts.

4.2 Independent
(i)   Apparently uncommitted persons — either expert in the relevant field (although not 'academic/ research' figures) or serving as unconnected lay persons intended to bring useful outside judgement;
(ii)   Retired persons (other than 'academic/ research' figures) who appear not to have entered another classified field.

● [The names of all 'outsiders' on groups (i.e., not ministers or civil servants ['Central government']) are listed alphabetically, below, to show their single or multiple memberships.]

MINISTRY OF AGRICULTURE, FISHERIES AND FOOD (MAFF)

Name	Affiliation	Classification
1 Agricultural Advisory Group To advice Agriculture ministers on key food, agricultural, environmental and rural policy issues.		
John Cousins (Chair)	• Executive Director, Farm Wildlife Advisory Group • Chair, Suffolk Wildlife Trust	Voluntary/charity
Lord Donoughue	• Parliamentary Secretary, MAFF (resigned July 1999)	Central government
Lord Eatwell	• President, Queens' College, Cambridge • Chair, Board of the Royal Ballet	Academic/research
Andrew Graham	• Acting Master, Balliol College, Oxford	Academic/research
Jill Johnstone	• Head of Policy, National Consumer Council	National public body
Philip Lowe	• Head of Centre for Rural Economy, University of Oxford	Academic/research
Professor John Marsh	• Former Head, Centre for Agriculture Strategy, University of Reading	Academic/research
Cathy McGlynn	• Special Adviser, MAFF	Central government
Jonathon Porritt	• Director, Forum for the Future • Former Director, Friends of the Earth	Voluntary/charity
Baronness Young of Old Scone	• Chair, English Nature • Vice-Chair, BBC Governors	National public body
2 Review of Bovine TB in Cattle and Badgers To advise Ministers on implementation of the Krebs Report by overseeing the design & analysis of the randomised experiment to test the effectiveness of badger culling as a means of controlling bovine TB.		
Professor John Bourne (Chair)	• Professor of Animal Health and former Professor of Veterinary Medicine, University of Bristol • Former Director, Institute for Animal Health	Academic/research
Dr Christl Donnelly (Deputy Chair)	• Research statistician, Wellcome Trust Centre for the Epidemiology of Infectious Disease, University of Oxford • Specialist in infectious disease modelling	Academic/research
Sir David Cox FRS	• Former Warden of Nuffield College, University of Oxford • A statistician, with experience of experimental design especially in a medical context	Academic/research
Professor George Gettinby	• Professor in the Department of Statistics and Modelling Science, University of Strathclyde • Specialist in experiment design for the evaluation of veterinary products	Academic/research
Professor Ivan Morrison	• Head, Division of Immunology and Pathology, Compton Laboratory of the Institute for Animal Health • Veterinarian and specialist in bovine immunology and disease pathogenesis with practical experience of field experiments	Academic/research
Dr Rosie Woodroffe	• Research fellow, Department of Zoology, University of Cambridge • Specialist in wildlife disease and badger ecology and behaviour	Academic/research
3 Review of Fishing Vessel Licensing To review the operation of the current arrangements for licensing of UK fishing vessels to establish whether they are necessary and if so how they may be improved.		
5 Representatives	• *National Federation of Fishermen's Organisations*	Trade association
5 Representatives	• *Scottish Fisherman's Federation*	Trade association
Representative	• *Northern Ireland Fishermen's Federation*	Trade association
Representative	• *Sea Fish Industry Authority*	National public body
Representative	• *Maritime and Coastguard Agency*	Central government
4 Review of the Public Analyst Service in England and Wales To review public analyst arrangements in England and Wales; to make recommendations on how best to provide the scientific and technical support needed by food authorities in respect of their food law enforcement responsibilities. Some 44 bodies invited to comment.		
Alan Turner (Chair)	• Independent consultant on food science, technology and law • Former senior examiner for the M.Chem.A. qualification (public analyst qualification) • Former Chair, Food and Drink Federation's Food Labelling and Law Panels	Private business
Professor Edward Abel	• President, Royal Society of Chemistry	Academic/research
Councillor Neil Bonnar	• Member, South Tyneside Metropolitan Borough Council	

	• Former Chair, Local Authorities Co-ordinating Body on Food and Trading Standards	Local government
Dorothy Craig	• Member, Food Advisory Committee • Member, Executive Committee of the National Federation of Consumer Groups • Chair, Food and Agriculture Working Party of Consumers in Europe Group	National public body
Dr Tom Gorsuch	• Former member, Food Advisory Committee • Former Chair, Food Processing Research Consultative Committee	Independent
Dr Catherine Humphries	• Chief Scientific Adviser, Co-operative Wholesale Society	Private business
Valerie Saint	• Legal adviser, Unilever UK Ltd. • Chair, Labelling Sub-Committee of the Food and Drink Federation and the Legislation and Technical Committee of the Ice Cream Federation	Private business

5 Review of the Current Rules on Quarantine of Imported Pet Animals

To assess the risk of introduction of rabies into the UK under the current policy for quarantine of pet animals and under alternative policies. Consultation of relevant bodies. A report of September 1998 recommended a passport scheme: accepted by the Government.

Professor Ian Kennedy (Chair)	• Professor of Health Law, Ethics and Policy, School of Public Policy, University College, London • Former President, Centre for Medical Law and Ethics, King's College, London • Chaired the Government's Advisory Group on the ethics of xenotransplantation (1995-96)	Academic/research
Dr Michel Aubert	• Centre for Veterinary Studies, Nancy, France	Academic/research
Dr Barbara Bannister	• Consultant in Infectious and Tropical Diseases, Royal Free Hospital, London	Academic/research
Paul DeVile	• Small animal veterinary practitioner in Eastbourne • Former President, British Veterinary Association • Former President, British Small Animals Veterinary Association • Former Chair, BVA Rabies Working Group	Private business
Dr Chris Dye	• Senior Epidemiologist, World Health Organization, Geneva	Academic/research
Dr Andrew Higgins	• Chief Executive and Scientific Director, Animal Health Trust	Academic/research
Professor Oswald Jarrett	• Professor of Comparative Virology, University of Glasgow	Academic/research
Professor Herbert Sewell	• Head of Immunology, University Hospital Medical School, Nottingham	Academic/research
Sir Joseph Smith	• Former Head, Public Health Laboratory Service • Former member of the Committee on Safety of Medicines	Independent

6 Review of Salmon and Freshwater Fisheries

To review existing policies and legislation in England and Wales concerning management & conservation of salmon, trout, eels & freshwater fish & make recommendations. Consultation during 1998 included national and regional discussions and hearings.

Professor Lynda Warren (Chair)	• Professor of Environmental Law, University of Wales	Academic/research
Dr Nick Giles	• Self employed consultant specialising in freshwater fisheries and wetland ecology management • Chair, Environment Agency's Southern Regional Fisheries Advisory Committee (RFAC) • Scientific adviser to the Salmon and Trout Association • Former Head of Wetlands Research, Game Conservancy Trust	Private business
John Golding	• Former junior minister 1976-79; Chair of the Employment Select Committee, 1979-82 • Fished on the River Dovey, the River Wye and Avington	Independent
Dr Keith Hendry	• Managing Director and senior fisheries biologist, APEM Ltd (consultancy) • Honorary Biologist, National Federation of Anglers	Private business
Derek Heselton	• Sea fisherman and salmon netsman • Chair, Salmon Committee, National Federation of Fishermen's Organisations • MAFF appointee, North Eastern Sea Fisheries Committee • Member, former Salmon Advisory Committee	Trade association
David Hodgkiss	• Businessman • Riparian owner on Rivers Eden and Derwent • Member, Salmon and Trout Association • Patron, the Tweed Foundation	Private business
Jean Howman	• Former Chair, Salmon and Trout Association • A founder of the Association of Stillwater Game Fishery Managers • Owns and runs a still water trout fishery	Private business
Jane James	• Director of the Anglers' Conservation Association	Voluntary/charity
Dr Mike Ladle	• Salmon and coarse fish ecologist, Institute of Freshwater Ecology • Author of books on coarse and sea fishing	Academic/research

Frank Lythgoe	• Vice President, National Federation of Anglers • Secretary, Warrington Anglers' Association	Voluntary/charity
David Moore	• Recreation development manager, Anglian Water • Committee member, Association of Stillwater Game Fishery Managers • Founder Member, Institute of Fisheries Management	Privatised business
Mervyn Mountjoy	• Skipper/owner of a stern trawler • Former salmon netsman • South West member, Salmon Committee, NFFO • Former MAFF appointee, Devon and Cornwall Sea Fisheries Committees	Privatised business
Pat O'Reilly	• Self employed management consultant • Chair, Environment Agency's Welsh RFAC	Private business
Stanley Payne	• Fisheries Manager, Castle Fisheries on the River Derwent • Chair, Derwent Owners' Association • Founder Member, Institute of Fisheries Management • Chair, South and West Cumberland Fisheries Association	Private business
Dr Anne Powell	• Partner, The Hamlet Partnership (conservation consultancy) • MAFF Fisheries appointee to the Environment Agency Board • Trustee and Director, World Wildlife Fund (UK) • Trustee, Thames Salmon Trust	Private business
Professor Kerry Turner	• Professor of Environmental Economics and Management, University of East Anglia • Member, Board of the former National Rivers Authority • Economic consultant to OECD, Environment Division	Academic/research
John Williams	• General Secretary, Birmingham Anglers' Association Ltd • Vice chair, Severn Fisheries Consultative Council • Associate member, Anglers' Conservation Association	Voluntary/charity

OFFICE OF THE ATTORNEY GENERAL (AG)

Name	Affiliation	Classification
1 Review of the Crown Prosecution Service		
Rt. Hon. Sir Iain Glidewell (Head)	• Former Lord Justice of Appeal	Independent
Sir Geoffrey Dear	• Former Her Majesty's Inspector of Constabulary • Former Assistant Commissioner, Metropolitan Police	Independent
Robert Macfarlane	• Former Chief Executive (SW Asia) British Oxygen Company and other directorships	Independent

CABINET OFFICE (CO)

Name	Affiliation	Classification
1 Better Regulation Taskforce To advise the government on action which improves the effectiveness and credibility of government regulation by ensuring that it is necessary, fair and affordable, and simple to understand and administer, taking particular account of the needs of small businesses and ordinary people. Listed by the Cabinet Office as an Advisory Public Body (ANDPB).		
Lord Haskins (Chair)	• Chair, Northern Foods plc • Chair, Express Dairies plc • Member, Interchange Steering Council (Cabinet Office) • Member, UK Round Table on Sustainable Development (DETR) • Member, CBI President's Council • Member, New Deal Task Force (DfEE) • Trustee, Demos • Trustee, National Civil Liberties Trust	Private business
Teresa Graham (Deputy Chair)	• Partner and Head of Business Services, Baker Tilly (Chartered Accountants) • Institute of Chartered Accountants' spokesperson for England and Wales on small and medium enterprises • Member, Advisory Committee, Office for National Statistics • A Director of Business Link London South • Member, Deregulation Task Force of the Conservative government 1994 – 1997	Private business
Stephen Alambritis	• Head of Press and Parliamentary Affairs, Federation of Small Businesses • Previous experience running a small family business	Private business
Sarah Anderson	• Chief Executive and majority shareholder of own company, Mayday Group (London-based employment agency providing catering staff) • Member, CBI Small and Medium Enterprise Council • A Training and Enterprise Council assessor • Chair, London Enterprise Agency	Private business
Allan Charlesworth	• Deputy Chief Constable of West Yorkshire Police (special responsibility for	

	corporate development and strategic planning) • Chair of several sub committees, Association of Chief Police Officers	Police
Hugh Field	• Director, BCB International (suppliers of medical and food products and camping equipment; 65 employees) • Chair, Cardiff Local Business Partnership	Private business
Ram Gidoomal	• Chair, Winning Communications (business consultants with expertise in equal opportunities, leadership training and ethnic business advice) • Chair, Business Link London South • Member, National Accreditation Advisory Board of Business Link • Member, executive committee of the Association of Charitable Foundations	Private business
Sir Simon Gourlay	• Farmer, former President, National Farmers Union • Chair, Conservation Grade Producers • Vice-chair, Herefordshire Health Authority • Partner, Maesbrook Nursing Home	Trade association
Pamela Meadows	• National Institute of Economic and Social Research • Europe Economics • Former government economist • Former Director, Policy Studies Institute	Academic/research
Dr Chai Patel	• Former Chief Executive, Care First Group plc (largest provider of residential homes, nursing homes and other long term care services) • Department of Health Benchmark Standards Group • Deputy Chair, Continuing Care Conference • Member, Residential Forum • Governor, National Institute of Social Work	Independent
Robert Purry	• Head of Tax, Grant Thornton	Private business
Janet Russell	• Environmental Services Manager, Kirklees Metropolitan Council • Former Vice-Chair, Chartered Institute of Environmental Health's Occupational Health and Safety Committee • Association of Metropolitan Authorities advisor on the Local Authority Co-ordinating Body on Trading Standards • Local Government Association advisor on the Health and Safely Executive/Local Authority Liaison Committee	Local government
Peter Salsbury	• Managing Director, General Merchandise Group (International Procurement and Continental Europe) Marks and Spencer • President, Institute of Employment Studies	Private business
Helena Shovelton	• Chair, National Association of Citizens Advice Bureaux • Member, Audit Commission • Member, Monopolies and Mergers Commission • Deputy Chair, Local Government Commission • Member, Independent Review Body for Banking and Mortgage Lending Codes	Voluntary/charity
Sue Slipman	• Director, Gas Consumers Council • Former Director, London Training and Enterprise Council • Former Director, National Council for One Parent Families	National public body
Ed Sweeney	• General Secretary, Banking Insurance and Finance Union • Member, Trades Union Congress General Council	Trade union

2 Interchange Steering Council

To provide strategic direction for the Interchange initiative between the Civil Service and other occupations; to act as a champion for interchange wherever possible; to review progress both by departments and other sectors in taking forward the initiative.

Lord Marshall (Chair)	• Former President, Confederation of British Industry • Chair, British Airways and other directorships • Chair, Task Force on Economic Instruments for Energy Use (HM Treasury)	Privatised business
Brian Briscoe	• Chief Executive, Local Government Association	Local government
Stuart Etherington	• Chief Executive, National Council of Voluntary Organisations	Voluntary/charity
Lord Haskins	• Chair, Northern Foods plc • Chair, Express Dairies plc • Chair, Better Regulation Task Force (Cabinet Office) • Member, UK Round Table on Sustainable Development (DETR) • Member, CBI President's Council • Member, New Deal Task Force (DfEE) • Trustee, Demos • Trustee, National Civil Liberties Trust	Private business
Sir Alan Langlands	• Chief Executive, National Health Service Executive	Central government
John Sacher	• Chair of Trustees, WIG • IPT Trustee	Voluntary/charity

| Peter Sinclair | • Chief Executive, Business Links Network Company | Private business |
| Diana Warwick (now Baroness Warwick) | • Chief Executive, Committee of Vice-Chancellors and Principals | Education |

3 People's Panel Advisory Group
To advise the Service First Unit (Cabinet Office) on issues relating to the use and development of the People's Panel public opinion survey

Professor Sara Arber	• Department of Sociology, University of Surrey	Academic/research
Mike Bartram	• Senior Policy Development Officer, National Consumer Council	National public body
Professor Julia Brannen	• Thomas Coram Research Institute, University of London	Academic/research
Michelle Heyworth	• Market Research Manager, British Airways	Privatised business
Nicola Simpson	• Director, Policy and Public Affairs, National Association of Citizens Advice Bureaux	Voluntary/charity

18 Social Exclusion Unit Policy Action Teams
To develop policy on tackling social exclusion, giving particular consideration to the needs of poor neighbourhoods.

4 'Getting the people to work': Policy Action Team 1: Jobs
(lead Department DfEE; original 'champion Minister' Andrew Smith)

Mark Neale (Chair)	• Department for Education and Employment	Central government
Bhupinda Anand	• Businessman • Member, New Deal Task Force	Private business
Jonathan Baldry	• Managing Director, Talent Training	Private business
Paul Bolt	• Department for Culture, Media and Sport	Central government
Sarah Brannan	• Director, Education and Employment, Centrepoint	Voluntary/charity
William Chapman	• Department of the Environment, Transport and the Regions	Central government
Val Chinn	• Director, Big Step	Voluntary/charity
Phil Clapp	• Social Exclusion Unit, Cabinet Office	Central government
Jeremy Crook	• Director, Black Training and Enterprise Group	Private business
Helen D'Arcy	• Department of Social Security	Central government
Chris Dolphin	• Home Office	Central government
Abu Fabunmi-Stone	• Businessman	Private business
Dan Finn	• University of Portsmouth	Academic/research
Chris Francis	• Department of Trade and Industry	Central government
Jeremy Groombridge	• Department of Social Security	Central government
John Hills	• London School of Economics	Academic/research
Alistair Kennard	• Department of Trade and Industry	Central government
Andrew Lewis	• HM Treasury	Central government
Shahid Malik	• Assistant Commissioner, Commission for Racial Equality	National public body
Bob Marshall	• Director, Glasgow Works	Voluntary/charity
Steven Martin	• Head of Research and Evaluation, Reed Employment	Private business
Geoff Mulgan	• No. 10 Policy Unit	Central government
Matthew Nicholas	• Department for Education and Employment	Central government
Simon Pellew	• Managing Director, PECAN Ltd	Private business
David Reardon	• Social Exclusion Unit, Cabinet Office	Central government
Cay Stratton	• Department for Education and Employment	Central government
Anne Weinstock	• Chief Executive, Rathbone Community Industry Ltd	Private business
Sharon Welch	• Director, Millenium Festival, London First	Private business
Bill Wells	• Department for Education and Employment	Central government
Richard Wragg	• Government Office for London	Central government

5 'Getting the people to work': Policy Action Team 2: Skills
(lead Department DfEE; original 'champion Minister' Baroness Blackstone)

| Derek Grover (Chair) | • Department for Education and Employment | Central government |
| Marcus Bell | • Department for Education and Employment | Central government |

Paul Bolt	• Department for Culture, Media and Sport	Central government
Phil Clapp	• Social Exclusion Unit, Cabinet Office	Central government
Ellen Cockburn	• Personnel Executive, Northern Foods	Private business
Jay Derrick	• Head of School, City and Islington College	Education
Bob Fryer	• Principal, Northern College • Chair, National Advisory Group on Continuing Education and Lifelong Learning	Education
Craig Harris	• Director, Education and Employment, National Association for the Care and Resettlement of Offenders	Voluntary/charity
Marion Headicar	• Department of the Environment, Transport and the Regions	Central government
Allan Mayo	• Department of Trade and Industry	Central government
Victoria McKechnie	• Human Resources Development Manager, Great North Eastern Railways	Privatised business
Andrew Olive	• HM Treasury	Central government
Haroon Saad	• Head of Equalities, Birmingham City Council	Local government
Tom Schuller	• Director, Centre for Continuing Education, University of Edinburgh	Academic/research
Michael Ward	• Director, Centre for Local Economic Strategies	Academic/research
Claire Tyler	• Department for Education and Employment	Central government

6 'Getting the people to work': Policy Action Team 3: Business
(lead Department HM Treasury; original 'champion Minister' Patricia Hewitt)

Philip Rutnam (Chair)	• HM Treasury	Central government
David Alexander	• HM Treasury	Central government
Gavin Bowen	• Department of Social Security	Central government
Amanda Brooks	• Department of Trade and Industry	Central government
Mark Davies	• Businessman	Private business
Eric Galvin	• Department for Education and Employment	Central government
Martin Hurst	• Department of the Environment, Transport and the Regions	Central government
Amanda Jordan	• Social Exclusion Unit, Cabinet Office	Central government
Maria Kenyon	• Department of Trade and Industry	Central government
Ed Mayo	• Executive Director, New Economics Foundation	Academic/research
Geoff Mulgan	• No. 10 Policy Unit	Central government
Atul Patel	• Social Exclusion Unit, Cabinet Office	Central government
David Reardon	• Social Exclusion Unit, Cabinet Office	Central government
Andrew Robinson	• Manager, Community Enterprise, National Westminster Bank	Private business
Caroline Shah	• Consultant • Board member, Richmond Churches Housing Association	Private business
Tim Sharp	• HM Treasury	Central government
Mark Smith	• Department of Trade and Industry	Central government
Daniel Storey	• HM Treasury	Central government
Richard Street	• Chief Executive, The Prince's Youth Business Trust	Voluntary/charity
Museji Takiolia	• Chair, Centre for Employment and Economic Development	Voluntary/charity
Sue Walsh	• Manager, Partnerships and Democracy, Watford Borough Council	Local government

7 'Getting the place to work': Policy Action Team 4: Neighbourhood Management
(lead Department Social Exclusion Unit; original 'champion Minister' Hilary Armstrong)

Jon Bright (Chair)	• Social Exclusion Unit, Cabinet Office	Central government
Dick Atkinson	• Director, Phoenix Centre • Chief Executive, Balsall Health Forum	Voluntary/charity
Matt Baggott	• Assistant Chief Constable, Community Affairs, West Midlands Police	Police
Harper Brown	• Director, Planning, Tees Health Authority	Health
Neale Coleman	• Housing Consultant, Paddington Housing Consultancy	Private business
Paul Collins	• Department of the Environment, Transport and the Regions	Central government
Cheryl Coppell	• Chief Executive, Slough Borough Council	Local government

David Cowans	• Group Chief Executive, North British Housing Association	Local public spending body
Jeremy Cowper	• Cabinet Office	Central government
Celia Dale	• Home Office	Central government
Amy Edwards	• Department of Health	Central government
Helen Ghosh	• Government Office for London	Central government
Yvonne Hutchinson	• Tenant representative, Housing Corporation Board	National public body
John Jones	• Headteacher, Ruffwood Community Comprehensive School, Merseyside	Education
Angus Kennedy	• Chief Executive, Castle Vale Housing Action Trust	Local public spending body
John Knight	• Head of Policy, Leonard Cheshire Foundation	Voluntary/charity
Bernard Mitton	• Department of Social Security	Central government
Ed Mountfield	• HM Treasury	Central government
John Roberts	• Department of the Environment, Transport and the Regions	Central government
Hugh Sharp	• Department for Education and Employment	Central government
John Tench	• Associate Director, Audit Commission	Central government
Liz Walton	• Social Exclusion Unit, CO	Central government
Andrew Webster	• Project Director, Joint Review (Social Services), Audit Commission	Central government
Will Wesson	• Chief Executive, Whitehall and Industry Group	Trade association
Tricia Zipfel	• Director, Priority Estates Project	Central government

8 'Getting the place to work': Policy Action Team 5: Housing Management
(lead Department DETR; original 'champion Minister' Hilary Armstrong)

Mike Gahagan (Chair)	• Department of the Environment, Transport and the Regions	Central government
Andrew Allberry	• Department of the Environment, Transport and the Regions	Central government
Michael Beverley	• Tenant and Board Member, London Borough of Kensington and Chelsea's Tenant Management Organisation	Voluntary/charity
John Binns	• Partner, Arthur Andersen	Private business
George Clark	• Department of the Environment, Transport and the Regions	Central government
Geoff Fordham	• Director, GFA Consulting	Private business
Charlie Forman	• Policy Section Head, London Housing Unit	Local government
Ross Fraser	• Director, Professional Practice, Chartered Institute of Housing	Professional association
James Gorringe	• Department of the Environment, Transport and the Regions	Central government
Roger Jarman	• Head, Housing Management, Housing Corporation	National public body
John Kettlewell	• Housing Finance Manager, Chartered Institute of Public Finance and Accountancy	Professional association
Keith Kirby	• Department of the Environment, Transport and the Regions	Central government
Paul Lautman	• Assistant Head of Housing, Local Government Association	Local government
Jeremy Moore	• HM Treasury	Central government
Darren Murphy	• Department of the Environment, Transport and the Regions	Central government
Pat Niner	• University of Birmingham	Academic/research
Atul Patel	• Social Exclusion Unit, Cabinet Office	Central government
Liz Potter	• Head, Housing Management and Support, National Housing Federation	Voluntary/charity
Pauline Prosser	• Department of the Environment, Transport and the Regions	Central government
Rachael Reynolds	• Home Office	Central government
David Sands	• Department of the Environment, Transport and the Regions	Central government
Anil Singh	• Secretary, Mannigham Housing Association	Local public spending body
Don Stewart	• Government Office for Yorkshire and Humberside	Central government
Janet Walden	• Department of Health	Central government
David Walker	• Chair, South Yorkshire Housing Association	Local public spending body

9 'Getting the place to work': Policy Action Team 6: Neighbourhood Wardens
(lead Department HO; original 'champion Minister' Paul Boateng)

Lynda Lockyer (Chair)	• Home Office	Central government
Ian Blair	• Chief Constable, Surrey Police	Police
John Curtis	• Government Office for the North West	Central government
Aman Dalvi	• Chief Executive, Ujima Housing Association	Local public spending body
Paul Doe	• Chief Executive, Shepherds Bush Housing Association	Local public spending body
David Fotheringham	• Principal Policy Officer, Chartered Institute of Housing	Professional association
Guy Gardener	• Social Exclusion Unit, Cabinet Office	Central government
Gary Glover	• Treasurer, Tenants and Residents Organization of England	Voluntary/charity
Peter Hampson	• Assistant Inspector of Constabulary, HM Inspectorate of Constabulary	Police
Sohail Husain	• Managing Consultant, Crime Concern	Private business
Ken Jones	• Assistant Chief Constable, Avon and Somerset Police	Police
Liz Lloyd	• No. 10 Policy Unit	Central government
Mark Neale	• Department for Education and Employment	Central government
Colin Passey	• Home Office	Central government
Atul Patel	• Social Exclusion Unit, Cabinet Office	Central government
Arnold Phillips	• Director, Housing, City and County of Swansea	Local government
Pauline Prosser	• Department of the Environment, Transport and the Regions	Central government
Joanna Simons	• Director, Housing, London Borough of Greenwich	Local government
Iain Walsh	• Home Office	Central government
Barry Webb	• Home Office	Central government
Stuart Whyte	• Regional Manager, Bradford and Northern Housing Association	Local public spending body
Sue Yoxall	• Chief Executive, National Neighbourhood Watch Association	Voluntary/charity

10. 'Getting the place to work': Policy Action Team 7: Unpopular Housing
(lead Department DETR; original 'champion Minister' Hilary Armstrong)

Mavis McDonald (Chair)	• Department of the Environment, Transport and the Regions	Central government
David Butler	• Chief Executive, Chartered Institute of Housing	Professional association
William Chapman	• Department of the Environment, Transport and the Regions	Central government
Hilary Chipping	• Department of the Environment, Transport and the Regions	Central government
Bob Dinwiddy	• Department of the Environment, Transport and the Regions	Central government
Bob Eagle	• Home Office	Central government
Mick Gahagan	• Department of the Environment, Transport and the Regions	Central government
Chris Holmes	• Director, Shelter	Voluntary/charity
Paul Johnstone	• HM Treasury	Central government
Paul Lees	• Department of Health	Central government
Andy McLellan	• Department for Culture, Media and Sport	Central government
Neil O'Connor	• Department of the Environment, Transport and the Regions	Central government
Prof Anne Power	• Dept. of Social Policy (Head of Housing), London School of Economics	Academic/research
Harry Seaton	• Director, Housing, Salford Metropolitan Borough Council	Local government
Max Steinberg	• Director, North West Region, Housing Corporation	National public body
Peter Styche	• Government Office for the North West	Central government
Liz Walton	• Social Exclusion Unit, Cabinet Office	Central government

11 'Getting the place to work': Policy Action Team 8: Anti-Social Behaviour
(lead Department SEU; original 'champion Minister' Paul Boateng)

Zena Peatfield (Chair)	• Social Exclusion Unit, Cabinet Office	Central government
Nicola Bacon	• Head of Policy, Shelter	Voluntary/charity
Ellis Blackmore	• Policy Advisor, Housing Corporation	National public body
Gill Cable	• Co-ordinator, Dundee Families Project	Voluntary/charity

John Cairncross	• Cabinet Office	Central government
Brigid Canavan	• Co-ordinator, Lambeth Community Mediation Project	Voluntary/charity
Christine Corrigan	• Department of Health	Central government
Ed Davies	• Lord Chancellor's Department	Central government
Helen Edwards	• Chief Executive, National Association for the Care and Resettlement of Offenders	Voluntary/charity
Naomi Eisenstadt	• Chief Executive, Family Services Unit	Voluntary/charity
Richard Evans	• Director, Social Services, Birmingham City Council • Association of Directors of Social Services	Local government
Duncan Forbes	• Legal Practice Manager, Herefordshire County Council	Local government
Stella Gardiner	• Co-ordinator, Cowgate Landlords Project	Voluntary/charity
Caroline Gitsham	• Co-ordinator, Pennywell Project	Voluntary/charity
Adrian Greenwood	• Consultant	Private business
Debbie Grice	• Home Office	Central government
Robert Jezzard	• Department of Health	Central government
Claudia Lewis-Moore	• Assistant Chief Probation Officer, Hereford and Worcester Probation Service	Central government
Naseem Malik	• Housing Solicitor, Oldham Metropolitan Borough Council	Local government
Atul Patel	• Social Exclusion Unit, Cabinet Office	Central government
Bill Pitt	• Head, Nuisance Strategy Group, Manchester City Council	Local government
Pauline Prosser	• Department of the Environment, Transport and the Regions	Central government
Matthew Quinn	• Government Office for the South West	Central government
David Reardon	• Social Exclusion Unit, Cabinet Office	Central government
Anne Richardson	• Department of Health	Central government
John Thompson	• Home Office	Central government
David Woodward	• Lord Chancellor's Department	Central government
Jeanette York	• Policy Officer, Local Government Association	Local government

12 'Getting the place to work': Policy Action Team 9: Community Self-Help
(lead Department HO; original 'champion Minister' Paul Boateng)

William Fittall (Chair)	• Home Office	Central government
Veena Bahl	• Department of Health	Central government
Phil Barton	• North West Regional Officer, Groundwork Trust	Voluntary/charity
Adele Blakebrough	• Director, Kaleidoscope Drug Project • Member, Community Action Network	Voluntary/charity
Alan Brown	• Department of the Environment, Transport and the Regions	Central government
Simon Dale	• Community worker, Douglas Valley Community, Wigan	Voluntary/charity
Richard Farnell	• University of Coventry	Academic/research
Mark Gale	• Co-ordinator, Gloucester Neighbourhood Projects Network	Voluntary/charity
Chris Hayes	• Department of Social Security	Central government
Phillipa Holland	• Government Office for the West Midlands	Central government
Gerard Lemos	• Consultant, Lemos and Crane	Private business
Jerry Marston	• Community Relations Manager, The Littlewoods Group	Private business
Andy McLellan	• Department for Culture, Media and Sport	Central government
Ronnie Moodley	• Chief Executive, African Refugees' Housing Association Group	Voluntary/charity
Geoff Mulgan	• No. 10 Policy Unit	Central government
George Nicholson	• Chair, Community Development Trusts Association	Voluntary/charity
Janice Owens	• Secretary, St. Martin's Resident Action Group, Hughes Estate, London Borough of Lambeth	Voluntary/charity
Jacquie Ross	• Social Exclusion Unit, Cabinet Office	Central government
Angela Sarkis	• Social Exclusion Unit, Cabinet Office	Central government
Sharon Scott	• Senior Grants Officer, National Lottery Charities Board	National public body

Howard Simmons	• Director, Community and Leisure Services, London Borough of Hounslow	Local government
Howard Webber	• Home Office	Central government
Chris Wells	• Department for Education and Employment	Central government
Alison West	• Director, Community Development Foundation	National public body
Charles Wood	• National Director, Community Matters	Voluntary/charity

13 'Getting the place to work': Policy Action Team 10: Arts and Sport
(lead Department DCMS; original 'champion Minister' Tony Banks)

Paul Bolt (Chair)	• Department for Culture, Media and Sport	Central government
Sue Ball	• Department for Culture, Media and Sport	Central government
Alan Brown	• Department of the Environment, Transport and the Regions	Central government
Joanna Carpenter	• Department for Culture, Media and Sport	Central government
Jim Darlington	• Government Office for the North East	Central government
Mick Everett	• Development Officer, Charlton Athletic Football Club	Private business
Marcia Fry	• Department of Health	Central government
Tina Glover	• Director, Junction Arts	Private business
Celia Greenwood	• Head, Weekend Arts and Sports Colleges	Voluntary/charity
Sally Hart	• Head of Policy, English Sports Council	National public body
Graham Hitchen	• Corporate Policy Director, Arts Council of England	National public body
Susan Johnson	• Department for Education and Employment	Central government
Francois Matarasso	• Consultant, Comedia	Private business
Bill Mather	• Chief Executive, Trafalgar Square 2000	Private business
Aileen McEvoy	• Head of Visual and Media Arts, North West Arts Board	Local public spending body
John Newbigin	• Special Adviser to the Secretary of State, Department for Culture, Media and Sport	Central government
Keith Nichol	• Department for Culture, Media and Sport	Central government
Mark Parkinson	• HM Treasury	Central government
Atul Patel	• Social Exclusion Unit, Cabinet Office	Central government
James Purnell	• No.10 Policy Unit	Central government
Maria Reader	• Policy Officer, Local Government Association	Local government
Jatinder Verma	• Artistic Director, Tara Arts Group	Voluntary/charity
Andy Worthington	• Director, Leisure Services and Tourism, Wirral Metropolitan Borough Council	Local government
Jenny Wostrack	• Women's Cricket Development Officer, London Community Cricket Association	Voluntary/charity

14 'A future for young people': Policy Action Team 11: Schools Plus
(lead Department DfEE; original 'champion Minister' Estelle Morris)

Rob Smith (Chair)	• Department for Education and Employment	Central government
Andrew Adonis	• No. 10 Policy Unit	Central government
Tony Allen	• Education Manager, Whitbread	Private business
Mog Ball	• Social researcher	Academic/research
Jon Bell	• Deputy Principal, Ilfracombe College	Education
Paul Collins	• Department of the Environment, Transport and the Regions	Central government
Paul Ennals	• Chief Executive, National Children's Bureau	Voluntary/charity
Moira Gibb	• Director, Social Services, London Borough of Kensington and Chelsea	Local government
John Graham	• Social Exclusion Unit, Cabinet Office	Central government
Sally Hinkley	• Department for Culture, Media and Sport	Central government
Susan Johnson	• Department for Education and Employment	Central government
Andy Miller	• Head of School Support, Focus Training and Enterprise Council	Local public spending body
Heidi Safia Mirza	• South Bank University • Member, Standards Task Force	Academic/research
David Muir	• University of North London	Academic/research
Pat Petch	• Chair, National Governors' Council	Voluntary/charity

Michael Peters	• Chief Education Officer, York City Council	Local government
David Reardon	• Social Exclusion Unit, Cabinet Office	Central government
David Roberts	• Department of Health	Central government
Andrew Sargent	• Government Office for London	Central government
Phil Street	• Director, Community Education Development Council	Voluntary/charity
Stuart Taylor	• HM Treasury	Central government
Philip Turner	• Headteacher, Westgate Community School, Newcastle	Education
Paul Wiles	• University of Sheffield	Academic/research
Vanessa Wiseman	• Headteacher, Langdon School, London Borough of Newham	Education

15 'A future for young people': Policy Action Team 12: Young People
(lead Department SEU; original 'champion Minister'   Paul Boateng)

Moira Wallace (Chair)	• Social Exclusion Unit, Cabinet Office	Central government
Caroline Abrahams	• Head of Public Policy, NCH Action for Children	Voluntary/charity
Victor Adebowale	• Chief Executive, Centrepoint	Voluntary/charity
Sarah Benioff	• National Programme Manager, Mentoring Plus, Crime Concern	Voluntary/charity
Tom Bentley	• Department for Education and Employment	Central government
Katharine Bramwell	• Home Office	Central government
Paul Bolt	• Department for Culture, Media and Sport	Central government
John Bynner	• Institute of Education, University of London	Academic/research
Balbir Chatrik	• Joint Director, Unemployment Unit and Youth Aid	Voluntary/charity
Sue Duncan	• Department of Social Security	Central government
David Forrester	• Department for Education and Employment	Central government
John Graham	• Social Exclusion Unit, Cabinet Office	Central government
Caroline Hassan	• Chief Executive, Watford Borough Council	Local government
Nicholas Holgate	• HM Treasury	Central government
Hilary Jackson	• Home Office	Central government
Andrew Lean	• Department of the Environment, Transport and the Regions	Central government
Adrian Leather	• Manager and Youthworker, Blackburn Youthworks	Voluntary/charity
Denise Platt	• Department of Health	Central government
David Reardon	• Social Exclusion Unit, Cabinet Office	Central government
Andrew Sargent	• Government Office for London	Central government
Rob Smith	• Department for Education and Employment	Central government
Mike Trace	• Cabinet Office	Central government
Phil Ward	• Corporate Affairs Executive, Northern Foods	Private business
Michael Watson	• Mentoring Project Co-ordinator, African-Caribbean Evengelical Alliance	Voluntary/charity
Martin Wheatley	• Social Exclusion Unit, Cabinet Office	Central government
Howard Williamson	• University of Cardiff	Academic/research
Peter Wilson	• Director, Young Minds	Voluntary/charity

16 'Access to services': Policy Action Team 13: Shops
(lead Department DH; original 'champion Minister' Tessa Jowell)

Eileen Rubery (Chair)	• Department of Health	Central government
Michael Bach	• Department of the Environment, Transport and the Regions	Central government
Mark Bradshaw	• Director, Operational Resources, British Retail Consortium	Trade association
Jeni Bremner	• Health Policy Officer, Local Government Association	Local government
Jane Corbett	• Resident, West Everton	Independent
Tricia Cresswell	• Director of Public Health, Newcastle and North Tyneside	Health
Andy Dexter	• Business consultant, DVL	Private business
Rachel Flowers	• Principal Health Development Officer, Coventry City Council	Local government

Lesley Forsdike	• Department of Trade and Industry	Central government
John Fuller	• Department for Education and Employment	Central government
Tim Lang	• Professor of Food Policy, Thames Valley University, London	Academic/research
Mary McGrath	• Institute of Grocery Distribution	Trade association
Cliff Newman	• Department of Social Security	Central government
Ballu Patel	• Consultant • Owner of Asian food business, Leicester	Private business
John Rabagliati	• Ministry of Agriculture, Fisheries and Food	Central government
Helen Steele	• Department of Health	Central government
Geoff Steeley	• Chair of Research, National Retail Planning Forum	Local government
Don Stewart	• Government Office for Yorkshire and Humberside	Central government
Marilyn Taylor	• Director, Orient Regeneration, Waltham Forest	Voluntary/charity
Ann Taggart	• HM Treasury	Central government
Liz Walton	• Social Exclusion Unit, Cabinet Office	Central government
Jackie Westlake	• Home Office	Central government
Heather White	• Department of Health	Central government
Brendan Yates	• NHS South West Region	Health

17 'Access to services': Policy Action Team 14: Financial Services
(lead Department HMT; original 'champion Minister' Patricia Hewitt)

David Alexander (Chair)	• HM Treasury	Central government
Alan Brown	• Department of the Environment, Transport and the Regions	Central government
Tania Burchardt	• London School of Economics	Academic/research
Ruth Calder	• Department of Social Security	Central government
Denise Caudle	• Government Office for the North East	Central government
Tony Challinor	• Community Development Officer, Cheshire County Council	Local government
Jeremy Jones	• HM Treasury	Central government
Amanda Jordan	• Social Exclusion Unit, Cabinet Office	Central government
Elaine Kempson	• University of Bristol	Academic/research
Liz Lawrence	• Social Exclusion Unit, Cabinet Office	Central government
Jim McCormick	• Research Director, Scottish Council Foundation	Voluntary/charity
Geoff Mulgan	• No. 10 Policy Unit	Central government
Shaun Mundy	• Head of UK Banks, Banking Department, Financial Services Authority	National public body
Amanda Paul	• Assistant Director, British Association of Social Settlements and Action Centres	Voluntary/charity
Susan Rice	• Head, Branch Banking, Bank of Scotland	Private business
Peter Robinson	• HM Treasury	Central government
David Sibbick	• Department of Trade and Industry	Central government
Susan Spencer	• Director, Birmingham Settlement	Voluntary/charity
Daniel Storey	• HM Treasury	Central government

18 'Access to services': Policy Action Team 15: Information Technology
(lead Department DTI; original 'champion Minister' Barbara Roche)

David Baxter (Chair)	• Department of Trade and Industry	Central government
John Adams	• IT Manager, Black Information Network	Voluntary/charity
Jeremy Crump	• Cabinet Office	Central government
Sue Davidson	• Director, Strategy and Business Development (UK), British Telecom	Privatised business
Chris Drew	• Chief Executive, Northern Infomatics	Private business
Tim Goodship	• Department of Trade and Industry	Central government
Graham Hall	• Chair Designate, Yorkshire and Humberside Regional Development Agency	Local public spending body
Kevin Harris	• Information Mananger, Community Development Foundation	National public body
Samantha Hellawell	• Community Programmes Manager, IBM	Private business

Charles Hughes	• Marketing Director, Services Division, ICL	Private business
John Humphreys	• Department of Trade and Industry	Central government
Liz Lawrence	• Social Exclusion Unit, Cabinet Office	Central government
Ken Lussey	• Department for Culture, Media and Sport	Central government
Neville Mackay	• Department for Culture, Media and Sport	Central government
Michael Mulquin	• Executive Director, Communities Online (Newham Online)	Voluntary/charity
Kevin Peers	• Assistant Director, Social Services, Knowsley Borough Council	Local government
Jeanette Pugh	• Department for Education and Employment	Central government
James Purnell	• No. 10 Policy Unit	Central government
Robin Ritzema	• Department for Education and Employment	Central government
John Roberts	• Department of the Environment, Transport and the Regions	Central government
Mark Smith	• Department of Trade and Industry	Central government
Martin Trees	• Chair, IT in the Community, Business in the Community	Voluntary/charity

19 'Making Government work better': Policy Action Team 16: Learning Lessons
(lead Department SEU; original 'champion Minister' Lord Falconer)

Jon Bright (Chair)	• Social Exclusion Unit, Cabinet Office	Central government
Richard Best	• Director, Joseph Rowntree Foundation	Voluntary/charity
Alison Blackburn	• Ministry of Agriculture, Fisheries and Food	Central government
Paul Bolt	• Department for Culture, Media and Sport	Central government
Jennie Carpenter	• Department of Health	Central government
William Chapman	• Department of the Environment, Transport and the Regions	Central government
Bob Chilton	• Director, Local Government Studies, Audit Commission	National public body
Richard Dennis	• HM Treasury	Central government
Sheila Drew-Smith	• Management Consultant	Private business
Graham Duncan	• Regeneration and Partnership Unit, London Borough of Hackney	Local government
Sue Goss	• Director, Public Services Development, Office for Public Management	Academic/research
David Grayson	• Chair, National Disability Council	National public body
Richard Harrison	• Department for Education and Employment	Central government
Robert Hughes	• Member, Local Government Commission for England	National public body
Penny Jones	• Director, PJR Ltd	Private business
Charles Leadbetter	• Consultant • Associate member, Demos	Private business
Katie Limm	• Department of Social Security	Central government
Judith Littlewood	• Department of the Environment, Transport and the Regions	Central government
Geoff Merchant	• Principal consultant, Civil Service College	Central government
Nalin Morjaria	• Director, Minds Eye	Voluntary/charity
Geoff Mulgan	• No. 10 Policy Unit	Central government
Steve Mycio	• Director of Housing Services, Deputy Chief Executive Manchester City Council	Local government
David Norgrove	• Divisional Director, Marks and Spencer	Private business
Stephen Putman	• Government Office for London	Central government
Alison Schofield	• Cabinet Office	Central government
David Smith	• Department of Trade and Industry	Central government
Joan Toovey	• Deputy Chief Executive, Stratford Development Partnership	Local public spending body
Liz Walton	• Social Exclusion Unit, Cabinet Office	Central government
Richard Weatherill	• Home Office	Central government

20 'Making Government work better': Policy Action Team 17: Joining It Up Locally
(lead Department DETR; original 'champion Minister' Hilary Armstrong)

Andrew Whetnall (Chair)	• Local Government Sponsorship Unit, Department for the Environment, Transport and the Regions	Central government

Harris Beider	• Executive Director, Federation of Black Housing Organisations	Voluntary/charity
Cynthia Bower	• Head, Policy Analysis, Birmingham Health Authority	Health
Helen D'Arcy	• Department of Social Security	Central government
Richard Dennis	• HM Treasury	Central government
Louise Dominian	• Social Exclusion Unit, Cabinet Office	Central government
Paul Douglas	• Department for Culture, Media and Sport	Central government
Jonathan Duke-Evans	• Home Office	Central government
Paul Evans	• Department of the Environment, Transport and the Regions	Central government
Peter Fanning	• Chief Executive, Public Private Partnerships Programme	Central government
Simon Fryer	• Cabinet Office	Central government
Robert Hill	• No. 10 Policy Unit	Central government
Stephen Hill	• Director, Capital Action	Private business
Neil Kinghan	• Director, Local Government Association	Local government
Geoff Mulgan	• No. 10 Policy Unit	Central government
David Ritchie	• Government Office for the West Midlands	Central government
Tim Sands	• Department of Health	Central government
David Smith	• Department of Trade and Industry	Central government
John Stevens	• Deputy Commissioner, Metropolitan Police	Police
Murray Stewart	• University of the West of England	Academic/research
Sukvinder Stubbs	• Director, Runnymede Trust	Voluntary/charity
Liz Walton	• Social Exclusion Unit, Cabinet Office	Central government
Peter Wanless	• Department for Education and Employment	Central government
Rose Wheeler	• Chief Executive, Society of Local Authority Chief Executives	Professional association

21 'Making Government work better': Policy Action Team 18: Better Information
(lead Department SEU; original 'champion Minister' Hilary Armstrong)

Moira Wallace (Chair)	• Social Exclusion Unit, Cabinet Office	Central government
Paul Allin	• Department for Culture, Media and Sport	Central government
Julia Atkins	• Director, Housing and Social Research, London Research Centre	Academic/research
Bob Barr	• University of Manchester • Director, Manchester Regional Research Laboratory	Academic/research
Richard Bartholomew	• Department for Education and Employment	Central government
Louise Dominian	• Social Exclusion Unit, Cabinet Office	Central government
Janet Dougharty	• Department of Trade and Industry	Central government
Keith Dugmore	• Director, Demographic Decisions	Private business
Philip Edwards	• Head, Social Policy Team, Local Government Management Board	Local government
David Fraser	• Department of Social Security	Central government
Zarina Kurtz	• Consultant, public health	Private business
Sam Mason	• Department of the Environment, Transport and the Regions	Central government
David Moxon	• Home Office	Central government
Mike Noble	• Course Director, Comparative Social Research, University of Oxford	Academic/research
Paul Orrett	• Senior Manager, Local Government Studies, Audit Commission	National public body
Atul Patel	• Social Exclusion Unit, Cabinet Office	Central government
John Pullinger	• Office for National Statistics	Central government
David Smith	• Department of Trade and Industry	Central government
Roger Sykes	• Co-ordinator, Central and Local Government Information Partnership • Local Government Association	Local government
Andy Taylor	• Senior Assistant Director, Leeds City Council	Local government
Richard Wilmer	• Department of Health	Central government

DEPARTMENT FOR CULTURE, MEDIA AND SPORT (DCMS)

Name	Affiliation	Classification
1 BBC License Fee Review Panel		
To review the BBC's financing, notably the license fee increase, up to 2006. Report published in August 1999: a consultation period to 31 October was announced.		
Gavyn Davies (Chair)	• Partner, Goldman Sachs • Economics commentator, *The Independent*	Private business
Helen Black	• Regional Head of Health, Southern Region, Unison	Trade union
Sir Alan Budd	• Member, Monetary Policy Committee, Bank of England • Former Head, Government Economic Service	National public body
Ruth Evans	• Former Director, the National Consumer Council	Voluntary/charity
Lord Gordon of Strathblane	• Chair, Scottish Radio Holdings • Vice Chair, Melody Radio • Former political editor, Scottish Television	Private business
David Lipsey (now Lord Lipsey)	• Political Editor, The Economist	Private business
Rabbi Julia Neuberger	• Chief Executive, The King's Fund	Voluntary/charity
Lord Newton of Braintree	• Professional Standards Director of the Institute of Directors • Former Leader of the House of Commons	Trade association
Heather Rabbatts	• Chief Executive, London Borough of Lambeth	Local government
2 Creative Industries Task Force		
To look for ways of maximising the economic impact of British goods and services in the creative sector.		
Rt Hon. Chris Smith MP (Chair)	• Secretary of State for Culture, Media and Sport	Central government
Richard Caborn MP	• Minister of State, Department for the Environment, Transport and the Regions	Central government
Derek Fatchett MP	• Minister of State, Foreign and Commonwealth Office	Central government
Sam Galbraith MP	• Under-Secretary of State, Scottish Office	Central government
Dawn Primarolo MP	• Paymaster General	Central government
Michael Wills MP	• Under-Secretary of State, Department of Trade and Industry	Central government
Lord Alli	• Managing Director, Planet 24 (TV Company)	Private business
Richard Branson	• Chair, Virgin Group	Private business
Robert Devereux	• Virgin Group	Private business
Janice Hughes	• Spectrum Strategy Consultants	Private business
Alan McGee	• Head, Creation Records	Private business
Lord Puttnam	• Film producer: Chairman, Enigma Productions Ltd.	Private business
Gail Rebuck	• Chair and Chief Executive, Random House	Private business
Eric Salama	• Group Director of Strategy, WPP (communications/marketing group) • Former Joint Managing Director, The Henley Centre (forecasting consultancy)	Private business
Paul Smith	• Designer	Private business
Representatives	*From the Cabinet Office; Department for Education and Employment; No 10 Policy Unit; Northern Ireland Office; Office of Science and Technology; Department of Social Security; Welsh Office; British Council*	Central government
3 Review of Film Policy		
To draw up an action plan for Government and industry based on the key objectives of doubling of domestic market share of British films; a larger and more diverse audience; training provision; sustained investment in the British film industry; export performance; inward investment.		
Stewart Till (Chair)	• President, Polygram International	Private business
Chris Auty	• Recorded Picture Company	Private business
Daniel Battsek	• Buena Vista International (UK)	Private business
Peter Broughan	• Bronco Films Ltd.	Private business
Dinah Caine	• Skillset	Private business
Charles Denton	• Arts Council of England	National public body
Duncan Kenworthy	• Toledo Pictures	Private business

Colin Leventhal	• HAL Films	Private business
Lynda Myles	• Pandora Productions	Private business
Wendy Palmer	• MGM (UK)	Private business
Ridley Scott	• Film director and Shepperton studios	Private business
Richard Segal	• Odeon Cinemas	Private business
Wilf Stevenson	• Director, The Smith Institute (political research) • Former Director, British Film Institute	Academic/research

4   Film Policy Action Committee
To carry through proposals of the Review of Film Policy.

Tom Clarke MP (Joint Chair)	• Films Minister, DCMS (replaced by Janet Anderson, MP, July 1998)	Central government
Stewart Till (Joint Chair)	• President, Polygram International	Private business
Chris Auty	• Recorded Picture Company	Private business
Daniel Battsek	• Buena Vista International (UK)	Private business
Peter Broughan	• Bronco Films Ltd.	Private business
David Bruce	• Author	Private business
Dinah Caine	• Skillset	Private business
Charles Denton	• Arts Council of England	National public body
David Elstein	• Chair, British Screen Advisory Council	Trade association
Trevor Etienne	• Actor and producer	Private business
Gary Ferguson	• Chair, British Video Association	Trade association
Nigel Green	• Entertainment	Private business
Peter Hewitt	• Arts Council of England	National public body
Duncan Kenworthy	• Toledo Pictures	Private business
Kevin Kinsella	• Director, Business Development, BSkyB	Private business
Colin Leventhal	• HAL Films	Private business
Steve Morrison	• Chief Executive, Granada Media Group	Private business
Lynda Myles	• Pandora Productions	Private business
Steve Norris	• British Film Commission	National public body
Wendy Palmer	• MGM (UK)	Private business
Simon Perry	• Chief Executive, British Screen Finance	Private business
Marc Samuelson	• Producers' Alliance for Cinema and Television	Trade association
Ridley Scott	• Film director and Shepperton studios	Private business
Richard Segal	• Odeon Cinemas	Private business
Ric Senat	• Senior Vice President, Warner Bros.	Private business
Wilf Stevenson	• Director, The Smith Institute (political research) • Former Director, British Film Institute	Academic/research
John Woodward	• Director, British Film Institute	National public body
David Thompson	• Head, Film and Single Drama, BBC	National public body

5   Film Finance Sub-Group

Colin Leventhal (Chair)	• HAL Films	Private business
Jonathan Davis	• London Economics	Private business
Charles Denton	• Arts Council of England	National public body
Michael Foster	• Ginger Productions (formerly ICM)	Private business
Billy Hinshelwood	• Marriott Harrison	Private business
Simon Perry	• British Screen	Private business
David Potter	• Chief Group Executive, Guinness Mahon Holdings	Private business
Sawtantar Sharma	• Stirling Cooke	Private business
Bob Watts	• KPMG (accountants and consultants)	Private business

6 Achieving 20% Market Share Sub-group

Duncan Kenworthy (Chair)	• Toledo Pictures	Private business
David Aukin	• HAL Films	Private business
Stuart Boreman	• UCI	Private business
Gary Ferguson	• 20th Century Fox	Private business
Nigel Green	• Entertainment Films	Private business
Andrew MacDonald	• Figment Films	Private business
Lynda Myles	• Pandora Productions	Private business
Richard Segal	• Odeon Cinemas	Private business
Baroness Smith	• President, Scottish Opera • Board member, Edinburgh International Festival	Voluntary/charity

7 Broadening the Audience Sub-Group

David Battsek (Chair)	• Buena Vista International (UK)	Private business
Peter Buckingham	• Oasis Cinemas	Private business
Eric Fellner	• Working Title	Private business
Romaine Hart	• Marine Pictures	Private business
Sara Keene	• Corbett & Keene	Private business
Jim Kelly	• Rainey Kelly Campbell Roalfe	Private business
Wilf Stevenson	• Director, The Smith Institute (political research) • Former Director, British Film Institute	Voluntary/charity
Margaret Taylor	• Virgin Cinemas	Private business

8 Inward Investment Sub-Group

Chris Auty (Chair)	• Recorded Picture Company	Private business
Christabel Albery	• London Film Commission	Local public spending body
Roger Bolton	• General Secretary, Broadcasting, Entertainment, Cinematograph and Theatre Union	Trade union
Dennis Davidson	• Dennis Davidson Associates	Private business
Mark Devereux	• Olswang	Private business
Steve Norris	• British Film Commission	National public body
Andrew Patrick	• NW of England Film Commission	Local public spending body
Sir Sydney Samuelson	• British Film Commission	National public body
Ridley Scott	• Film director & Shepperton studios	Private business
Ric Senat	• Warner Bros.	Private business
Paul Webster	• Channel 4	Private business
John Woodward	• British Film Institute	National public body

9 Export Sub-Group

Wendy Palmer (Chair)	• MGM (UK)	Private business
Tim Bevan	• Working Title	Private business
Trea Hoving	• HAL Films	Private business
Terry Ilott	• Bridge Media	Private business
Julia Palau	• J&M Entertainment	Private business
Nik Powell	• Scala Productions	Private business
Jonathan Rutter	• McDonald & Rutter	Private business

10 Training and Education Sub-Group

Dinah Caine (Chair)	• Skillset	Private business
Peter Broughan	• Bronco Films Ltd.	Private business
Timothy Burrill	• Pathe	Private business
Jane Frazer	• Working Title	Private business
Diane Freeman	• Producers' Alliance for Cinema and Television	Trade association

Roy Lockett	• Broadcasting, Entertainment, Cinematograph and Theatre Union	Trade union
Brian Reilly	• United International Pictures	Private business
Marc Samuelson	• Samuelson Productions	Private business
Michael Samuelson	• Michael Samuelson Lighting	Private business
Neil Watson	• Consultant	Private business

11 Football Task Force

To investigate and recommend new measures to deal with the public's concerns on issues such as racism, ticket prices, disabled access and the increasing commercialisation of football. Listed by DCMS as an Advisory Public Body (ANDPB).

Rt Hon David Mellor QC (Chair)	• Former Secretary of State for National Heritage • Broadcaster and journalist on sports affairs	Private business
Richard (now Lord) Faulkner (Vice Chair)	• Chair, Sports Grounds Initiative • Former deputy chair, the Football Trust	Voluntary/charity
John Barnwell	• Chief Executive, League Managers' Association	Trade association
Graham Bean (until 1998)	• Chair, Football Supporters' Association (when appointed)	Voluntary/charity
Trevor Brooking	• Acting Chair, English Sports Council	National public body
Cllr Chris Heinitz	• Local Government Association • South Yorkshire County Council	Local government
Steve Heneghan (until 1998)	• Chair, National Association of Disabled Supporters Clubs (when appointed)	Voluntary/charity
Tony Kershaw	• Chair, National Federation of Football Supporters Clubs	Voluntary/charity
Peter Leaver QC (until 1999)	• Chief Executive, FA Premier League (when appointed)	Trade association
Eleanor Oldroyd	• Journalist, BBC Radio Five Live	Independent
Sir Herman Ouseley	• Chair, Commission for Racial Equality	National public body
David Phillips	• Association of Premier and Football League Match Officials	Trade association
Alison Pilling (from 1998)	• Football Supporters Association	Voluntary/charity
David Sheepshanks	• Chair, The Football League	Trade association
Gordon Taylor (resigned January 1999)	• Professional Footballers' Association	Trade union
Rogan Taylor	• Head, Football Research Unit, University of Liverpool	Academic/research
Sir Rodney Walker (until 1998)	• Chair, English Sports Council (when appointed) • Chair, Rugby Football League	National public body
Keith Wiseman (until 1998)	• Chair, Football Association (when appointed)	Trade association
Colin Jones (observer)	• Sport and Recreation Division, DCMS	Central government
Andrew Burnham (Secretary)	• Secretariat contracted to the Football Trust	

12 Football Task Force Working Group

Rt. Hon David Mellor QC (Chair)	• Former Secretary of State for National Heritage • Broadcaster and journalist on sports affairs	Private business
Richard (now Lord) Faulkner (Vice Chair)	• Chair, Sports Grounds Initiative • Former deputy chair, the Football Trust	Voluntary/charity
Dr Adam Brown	• Manchester Metropolitan University	Academic/research
David Davies	• Acting Chief Executive and former Director, Public Affairs, The Football Association	Trade association
Robbie Earle	• Premier League player	Private business
Peter Leaver QC (until 1999)	• Chief Executive, FA Premier League (when appointed)	Trade association
Peter Lee	• Chief Executive, The Football Trust	Voluntary/charity
Eleanor Oldroyd	• Journalist, BBC Radio Five Live	Independent
Uriah Rennie	• Premier League referee	Independent
Sir John Smith	• Consultant, Football Association • Former Deputy Chief Commissioner, Metropolitan Police	Independent
Sir Roland Smith	• Chair, Manchester United plc	Private business
Pamela Taylor	• Chief Executive, Water Companies Association	Trade association

13 Working Party on Legal Deposit

To advise on how an effective national archive of non-print material might be achieved; draw up and agree a voluntary code of practice to achieve deposit of electronic and microfilm publications and advise on the scope for developing the existing arrangements for the deposit of printed publications.

Sir Anthony Kenny (Chair)	• Warden, Rhodes House, Oxford • Professorial Fellow, St. John's College, Oxford	Academic/research
Clive Bradley	• Publishers' Association	Trade association
Peter Fox	• University of Cambridge	Academic/research
Steven Hall	• Chadwyck-Healey Ltd	Private business
Clive Jeavons	• British Film Institute	National public body
Andrew Lucas	• Reuters	Private business
Ian McGowan	• National Library of Scotland	National public body
Andrew Phillips	• British Library	National public body
Norman Russell	• Queen's University of Belfast	Academic/research
Geoff Smith	• British Library	National public body
Anthony Watkinson	• Thomson Science and Professional	Private business
Stella Pilling (secretariat)	• DCMS	Central government

14 Music Industry Forum

To discuss problems in the music industry, notably copyright and piracy protection.

Rt. Hon. Chris Smith MP (Chair)	• Secretary of State for Culture, Media and Sport	Central government
Richard Constant	• Polygram International	Private business
Rob Dickens	• Chair, Warner Music (UK)	Private business
John Glover	• International Managers' Forum	Trade association
Prof Edward Gregson	• Principal, Royal Northern College of Music • Writer Director, Performing Rights Society	Academic/research
Andy Heath	• Momentum Music	Private business
Mick Hucknall	• Songwriter and performer, Simply Red	Private business
Kanya King	• Music of Black Origin Awards	Trade association
Sir George Martin (resigned 1998)	• Chair, AIR Group • Record producer	Private business
Alan McGee	• Creation Records • Member, Creative Industries Task Force, DCMS	Private business
Martin Mills	• Beggars' Banquet	Private business
Brian McLaughlan	• His Master's Voice (UK)	Private business
Tim Parsons	• Midland Concert Promotions	Private business
Peter Reichardt	• EMI Music Publishing	Private business
Sir Tim Rice	• Lyricist	Private business
Dennis Scard	• Musicians' Union	Trade union
David Fawcett (observer)	• Secretary, Creative Industries Task Force, DCMS	Central government
Phillip Stevens (secretary)	• Head of Media Branch 1 (Press and Music Business Sponsorship) DCMS	Central government

15 Independent Review of the Future of the Royal Opera House Companies and the English National Opera

To ensure the highest standards of excellence in performance; to protect and nurture the distinctive artistic styles of each of the companies; to improve access to their work; to ensure maximum value for public money; and to secure the financial stability of the companies. Working Group members in support of Sir Richard Eyre.

Sir Richard Eyre (Chair)	• Theatre, film and TV director • Former Artistic Director, Royal National Theatre • Governor, BBC	Independent
David Brierly	• General Manager, Royal Shakespeare Company	Voluntary/charity
Hilary Carty	• Director of Dance, Arts Council of England	National public body
Mark Elder	• Conductor	Independent
Matthew Evans	• Chair, Faber and Faber Ltd. • Chair, Library and Information Commission • Member, Arts Council National Lottery Advisory Panel	Private business

Gavin Henderson	• Chair, Arts Council of England Music Panel • Principal, Trinity College of Music	National public body
Melanie Leech	• Head, Broadcasting and Media Group, former Head, Arts Division, Department of Culture, Media and Sport	Central government
Lady (Deborah) MacMillan	• Member, Arts Council of England • Ex-member, Royal Opera House's Ballet Board • Widow of Sir Kenneth MacMillan (ballet director, choreographer)	National public body
Kathyrn McDowell	• Director of Music, Arts Council of England	National public body
Colin Nears	• Chair, Birmingham Royal Ballet Board • Former Chair, Advisory Panel on Dance, the former Arts Council of Great Britain • Former Director, Royal Opera House • Former member and deputy chair, Royal Opera House's Ballet Board	Local public spending body
John Newbigin	• Special adviser to the Secretary of State for Culture, Media and Sport on arts, education and lottery	Central government
Trevor Phillips	• Chair, London Arts Board • Producer, Factual Programmes, London Weekend Television	Local public spending body
Michael Ratcliffe	• Freelance arts journalist	Independent

'Participants':

Graham Vick	• Conductor and director • Freelance links with Royal Opera House and English National Opera	Independent
Ian Albery	• Sadler's Wells Theatre	Voluntary/charity
Mary Allen	• Royal Opera House	Voluntary/charity
Pelham Allen	• Royal Opera House	Voluntary/charity
Michael Berkeley	• Royal Opera House	Voluntary/charity
Bob Boas	• English National Opera	Voluntary/charity
Paul Daniel	• English National Opera	Voluntary/charity
Carol McPhee	• English National Ballet	Voluntary/charity

16 Review of the List of Nationally Important Sporting Events Which Must be Made Available on Free-to-Air Terrestrial TV Channels
To review the current list.

Lord Gordon of Strathblane (Chair)	• Chair, Scottish Radio Holdings • Vice Chair, Melody Radio • Former political editor, Scottish Television	Private business
Alistair Burt	• Former Minister of State, Department of Social Security (1995-97)	Independent
Jack Charlton	• Former manager, Republic of Ireland football team • Former manager, Middlesborough and Newcastle Football Clubs	Independent
Steve Cram	• Television and radio broadcaster • Member, the Sports Council • Former world class athlete	Private business
Kate Hoey MP	• Labour MP for Vauxhall since 1989 (since appointed a junior minister) • Committee member, Surrey County Cricket Club • Former athlete	Independent
Michael Parkinson	• Journalist, broadcaster and sports enthusiast	Independent
Clive Sherling	• Chairman of the Football Licensing Authority • Former Chairman of the Sports Aid Foundation • Partner at Arthur Andersen (accountants) until 1987	National public body
Professor David Wallace	• Vice-Chancellor, University of Loughborough • Chair, (since 1991) Task Force on Sport in Higher Education since 1991	Education

17 Task Force on Alternatives to Tobacco Sponsorship
To assist sports to identify and obtain alternative sponsors.

Tony Banks MP (Chair)	• Minister for Sport and Heritage, Department of Culture, Media and Sport	Central government
Derek Etherington	• Sports sponsorship consultant to Department of Culture, Media and Sport	Private business
Maurice Lindsay	• Central Council for Physical Recreation • Rugby League	National public body
Gordon Macallum	• Virgin Group	Private business
Mike Reynolds	• Institute of Sports Sponsorship	Trade association

| Jon Smith | • First Artist Corporation | Private business |

18   Tourism Forum

To enhance the quality of the relevant industries and promote their value to the economy. A new public body, the English Tourism Council, has resulted.

Rt. Hon. Chris Smith MP (Chair)	• Secretary of State for Culture, Media and Sport	Central government
Peter Agar	• Deputy Director General, Confederation of British Industry	Trade association
Pam Alexander	• Chief Executive, English Heritage	National public body
Charles Allen	• Chief Executive, Granada Group plc	Private business
Robert Ayling	• Chief Executive, British Airways	Privatised business
Tim Bartlett	• Chief Executive, English Tourist Board	National public body
Brian Barrett	• Chief Executive, Virgin Rail Group Ltd.	Privatised business
David Beeton	• Chief Executive, Historic Royal Palaces Agency	Central government
Bill Breakell	• Tourism Officer, North Yorkshire Moors National Park Authority	National public body
Alan Britten	• Member, British Tourist Authority	National public body
Lewis Bronze	• Managing Director, Bronze Productions	Private business
Brendan Burns	• Vice Chair (Policy), Federation of Small Businesses	Trade association
Peter Chappelow	• Managing Director, Holiday Cottages Group; member, English Tourist Board	Trade association
Margaret Clarke	• Director of Policy, Rural Development Commission	National public body
Donna Covey	• National Officer, General and Municipal Boilermakers Union	Trade union
Gary Crossley	• Publisher, caterer and hotelkeeper	Private business
Graham Devlin	• Deputy Secretary General, Arts Council of England	National public body
Martin Drury	• Director General, National Trust	Voluntary/charity
Michael Elliot	• Chief Executive, Heart of England Tourist Board	Local public spending body
Peter Ford	• Chair, London Transport	National public body
Steven Freudmann	• President, Association of British Travel Agents	Trade association
Peter Hampson	• Director, British Resorts Association	Trade association
David Harbourne	• Former Chief Executive, Hospitality Training Foundation	Independent
Nicola Hayward	• Seaview Hotel and Restaurant, Isle of Wight	Private business
Sir Denys Henderson	• Chair, Rank Organisation plc	Private business
Michael Hirst	• Chair, Joint Hospitality Industry Congress	Trade association
Gulshan Jaffer	• Hotel La Place, London	Private business
John Jarvis	• Chair and Chief Executive, Jarvis Hotels; member, British Tourist Association Board	Private business
Michael Jolly	• Chair and Chief Executive, Tussauds Group	Private business
Conrad Lashley	• Chair, Council for Hospitality Management Education	Trade association
John Lee	• Chair, Association of Leading Visitor Attractions	Trade association
Geoffrey Lipman	• President, World Travel and Tourism Council	Trade association
Jeremy Logie	• Chief Executive, British Hospitality Association	Trade association
David Lunn	• Member, British Tourist Authority	National public body
Ken Male	• Managing Director, Bournemouth Tourism	Trade association
Tim Mason	• Director, Museum and Galleries Commission	National public body
Patrick McKenna	• Member, British Tourist Authority	National public body
Peter Moore	• Managing Director, Centerparcs UK Ltd.	Private business
Stephen Moss	• Chair, Springboard UK	Voluntary/charity
Dorothy Naylor	• Chief Executive, North West Tourist Board	Local public spending body
Eve Pollard	• Member, English Tourist Board • Journalist	National public body
Cllr John Price	• Chair, Tourism Panel, Local Government Association	Local government
David Quarmby	• Chair, British Tourist Authority; member, English Tourist Board	National public body

Rupert Rhymes	• Chief Executive, Theatrical Management Association	Trade association
Ken Robinson	• Managing Director, Ventures Consultancy • Tourism Society	Private business
Jennifer Robson	• Member, English Tourist Board	National public body
Anthony Sell	• Chief Executive, British Tourist Authority	National public body
James Spencer	• Director General, British Holiday and Home Parks Association	Trade association
Phil Swann	• Head of Environment and Development, Local Government Association	Local government
Bob Taylor	• Chair, Tourism for All Consortium	Trade association
David Thomas	• Chief Executive, Whitbread plc	Private business
Richard Tobias	• Chief Executive, British Incoming Tour Operators Association	Trade association
Akbar Verjee	• Manager, Oki Hotel Kensington	Private business
Richard Wakeford	• Chief Executive, Countryside Commission	National public body
Howard Wells	• Chief Executive, UK Sports Council	National public body
Des Wilson	• Director of Corporate and Public Affairs, British Airports Authority	Privatised business
David Wood	• Chief Executive, Hotel and Catering International Management Association	Trade association
Patricia Yates	• Editor, Holiday Which ?, Consumers' Association	Voluntary/charity

19 Tourism Forum Communications Strategy Working Group

Charles Allen (Chair)	• Granada Group	Private business
Judith Anthony	• Thames Valley Economic Partnership	Trade association
Colin Browne	• British Broadcasting Corporation	Independent
Gary Crossley	• Caterer and Hotelkeeper	Private business
Sandie Dawe	• British Tourist Authority	National public body
Derek Dear	• British Airways	Privatised business
Harvey Elliott	• The Times	Independent
Jim Graham	• Border Television	Private business
David Harbourne	• Former Chief Executive, Hospitality Training Foundation	Independent
Simon Johnson	• Barclays de Zoete Wedd (now Barclays Capital)	Private business
Ray Kelly	• Carat UK	Private business
Lyn Lavers	• Distinctive Publishing	Private business
Jeremy Logie	• British Hospitality Association	Trade association
Ken McCulloch	• MHM	Private business
Professor Peter Jones	• University of Bournemouth	Academic/research
Eve Pollard	• Member, English Tourist Board • Journalist	National public body
Ann Scott	• Ann Scott Associates	Private business
Diane Summers	• Financial Times	Independent
Clare Walker	• Janus Group	Private business
Roy Tutty (observer)	• Official, DCMS	Central government

20 Tourism Forum Whitehall Issues Working Group

Ken Robinson (Chair)	• Ventures Consultancy	Private business
Peter Agar	• Confederation of British Industry	Trade association
Ailsa Blaire	• Local Government Association	Local government
Colin Clark	• Horwath and Horwath	Private business
Sue Garland	• British Tourist Authority • English Tourist Board	National public body
Barry Goddard	• Council for Travel and Tourism	Trade association
Peter Hampson	• British Resorts Association	Trade association
Brian Handley	• Yorkshire Tourist Board	Local public spending body
Michael Hirst	• Joint Hospitality Industry Congress	Trade association

John Lee	• Association of Leading Visitor Attractions	Trade association
Jeremy Logie	• British Hospitality Association	Trade association
James Spencer	• British Holiday and Home Parks Association	Trade association
Barbara Phillips (observer)	• Tourism Division, DCMS	Central government

21 Tourism Forum Business Tourism Working Group

Michael Hirst (Chair)	• Joint Hospitality Industry Congress	Trade association
Peter Agar	• Confederation of British Industry	Trade association
Robert Ayling	• British Airways	Privatised business
Barry Cleverdon	• National Exhibition Centre	Private business
Sarah Dale	• Sarah Dale Travel	Private business
Michael Edwards	• American Express	Private business
Sir John Egan	• London Tourist Board	Local public spending body
Carole Forman	• British University Accommodation Consortium	Trade association
David Hackett	• The Marketing Organisation	Private business
Albert Hampson	• Automobile Association	Private business
John Jarvis	• Chair and Chief Executive, Jarvis Hotels; member, British Tourist Association Board	Private business
Jack Monro	• Glasgow Tourist Board	Local public spending body
Mike Platt	• Hogg Robinson	Private business
Peter Rand	• Rand Group	Private business
Tony Rogers	• British Association of Conference Destinations	Trade association
Georges Sampeur	• Avis	Private business
Anthony Sell	• British Tourist Authority	National public body
Michael Skapinker	• Financial Times	Independent
Mike Toynbee	• Executive Travel	Private business
Robert Watson	• British Telecom	Privatised business
Ivor Warburton	• InterCity West Coast	Privatised business
Roy Tutty (observer)	• Official, DCMS	Central government

22 Tourism Forum Visitor Attractions Working Group

John Lee (Chair)	• English Tourist Board • Association of Leading Visitor Attractions	National public body
Michael Ann	• English Tourist Board • Drusillas Park	National public body
David Beeton	• Historic Royal Palaces Agency	Central government
Brian Handley	• Yorkshire Tourist Board	Local public spending body
Michael Jolly	• Tussauds Group	Private business
Ken Robinson	• Ventures Consultancy	Private business
Martin Sandbach	• English Tourist Board	National public body
Patricia Yates	• Editor, Holiday Which?, Consumers' Association	Voluntary/charity
Hugh Corner	• Museums and Galleries Division, DCMS	Central government
Stephen Creigh-Tyte	• Official, Economics Branch, DCMS	Central government
John Murphy	• Official, DCMS	Central government
Nigel Pittman	• Official, Buildings, Monuments and Sites Division, DCMS	Central government
Richard Thomas	• Official, Lottery Policy Branch, DCMS	Central government

23 Tourism Forum Human Resources or 'People' Working Group

Peter Moore (Chair)	• Center Parcs • English Tourist Board	Private business
Mary Curnock-Cook	• BII	Private business
Matthew Farrow	• Confederation of British Industry	Trade association
David Harbourne	• Former Chief Executive, Hospitality Training Foundation	Independent

Nicola Hayward	• Seaview Hotel	Private business
Conrad Lashley	• Council for Hospitality Management Education	Trade association
Stephen Moss	• Springboard UK	Voluntary/charity
Elaine Noble	• English Tourist Board • British Tourist Authority	National public body
Kim Parrish	• Scottish and Newcastle Breweries	Private business
Pauline Wells	• Tussauds Group	Private business
David Wood	• Hotel Catering and International Management Association	Trade association

24 Tourism Forum Presentation of Heritage and Culture Group

David Quarmby (Chair)	• British Tourist Authority; member, English Tourist Board	National public body
Mary Allen	• Arts Council of England	National public body
Robert Anderson	• British Museum	National public body
David Beeton	• Historic Royal Palaces Agency	Central government
Martin Drury	• National Trust	Voluntary/charity
Graham Greene	• British Museum	National public body
James Joll	• Museum and Galleries Commission	National public body
Timothy Mason	• Museum and Galleries Commission	National public body
Anthony Sell	• British Tourist Authority	National public body
Sir Jocelyn Stevens	• English Heritage	National public body
Michael Taylor	• National Trust	Voluntary/charity
John Tod	• British Council	National public body
Damien Whitmore	• Tate Gallery	National public body

25 Tourism Forum Strategic Planning Working Group

Charles Allen	• Granada Group	Private business
Michael Elliot	• Heart of England Tourist Board	Local public spending body
Michael Hirst	• Joint Hospitality Industry Congress	Trade association
Michael Jolly	• Tussauds Group	Private business
John Lee	• Association of Leading Visitor Attractions	Trade association
Geoffrey Lipman	• World Travel and Tourism Council	Trade association
Jeremy Logie	• British Hospitality Association	Trade association
Peter Moore	• Center Parcs	Private business
David Quarmby	• British Tourist Authority; member, English Tourist Board	National public body
Cllr John Price	• Local Government Association	Local government
Ken Robinson	• Ventures Consultancy	Private business

26 Tourism Forum Widening Access to Tourism Working Group

Jeremy Logie (Chair)	• British Hospitality Association	Trade association
John Bamsey	• Hilton UK	Private business
Alan Bishop	• National Caravan Council	Trade association
Roger de Haan	• Saga Holidays	Private business
Peter Holland	• Disability Partnership	Voluntary/charity
Jenny How	• Cheshire County Council	Local government
Sir William Lawrence	• Heart of England Tourist Board	Local public spending body
Tim Mason	• Museums and Galleries Commission	National public body
Stephen Mills	• English Tourist Board	National public body
David Phillips	• Holiday Care Service	Private business
Peter Taylor	• Millennium and Copthorne Hotels	Private business
Maundy Todd	• Tourism for All	Trade association
Roddy Watt	• Berkeley Scott Group	Private business

Phil White	• National Express Group	Private business
Rosemary Griggs (observer)	• Official, DCMS	Central government

27 Tourism Forum Domestic Tourism Working Group

Cllr John Price (Chair)	• Local Government Association	Local government
Bob Ackland	• North Somerset District Council	Local government
Tim Bartlett	• English Tourist Board	National public body
Brendan Burns	• Federation of Small Businesses	Trade association
Jerry Fowden	• Rank Group plc	Private business
Peter Hampson	• British Resorts Association	Trade association
Geoffrey Lipman	• World Travel and Tourism Council	Trade association
Professor Victor Middleton	• Oxford Brookes University	Academic/research
Dorothy Naylor	• North West Tourist Board	Local public spending body

28 Tourism Forum Domestic Tourism Working Group: Quality Sub-Group

Jerry Fowden (Chair)	• Rank Group plc	Private business
Tim Bartlett	• English Tourist Board	National public body
Peter Hampson	• British Resorts Association	Trade association
Nicola Hayward	• Seaview Hotel, Isle of Wight	Private business
Dorothy Naylor	• North West Tourist Board	Local public spending body
James Spencer	• British Holiday and Home Parks Association	Trade association
Patricia Yates	• Holiday Which, Consumers' Association	Voluntary/charity

29 Tourism Forum Domestic Tourism Working Group: Distribution Sub-Group

Brendan Burns (Chair)	• Federation of Small Businesses	Trade association
Bob Ackland	• North Somerset District Council	Local government
Brian Barrett	• Virgin Rail Group	Privatised business
Peter Chappelow	• Managing Director, Holiday Cottages Group; member, English Tourist Board	Private business
Nick Cust	• Superbreak	Private business
Colin Doyle	• Countrywide Holidays	Private business
Steven Freudmann	• Association of British Travel Agents	Trade association
Ken Male	• Bournemouth Tourism	Trade association
Dorothy Naylor	• North West Tourist Board	Local public spending body
Martin Sandbach	• English Tourist Board	Local public spending body
Richard Tobias	• British Incoming Tour Operators Association	Trade association

30 Tourism Forum Domestic Tourism Working Group: Sustainability Sub-Group

Geoffrey Lipman (Chair)	• President, World Travel and Tourism Council	Trade association
Bill Breakell	• Tourism Officer, North Yorks Moors National Park Authority	Local public spending body
Margaret Clarke	• Rural Development Commission	National public body
Chris Collier	• Cumbria Tourist Board	Local public spending body
John Dawson	• Automobile Association	Private business
David Lunn	• Windsor District Council	Local government
Professor Victor Middleton	• Oxford Brookes University	Academic/research
Stephen Mills	• English Tourist Board	National public body
Dorothy Naylor	• North West Tourist Board	Local public spending body
Jonathon Porritt	• Forum for the Future	Voluntary/charity
Richard Wakeford	• Countryside Commission	National public body
Tim Whitehead	• English Riviera Tourist Board	Local public spending body
Alex Youel	• National Trust	Voluntary/charity
Stephen Hodgson (observer)	• Official, DCMS	Central government

MINISTRY OF DEFENCE (MOD)

Name	Affiliation	Classification

1 Independent Panel on Gulf Veterans' Illnesses Interactions Research
To investigate the possible adverse health effects of the combination of vaccines and tablets which were given to troops in the Gulf War to protect them against the threat of biological and chemical warfare.

Name	Affiliation	Classification
Professor Harrison Spencer	• London School of Hygiene and Tropical Medicine	Academic/Research
Professor J.E. Banatvala	• St. Thomas's Hospital, London	Academic/research
Professor P. Beverley	• The Edward Jenner Institute for Vaccine Research	Academic/research
Dr. J. Bird	• Burden Neurological Hospital	Academic/research
Dr A. Boylston	• Molecular Medicine Unit, St. James's Hospital, Leeds	Academic/research
Dr P. Fawcett	• Department of Clinical Neurophysiology, Newcastle General Hospital	Academic/research
Professor A. Grossman	• Department of Endocrinology, St. Bartholomew's Hospital, London	Academic/research
Professor M. Hooper	• University of Sunderland (nominated by ex-servicemen)	Academic/research
Dr N. Jones	• Royal British Legion, London (nominated by ex-servicemen)	Voluntary/charity
Professor S. Lightman	• Department of Medicine, Bristol Royal Infirmary	Academic/research
Dr C. Martyn	• MRC Environmental Epidemiology Unit, University of Southampton	Academic/research
Dr E. Miller	• Communicable Diseases Surveillance Centre, Colindale, London	Academic/research
Dr D. Ray	• Centre for Mechanisms of Human Toxicity, University of Leicester	Academic/research
Dr G. Schild	• National Institute of Biological Standards and Control	Academic/research
Professor Sedgwick	• Wessex Neurological Centre, University of Southampton	Academic/research
Professor A. Silman	• Agricultural Research Council Epidemiology Research Unit, Manchester University Medical School	Academic/research

2 Smart Procurement Partnerships Group
To carry through a thorough reform of the equipment procurement process.

Name	Affiliation	Classification
John Spellar MP (Joint Chair)	• Parliamentary Secretary, Ministry of Defence	Central government
Kevin Smith (Joint Chair)	• Defence Industry Council	Trade association
Industry representatives included:		
Alan Jones	• Defence Industry Council	Trade association
Sir David Lees	• Defence Industry Council • Member, National Defence Industries Council • Managing Director (since chairman) GKN plc • Director, Bank of England	Trade association

Military contracting firms' management and technical staff seconded (full or part-time and unpaid) to MoD's Procurement Executive to advise and participate in Smart Procurement work have included:

Name	Affiliation	Classification
Colin Howard	• GEC Marconi	Private business
Robert Mair	• Rolls Royce	Private business
Warren North	• Widney Aish	Private business
Bob Smith	• British Aerospace	Private business

3 Strategic Defence Review Expert Panel
This major internal policy review (established May 1997; completed May 1998; report published July 1998) entailed several seminars for interested groups and persons together with limited consultations with an invited group known as the 'Expert Panel'.

Name	Affiliation	Classification
Sir Michael Alexander	• Chair, Royal United Services Institute • former ambassador to NATO	Independent
Lady Balfour of Burleigh	• Political historian • Chair, Cable and Wireless Resource Ltd	Independent
Janet Cohen	• Director, Charterhouse Bank • Governor, BBC	Private business
Professor Lawrence Freedman	• Department of War Studies, King's College, University of London	Academic/research
Air Marshall Sir Timothy Garden	• Director, Royal Institute of International Affairs • former Assistant Chief of Air Staff, Ministry of Defence	Academic/research

Lord Gladwin	• Member, Armed Forces Pay Review Body • former Regional Secretary, General and Municipal Workers Union	Independent
Dr James Gow	• King's College, University of London	Academic/research
Professor Colin Gray	• Director of Security Studies, University of Hull	Academic/research
Simon Jenkins	• Journalist; former editor, *The Times* and *Evening Standard*	Independent
Richard Lapthorne	• Vice chairman, British Aerospace plc • member, Industrial Development Advisory Board (Department of Trade and Industry)	Privatised business
Dr Patricia Lewis	• Director, UN Institute for Disarmament Research • former Director, Verification Technology Information Centre	Academic/research
Admiral of the Fleet Sir Julian Oswald	• Chairman, Aerosystems International • former Chief, Naval Staff, Ministry of Defence	Private business
Trevor Phillips	• Producer, Factual Programmes, London Weekend Television • Chair, London Arts Board	Independent
Sir Michael Quinlan	• Director, the Ditchley Foundation • former Permanent Secretary, Ministry of Defence	Independent
John Rose	• Chief Executive, Rolls Royce plc	Private business
Dr Alan Rudge	• Chairman, W.S. Atkins plc and ERA Technology Ltd • Chairman, Engineering and Physical Sciences Research Council	Private business
Colonel Terence Taylor	• Assistant Director, International Institute of Strategic Studies	Academic/research
Field Marshall Lord Vincent	• Former Chief of the Defence Staff • former chair, NATO Military Committee	Independent

4   Strategic Defence Review: technical and specialist groups
Many informal, ad hoc, links between MoD and the defence (and defence industry) 'communities' were developed for Strategic Defence Review purposes. One illustrative example was:

The Procurement Consultation Group

John Howe (Chair)	• Deputy Chief, Defence Procurement (Support), MoD (latterly, Deputy Chief Executive, Procurement Executive, MoD)	Central government

Representatives of industry (Defence Industry Council) and MoD officials

DEPARTMENT FOR EDUCATION AND EMPLOYMENT (DFEE)
(i)   Education issues

Name	Affiliation	Classification

1   Adult and Community Learning Fund Advisory Group
Announced August 1998: to advise DfEE on grant applications to this fund during its life (1998-2001).

Marcus Bell (Chair)	• Team Leader, Lifelong Learning Access and Promotion team, DfEE	Central government
Maureen Banbury	• Her Majesty's Inspector of Schools, OFSTED	Central government
Jane Cowell	• Vice-Principal, Warrington Collegiate Institute	Education
Professor Bob Fryer	• Principal, Northern College	Education
Haroon Saad	• Head, Equality Department, Birmingham City Council	Local government
Peter Shuker	• Principal, Darlington College	Education
Marge Ben Tovim	• Assistant Principal, Liverpool Community College	Education

2   Advance Skills Teacher Working Group
To advise on implementing the Advanced Skills Teacher Policy. Announced March 1998, at the NUT's suggestion, as an ongoing group with no set report date.

Nick Sanders (Chair)	• Director, Schools Curriculum, Funding and Teachers Group	Central government
Representatives (Observer)	• National Union of Teachers and other interested bodies • *from Education Department, Welsh Office*	

3   Review of Reducing the Bureaucratic Burden on Teachers
To identify ways of reducing the bureaucratic burden on teachers within the existing statutory framework. Reported January 1998 but maintains an informal network.

Peter Owen (Chair)	• Director General, Schools Directorate, DfEE	Central government
Denis Allnut	• Director, Analytical Services, DfEE	Central government
John Bangs	• Assistant Secretary, National Union of Teachers	Trade union
Colin Broomfield	• Honorary Secretary, Secondary Heads' Association	Professional association

Tony Cann	• Chair, Promethean Ltd	Private business
Michael Collier	• Chief Executive, Funding Agency for Schools	National public body
Gwenlian Evans	• Deputy General Secretary, Association of Teachers and Lecturers	Trade union
John Fowler	• Local Government Association	Local government
Nigel de Gruchy	• General Secretary, National Association of Schoolmasters/Union of Women Teachers	Trade union
Greg Hill	• Education Officer for IT, Metropolitan Borough of Solihull	Local government
Stephen Hillier	• Head of Corporate Management, Teacher Training Agency	Central government
David Jones	• Acting General Secretary, Professional Association of Teachers	Professional association
Tony Mills	• Assistant Chief Executive, the former School Curriculum and Assessment Authority	National public body
Colin Muid	• Deputy Director, Central IT Unit, Cabinet Office	Central government
Pat Petch	• Chair, National Governors' Council	Voluntary/charity
Nick Sanders	• Director, School Curriculum, Funding and Teachers Group, DfEE	Central government
Rowie Shaw	• Director of Professional Services, National Association of Head Teachers	Professional association
John Taylor	• Office for Standards in Education	Central government
Graham Walker	• Senior Partner, Arthur Andersen (accountants and consultants)	Private business

4 Advisory Group on Education for Citizenship and the Teaching of Democracy in Schools

To advise on effective education in schools for citizenship and participation in democracy. Initial report March 1998. Final report September 1998. Government proposals arising from it were published for consultation in May 1999, within general consultation on the new National Curriculum.

Professor Bernard Crick (Chair)	• Professor Emeritus, University of London	Academic/research
Elaine Appelbee	• Member, General Synod, Church of England	Independent
Lord Baker	• Former Chair, Hansard Society for Parliamentary Government • Former Secretary of State for Education and Home Secretary	Independent
Tom Bentley	• Executive Assistant, Demos	Academic/research
Michael Brunson	• Political Editor, Independent Television News	Independent
Heather Daulphin	• Director, Post-16 Studies, Hampstead School, London	Education
Mavis Grant	• Head, Mary Trevelyan Primary School, Newcastle-upon-Tyne	Education
Elisabeth Hoodless	• Chief Executive, Community Service Volunteers	Voluntary/charity
Sir Donald Limon	• Clerk of the House, House of Commons, representing the Speaker	Independent
Jan Newton	• Chief Executive, Citzenship Foundation	Voluntary/charity
Dr Alex Porter	• Former Lecturer in Education (Politics), Institute of Education	Academic/research
Usha Prashar	• Chair, Parole Board	National public body
Graham Robb	• Head, Lode Heath Secondary School, Solihull; appointed HM Chief Inspector for Careers Education, April 1998	Education
Marianne Talbot	• Lecturer in Philosophy, Brasenose College, Oxford	Academic/research
Sir Stephen Tumim	• Former HM Chief Inspector of Prisons in England and Wales	Independent
Phil Turner (until 1998)	• Former Assistant Education Officer, London Borough of Redbridge	Independent
Scott Harrison (observer)	• Office for Standards in Education	Central government
Stephen Harrison (observer)	• Teacher Training Agency	National public body
Phil Snell (observer)	• Department for Education and Employment	Central government
Chris Jones (observer)	• Head, National Curriculum Review Division, Qualifications and Curriculum Authority	National public body
David Kerr (observer)	• Professional Officer, National Foundation for Educational Research (seconded to QCA)	Academic/research
Liz Craft (secretariat and project manager)	• Qualifications and Curriculum Authority	National public body

5 National Advisory Group on Continuing Education and Lifelong Learning

Established in July 1997 to advise on matters concerning adult learning and extending lifelong learning to contribute to improvements in employability, social cohesion, independent living and citizenship.

Prof. Bob Fryer (Chair)	• Principal, Northern College	Education
Alan Tuckett (Vice-Chair)	• National Institute for Adult and Continuing Education	Professional association

Cliff Allen	• Higher Education Funding Council for England	National public body
Maureen Banbury	• Ofsted	Central government
Jacqui Bufton	• Gloucestershire LEA • Workers' Education Association	Education
Kirstie Donnelly	• Manchester Training and Enterprise Council	Local public spending body
Felicity Everiss	• DfEE	Central government
Professor John Field	• University of Warwick	Academic/research
Dr Dan Finn	• University of Portsmouth	Academic/research
Professor Hywel Francis	• University of Wales	Academic/research
Leisha Fullick	• London Borough of Islington	Local government
Pat Gale	• Darlington College of Technology	Education
Lucia Jones	• BBC	National public body
Paul Nolan	• Workers' Education Association, Northern Ireland	Education
Sarah Perman	• Trades Union Congress	Trade union
Professor Naomi Sargent	• Open University	Academic/research
Professor Tom Schuller	• Birkbeck College, University of London	Academic/research
Professor Peter Scott	• University of Kingston upon Thames	Academic/research
Janice Shiner	• Further Education Funding Council	National public body
Maggie Semple	• The New Millennium Experience Company	Private business
Gordon Stokes	• North Warwickshire and Hinckley College	Education
David Taylor	• Potterton Myson	Private business
Secretariat:		
Mike Evans	• DfEE	Central government
Dennis Carrington	• DfEE	Central government

6-11 Working Groups: Changing Cultures and Cultural Change:
Chair, Leisha Fullick (London Borough of Islington); Stimulating Demand for Lifelong Learning: Chair, Professor Tom Schuller (Birkbeck College); Reviewing Lifelong Learning and the Benefits System: Chair, Dr Dan Finn (University of Portsmouth); Supporting Family Learning: Chair, Jacqui Bufton (Gloucestershire LEA); Building Community, Citizenship and Civil Society: Joint chairs, Professor John Field (University of Warwick), Paul Nolan (Workers' Education Association, Northern Ireland); Creating Effective Local and Regional Partnerships: Chair, Professor Naomi Sargant (Open University).

12 National Advisory Committee on Creative and Cultural Education [joint with DCMS]
Established in February 1998 to recommend on formal and informal education for young people's cultural development and review current provision. Report ('*All our Futures: Creativity, Culture and Education*') published July 1999.

Professor Ken Robinson (Chair)	• University of Warwick	Academic/research
Professor Eric Bolton	• Former Senior Chief Inspector of Schools	Independent
Dawn French	• Actress	Independent
Lindsey Fryer	• Deputy chair, ENGAGE (visual arts) • Education Officer, Arnolfini Gallery, Bristol	Voluntary/charity
Professor Susan Greenfield	• University of Oxford	Academic/research
Valerie Hannon	• Chief Education Officer, Derbyshire County Council	Local government
Lenny Henry	• Actor	Independent
Dawn Holgate	• Phoenix Dance Company	Independent
Dame Tamsyn Imison	• Head, Hampstead School, London	Education
Clive Jones	• Chief Executive, Carlton Television	Private business
Jude Kelly	• Artistic Director, West Yorkshire Playhouse, Leeds	Independent
Professor Sir Harry Kroto	• University of Sussex	Independent
Professor Lewis Minkin	• Northern Institute of Continuing Education	Education
Sir Claus Moser	• Chairman, the Basic Skills Agency	National public body
Sir Simon Rattle	• Conductor	Independent
Lord Stone of Blackheath	• Chief Executive, Marks and Spencer plc	Private business

| Professor Helen Storey | • Fashion designer | Independent |
| Carol Traynor | • Head, St Boniface RC Primary School, Salford | Education |

13 Inter-Agency Forum for Promoting the Education and Attainment of Looked-After Children

Established April 1998 to discuss draft guidance issued by DfEE/Department of Health on the education of children looked after by local authorities and then to discuss feedback from the consultation exercise. Last met July 1998; will reconvene in September 1999.

Rob Smith (Chair)	• Director, Pupils, Parents and Youth Group, DfEE	Central government
Jane Allberry	• Social Care Group, Department of Health	Central government
Caroline Boswell	• First Key	Voluntary/charity
Clare Chaimberlain	• Housing and Social Services, London Borough of Kensington and Chelsea	Local government
Susanna Cheal	• Director, The Who Cares? Trust	Voluntary/charity
Don Coleman	• Royal Philanthropic Rainer Society	Voluntary/charity
Barbara Fletcher	• Policy Officer, Education, Local Government Association	Local government
Jenny Hand	• National Youth Agency	Voluntary/charity
Peter Hardman	• Director, First Key	Voluntary/charity
Steve Harwood	• Child Care Department, Barnados	Voluntary/charity
Richard Jones	• Director, St Helen's District Council Social Services Department	Local government
David McGahey	• Director of Education, Buckinghamshire County Council	Local government
Zena Peatfield	• Social Exclusion Unit, Cabinet Office	Central government
Pat Verity	• National Foster Care Association	Voluntary/charity
Phil Yhoudan	• National Children's Bureau	Voluntary/charity

14 Raising Ethnic Minority Pupil Achievement Advisory Group (also 'Ethnic Minority Pupils Achievement Group')

To provide a forum to discuss issues related to the education and achievement of ethnic minority pupils and ensure that action set out in the White Paper is fully implemented, working to the Standards Task Force and the Standards and Efficiency Unit of DfEE.

Charles Clarke MP (Chair)	• Parliamentary Under-Secretary of State for School Standards, DfEE	Central government
Sukhvinder Stubbs (Deputy Chair)	• Chief Executive, The Runnymede Trust	Voluntary/charity
Professor Michael Barber	• Head, DfEE Standards and Effectiveness Unit, DfEE; Senior Policy Adviser	Central government
Yasmin Bevan	• Headteacher, Foundry Primary School, Birmingham	Education
Kay Driver	• General Secretary, Professional Association of Teachers	Professional association
Sandy Finnigan	• Chief Executive, Careers Bradford Ltd	Private business
Samidha Garg	• Principal Officer, Race Equality, National Union of Teachers	Trade union
Dame Tamsyn Imison	• Headteacher, Hampstead School	Education
Christine Keates	• Chair, National Equal Opportunities Committee, National Association of School Masters/Union of Women Teachers	Trade union
C. Kiddle	• Co-ordinator, Devon Consortium Traveller Education Service	Voluntary/charity
Peter Mercer	• General Secretary, East Anglian Gypsy Council	Voluntary/charity
Anthea Millett	• Chief Executive, Teacher Training Agency	National public body
Sir Herman Ouseley	• Chair, Commission for Racial Equality	National public body
Paul Patrick	• Headteacher, Cardinal Wiseman Roman Catholic High School, Middlesex	Education
Michael Peters	• Director, Educational Services, City of York Council	Local government
Jim Rose	• Director of Inspection, Ofsted	Central government
Rowie Shaw	• Director, Professional Services, National Association of Head Teachers	Professional association
Peter Smith	• General Secretary, Association of Teachers and Lecturers	Trade union
Anne Sofer	• Local Government Association	Local government
Hugh South	• Chair, NALDIC	Professional association
Chris Vieler-Porter	• Chair, ALAOME	Professional association
Judith Wade	• Principal Manager, Equal Opportunities and Access, Qualifications and Curriculum Authority	National public body

15 Further Education Student Support Advisory Group

To advise on new arrangements for financial support for students in further education most in need to replace s.2 discretionary awards and to propose criteria for payments and student eligibility. Consultation on its report of June 1998 led to a final published report in November 1998.

Cllr Graham Lane (Chair)	• Chair, Education Committee, Local Government Association	Local government
Dr John Brennan	• Director of Further Education Development, Association of Colleges	Local government
Sue Cara	• Associate Director, Programmes and Policy, National Institute of Adult Continuing Education	Professional association
Beverley Evans	• Divisional Manager, 16-19 Student Support, DfEE	Central government
Geoff Hall	• Director, Funding and Strategy, Further Education Funding Council	National public body
Lynne How	• Principal, Redcar and Cleveland College	Education
Dr Phillip Hunter	• Director of Education, Staffordshire County Council	Local government
Cllr Jeff Jones	• Education Spokesperson, Welsh Local Government Association	Local government
Cllr Peter Lawrence	• Buckinghamshire County Council	Local government
Dr Anne Sims	• Research Officer, Student Financial Support, National Union of Students	Voluntary/charity
Nick Tooze	• Team Leader, Individual Learning Division, DfEE	Central government
Nigel Trim	• Administrative Assistant for Financial Services, Manchester City Council	Local government
Annette Zera	• Principal, Tower Hamlets College	Education

16 Gifted and Talented Children Advisory Group

To develop a strategy for the early identification and support of able and talented children and how the Government's policies can contribute to the education of gifted and talented children. A pilot scheme for additional teaching was announced in June 1999.

Tim Dracup (Chair)	• Team leader, Gifted and Talented Children, DfEE	Central government
Ann Bridgland	• Co-ordinator, Able Pupil Programme and Adviser for Continuing Professional Development, West Sussex County Council	Local government
Peter Carey	• Chief Executive, National Association for Gifted Children	Voluntary/charity
Alastair Clarke	• Co-ordinator, Very Able Pupils and Senior Teacher, Mark Hall School, Harlow, Essex	Education
Dr Deborah Eyre	• President, National Association for Able Children in Education • Head, Centre for Able Pupils, Westminster College, University of Oxford	Academic/research
Professor Joan Freeman	• Visiting Professor, Middlesex University • Founding President, European Council for High Ability	Academic/research
Gwen Goodhew	• Director, Wirral Able Children Centre, Calday Grange Grammar School, West Kirby	Local public spending body
Clare Lorenz	• Vice Chair, Support Society for Children of High Intelligence	Voluntary/charity
Ian McNiff	• Chair, Support Society for Children of High Intelligence • Head, St Jude's RC Primary School Fareham, Hampshire	Education
Professor Diane Montgomery	• Emeritus Professor of Education, Middlesex University • Director of a Learning Difficulties Research Project	Academic/research
Dr Ray Peacock	• President, National Association for Gifted Children	Voluntary/charity
John Senior	• Education Manager (South East) New Millennium Experience Company • Chair, Science and Technology Regional Organisation for Surrey • Co-founder, GIFT (a company providing courses for gifted children)	Private business
Dr Michael Stopper	• County Co-ordinator, Gifted and Able Children, Lincolnshire County Council	Local government
Barry Tears	• Consultant on able and talented children • Member, Executive Committee, National Association for Able Children in Education	Private business
Chris Tipple	• Director of Education, Northumberland County Council	Local government
Julian Whybra	• Educational consultant and Managing Director of GIFT	Private business
Dr David Winkley	• Director, National Primary Trust • Member, Standards Task Force (DfEE) • Former Head, Grove Primary School, Handsworth Wood, Birmingham	Education
Observers	• OFSTED, Quality and Curriculum Authority; BECTA	

17 Advisory Group on Independent/State School Partnerships

Established in November 19978 to consider affordable and acceptable ways of developing partnerships locally between the maintained and independent school sectors for the benefit of pupils and the community. Final report, 'Building Bridges', (October 1998) was accepted in full by the Government and a successor group was announced.

Chris Parker (Chair)	• Headmaster, Nottingham High School	Education

Jane Billing	• Principal, Arts Educational School, Tring	Education
Peter Blake	• Chair, Young People and Sport Task Force • Former Head, The Windsor Boys' School	Education
Steve Chinn	• Principal, Mark College, Mark, Somerset	Education
Quentin Edwards	• Headmaster, Bilton Grange, Dunchurch, Rugby	Education
Philip Hunter	• Director of Education, Staffordshire County Council • President, Society of Education Officers	Local government
Rosalind McCarthy	• Head, Cobham Hall, Cobham, Kent	Education
Dr David Winkley	• National Director, The National Primary Trust • Former Head, Grove Primary School, Handsworth Wood, Birmingham • Member, Standards Task Force	Education
Helen Bennett (Secretariat)	• Independent/State Schools Partnership Team, DfEE	Central government
Stuart Dickenson (Secretariat)	• Independent/State Schools Partnership Team, DfEE	Central government
Stephen Mangan (Secretariat)	• Independent/State Schools Partnership Team, DfEE	Central government
Gale McNiff (Secretariat)	• Independent/State Schools Partnership Team, DfEE	Central government
Michael Phipps (Secretariat)	• Divisional Manager for Pupil Welfare and Opportunities and Registrar of Independent Schools for England, DfEE	Central government

18 Independent/State School Partnerships Advisory (Successor) Group
Established in December 1998 to oversee implementation of the above group's report 'Building Bridges', which was fully accepted by the Government.

Chris Parker (Chair)	• Headmaster, Nottingham High School	Education
Steve Chinn	• Principal, Mark College, Mark, Somerset	Education
Elizabeth Clark	• Teacher, Turnford School, Waltham Cross, London	Education
Roger Durston	• Director of Music, Wells Cathedral School	Education
Bob Evans	• Head teacher, Osmotherley County Primary School	Education
Susan Freestone	• Head teacher, Sibford Schools, Oxfordshire	Education
Patricia Langham	• Head, Wakefield Girls' High School	Education
Mary Richardson	• Head teacher, Jesus and Mary Language College, Brent, London	Education
Dr David Winkley	• Director, National Primary Trust • Member, Standards Task Force (DfEE) • Former Head, Grove Primary School, Handsworth Wood, Birmingham	Education
Eric Wood	• Chief Education Officer, Warwickshire County Council	Local government

19 Advisory Group on the Development of Individual Learning Accounts
To advise on the development and implementation of ILAs and to act as their advocate.

Representatives of:	• *Campaign for Learning*	Voluntary/charity
	• *Confederation of British Industry*	Trade association
	• *Engineering Employers' Federation*	Trade association
	• *Further Education Funding Council*	National public body
	• *Huddersfield Technical College*	Education
	• *Institute of Personnel and Development*	Professional association
	• *Lewisham College, London*	Education
	• *Manchester Training and Enterprise Council*	Local public spending body
	• *Midland Bank plc*	Private business
	• *National Council of National Training Organisations*	Trade association
	• *NICEC*	Education
	• *NatWest UK*	Private business
	• *Northern Ireland Training and Employment Agency*	Central government
	• *Post Office Counters*	National public body
	• *Royal Bank of Scotland*	Private business
	• *Scottish Enterprise*	National public body

• Tesco plc		Private business
• TEC National Council		Trade association
• Inland Revenue		Central government
• Department of Social Security		Central government
• Scottish Office		Central government
• HM Treasury		Central government
• Welsh Office		Central government

20 Literacy Task Force

To provide advice on how to raise standards of literacy in primary schools over a 5-10 year period. Primary schools began a national literacy strategy, including the 'reading hour' in 1998. See also the National Year of Reading Task Force.

Professor Michael Barber (Chair)	• Head, DfEE Standards and Effectiveness Unit, DfEE; Senior Policy Adviser	Central government
John Botham	• Head teacher, Greenwood Junior School, Nottingham	Education
Ken Follett	• Novelist	Independent
Simon Goodenough	• Chair, Governors, Queen Elizabeth Community College, Devon	Education
Mary Gray	• Retired head teacher, Fair Furlong School, Bristol	Education
David Pitt-Watson	• Deloitte & Touche (accountants and consultants)	Private business
Professor David Reynolds	• Professor of Education, University of Newcastle	Academic/research
Anne Waterhouse	• Head, a small County Primary School, Ormskirk, Lancashire	Education
Diane Wright	• Parent	Independent

21 Literacy and Numeracy Strategy Group

Established, without time limit, in Spring 1998 to monitor and advise on projects of the LNS in the context of other education objectives and developments, including international research and programmes, particularly avoiding overloading schools; to monitor the Ontario Institute's research; to advise on the national targets for 2002.

Professor Michael Barber (Chair)	• Head, DfEE Standards and Effectiveness Unit; Senior Policy Adviser	Central government
John Botham	• Director, Education Action Zone, Sheffield	Education
David Hawker	• Head, Curriculum and Assessment Division, Qualifications and Curriculum Authority	National public body
Annabel Hemstedt	• Deputy Director, Basic Skills Agency	Education
Patricia Hull	• Head, Central Foundation Girls' School, Tower Hamlets, London	Education
Do Hulse	• Literacy Consultant, Sheffield local education authority	Education
Neil McIntosh	• Chief Executive, Centre for British Teachers	Private business
Marion Murray	• Deputy head, Manor Park First School, Dorset	Education
Sue Pearson	• Head teacher, Lache County Junior School, Cheshire	Education
Lindsey Peer	• Education Director, British Dyslexia Association	Voluntary/charity
Pat Petch	• Chair, National Governors' Council	Education
Professor David Reynolds	• Professor of Education, University of Newcastle; • Chair, Numeracy Task Force	Academic/research
Carol Robinson	• Head teacher, William Ford Junior School, Barking and Dagenham, London	Education
Jim Rose	• Director of Inspections, Ofsted	Central government
Graham Smart	• Chair, Mathematics Advisers Association	Professional association
John Stannard	• Director, National Literacy Strategy	Education
Anita Straker	• Director, National Literacy Strategy	Education
Frankie Sulke	• Head, Teacher Training, Teacher Training Agency	National public body
Ian Berry	• Head, Curriculum and Assessment Division, DfEE	Central government
Christina Bienkowska	• Head, Teacher Supply, Training and Quality Division, DfEE	Central government
Stephen Crowne	• Head, Special Education Needs Division, DfEE	Central government
Ralph Tabberer	• Head, Education and Training Technology Division, DfEE	Central government
Sandy Adamson	• Head, Standards Division, Standards and Effectiveness Unit, DfEE	Central government
Alison Jeffery	• Standards and Effectiveness Unit, DfEE	Central government
Dawn Taylor	• National Literacy Team Leader, Standards and Effectiveness Unit, DfEE	Central government

| Lucy Welch | • National Numeracy Team Leader, Standards and Effectiveness Unit, DfEE | Central government |
| Dave Sleep | • Literacy and Numeracy Operations Teams Leader, Standards and Effectiveness Unit, DfEE | Central government |

22 National Year of Reading Task Force

To advise on planning the year (September 1998-99), drawing on experts in media, publishing, bookselling, etc. Further literacy initiatives were announced in August 1999. The year was part of the National Literacy Strategy.

Ken Follett (Chair)	• Writer	Independent
Sandy Adamson	• Head of Standards Division, Standards and Effectiveness Unit, DfEE	Central government
Liz Attenborough	• Project Director, National Year of Reading	Voluntary/charity
Professor Michael Barber	• Head, Standards and Effectiveness Unit, DfEE; Senior Policy Adviser	Central government
Tim Blythe	• Group Corporate Affairs, WH Smith	Private business
Neil McClelland	• Director, National Literacy Trust	Voluntary/charity
Richard Osmond	• Former Director, CBI	Independent
Dawn Taylor	• Team Leader, National Literacy Strategy, DfEE	Central government

23 New Start Advisory Group

Established in June 1997, following on from the Re-launch Strategy Advisory Group of January 1995, to advise on the implementation and development of the New Start initiative and the Partnership Projects. Two sub-groups on Monitoring and Evaluation and on Equal Opportunities have supported the Group's work.

Rob Smith (Chair)	• Director, Pupil Support and Inclusion Group, DfEE	Central government
A. Anderson	• National Council of National Training Organisations	Trade association
J. Bennett	• Local Government Association	Local government
F. Bosvieux	• Confederation of British Industry	Trade association
J. Brennon	• Association of Colleges	Education
P. Clarke	• Government Office for the West Midlands	Central government
A. Davies	• Training for Young People, DfEE	Central government
T. Evans	• Northern Ireland Training & Employment Agency	Central government
R. Fawcett	• Secondary Heads Association	Professional association
B. Garland	• Community Service Volunteers	Voluntary/charity
S. James	• British Chamber of Commerce	Trade association
C. Jendoubi	• Department of Education, Northern Ireland	Central government
J. Landeryou	• Training Standards Council	Professional association
M. Lord	• Training and Enterprise Councils National Council	Trade association
C. Loveland	• National Council for Voluntary Organisations	Voluntary/charity
A. McGowan	• Career Services National Association	Professional association
D. McMahon	• Prince's Action Trust	Voluntary/charity
L. Morphy	• Prince's Trust	Voluntary/charity
J. Normington	• Association of Colleges	Education
S. Olleranshaw	• Commission for Racial Equality	National public body
I. Pearce	• Business in the Community	Voluntary/charity
S. Perman	• Trades Union Congress	Trade union
C. Reindorp	• Carnegie Young People's Initiative	Voluntary/charity
A. Reisenberger	• Further Education Development Agency	Education
P. Russell	• Scottish Office	Central government
J. Sharman	• Equal Opportunities Commission	National public body
J. Snaith	• J. Sainsbury plc	Private business
M. Stephenson	• Include (formerly Cities in Schools)	Voluntary/charity
F. Stoner	• Consultant	Private business
M. Vaughan-Huxley	• Inspectorate, Further Education Funding Council for England	National public body
B. Waller	• Welsh Office	Central government
B. Waters	• SKILL	Voluntary/charity

K. Weller	• Qualifications and Curriculum Authority	National public body
D. West	• Office for Standards in Education	Central government
T. Williams	• National Association of Head Teachers	Professional association
T. Wylie	• National Youth Agency	Voluntary/charity

24 Monitoring and Evaluation Sub-group

Michael Chaplin (Chair)	• DfEE	Central government
Paul Johnson	• Ofsted	Central government
John Landeryou	• Training Standards Council	Professional association
Iain Mackie	• GHK	Private business
Richard Persons	• DfEE	Central government
Sue Stone	• DfEE	Central government
Merillie Vaughan-Huxley	• Inspectorate, Further Education Funding Council for England	National public body

25 Equal opportunities Sub-group

Jonathan Yewdall (Chair)	• DfEE	Central government
Peter Clarke	• Government Office for the West Midlands	Central government
John Cornwall	• Education consultant	Private business
Bhal Dillon	• Training and Enterprise Councils National Council	Trade association
Liz Maudslay	• SKILL	Voluntary/charity
Parmjeet Panaseer	• Commission for Racial Equality	National public body
John Sharman	• Equal Opportunities Commission	National public body
Merillie Vaughan-Huxley	• Inspectorate, Further Education Funding Council for England	National public body
Kamila Zahno	• Consultant	Private business

26 Numeracy Task Force

To advise on raising standards of numeracy in schools. Report of January 1998 (Numeracy Matters), published for consultation, January-March. DfEE funded some 50 special numeracy summer schools in 1998 and 300 in 1999, starting with the weakest maths results. From September 1999, the new national numeracy strategy will require a daily 'numeracy hour'.

Professor David Reynolds (Chair)	• Professor of School Effectiveness, University of Newcastle	Academic/research
Martin Armstrong	• Deputy Head Teacher, Marlwood School, South Gloucestershire	Education
Professor Margaret Brown	• Professor of Mathematics, School of Education, Kings College, London	Academic/research
Professor David Burghes	• Centre of Innovation in Mathematics Training, University of Exeter	Academic/research
Margaret Dawes	• KPMG (accountants and consultants)	Private business
Patricia Petch	• National Governors Council	Education
Carol Robinson	• Head, William Ford Primary School, Barking and Dagenham	Education
Professor Christopher Robson	• Professor of Pure Mathematics, University of Leeds	Academic/research
Anita Straker	• Director, National Numeracy Project	Voluntary/charity
Ann Waterhouse	• Head, A small County Primary School, Ormskirk, Lancashire	Education
Sandy Adamson (Observer)	• DfEE	Central government
Richard Browne (from Nov 1997, Observer)	• Qualifications and Curriculum Authority	National public body
Nigel Bufton (Observer)	• Office of Standards in Education	Central government
Julian Critchley (Observer)	• DfEE	Central government
Daniel Muijs (Observer)	• Research Associate, University of Newcastle	Academic/research
Dave Sleep (Observer)	• DfEE	Central government
Francis Sulke (Observer)	• Teacher Training Agency	National public body
Barbara Tucker (Observer)	• DfEE	Central government
Angela Walsh (until Nov 1997, Observer)	• Qualifications and Curriculum Authority	National public body

27 Personal, Social and Health Education (PSHE) Advisory Group [joint with Department of Health]

Established in May 1998 to advise on the aims, design and curriculum context of PSHE, particularly the study of citizenship and democracy. New policies against teenage pregnancies were announced in June 1999. A White Paper covering PSHE, within public health, was published in July 1999.

Estelle Morris MP (Co-Chair)	• Minister of State for School Standards, DfEE	Central government
Rt. Hon Tessa Jowell, MP (Co-Chair)	• Minister of State for Public Health, Department of Health	Central government
Jane Jenks (Vice-Chair)	• Co-ordinator, Gulbenkian Foundation's PASSPORT Project • Co-ordinator, Healthy Schools Award, Wandsworth, London	Voluntary/charity
Professor Michael Barber	• Head, Standards and Effectiveness Unit, DfEE; Senior Policy Adviser	Central government
John Bennett	• Chair, National Health Education and Liaison Group • Adviser, Coventry local education authority	Education
Dave Brockington	• Award Scheme, Development and Accreditation Network	Education
Estelle Corbyn	• PSHE Co-ordinator, Stokesley School North Yorkshire	Education
Dr Paula Grey	• Director of Public Health, North Cheshire Health Authority	Health
Peter Griffiths	• Ofsted	Central government
Miralee Hackshaw	• Head teacher, Dalmain School, Lewisham, London	Education
Stephen Harrison	• Teacher Training Agency	National public body
Tina Harvey	• Head teacher, St Anne's School, Merton, London	Education
Lorraine Hoare	• Health Education Authority	National public body
Louise Horseman	• President, Participation Education Groups	Voluntary/charity
Phil Hope, MP	• Labour MP for Corby • Children's Society education project and pack designer	Independent
Chris Jones	• Qualifications and Curriculum Authority	National public body
Hansa Patel Kanwar	• Member, Task Group on Vulnerable and Hard to Reach Groups (Department of Health)	Education
David Kerr	• Professional Officer, National Foundation for Education Research	Academic/research
Tony Lamb	• Archdiocese of Liverpool	Education
Nick Peacey	• Special Educational Needs Joint Initiative on Training	Education
Sue Plant	• Chair, Sex and Relationships Task Group (Department of Health) • Chair, National Standing Committee of Advisers, Inspectors and Consultants of Personal and Social Education; • Chair, Sex Education Forum	Education
John Reavely	• Head teacher, Evelyn's Community School, Middlesex	Education
Sandra Shipton	• Head teacher, Edgwick Community Primary School, Coventry	Education
Marianne Talbot	• Consultant for QCA pilot project on Spiritual, Moral, Social and Cultural Development • Lecturer in Philosophy, Brasenose College, University of Oxford	Academic/research
Chris Watkins	• Institute of Education, Universityof London	Academic/research
Tom Wylie	• National Youth Agency	Voluntary/charity

28 PSHE Advisory Group: Panel of Expert Advisers

Gill Lenderyou (Co-chair)	• Sex Education Forum	Education
Ruth Joyce (Co-chair)	• Drug Education Forum	Education
Nigel Bennett	• Barnado's	Voluntary/charity
Pat Dark	• NHS Executive	Central government
Hetty Einzig	• Parenting Forum	Voluntary/charity
Viv Evans	• TACADE	Voluntary/charity
Martin Gomberg	• Education Officer, Royal Society for the Prevention of Accidents	Voluntary/charity
Carol Healy	• Health Education Authority	National public body
Nick Jones	• Education Officer, Council for Environmental Education	Voluntary/charity
John Lloyd	• Health Education Adviser, Birmingham local education authority	Education
Gill Nott	• Chair, Personal Finance Education Group	Voluntary/charity

James Park	• Antidote	Voluntary/charity
Dilys Went	• Brook Advisory Centres	Voluntary/charity
Ann Weyman	• Family Planning Association	Voluntary/charity

29 Working Group on Effective Post-School Basic Skills Provision

Established in May 1998 to advise the Government on how best to double help for basic literacy and numeracy skills amongst adults so that over 500,000 adults a year are being helped by 2002. Reported March 1999 (A Fresh Start: Basic Skills for Adults). Baroness Blackstone (Minister of State, DfEE) is chairing a 'strategy group to take forward the report's findings', supported by a Technical Implementation Group.

Sir Claus Moser (Chair)	• Chair, Basic Skills Agency • Chair, British Museum Development Trust	National public body
Professor Michael Barber	• Head, Standards and Effectiveness Unit, DfEE; Senior Policy Adviser	Central government
Steven Broomhead	• Chief Executive, Warrington Borough Council	Local government
Professor John Bynner	• Professor of Social Statistics, City University, London	Academic/research
Mike Carnaby	• Adult learner, Sheffield Hallam University	Independent
Professor Bob Fryer	• Principal, Northern College • Chair, National Advisory Group for Continuing Education and Lifelong Learning	Education
Nick Henwood	• Director, Education and Library Services, Kent County Council	Local government
Jean Irvine	• Group Personnel Strategy Director, Post Office	National public body
Professor Richard Layard	• Professor of Economics and Director, Centre for Economic Performance, London School of Economics	Academic/research
Andrea Mearing	• Director of Student Services, Norfolk County Council	Local government
Sir David Nicholas	• Former Chair, Independent Television News	Independent
Sarah Perman	• Policy Officer, Economic and Social Affairs Department, Trades Union Congress	Trade union
Annette Zera	• Principal, Tower Hamlets College	Education
Derek Grover (Assessor)	• Director for Skills and Lifelong Learning, DfEE	Central government
Alan Wells (Adviser)	• Director, Basic Skills Agency	National public body

30 Scottish Fee Support Review Body

To review the grant arrangements for fees due in the final year of Scottish universities' first degree courses.

Sir George Quigley (Chair)	• Chairman, Ulster Bank • Member, Qualifications and Curriculum Authority	Private business
Lord Burns	• former Permanent Secretary, HM Treasury	Independent
Professor Michael Hamlin	• former Vice Chancellor, University of Dundee	Independent
Sir Philip Jones	• Chairman, Higher Education Funding Council for Wales	National public body

31 National Advisory Group on Special Educational Needs (SEN) (and two Working Groups)

To take forward the Government's commitments on raising the standard of education for children with special educational needs.

Charles Clarke MP (Chair)	• Parliamentary Under Secretary of State for School Standards, DfEE	Central government
Paul Ennals (Vice-Chair)	• Director, Education and Employment, Royal National Institute for the Blind • Chair, Council for Disabled Children	Voluntary/charity
Gordon Bull	• Principal, Newbury College, Berkshire	Education
Gillian Dawson	• SEN Co-ordinator, Sandford Primary School, Leeds Local Education Authority (LEA)	Education
Michael De Val	• Director of Education, Torfaen County Borough Council	Local government
Clive Danks	• Special Needs adviser, Birmingham LEA	Education
Professor Alan Dyson	• Special Needs Research Centre, University of Newcastle upon Tyne	Academic/research
Tim Exell	• Headteacher, Wendover House School, Buckinghamshire LEA	Education
Glenys Fox	• Principal Educational Psychologist, Poole LEA	Education
Chrissie Garrett	• SEN Co-ordinator, Banbury Secondary School, Oxfordshire LEA • Member, Standards Task Force	Education
Moira Gibb	• Director, Social Services, Royal Borough of Kensington and Chelsea	Local government
Paul Lincoln	• Director of Learning Services (Chief Education Officer), Essex LEA	Local government
Pauline Maddison	• Chief Education Services Officer, Bexley LEA	Local government
Robina Mallett	• Parent of two children with SEN	

	• Carer Support Officer • Officer and Committee member, Supportive Parents for Special Children	Voluntary/charity
Vincent McDonnell	• Chief Education Officer, Richmond-upon-Thames LEA • Chair, SEN Committee of Society of Education Officers	Local government
Richard Rieser	• Teacher, Hackney LEA • Chair, Alliance for Inclusive Education • Treasurer, Greater London Branch of the National Association of SEN	Education
Dr Philippa Russell	• Director, Council for Disabled Children	Voluntary/charity
Dela Smith	• Headteacher, Beaumont Hill Special School, Darlington LEA	Education
Sandra Tomlinson	• Vice Chair, National Governors' Council • Chair, Sheffield Association of School Governing Bodies	Voluntary/charity
Vanessa Wiseman	• Headteacher, Langdon Secondary School, Newham LEA	Education
Observers	*From Department of Health, Ofsted, OHMCI (Wales), Qualifications and Curriculum Authority, Special Educational Needs Tribunal, Teacher Training Agency and Welsh Office Education Department*	Central government

32 SEN Working Group on the Future Role and Training of Educational Psychologists

Stephen Crowne (Chair)	• Divisional Manager, SEN Division, DfEE	Central government
Anne Chan	• Assistant Director, Southwark Social Services	Local government
Pat Chick	• Parent Partnership Officer, Lancashire Parent Partnership	Voluntary/charity
Dawn Cox	• Headteacher, Caversham Park Primary School, Reading	Education
Glenys Fox	• Principal Educational Psychologist, Borough of Poole • Member, NAGSEN	Education
Irvine Gersch	• Principal Educational Psychologist, London Borough of Waltham Forest	Education
Roy Howarth	• Headteacher, Northern House School, Oxford	Education
Max Hunt	• Chief Education Officer, Metropolitan Borough of Stockport	Local government
Jackie Lown	• Educational Psychologist, York City Council	Education
Chris Marshall	• Head of SEN Team, Ofsted	Central government
Sue Morris	• EP National Tutors Group, School of Education, University of Birmingham	Academic/research
Jacqueline Nicholson	• Consultant Community Paediatrician, Derby City Hospital NHS Trust	Health
Caroline Roaf	• Lord Williams School, Oxford	Education
Rob Stoker	• Chair, Division of Education and Child Psychology, British Psychological Society	Professional association
John Wallis	• President, Association of Educational Psychologists	Professional association
Christine Webb	• Local Government Management Board	Local government
Mike Wilson	• Assistant Director of Education (Pupil Services), West Sussex County Council	Local government
Kevin Aitchison (Secretariat)	• DfEE	Central government
Carol Radley (Secretariat)	• DfEE	Central government

33 SEN Working Group on Provision of Speech and Language Therapy Services

Brian Norbury (Chair)	• Chair, Opportunities and Networks in Southwark (London) • Former Under Secretary, Department of Education	Voluntary/charity
John Adler	• Sheffield Children's Hospital	Health
Pippa Cook	• Royal Hampshire County Hospital	Health
Janet Dunn	• John Horniman School	Education
Lesley Feakes	• The Brow County Primary School	Education
James Law	• City University, London	Academic/research
James McLeod	• Wakefield Local Education Authority	Local government
Kate Ripley	• Senior Educational Psychologist, East Sussex LEA	Education
Sue Roulstone	• Royal College of Speech and Language Therapists	Professional association
Tessa Sambrook	• AFASIC	Professional association
Brian Slater	• Norfolk LEA	Local government
Vanessa Wiseman	• Headteacher, Langdon Secondary School, Newham LEA	Education
Stephen Crowne	• DfEE	Central government

Stefano Pozzi	• DfEE	Central government
Alison Britton (Secretariat)	• DfEE	Central government
Michelle Reid (Secretariat)	• DfEE	Central government
Julia Ritchie (Observer)	• Speech and Language Therapy Officer, Department of Health	Central government
Kim Sibley (Observer)	• DfEE	Central government
Keith Young (Observer)	• Department of Health	Central government

34 Standards Task Force

To advise the Secretary of State on the development and implementation of policies to improve school standards and to keep him abreast of best practice, nationally and internationally.

Rt. Hon David Blunkett MP (Chair)	• Secretary of State, Education and Employment	Central government
Estelle Morris (Deputy Chair)	• Minister for School Standards, DfEE	Central government
Professor Tim Brighouse (original Vice-Chair)	• Chief Education Officer, City of Birmingham • Member, Development Awareness Working Group	Local government
Professor David Hargreaves (Vice Chair)	• School of Education, University of Cambridge	Academic/research
Chris Woodhead	• Her Majesty's Chief Inspector of Schools, Office of Standards in Education (OFSTED)	Central government
Carol Adams	• Chief Education Officer, Shropshire County Council	Local government
William Atkinson	• Head, Phoenix High School, Shepherd's Bush, London	Education
John Baker	• Chair, National Power	Privatised business
David Bell	• Chief Education Officer, Newcastle-Upon-Tyne City Council	Local government
Carole Evans	• Head, Priory School, Slough	Education
Chrissie Garrett	• Assistant Principal, Banbury School, Banbury	Education
Professor Stephen Heppell	• Ultra-Lab, Anglia Polytechnic University, Chelmsford	Academic/research
Jill Kieran	• Deputy Head, Whiteheath Infant School, Ruislip, Middlesex	Education
Professor Simon Lee	• Liverpool Hope University College	Education
Janet Major	• Teacher, Bungay High School, Bungay, Suffolk	Education
Professor John McBeath	• University of Strathclyde, Glasgow	Academic/research
Anthea Millett	• Chief Executive, Teacher Training Agency	National public body
Dr Heidi Safia Mirza	• South Bank Univeristy, London	Academic/research
Peter Owen	• Director General of Schools Directorate, DfEE	Central government
Sue Pearson	• Head, Lache County Junior School, Chester	Education
Lord Puttnam	• Chair, Enigma Productions	Private business
Dr Nick Tate	• Chief Executive, Qualifications and Curriculum Authority	National public body
Janet Warwick	• Head, Rhyn Park School, Oswestry, Shropshire	Education
Dr David Winkley	• National Director, The National Primary Trust • Member, National School Standards Task Force (DfEE) • Former Head, Grove Primary School, Handsworth Wood, Birmingham	Education
Professor Michael Barber (Secretary)	• Head, DfEE Standards and Effectiveness Unit, DfEE; Senior Policy Adviser	Central government
Study Support Team Advisory Group	Establish in 1997 to support DfEE officials preparing a report on out-of-school study support. Findings were offered for consultation in early summer, 1998 and Extending Opportunity: a National Framework for Study Support was published in 1999. The Advisory Group consisted of a Working Group and a Practitioners' Group. Their remit was to develop a framework for effective learning opportunities outside school hours to complement and support classroom teaching.	

35 Study Support: Working Group

Rob Smith (Chair)	• Director, Pupils, Parents and Youth Group, DfEE	Central government
Dr Kay Andrews	• Director, Education Extra	Voluntary/charity
Tom Bentley	• Executive Assistant, Demos	Academic/research
Maggie Farrar	• Principal, University of the First Age	Education
Cliff Gould	• Team Manager, Secondary, Ofsted	Central government

Olivia Grant	• Chief Executive, Tyneside TEC	Local public spending body
Rex Hall	• Partnership Strategy Manager, Tower Hamlets Education Business Partnership	Education
Nick Henwood	• Strategic Director, Education and Libraries, Kent County Council	Local government
Susan Johnson	• Divisional Manager, Pupil Motivation and Business and Community Links Division, DfEE	Central government
Molly Lowell	• Study Support Manager, The Prince's Trust	Voluntary/charity
Professor John MacBeath	• Director, Quality in Education Centre, University of Strathclyde	Academic/research
Ann McNicholl	• Out of School Hours Learning Activities Team, DfEE	Central government
Tim Oates	• Principal Research Manager, Qualifications and Curriculum Authority	National public body
Ian Pearce	• Director of Education, Business in the Community	Voluntary/charity
Shan Scott	• Team Leader, Out of School Hours Learning Activities Team, DfEE	Central government
Tom Wylie	• Chief Executive, National Youth Agency	Voluntary/charity

36 Study Support: Practitioners' Group

Shan Scott (Chair)	• Team Leader, Out of School Hours Learning Activities Team, DfEE	Central government
Carolyn Brown	• Head, Sarah Bonnell School, Newham, London	Education
Helen Buchannon	• Head, St Clement's Primary School, Salford	Education
Jim Castle	• Out of School Manager, Somerset County Council	Local government
Ingrid Fisher	• Senior Education Officer, Devon County Council	Local government
James Forte	• Director of Community Broking, KPMG	Private business
Jame Fulford	• Head, Winton Primary School, Islington, London	Education
Chrissie Garrett	• Assistant Principal, Banbury School Banbury	Education
John Goffee	• County Youth and Community Officer, Lancashire County Council	Local government
Christine Hall	• Head of Services, Communication and Young People's Services, Hertfordshire County Council	Local government
Bill Jordan	• Head, Dyke House Comprehensive School, Hartlepool	Education
Elizabeth Lynch	• Director, Tower Hamlets Summer University	Education
Diana Mackie	• Head, Castlechurch Primary School Staffordshire	Education
Pat Petch	• Chair, National Governors Council	Education
Neil Rees-Davies	• Head, Halstead Place School, Kent	Education
Glynn Roberts	• Head of Centre, Birmingham Outdoor Education Centre	Education
Philip Turner	• Head, West Gate Community School, Newcastle	Education

(ii) Employment and Training issues:

37 Careers Education and Guidance Consultative Advisory Group
To provide a forum on the long term strategy of careers education and guidance in England, using ad hoc working groups of Group members.

Steve Geary (Chair)	• Director, Careers and Information Division, DfEE	Central government
John Allen	• Qualifications and Curriculum Authority	National public body
Martin Allerston	• Somerset Training and Enterprise Council	Local public spending body
David Andrews	• National Association of Careers Guidance Teachers	Professional association
Anthony Barnes	• National Association of Careers Guidance Teachers	Professional association
Alan Beale	• Government Office East Midlands	Central government
Julia Bennett	• Local Government Association	Local government
Colin Brown	• Scottish Office	Central government
David Brownlee	• Careers Service National Association	Professional association
Ray Collier	• Careers Association of Wales	Professional association
Chris Evans	• Careers Service National Association	Professional association
Tom Evans	• Northern Ireland Training and Employment Agency	Central government
Steve Fountain	• London Council of Training and Enterprise Councils • North London TEC	Local public spending body
Russ Gillam	• Careers Service National Association	Professional association

Leigh Henderson	• National Advisory Council for Careers and Educational Guidance	Education
Merrillie Vaughan Huxley	• Further Education Funding Council	National public body
Bill Massam	• Ofsted	Central government
Gareth Matthewson	• National Association of Head Teachers	Professional association
Paul O'Shea	• Secondary Heads Association	Professional association
Franki Ord	• Government Office London	Central government
Bryony Pawinska	• Institute of Careers Guidance	Professional association
Dr Tony Peters	• Careers Guidance Branch, Welsh Office	Central government
Graham Robb	• Careers Service Chief Inspector, DfEE	Central government
Sue Samson	• West Sussex County Council	Local government
John Stuart	• Independent Schools Careers Organisation	Education
John Wilkins	• Careers and Information, DfEE	Central government
Michael Wright	• Association of Colleges	Education
Secretary:		
Fiona George	• Careers and Information Service, DfEE	Central government

38 Careers Service Special Needs Task Force

To improve the standard of careers guidance which is available for young people with special needs following the recommendations of a performance assessment. Announced December 1997. Sub-groups on Organisation, Training and Information were created.

Linda Ammon (Chair)	• DfEE Choice and Careers Division	Central government
Pat Bagshaw	• Woodside Community School	Education
Julia Bennett	• Local Government Association	Local government
Janice Burton	• DfEE	Central government
Denise Fielding	• Thurrock Technical College	Education
Joan Giles	• Ofsted	Central government
Chris Hutchings	• DfEE, CCD Careers Policy Team	Central government
David Lee	• DfEE	Central government
Roger Little	• Careers Service National Organisation	Professional association
Fiona Moir	• Ellesmere College	Education
Angela Rawson	• Lancashire County Council	Local government
Mike Reeves	• Institute of Careers Guidance	Voluntary/charity
Dr Michael Smith	• National STAR Centre College of Further Education	Education
David Stuart	• Employment Service Head Office	Central government
Lindy Syson	• Further Education Funding Council	National public body
Barbara Walters	• SKILL (National Bureau for Students with Disabilities)	Voluntary/charity
John Wilkins	• DfEE Careers Policy Team	Central government

39 Disability Rights Task Force

To implement comprehensive and enforceable civil rights for disabled people, pending the Disability Rights Commission (1 April 2000). Half the members have a disability. Listed by DfEE as an Advisory Public Body (ANDPB).

Margaret Hodge MP (Chair)	• Parliamentary Under Secretary (Minister for the Disabled), DfEE	Central government
Stephen Alambritis	• Head of Press and Parliamentary Affairs, Federation of Small Businesses	Trade association
Bob Benson	• Director, Disability Scotland	Voluntary/charity
Jane Campbell	• Member, National Centre for Independent Living • Member, British Council of Organisations of Disabled People • Member, Disability Benefits Forum (DSS)	Voluntary/charity
Caroline Gooding	• Member, Trades Union Disability Alliance	Trade union
David Grayson	• Chair, National Disability Council • Member, Business Links National Advisory Panel • Director, Business in the Community	National public body
Rachel Hurst	• Chair, Rights Now • Member, Disability Benefits Forum (DSS)	Voluntary/charity

David Jenkins	• General Secretary, Welsh TUC	Trade union
Su Jenkins	• Legal Adviser, J Sainsbury plc	Private business
Brian Lamb	• Head of Public Affairs, Scope (cerebral palsy charity) • Member, Disability Benefits Forum (DSS)	Voluntary/charity
Colin Low	• Vice Chair, Royal National Institute for the Blind • Member, Disability Benefits Forum (DSS)	Voluntary/charity
Tracey-Jane Malthouse	• Employment Research Executive, Institute of Directors	Trade association
Joe Mann	• General Secretary, National League of the Blind and Disabled	Voluntary/charity
Bert Massie	• Director, Royal Association for Disability And Rehabilitation	Voluntary/charity
Denise Platt	• Department of Health	Central government
Brian Pomeroy	• Senior Partner, Deloitte and Touche Consulting Group	Private business
Philippa Russell	• Director, Council for Disabled Children	Voluntary/charity
Liz Sayce	• Policy Director, Mind (mental health charity)	Voluntary/charity
Susan Scott-Parker	• Chief Executive, Employers' Forum on Disability	Trade association
Ranjit Sondhi	• Former Deputy Chair, Commission for Racial Equality	Independent
James Strachan	• Chief Executive, Royal National Institute for Deaf People • Member, Disability Benefits Forum (DSS)	Voluntary/charity
Keith Welton	• Group Chief Executive, Mid Yorkshire Chamber of Commerce and Industry Ltd.	Trade association
Monica Wilson	• Chief Executive, Disability Action	Voluntary/charity
Richard Wood	• Chief Executive, British Council of Organisations of Disabled People • Member, Disability Benefits Forum (DSS)	Voluntary/charity

40 Disabled People in Employment and Training Advisory Committee

Established in June 1998 to advise on securing equality of participation in employment, self-employment and training opportunities for disabled people, including necessary research support and the value of DfEE's services to disabled people. Annual progress reports are requested.

Alan Smith (Chair)	• Director, Indigo Multimedia Ltd	Private business
David Bradford	• Welfare Rights Officer, Norfolk County Council	Local government
Sharon Collins	• Director of Employment, Royal National Institute for the Deaf	Voluntary/charity
John Cornwall	• Education consultant	Private business
Raymond Fletcher	• Personnel Director, Remploy Ltd	National public body
Rosemary Hallam	• Director, RESTORE	Voluntary/charity
Diana Holland	• National Secretary, Transport and General Workers Union	Trade union
Roger Little	• Chief Executive, Hereford and Worcester Careers Service	Local public spending body
Sue Maynard-Campbell	• Director, Equal Ability Ltd	Private business
Tim Pape	• Director General, Shaw Trust	Voluntary/charity
Susan Scott-Parker	• Former Chief Executive, Employers Forum on Disability	Trade association
Ian Sneddon	• Public Relations Manager, ZENECA Grangemouth	Private business
Kenneth Stevens	• Regional Organiser, Federation of Small Businesses	Trade association

41 Key Skills National Strategy Group

To develop a national strategy for 16-19 year olds' Key Skills towards a single national KS qualification in 2000 and to monitor progress.

John West (Chair)	• Divisional Manager, Qualifications for Work, DfEE	Central government
Adrian Anderson	• National Training Organisations National Council	Trade association
Keith Brumfitt	• Teacher Training Agency	National public body
Julia Duckworth	• DfEE	Central government
Steve Emms	• DfEE	Central government
Dave Gould	• Qualifications and Curriculum Authority	National pubic body
Tricia Fettes	• Qualifications and Curriculum Authority	National public body
Helen Hadden	• DfEE	Central government
Brian Helsdon	• DfEE	Central government
Savita Kapoor	• Joint Council of Awarding Bodies	Education

Carline Mager	• Further Education Development Association	Education
Ron McLone	• Joint Forum for the GCSE and GCE Awarding Bodies	Education
Chris Wood	• Qualification Curriculum Authority	National public body

42 New Deal Task Force

To ensure the design of the New Deal takes full account of the requirements of employers and the wider community; to harness the energy and commitment of all sections of society, and particularly the business community, behind the New Deal. The remit was broadened to the long term unemployed aged 25+, lone parents and the disabled. A review was planned for May, 1999. Listed by DfEE as an Advisory Public Body (ANDPB).

Sir Peter Davis (Chair)	• Chief Executive, Prudential Assurance	Private business
Victor Adebowale	• Chief Executive, Centrepoint	Voluntary/charity
Shami Ahmed	• Joe Bloggs Jeans Ltd	Private business
Rodney Bickerstaffe	• General Secretary, Unison	Trade union
Helen Edwards	• Chief Executive, National Association for the Care and Rehabilitation of Offenders	Voluntary/charity
Sir John Harman	• Leader, Kirklees Metropolitan Council	Local government
Lord Haskins	• Chair, Northern Foods plc • Chair, Express Dairies plc • Chair, Better Regulation Task Force (Cabinet Office) • Member, Interchange Steering Council (Cabinet Office) • Member, UK Round Table on Sustainable Development (DETR) • Member, CBI President's Council • Trustee, Demos • Trustee, National Civil Liberties Trust	Private business
Paul Loveluck	• Chief Executive, Hyder plc • Chair, Wales New Deal Advisory Task Force	Private business
Ian McAllister	• Chair, Ford UK	Private business
Bill McGinnis	• Chairman, Sperrin Metal Products • Chair, Training and Employment Agency (NI) • Chair, Northern Ireland New Deal Task Force	Private business
Dr Alison Millward	• Chair, Groundwork Black Country	Voluntary/charity
Stephanie Monk	• Group Human Resources Director, Granada Group plc	Private business
Bill Morris	• General Secretary, Transport and General Workers' Union	Trade union
John Roberts	• Chief Executive, The Post Office • Member, Training and Enterprise Councils Assessors Committee	National public body
Valerie Scoular	• Director of Customer Services, British Airways	Privatised business
Jenny Shackleton	• Principal, Wirral Metropolitan College	Education
Tom Shebbeare	• Director, Prince's Trust	Voluntary/charity
Michael Wemms	• Managing Director, Operations, Tesco plc	Private business

43 New Deal Task Force Advisory Group

To advise the New Deal Task Force on questions of design and delivery on the New Deal programmes. An initial two-year life was to be reviewed in May 1999.

Sir Peter Davis (Chair)	• Chief Executive, Prudential Assurance	Private business
John Bright	• Crime Concern Trust	Voluntary/charity
Rita Britton	• Director, Pollyanna, Barnsley	Private business
Christine Carling	• Director, National Association of Councils for Voluntary Service	Voluntary/charity
Paul Convery	• Director, Unemployment Unit, Training and Enterprise Network	Voluntary/charity
Andrea Cook	• Director, National Energy Action	Voluntary/charity
Jeremy Crook	• Director, Black Training and Enterprise Group	Voluntary/charity
John Davidson	• Former Chief Executive, Groundwork	Independent
Ann-Marie Dixon-Barrow	• Programme Director, Project Fullemploy	Voluntary/charity
David Eade	• Chief Executive, Barnsley College	Education
Stuart Etherington	• Chief Executive, National Council for Voluntary Organisations	Voluntary/charity
Dan Finn	• University of Portsmouth	Academic/research
Carolyn Hayman	• Chief Executive, Foyer Federation for Youth	Voluntary/charity
Chris Humphries	• Chief Executive, Training and Enterprise Councils National Council	Trade association

Amanda Jordan	• Natwest plc	Private business
Prof. Richard Layard	• London School of Economics	Academic/research
Bert Massie	• Director, Royal Association for Disability and Rehabilitation	Voluntary/charity
Samantha Peters	• General Secretary, British Youth Council	Voluntary/charity
Iain Roxborough	• Chief Executive, Coventry City Council	Local government
Judith Rutherford	• Director, London Training and Enterprise Council	Local public spending body
Alan Sinclair	• Chief Executive, Wise Group	Private business
Michael Ward	• Director, Centre for Local Economic Strategies	Academic/research
Howard Williams	• University of Cardiff	Academic/research
Chris Woodcock	• Head, Corporate Affairs, Kellogg's	Private business
Shelagh Wooliscroft	• General Secretary, Careers Service National Association	Professional association

44 Performance Indicators Consultative Group
To develop these for the 16-19 group for various qualifications from school, FE and the workplace. A continuing consultative forum.

John Eliott (Chair)	• Divisional Manager, Youth and FE, DfEE	Central government
Representatives	• *Qualifications and Curriculum Authority; Ofsted; Local Government Association; TEC National Council; FE Funding Council;* et al	

45 Performance Indicators Cost Analysis Consultative Group
Reports to the PI Consultative Group on agreed analyses of comparative costs of post-16 qualifications packages, which are published.

John Eliot (Chair)	• Divisional Manager, Youth and FE, DfEE	Central government
Representatives	• *Qualifications and Curriculum Authority; Ofsted; Local Government Association; TEC National Council; FE Funding Council;* et al	

46 Race Employment and Education Forum (Reef) Advisory Group
Announced September 1998 (first meeting October) to advise on the progress of ethnic minorities in the labour market, including the relationship between employment, education and training.

Nadim Ahmad	• Principal Policy Officer (Racial Equality), Newcastle upon Tyne City Council	Local government
Stephen Alambritis	• Head, Parliamentary Affairs, Federation of Small Businesses	Trade association
Sher Azam	• Self-employed Bradford businessman	Private business
Wally Brown	• Principal, City of Liverpool Community College	Education
Andrea Callender	• Campaign Director, Race for Opportunity	Voluntary/charity
John Cridland	• Director, Human Resources Policy, Confederation of British Industry	Trade association
Sandy Finnigan	• Chief Executive, Careers Bradford Ltd	Private business
Len Jackson	• Managing Director, Pork Farm Bowyers	Private business
Mei Sim Lai	• Partner and Director, Pridie Brewster Chartered Accountants	Private business
Kaliani Lyle	• Director, Citizens' Advice Scotland	Voluntary/charity
Thalia Marriott	• Deputy Principal, South Thames College	Education
Gloria Mills	• National Equalities Officer, Unison	Trade union
Professor Tariq Modood	• Professor of Sociology, University of Bristol	Academic/research
Sir Herman Ouseley	• Chair, Commission for Racial Quality	National public body
Clyde Pile	• Managing Director, Glass Processing Midlands	Private business
Mohammed Shafiq	• Equal Opportunities Manager, Training and Enterprise, Greater Peterborough Chamber of Commerce	Trade association
Sanjeev Sharma	• Human Resources Director, Property Division, Prudential Portfolio Managers	Private business
Cherry Short	• Chair, Cardiff and Vale Race Equality Council	Local public spending body
Sukhvinder Stubbs	• Chief Executive, Runnymede Trust	Voluntary/charity
Christine Taylor-Özgen	• Head of Training and Employment, Refugee Council	Voluntary/charity
Professor Gajendra Verma	• Professor of Education, University of Manchester	Academic/research

47   16-19 Performance Indicator Consultative Group

Established in 1997, with no end-date, to develop common indicators of training and education performance permitting young people's training options, training funding arrangements, training quality assurance and management information all to be more clearly defined and compared.

John Eliott (Chair)	• Team Leader, Youth and Further Education Team, DfEE	Central government
Derek Adams	• Head of Further and Higher Education Division, Welsh Office Education Department	Central government
Leslie Ash	• Department for Education, Northern Ireland Office	Central government
Catherine Benfield	• Higher Education Statistics Agency	National public body
Julie Bennett	• Education Section, Local Government Association	Local government
Martin Boyle	• Education Statistics, Scottish Office	Central government
Dr John Brennan	• Director, Further Education Development, Association of Colleges	Education
Chris Bryant	• Head, Research and Analysis, Ofsted	Central government
Janis Grant	• Head, Value for Money Unit, Funding Agency for Schools	National public body
Ricahrd G. Hart	• Head, Further Education Funding Division, Further Education Funding Council for Wales	National public body
Caroline Kempner	• Further Education Funding Council	National public body
Allister McGowan	• Chief Executive, Herts Careers Service Ltd	Privatised business
Andrew Olive	• HM Treasury	Central government
Janet Plested	• Training and Enterprise Councils National Council	Trade association
Anna Reisenberger	• Further Education Development Agency	Education
Mike Snell	• Principal, Brockenhurst College, Hampshire	Education
Louise Stern	• Qualifications and Curriculum Authority	National public body
Chris Thompson	• Training and Employment Agency for Northern Ireland	National public body
John Thompson	• Director of Policy, Higher Education Funding Council	National public body

48   Skills Task Force

To advise on a National Skills Agenda aimed at tackling a crucial issue for the economic success of the country. Estimated report date: 2000. Listed by DfEE as an Advisory Public Body (ANDPB).

Chris Humphries (Chair)	• Chief Executive, Training and Enterprise Councils National Council	Trade association
Gary Allen	• Chief Executive IMI plc	Private business
Llew Avis	• Personnel Director, Siemens Semiconductor manufacturing plant, Newcastle • Chair, BCC Task Force on Skills	Private business
Rita Britton	• Polyannas, Barnsley	Private business
Tony Dubbins	• General Director, Print Workers' Union	Trade union
John Edmonds	• General Secretary, Union for General, Municipal and Boilermakers	Trade union
Denise Hall	• General Manager, Education, British Telecom	Private business
Ken Jackson	• General Secretary, Amalgamated Engineering and Electrical Union	Trade union
Deanne Julius	• Bank of England	National public body
Eddie MacIntyre	• Principal, Birmingham College of Food, Tourism and Creative Studies	Education
Ashwin Mistry	• Managing Director, Brett and Randall, Insurance Brokers • Member, boards of Leicestershire Training and Enterprise Council, Careers Service, Ambulance Service and NHS Trust	Private business
John Palmer	• Chair, Steel Training Ltd. • Former Managing Director, Firsteel Group of Walsall	Private business
Peter Rainbird	• Deputy Chair, Construction Industry Training Board • Chair, Essex Training and Enterprise Council	National public body
Iain Roxburgh	• Chief Executive, Coventry City Council	Local government
Sharon Studer	• General Manager, 3 COM (Remote Access)	Private business
Julia Tinsley	• Pitman Training Centre, Sheffield	Private business
Adair Turner	• Director-General, Confederation of British Industry	Trade association
Leslie Wagner	• Leeds Metropolitan University • Leads for Committee of Vice-Chancellors and Principals on employment issues	Academic/research
Anne Weinstock	• Rathbone CI	Voluntary/charity

49 Information Technology Skills Strategy Group

Established in January 1998 as part of the Skills Task Force following its identification of skills needs in the IT and electronics sectors as a national priority, to develop a National Skills Strategy for the information technology, electronics and communications sector. The group will report to DfEE and the Department of Trade and Industry – also to the Information Age Partnership.

Alan Stevens (Chair)	• Chief Executive, Electronic Data Systems Ltd	Private business
Roy Bliss	• Demon Internet Ltd	Private business
David Brown	• Motorola Ltd	Private business
David Burrows	• Microsoft Ltd	Private business
Bob Duncan	• Electronic & Software Services National Training Organisation	Trade association
Colin Flint	• Solihull College	Education
Wendy Hall	• University of Southampton	Academic/research
Kevin Harden	• Lloyds-TSB Group	Private business
Gillian Langford	• Teacher Training Agency	National public body
John Leighfield	• AISS	Private business
Bob Nelson	• BBC	National public body
Anselm de Pleave	• Electronic Data Systems Ltd	Private business
Anne Russell	• Information Technology National Training Organisation	Trade association
Judith Scott	• British Computer Society	Professional association
Sharon Studer	• 3 COM Europe Ltd	Private business
Keith Telford	• IBM (UK) Ltd	Private business
David Thomas	• British Telecom	Privatised business
Peter Waller	• Spring Group plc	Private business
Geoff Mason (Consultant)	• National Institute for Economic and Social Research	Academic/research
John Temple (Secretariat)	• DfEE	Central government
Glenna Pryor (Secretariat)	• DfEE	Central government
Paul Williams (Secretariat)	• DTI	Central government

50 Steering Group of the Review of the Role of TECs/CCTEs in Delivering the Government's Education, Training and Enterprise Objectives

Established in May 1998 to oversee and advise on a programme to develop proposals on the future role, purpose, funding, contracting and organisation of Training and Enterprise Councils in delivering the Government's education, training and enterprise objectives; including specifically the development of new strategic guidance. A 'Bureaucracy Advisory Group' (also known as a 'funding sub-group') studied simplifying TEC funding in support of this Review. It was co-chaired by John Hedger and Christopher Humphries (Chief Executive, TEC National Council; latterly Director General, British Chamber of Commerce). Abolition of TECs was announced in a White Paper, 'Learning to Succeed', 30 June 1999.

John Hedger (Chair)	• Director, Operations Directorate, DfEE	Central government
Richard Ferre, Chris Humphries, Lindsey Simpson, Richard Guy and David Cragg	• Representing Training and Enterprise Councils	Local public spending body

51 University for Industry Design and Implementation Advisory Group

To advise the Secretary of State on the design and implementation of the University for Industry as a public/private partnership in support of improved employability and competitiveness. Announced August 1997; final report, November 1997.

David Brown (Chair)	• Chair, Motorola Ltd	Private business
Michael Wills MP	• Under-Secretary of State, Department of Trade and Industry	Central government
John Gray	• Principal, Newark and Sherwood College	Education
Sir Geoffrey Holland	• Vice-Chancellor, University of Exeter	Education
Chris Humphries	• Chief Executive, TEC National Council	Trade association
Lesley James	• Director, Human Resources, Tesco	Private business
Diane Laurillard	• Pro Vice-Chancellor, Open University	Education
John Lloyd	• National Education and Development Officer, Amalgamated Engineering and Electrical Union	Trade union
Margaret Salmon	• Director of Personnel, BBC	National public body

Cob Stenham	• Former Chair, Arjo Wiggins Appleton plc	Independent
Wilf Stevenson	• Director, The Smith Institute (political research) • Former Director, British Film Institute	Academic/research
Bernard Tyler	• Manager (Education and Training Development) Northern Europe, Ford Motor Co.	Private business
Peter Welch	• Chair, WSP Group • Deputy Chair, Holliday Chemicals Holdings	Private business

DEPARTMENT OF THE ENVIRONMENT, TRANSPORT AND THE REGIONS (DETR)
(i) External advisory groups on Environment issues

Name	Affiliation	Classification

1 Air Quality Forum
To provide stakeholders' views on the official reviews of the National Air Quality Strategy and the Expert Panel on Air Quality Standards. No reporting function.

Brian Hackland (Chair)	• Head, Air and Environment Quality Division, DETR	Central government
John Aitchison	• Scottish Council for Development and Industry	Trade association
Jane Allan	• Scottish Environment Protection Agency	Central government
Alan Barnard	• Environmental Industries Commission	Trade association
George Barrett	• Electricity Association	Trade association
Martin Bigg	• Environment Agency	Central government
Tony Bosworth	• Friends of the Earth	Voluntary/charity
Mark Branwyn	• Association of London Government	Local government
Alan Broadley	• Royal Environmental Health Institute of Scotland	Professional association
Simon Chapman	• Freight Transport Association	Trade association
James Collingwood	• Air and Environment Quality Division, DETR	Central government
Stephanie Coster	• Air and Environment Quality Division, DETR	Central government
John Crook	• Department of Health	Central government
Mike Etkind	• Air and Environment Quality Division, DETR	Central government
Mike Frend	• UK Petroleum Industry Association	Trade association
Christopher Fry	• Local Government Association	Local government
Chris Gadsen	• HM Treasury	Central government
Roy Harrison	• Expert Group on Airborne Particles	National public body
Christine Hemming	• Federation of Small Businesses	Trade association
Julie Hesketh	• Confederation of British Industry	Trade assocation
Wilf Howe	• Chemical Industries Association	Trade association
Graham Jukes	• Chartered Institute for Environmental Health	Professional association
Brian Kelly	• Confederation of Scottish Local Authorities	Local government
Ken Ledgerwood	• Environmental and Heritage Service, Department of Environment, Northern Ireland Office	Central government
Chris Leigh	• Air and Environment Quality Division, DETR	Central government
Roger Lightbody	• Department of Environment, Northern Ireland Office	Central government
Liz Lloyd	• No. 10 Policy Unit	Central government
Cathy McKenzie	• Transport 2000	Voluntary/charity
Peter Madden	• Green Alliance	Voluntary/charity
Martin Maeso	• Automobile Association	Private business
Alison Monroe	• Government Office for London	Central government
David Morgan	• Department of Trade and Industry	Central government
Huw Morgan	• Welsh Local Government Association	Local government
Noel Olsen	• British Medical Association	Professional association
Mike Parker	• Director-General, Nexus (Tyne and Wear Passenger Transport Executive)	Local government
David Pocklington	• Society of Motor Manufacturers and Traders	Trade association

Andrew Powell-Chandler	• Welsh Office	Central government
Vivienne Press	• British Heart Foundation	Voluntary/charity
Frank Price	• National Society for Clean Air	Voluntary/charity
Ann Reid	• Royal Automobile Club	Private business
Geoff Sadler	• Cabinet Office	Central government
Steven Salmon	• Confederation of Passenger Transport	Trade association
Tabitha Stebbings	• British Airports Authority	Privatised business
Simon Taggart	• British Lung Foundation	Voluntary/charity
Kim Tichias	• Health and Safety Executive	Central government
Janice Walter	• Air and Environment Quality Division, DETR	Central government
Joyce Whytock	• Scottish Office	Central government
Diana Wilkins	• MAFF	Central government
Tim Williamson	• National Society for Clean Air	Voluntary/charity
Robin Wilson	• Head, Environment Protection Economics, DETR	Central government

2   The Business Forum

Part of the Local Government Finance Review, looking into options for localising business rates and possibly returning them to local authority control.

Representatives from the CBI, the Institute of Directors, Association of British Chambers of Commerce, British Property Federation, British Retail Consortium, Engineering Industries Association, Chemical Industries Association, Machinery Users Association, Property Managers Association, Alliance of Independent Retailers, Federation of Small Business, Forum of Private Business and Small Business Bureau.

3   Cleaner Vehicles Task Force

To create a new partnership between Government and the private sector to promote environmentally friendly vehicles that people and businesses will want to buy and drive.

Rt. Hon. Gavin Strang MP (Joint Chair)	• Minister of Transport (replaced by subsequent Ministers of Transport from July 1998)	Central government
Ian McAllister (Joint Chair)	• President, Society of Motor Manufacturers and Traders • Managing Director and Chair, Ford UK	Private business
Rt. Hon. John Battle MP	• Minister for Energy	Central government
Rt. Hon. Michael Meacher MP	• Minister for the Environment	Central government
Mike Baunton	• Managing Director, Varity Perkins (diesel engine manufacturers)	Private business
Sir Trevor Chinn	• Chief Executive, Lex Services	Private business
David Green	• Director General, Freight Transport Association	Trade association
Michael Gwilt (until 1998)	• Chief Executive, Arriva Bus and Coach Group (when appointed)	Private business
Nigel Haigh	• Director, Institute for European Environmental Policy	Voluntary/charity
Walter Hasselkus (until 1999)	• Chair and Chief Executive, Rover Group (when appointed)	Private business
Stuart Holland	• Chief Executive, Alternative Traffic in Towns	Private business
Neil Johnson	• Chief Executive, Royal Automobile Club	Private business
David Lea	• Assistant General Secretary, Trades Union Congress	Trade union
Sir Robert May, FRS	• Chief Scientific Adviser to the Government	Central government
Mike Parker	• Director-General, Nexus (Tyne and Wear Passenger Transport Executive)	Local government
Keith Taylor	• Chair, and Chief Executive, Esso UK	Private business

4   Cleaner Vehicles Task Force Main Working Group

Iain Todd (Joint Chair)	• DETR	Central government
Nigel Davies (Joint Chair)	• Head of Intelligent Transport Systems and Services Ventures, RAC	Private business
Simon Brown	• Principal Engineer, London Transport Buses	National public body
Tim Brown	• Development Officer, National Society for Clean Air	Voluntary/charity
Andrew Davis	• Director, Environmental Transport Association	Trade association
Tony Downes	• Environmental Consultant, Perkins	Private business
Hugh Edwards	• Vehicle Inspectorate	Central government

Paul Everitt	• Society of Motor Manufacturers and Traders	Trade association
John Field	• Manager, Vehicle Environmental Engineering, Ford UK plc	Private business
Peter Fryer	• Environmental Quality Manager, Bristol City Council	Local government
Donna Green	• Manager, Environmental Programmes, Rover Group	Private business
Roger Higman	• Atmosphere and Transport Senior Campaigner, Friends of the Earth	Voluntary/charity
James Hookham	• Executive Director, Transport Policy, Freight Transport Association	Trade association
Chris Hunt	• Company Secretary, UK Petroleum Industries Association	Trade association
Chris Jones	• Diagnostics Development Manager, RAC	Private business
Hannah Jones	• Johnson Matthey	Private business
James Langley	• Client Development Manager, PHH Group (Cendant Corporation)	Private business
David Lea	• Assistant General Secretary, TUC	Trade union
Nicola Leahy	• Environmental Affairs Manager, Vauxhall Motors	Private business
David Leibling	• Head of Corporate Communications, Lex Services plc	Private business
Kathy Lockyer	• Interpreter, Honda	Private business
Robin MacKonochie	• External Affairs Manager, British Vehicle Renting and Leasing Association	Trade association
Martin Maeso	• Assistant Head, Research and Environmental Policy, Automobile Association	Private business
Stephen Marks	• Executive Director, Alter-Europe	Private business
David Martin	• Technology Environment, Atomic Energy Authority	Privatised business
Michael Monaghan	• Technical Director, Ricardo Consulting Engineering Ltd	Private business
Jonathan Murray	• Manager of Transport Policies, Energy Savings Trust	Voluntary/charity
N. Nakamura	• Head of Research and Development, Honda UK	Private business
Leith Penny	• Director, Environment, Westminster City Council	Local government
Roger Poole	• Department of Trade and Industry	Central government
Don Potts	• Environmental Adviser, Volvo Cars UK Ltd	Private business
Hugh Roberts	• Director, Independent Garage Association	Trade association
Teresa Smallbone	• National Consumer Council	National public body

5   Fleet Purchasing Guidance Subgroup

Veronica Henry Darius	• Managing Director, Market Power Communications	Private business
Steve Hawkes	• Technical Marketing Strategy Manager, Rover Group	Private business
James Langley	• Client Development Manager, PHH Group (Cendant Corporation)	Private business
David Leibling	• Head, Corporate Communications, Lex Services plc	Private business
Torsten Leidiger	• Policy and Technical Adviser, Ark Environmental Foundation	Voluntary/charity
Robin MacKonochie	• External Affairs Manager, British Vehicle Renting and Leasing Association	Trade association
Don Potts	• Environmental Adviser, Volvo Cars UK Ltd	Private business

6   Alternative Fuels Subgroup

Jonathan Murray (Convenor)	• Energy Savings Trust	Voluntary/charity
Tim Brown	• National Society for Clean Air	Voluntary/charity
Geoff Callow	• Motor Industry Research Association	Trade association
Geoff Day	• Freight Transport Association	Trade association
Tom Fidell	• Liquid Petroleum Gas Association	Trade association
Philip Heseltine	• Mersey Travel Passenger Transport Executive	Local government
Nancy Hofmeister	• Ford UK plc	Private business
David Owen	• Powergen	Privatised business
Fred Parker	• NGVA	Trade association
Keith Reid	• Royal Mail	National public body
Jon Singer	• Society of Motor Manufacturers and Traders	Trade association
Paul Sterling	• Electricity Association	Trade association
Neil Wallis	• Energy Savings Trust	Voluntary/charity

Malcom Watson	• UK Petroleum Industries Association	Trade association
Angela Wigley	• Rover Group plc	Private business

7 Information and Labelling Subgroup

Roger Higman (Convenor)	• Atmosphere and Transport Senior Campaigner, Friends of the Earth	Voluntary/charity
Simon Brown	• Principal Engineer, London Transport Buses	National public body
Brenda Creavin	• Technical Manager, Society of Motor Manufacturers and Traders	Trade association
Nigel Davies	• Head, Intelligent Transport Systems and Services Ventures, RAC	Private business
Donna Green	• Manager, Environmental Programmes, Rover Group plc	Private business
Andy Grimm	• Head, Planning and Development, Vehicle Certification Agency	Central government
John Lippe	• Ford UK	Private business
Martin Maeso	• Assistant Head, Research and Environmental Policy, Automobile Association	Private business
Don Potts	• Environmental Adviser, Volvo Cars UK Ltd	Private business
Teresa Smallbone	• National Consumer Council	National public body

8 Technology and Testing Subgroup

Tony Downes (Convenor)	• Environmental Consultant, Perkins	Private business
Andy Bailey	• Rover Group plc	Private business
Simon Brown	• Principal Engineer, London Transport Buses	National public body
Brendan Creavin	• Society of Motor Manufacturers and Traders	Trade association
Andrew Davis	• Director, Environmental Transport Association	Voluntary/charity
Geoff Day	• Freight Transport Association	Trade association
Hugh Edwards	• Vehicle Inspectorate	Central government
Robert Evans	• Johnson Matthey plc	Private business
Hannah Jones	• Johnson Matthey plc	Private business
Andrew Mercer	• Shell UK	Private business
David Muir	• Bristol City Council	Local government
John Stubbs	• Automobile Association	Private business

9 Forecourt Emissions Testing Subgroup

Chris Hunt (Convenor)	• Company Secretary, UK Petroleum Industries Association	Trade association
Nigel Davies	• Head, Intelligent Transport Systems and Services Ventures, RAC	Private business
Martin Maeso	• Assistant Head, Research and Environmental Policy, Automobile Association	Private business
John Nelson	• Garage Equipment Association	Trade association
Colin Parlett	• Retail Motor Industry Federation	Trade association
David Pocklington	• Manager, Environment Group, SMMT	Trade association

10 Coalfields Task Force
To examine options for revitalising former coalfield communities in England.

Paula Hay-Plumb (Chair)	• Managing Director Operations, English Partnerships (Government regeneration and inward investment agency)	National public body
Stephen Fothergill (Deputy Chair)	• Director, Coalfield Communities Campaign	Local government
Trevor Beattie	• Head, Policy and Planning, English Partnerships	National public body
Michael Brabham	• Executive Director, Groundwork Cresswell	Private business
Chris Collison	• Director of Development Services, Mansfield District Council	Local government
John Edwards	• Chief Executive, Barnsley Metropolitan Borough Council	Local government
Paul Evans	• Director of Regeneration, DETR	Central government
Peter McNestry	• General Secretary, National Association of Colliery, Overmen, Deputies and Shotfirers	Trade union
Alan Morgan	• Bishop of Sherwood • Chair, Sherwood Coalfield Community Foundation	Voluntary/charity
Hugh Sharp	• Divisional Manager, Department for Education and Employment	Central government

David Shelton	• Projects Director, English Partnerships	National public body
David Smith	• Director, Regional Policy, Department of Trade and Industry	Central government
Kingsley Smith	• Chief Executive, Durham County Council	Local government

11 Composting Development Group

Established in November 1997 to promote the marketing of compost in order (inter alia) to meet EU requirements for reducing landfilled disposal of organic waste. A report of July 1998 went out to consultation among local authority and trade organisations.

Tony Anderson (Chair)	• DETR	Central government
Hugh Bulson	• Organic Resource Agency	Trade association
Lizzy Carlyle	• Ministry of Agriculture, Fisheries and Food	Central government
Bob Evans	• National Farmers' Union	Trade association
John Jardine	• County Mulch Company	Private business
Helen Jones	• DETR	Central government
Philip Metcalfe	• Agricultural Development Advisory Services (Western)	Central government
Michael Walker	• Composting Association	Trade association
Pat Wheeler	• ETSU	Trade association

12 Advisory Group on the Fundamental Policy Review of Compulsory Purchase

Established in 1998 to advise on this review of current methods and legislation on compulsory purchasing and disposals of redundant land.

Graham Cory (Chair)	• Plans and Projects Division, DETR	Central government
Stephen Bowman	• Director, Union Property	Private business
Tony Chase	• Partner, Gerald Eve (chartered surveyors)	Private business
Andy Clark	• Local Government Association	Local government
Barry Denyer-Green	• Barrister	Independent
John Henderson	• Property Industry Group	Trade association
Carl Hopkins	• Solicitor	Independent
William McKee	• British Property Federation	Trade association
Professor Victor Moore	• Department of Law, University of Reading	Academic/research
Steve Mycio	• Director of Housing, Deputy Chief Executive, Manchester City Council	Local government
Alistair Paterson	• Scottish Power	Privatised business
Dr Brian Raggett	• Hillier Parker (property consultants and agents)	Private business
Guy Roots, QC	• Barrister	Independent
Professor Jeremy Rowan-Robinson	• University of Aberdeen	Academic/research
Michael Seals	• Property Industry Group	Trade association

13 Consultative Committee on Construction Industry Statistics

Established in 1998 to consider and advise upon this field

Alan Crane (Chair)	• Christiani and Nielson	Private business
Pauline Borland	• Federation of Master Builders	Trade association
Colin Brett	• House Builders Federation	Trade association
Stuart Burchell	• Constructors Liaison Group	Trade association
Jacquie Cannon	• Construction Forecasting and Research	Private business
Linda Gilardoni	• Construction Industry Training Board	National public body
Anne King	• Building Services Research and Information Association	Trade association
Martin Lockwood	• Construction Industry Council	Trade association
Ian Maclean	• Statistics Users Council	Trade association
Jerry McLaughlin	• Quarry Products Association	Trade association
Peter Matthews	• Building Merchants Federation	Trade association
Nina Ovanessian	• National Council of Building Materials Producers	Trade association
Matthew Ryall	• Royal Institution of Chartered Surveyors	Professional association

Owen Simon	• Institution of Civil Engineers	Professional association
John Stewart	• House Builders Federation	Trade association
Jim Turner	• Construction Forecasting and Research	Private business
Allan Wilen	• National Council of Building Materials Producers	Trade association
Mindy Wilson	• Association of Consulting Engineers	Professional association

14 Construction Task Force

To advise on improving productivity in the construction industry from the client's perspective. The report 'Rethinking Construction' led to new industry bodies and demonstration projects on productive building.

Sir John Egan (Chair)	• Chief Executive, British Airports Authority plc	Privatised business
Ian Gibson	• Managing Director, Nissan UK	Private business
David Gye	• Advisory Director, Morgan Stanley and Co Ltd	Private business
Professor Daniel Jones	• Director, Lean Enterprise Research Centre, Cardiff Business School	Academic/research
Anthony Mayer	• Chief Executive, Housing Corporation	National public body
Sir Nigel Mobbs	• Chief Executive, Slough Estates plc • Chair, Bovis Homes	Private business
Sir Brian Moffatt	• Chief Executive, British Steel plc	Privatised business
Alan Parker	• Managing Director, Whitbread Hotels	Private business
Mike Raycraft	• Property Services Director, Tesco Stores Ltd	Private business
David Warburton	• Senior National Officer, General and Municipal Boilermakers Union	Trade union
G. Nightingale (Secretary)	• Construction Directorate, DETR	Central government

15 Cowboy Builders Working Group

Established in July 1998 (first meeting September) to develop the 'quality marking' of builders and their trade associations as proposed in DETR's consultation paper 'Combating Cowboy Builders', while also considering consumer education and effective advertising about this advance. Draft recommendations were given limited circulation in early 1999 and an interim report published: a final report is expected in August 1999.

Anthony Merricks (Chair)	• Director, Balfour Beatty	Private business
Ian Davis	• Federation of Master Builders	Trade association
Ian Edwards	• Office of Fair Trading	Central government
Ian Foulkes	• Local Government Association	Local government
Ron Gainsford	• LACOTS (Local Authority Trading Standards Body)	Local government
Keith Hale	• LACOTS (Local Authority Trading Standards Body)	Local government
Colin Harding	• National Federation of Builders	Trade association
Frances Harrison	• National Consumer Council	National public body
John Hobson	• DETR	Central government
Sir Michael Latham	• Director, Wilmot Dixon • Consultant, construction industry	Private business
Rod Maceacrene	• National House-Building Council	Trade association
Peter Martin	• Construction Industry Training Board	National public body
Stephen Moon	• Chief Executive, National Federation of Builders	Trade association
Chris Mounsey	• Association of Building Insurers	Trade association
Terry Rochester	• Construction Clients Forum	Trade association
Peter Shiells	• Constructors Liaison Group	Trade association
Chris Shuttleworth	• Institute of Building Control	Trade association
Trevor Single	• DTI	Central government
Bill Swan	• Capita	Private business
Andy Watts	• Institute of Plumbing	Trade association
Graham Watts	• Construction Industry Council	Trade association

16 Sub-group 1: Trade Association Accreditation

| Sir Michael Latham (Chair) | • Director, Wilmot Dixon;
• Consultant, construction industry | Private business |
| David Ballard | • Glass and Glazing Federation | Trade association |

Jane Beaumont	• UK Accreditation Service	Private business
Brian Flint	• Federation of Master Builders	Trade association
Colin Garton	• Capita	Private business
John Harrower	• Special Engineering Contractors Group	Trade association
Martin Horsler	• Association of Building Insurers	Trade association
Stephen Moon	• Chief Executive, National Federation of Builders	Trade association
Fraser Watts	• Aon Insurance	Private business

17   Sub-group 2: **Accredited Constructors Scheme**

Colin Harding (Chair)	• National Federation of Builders	Trade association
David Brieley	• Institute of Building Control	Trade association
Colin Farrow	• National Federation of Builders	Trade association
Brian Flint	• Federation of Master Builders	Trade association
Simon Mitchell	• Institute of Plumbing	Trade association
Brian Newell	• National Specialist Contractors Council	Trade association
Nigel Pound	• Federation of Master Builders	Trade association
Denzil Slumbers	• Special Engineering Contractors Group	Trade association

18   Sub-group 3: **Approved Lists and Consumer Education**

Stephen Moon (Chair)	• Chief Executive, National Federation of Builders	Trade association
Edward Cowan	• National Federation of Roofing Contractors	Trade association
Ian Foulkes	• Local Government Association	Local government
Colin Garton	• Capita	Private business
Keith Hale	• LACOTS (Local Authority Trading Standards Body)	Local government
Frances Harrison	• National Consumer Council	National public body
Chris Mounsey	• Association of Building Insurers	Trade association
Arthur Over	• Special Engineering Contractors Group	Trade association
Derrick Ovington	• Federation of Master Builders	Trade association
Phil Sharman	• GESA Assistance	Private business
Chris Shuttleworth	• Institute of Building Control	Trade association
Bill Swan	• Capital	Private business
John Thorpe	• DTI	Central government
Alan Wilson	• Scotland and Northern Ireland Plumbing and Electricians Federation	Trade association

19   Sub-group 4: **Warranty, Dispute Resolution and Disciplinary Procedures**

Ian Davis (Chair)	• Federation of Master Builders	Trade association
Mark Broughton-Taylor	• Federation of Master Builders	Trade association
Colin Garton	• Capita	Private business
Glyn Jackson	• National House Building Council	Trade association
David McCullogh	• Institute of Building Control	Trade association
Julien Parrot	• Construction Industry Council	Trade association
Rod Pettigrew	• Heating and Ventilation Contractors Association	Trade association
Mike Rapley	• Association of Building Insurers	Trade association
David Tym	• Electrical Contractors Association	Trade association
Andy Watts	• Institute of Plumbing	Trade association
Kelvin Williams	• Local Government Association • LACOTS (Local Authority Trading Standards Body)	Local government

20   **Design Advisory Group**
Established in September 1998 to give expert architectural advice on the buildings to be provided for the new elected London government.

Sir Michael Hopkins (Chair)	• Michael Hopkins and Partners (architects)	Private business
Paul Finch	• Editor, *The Architect's Journal*	Independent

Lucy Musgrave	• Director, The Architecture Foundation	Voluntary/charity
Pankaj Patel	• Partner, Patel Taylor (architects)	Private business
Jane Priestmann	• Independent design consultant	Independent

21 Hedgerows Regulations Review Group

To review how the Hedgerows Regulations 1997 might be strengthened to provide more effective protection from removal for hedgerows in general and important hedgerows in particular.

Diana Kahn (Chair)	• Head, Rural Development Division, DETR	Central government
Judy Allfrey	• Head, Conservation and Rural Development Division, MAFF	Central government
Hannah Bartram	• Royal Society for the Protection of Birds	Voluntary/charity
Tony Burton	• Council for the Protection of Rural England	Voluntary/charity
Stuart Campbell	• The Electricity Association	Trade association
Andrew Clark	• National Farmers Union	Trade association
Allison Crofts	• The Wildlife Trusts	Voluntary/charity
Tim Dorkin	• Welsh Office	Central government
Janet Dwyer	• Countryside Commission	National public body
Graham Fairclough	• English Heritage	National public body
David Gear	• Countryside Commission	National public body
Frances Griffiths	• Council for British Archaeology	Voluntary/charity
Jim Harrisson	• Local Government Association	Local government
John Menon	• Farmers Union of Wales	Trade association
Hilary Miller	• Countryside Council for Wales	National public body
Sian Phipps	• Council for the Protection of Rural England	Voluntary/charity
Christine Reid	• English Nature	National public body
Geoffrey Sinclair	• Wales Wildlife and Countryside Link	Voluntary/charity
Merfyn Williams	• Campaign for the Protection of Rural Wales	Voluntary/charity
Gavin Wilson	• Local Government Association	Local government
Alan Woods	• Country Landowners Association	Trade association

22 Ministerial Task Group (and Review) on the Home Buying and Selling Process

Rt. Hon. Hilary Armstrong MP (Chair)	• Minister for Local Government and Housing, DETR	Central government
Nigel Griffiths MP	• Junior minister, Consumer Affairs, DTI (replaced by Kim Howells MP, July 1998)	Central government
Geoff Hoon MP	• Parliamentary Secretary (later Minister of State) Lord Chancellor's Department	Central government
Steering Group Representatives:	*from DETR, LCD, DTI, Office of Fair Trading, Land Registry, Law Society, Law Society of Scotland, Royal Institution of Chartered Surveyors, Incorporated Society of Valuers and Auctioneers, Council of Mortgage Lenders, National Association of Estate Agents, Consumers' Association.*	

23 Housing Fitness Standard Review Steering Group

Established in September 1998, with no set period, to steer DETR's research on this topic; to advise on technical guidance to fitness ratings, on enforcement and on how ratings can help monitor housing condition. Pilot work on new ratings is contracted with the University of Warwick.

Rachel Sharpe (Chair)	• Head, Housing Policy, Renewal and Ownership, DETR	Central government
Mike Amey	• Housing Policy, Renewal and Ownership, DETR	Central government
Stephen Battersby	• University of Warwick	Academic/research
Roger Burridge	• University of Warwick	Academic/research
Paul Everall	• Head, Building Regulations, DETR	Central government
Mike Faulkner	• Head, Housing Private Rented Sector, DETR	Central government
John Flower	• Housing Policy, Renewal and Ownership, DETR	Central government
Brendon Hillbourne	• Welsh Office	Central government
Paul Lees	• Department of Health	Central government
Sarah Millington	• Legal Division, DETR	Central government
Richard Moore	• Research Analysis and Evaluation, DETR	Central government

David Ormandy	• University of Warwick	Academic/research
Gary Raw	• Building Research Establishment	Privatised business
David Scott	• Housing Policy, Renewal and Ownership, DETR	Central government
Clive Singh	• Department of Social Security	Central government

Other organisations represented:

	• Allerdale Borough Council	Local government
	• Anchor Housing Association	Local public spending body
	• Bristol City Council	Local government
	• British Property Federation	Trade association
	• Caerphilly Borough Council	Local government
	• Focus Housing Association	Local public spending body
	• London Borough of Kensington and Chelsea	Local government
	• University of Loughborough	Academic/research
	• Sandwell Metropolitan Borough Council	Local government

24 Housing Revenue Account Resource Accounting Technical Advisory Group

Established in May 1998 to devise a scheme for capital charging in the HRA which will (inter alia) permit greater transparency; closer comparison with social housing; a possible corporate base for local authority housing; more efficient capital allocation and management. A consultation paper and pilot scheme during 1999-2000 were planned.

Hilary Chipping (Chair)	• Head, Local Authority Housing Division, DETR	Central government

Representatives of the Association of London Government:

Ernie Jarvis	• London Borough of Wandsworth	Local government
John Kettlewell	• London Borough of Tower Hamlets	Local government
Peter O'Kane	• London Housing Unit	Local government

Representative of the Audit Commission:

Grant Patterson	• The Audit Commission	National public body

Representative of the CIPFA:

Maureen Wellen	• Chartered Institute of Public Finance and Accounting	Professional association

Representatives of the Local Government Association:

Hilary Keenan	• Derby City Council	Local government
Paul Lautman	• Local Government Association	Local government
Ken Lee	• West Lancashire District Council	Local government
Steve Warburton	• Sheffield City Council	Local government
Alan Westwood	• Salford Metropolitan Borough Council	Local government

Representative of the Royal Institution of Chartered Surveyors:

Betty Albon	• St. Edmundsbury Borough Council	Professional association

Representative of the Valuation Office:

Brian Loder	• The Valuation Office, Board of Inland Revenue	Central government

Representative of HM Treasury:

Paul Johnston	• HM Treasury	Central government

DETR officials:

John Apps	• Local Authority Housing (LAH) Division	Central government
Susan Deville	• LAH	Central government
Michael Harryman	• LAH	Central government
Anne Kirkham	• RAE Division	Central government
Charles Pickering	• LAH	Central government
Paul Seaborne	• LAH	Central government
Margaret Slack	• LAH	Central government
Jeff Thompson	• Housing and Urban Economics Division	Central government
Darren Wells	• Local Government Capital Finance Division	Central government

25 Housing Sounding Board

An informal forum for discussing key issues in housing including some of those considered as part of the Comprehensive Spending Review, 1997-98.

Rt. Hon. Hilary Armstrong, MP (Chair)	• Minister for Local Government and Housing, DETR	Central government
Brian Briscoe	• Chief Executive, Local Government Association	Local government
Chris Brown	• Royal Institute of Chartered Surveyors	Professional association
Roger Dobson	• Institute of Civil Engineers	Professional association
Michael Gwilym	• Director, Civic Trust	Voluntary/charity
Roger Higman	• Atmosphere and Transport Senior Campaigner, Friends of the Earth	Voluntary/charity
Chris Holmes	• Director, Shelter	Voluntary/charity
Roger Humber	• Director General, House Builders' Federation	Trade association
Alistair Jackson	• National Housing Federation	Trade association
Alan Kilburn	• Chief Executive, Home Housing Association	Voluntary/charity
Samantha McDonough	• Royal Institute of British Architects	Professional association
Steve Mycio	• Director of Housing, Deputy Chief Executive, Manchester City Council	Local government
Mike Ockenden	• Managing Director, Barclays Mortgages	Private business
John Perry	• Chartered Institute of Housing	Professional association
Professor Anne Power	• Department of Social Policy (Head of Housing) London School of Economics	Academic/research
Heather Rabbatts	• Chief Executive, Lambeth London Borough	Local government
John Routledge	• Urban Forum	Voluntary/charity
Robert Upton	• Royal Town Planning Institute	Professional association
Steve Wilcox	• Centre for Housing Policy, University of York • Associate Director of HACAS	Academic/research

26 Leylandii Working Group

Established in September 1998 to produce a voluntary code of practice on the sale, use and maintenance of domestic hedge plants and to recommend on the ownership of the code and its dissemination. Reported in June 1999.

Diana Kahn (Chair)	• Divisional Manager, Rural Development Division, DETR	Central government
Representatives of:	• Arboricultural Association	Trade association
	• British Association of Landscape Industries	Trade association
	• Consumers' Association	Voluntary/charity
	• Horticultural Trades Association	Trade association
	• Joint Council for Landscape Industries	Trade association
	• The Landscape Institute	Professional association
	• Local Government Association	Local government
	• Royal Horticultural Society	Voluntary/charity
	• House Builders Federation	Trade association
	• Burall Floraprint	Private business

27 Market Development Group (for recycled goods and materials)

Established July 1998 to propose to central and local government, industry and voluntary groups how these markets might expand, including taxes, levies and obligations to promote recycling on original producers. A report was expected in early summer 1999.

Lisette Simcock (Chair)	• Waste Policy, DETR	Central government
Carolyn Abel	• Recycling Policy, DTI	Central government
Tony Anderson	• Waste Policy, DETR	Central government
Bryan Bateman	• The Paper Federation of Great Britain	Trade association
Sian Bunn	• Wespak	Private business
Robin Curry	• Institute of Wastes Management	Professional association
David Davis	• Enviros-RIS	Private business
Laura Fellowes	• Environment Protection Economics, DETR	Central government
Ray Georgeson	• Waste Watch	Voluntary/charity

Ivan Good	• Environmental Services Association	Trade association
Alex Griffin	• Aluminium Federation	Trade association
Tony Hammond	• Local Authority Recycling Advisory Committee	Local government
Kamilla Horak	• VALPAK	Private business
Sheila McKinley	• Packaging Unit, DETR	Central government
Louise Mitchell	• Waste Policy, DETR	Central government
Alison Morris	• British Glass Manufacturers Confederation	Trade association
Adrian Myers	• British Steel Packaging Recycling Unit	Privatised business
Steve Ogilvie	• Recycling Advisory Unit, Atomic Energy Authority Technology	Privatised business
Andrew Simmons	• Recycling of Used Plastic Containers	Voluntary/charity
Ian White	• Environment Agency	Central government
Anne Wilkins (Secretary)	• Waste Policy, DETR	Central government

28 Park Homes Working Party

Established in Autumn 1998 to review caravan and mobile home legislation and the promotion of best practice by the park homes industry. A report was expected by Spring 1999.

Michael Faulkner (Chair)	• DETR	Central government
Alan Bishop	• National Park Homes Council	Trade association
Rita Bolus	• Welsh Office	Central government
Brian Doick	• National Association of Park Home Residents	Voluntary/charity
Neil Eaton	• Local Government Association • Coventry City Council	Local government
Ken Lewis	• British Park Homes Residents Association	Voluntary/charity
Howard Price	• Chartered Institute of Environmental Health	Professional association
Richard Samuel	• Local Government Association • Sevenoaks District Council	Local government
James Spencer	• British Holiday and Home Parks Association	Trade association
Roy Waite	• Independent Park Homes Advisory Service	Private business
Lorraine Watson	• Local Government Association	Local government
Secretary: Robert Miles	• DETR	Central government

29 Sustainable Development Education Panel (joint with DfEE)

Established in February 1998 to consider and make recommendations on education for sustainable development in the education sector, at work, during recreation and at home. An interim report of July 1998 was followed by a First Annual Report 1998 in 1999. The Panel is a standing joint advisory body of DETR and DfEE: listed as an ANDPB in Public Bodies 1998.

Sir Geoffrey Holland (Chair)	• Vice-Chancellor, University of Exeter • Former Permanent Secretary, Department of Education and Science	Education
Dr Shirely Ali Khan	• Forum for the Future	Voluntary/charity
Prof. Graham Ashworth	• Going for Green Ltd	Voluntary/charity
Roy Atkinson	• Northamptonshire County Council	Local government
Heather Barrett-Mold	• Capel Manor Horticultural and Environmental Centre	Education
Douglas Bourn	• Development Education Association • Member, Development Awareness Working Group (Dept. for International Development)	Education
Dr Neil Chalmers	• Director, Natural History Museum	National public body
Jean Cook	• Further Education Funding Council	National public body
Peter Downes	• Secondary Heads Association	Education
Ruth Evans	• Director, National Consumer Council	National public body
Olivia Grant	• Chief Executive, Tyneside Training and Enterprise Council	Local public spending body
Rosemary Gray	• Principal, Walsall College of Arts and Technology	Education
Libby Grundy	• Council for Environmental Education • Member Development Awareness Working Group (DFID)	Voluntary/charity
Anne Harley	• Royal Society for the Protection of Birds	Voluntary/charity
Michael Knapp	• Edexcel and joint Awarding Bodies Council	Voluntary/charity

Alan Knight	• Head of Environment, B&Q plc	Private business
Bill Lucas	• Campaign for Learning	Voluntary/charity
Peter Martin	• World Wide Fund for Nature	Voluntary/charity
Prof. Peter Toyne	• Liverpool John Moores University	Academic/research
Alan Tuckett	• Director, National Institute for Adult and Continuing Education	Education
John Westaway	• Qualifications and Curriculum Authority • Member, Development Awareness Working Group (DFID)	National public body
Miles Wilson	• Environment Agency	Central government
Tom Wylie	• Chief Executive, National Youth Agency • Member, Development Awareness Working Group (DFID)	Voluntary/charity
Joint Secretaries:		
Gill Beauchamp	• DfEE	Central government
Helen Morris	• DETR	Central government

30   Thaumasite Expert Group

Established in April 1998 to investigate and recommend measures to address the risk of the thaumasite form of sulphate attack on concrete. The group reported in January 1999 having formally consulted a total of 32 further experts on the staffs of six private firms, four trade associations and five universities or associated research bodies.

Professor Leslie Clark (Chair)	• President, Institution of Structural Engineers	Professional association
Chris Curtis	• Quarry Products Association	Trade association
Neil Dutton	• Council of Mortgage Lenders • Royal Institution of Chartered Surveyors	Trade association
John Haynes	• National House-Building Council	Trade association
Dr Don Hobbs	• British Cement Association	Trade association
N. Loudon	• The Highways Agency	Central government
Dr Philip Nixon	• Building Research Establishment	Privatised business
John Patch	• Federation of Piling Specialists • Association of Specialist Underpinning Contractors	Trade association
Dr Bill Price	• Association of Consulting Engineers	Professional association
Dr Peter Robery	• Institution of Civil Engineers	Professional association
Terry Rochester	• Construction Clients' Forum	Trade association
David Slater	• The Concrete Society	Trade association
Roy Thurgood	• DETR	Central government
Secretary		
Chris Judge	• Building Research Establishment	Privatised business
Contributing technical experts:		
Dr N.J. Crammond	• Building Research Establishment	Privatised business
T.I. Longworth	• Building Research Establishment	Privatised business

31   Urban Task Force

Established April 1998 to help the Government identify the means of encouraging urban revival by incentives to encourage the re-use of brownfield sites in towns and cities where housing could be built to ease pressure on greenfield areas. Published a Prospectus (July 1998); interim report (January 1999): final report published in June 1999 (Towards an Urban Renaissance). The group will continue informally. A road show is in action, jointly funded by DETR and Ove Arup (engineers).

Lord Rogers (Chair)	• Richard Rogers Partnership (architects)	Private business
Anthony Mayer (Vice-Chairman)	• Chief Executive, Housing Corporation	National public body
Richard Burdett	• Director, City Policy, London School of Economics	Academic/research
Tony Burton	• Assistant Director (Policy), Council for the Protection of Rural England	Voluntary/charity
Alan Cherry	• Chair, Countryside Property plc	Private business
Martin Crookston	• Director, Llewelyn Davies (architects and planners)	Private business
Anthony Dunnett	• Chief Executive, English Partnerships	National public body
Sir Peter Hall	• Bartlett Professor of Planning, University College London	Academic/research

Stuart Lipton (Since Nov 1998 – advisory role only. Replaced by Phil Kirby)	• Chief Executive, Stanhope Property Developers • Deputy Chair, The Architecture Foundation • Chair, Commission on Architecture and the Built Environment	Private business
Phil Kirby	• Head of British Gas Properties	Private business
David Lunts	• Chief Executive, Urban Villages Forum	Voluntary/charity
Professor Anne Power	• Department of Social Policy (Head of Housing) London School of Economics	Academic/research
Wendy Thomson	• Chief Executive, London Borough of Newham	Local government
Sir Crispin Tickell	• Convenor, Government Panel on Sustainable Development	Independent
Lorna Walker	• Director, Ove Arup (engineers and architects)	Private business

32 Working Group One: 'Defining the Product'

Richard Fielden	• Senior Partner, Fielden, Clegg Architects	Private business
Peter Headicar	• Planning Department, Oxford Brookes University	Academic/research
Roger Levett	• Director, CAG Consultants	Private business
Richard MacCormac	• MacCormac, Jamieson and Prichard (architects)	Private business
Fred Manson	• Director of Regeneration and Environment, London Borough of Southwark	Local government
Tony Ridley	• Head of Civil Engineering Department, Imperial College, London	Academic/research
Michael Ward	• Director, CLES	Private business
Roger Zogolovitch	• Alsop Zogolovitch (architects)	Private business
Sir Jack Zunz	• Consultant, Ove Arup (engineers and architects)	Private business

33 Working Group Two: 'Liberating the Process'

Roger Aldridge	• Director of Estates & Store Development, Marks & Spencer plc	Private business
Mike Appleton	• AMEC Development	Private business
Tom Bloxham	• Chairman Urban Splash Properties Ltd.	Private business
Clive Dutton	• Head of Regeneration, Sandwell Metropolitan Borough Council	Local government
Imtiaz Farookhi	• Chief Executive, National House-Building Council	Trade association
Nicky Gavron	• Local Government Association	Local government
Marie Hodgson	• Head of Special Projects, English Partnerships	National public body
Sam Richards	• Local Government Association	Local government
Dickon Robinson	• Peabody Trust (social housing providers)	Voluntary/charity
Les Sparks	• Director of Planning and Architecture, Birmingham City Council	Local government
Tony Struthers	• Director of Development Services, Salford Metropolitan Borough Council	Local government

34 Working Group Three: 'Providing the Finance'

Chris Brown	• AMEC Development	Private business
Ben Denton	• Director, Abros	Private business
Professor Malcolm Grant	• Chair, Local Government Boundary Commission • Department of Land Economy, University of Cambridge	National public body
Maurice Hochschild	• Director, European Capital	Private business
Doug Johnson	• Director of Finance, Newcastle Upon Tyne City Council	Local government
David McKeith	• Tax partner, Pricewaterhouse Coopers (Manchester)	Private business
Adrian Montague	• Chief Executive, Private Finance task force, HM Treasury	Central government
Professor Brian Robson	• Professor of Geography, University of Manchester	Academic/research
Rosalind Rowe	• Director, Real Estate Group, Pricewaterhouse Coopers	Private business
Tony Travers	• Director of Greater London Group, London School of Economics	Academic/research

35 Institutional Sounding Board

Established to be confidentially briefed on The Urban Task Force's work and emerging conclusions and to give interim reactions on behalf of the relevant bodies through their chief or senior officials. These included:

Brian Briscoe	• Local Government Association	Local government
Chris Brown	• Royal Institution of Chartered Surveyors	Professional association
Roger Dobson	• Institution of Civil Engineers	Professional association

Michael Gwilym	• Civic Trust	Voluntary/charity
Roger Higman	• Friends of the Earth	Voluntary/charity
Chris Holmes	• Shelter	Voluntary/charity
Roger Humber	• National Housebuilders' Federation	Trade association
Alistair Jackson	• National Housing Federation	Trade association
Samantha McDonough	• Royal Institute of British Architects	Professional association
John Perry	• Chartered Institute of Housing	Professional association
John Routledge	• Urban Forum	Voluntary/charity
Robert Upton	• Royal Town Planning Institute	Professional association

(i)   Transport issues

36   Review of the Rolling Stock Leasing Market

John Swift QC	• Rail Regulator, Office of the Rail Regulator	Central government

37   Lord Donaldson's Review of Salvage and Intervention and their Command and Control
To review salvage operations where there is a risk of marine pollution.

Lord Donaldson	• Former Master of the Rolls	Independent
Professor Alasdair McIntyre (Assessor)	• Department of Zoology, University of Aberdeen	Academic/research
Michael Ellis (Assessor)	• General Manager, the Salvage Association	Trade association

38   Shipping Working Group
To promote economic and environmental benefits from an expanding UK merchant fleet, with higher employment and training levels for UK seafarers. The report was unpublished but incorporated into the White Paper 'British Shipping: Charting a New Course' (December 1998). A further Shipping Task Force (with three 'catalyst groups' on training, employment and environmental benefits) was launched early in 1999 with the same 'outsiders'. An agreed plan to try to double the UK's registered tonnage to ½ m. tons under a new tax regime was announced in August, 1999 together with P and O line's intention to double their own training programme.

Roger Clarke (Chair)	• Director, Shipping and Ports, DETR	Central government
Representatives	• Chamber of Shipping; maritime trade unions (NUMAST, RMT, TGWU); DfEE, MoD, DSS, DTI and FCO	

39   Fundamental Review of Transport Policy
To provide integrated and expert advice on how best to define, implement, organise and fund successful and practical integrated transport strategies. The Chair and Stephen Joseph were included in a new Commission for Integrated Transport in 1999 to monitor the White Paper of July 1998. (See also List 1.2)

Professor David Begg	• Chair of Transport Management, Business School, The Robert Gordon University, Aberdeen	Academic/research
Professor Carmen Hass-Klau	• Civil Engineering Department, Wuppertal University, Germany	Academic/research
Stephen Joseph	• Executive Director, Transport 2000	Voluntary/charity
Joyce Mamode	• Transport Trade Union Group (HGVs), Transport and General Workers Union	Trade union
Dr Susan Owens	• Department of Geography, University of Cambridge	Academic/research
Charles Rice	• P&O Trans European	Private business
Michael Roberts	• Head of Industrial Policy Group, Confederation of British Industry	Trade association
Bill Tyson	• Greater Manchester Passenger Transport Executive	Local government

FOREIGN AND COMMONWEALTH OFFICE (FCO)

Name	*Affiliation*	*Classification*

1   Panel 2000 Advisory Group
To produce a strategy for projecting a positive identity for Britain; to pull together all strands of public diplomacy, FCO, British Council, private sector; to monitor perceptions overseas; to ensure that the FCO projects an open and modern image at home and abroad.

Derek Fatchett MP (Chair)	• Minister of State, FCO	Central government
Lord Alli	• Managing Director, Planet 24 (TV Company)	Private business
Ms Zeinab Badawi	• News presenter, Channel 4	Independent
Martin Bell MP	• MP (Independent) for Tatton	Independent
Baroness Blackstone	• Minister of State, DfEE	Central government

Baroness Chalker of Wallasey	• Former Minister for Overseas Development, FCO	Independent
Lord Clinton Davis	• Appointed as Minister of State, DTI (1997-8); remains on the Group	Central government
Frances De Souza	• Article 19 (anti-censorship interest group)	Voluntary/charity
David Drewry	• Director General, British Council	National public body
Mark Fisher MP	• Appointed as Minister, Department for Culture, Media and Sport; remains on the Group	Central government
Andrew Fraser	• Invest in Britain Bureau	Central government
Claire Fulton	• Eastern Department, FCO	Central government
Priya Guha	• Aviation and Maritime Department, FCO	Central government
Tom Harris	• Director General, Export Promotion, DTI	Central government
Sir Michael Jay	• HM Ambassador, Paris	Central government
David John	• Chairman, British Oxygen Company Group	Private business
Sir John Kerr	• Permanent Under Secretary, FCO	Central government
Mark Leonard	• Demos	Academic/research
Lord Levy	• MG Records	Private business
Roger Liddle	• Policy Unit, Prime Minister's Office	Central government
Ms Vivien Life	• Latin America Department, FCO	Central government
Lord Marshall British Industry (1996-98)	• Chair, British Airways • Privatised business	President, Confederation of
Stella McCartney	• Fashion designer, Chloe	Private business
Ruth Mackenzie	• General Director, Scottish Opera	Voluntary/charity
Lord Paul	• Chair, Caparo Group Ltd.	Private business
David Quarmby	• Chair, British Tourist Authority	National public body
Mrs Shahwar Sadeque	• Consultant	Private business
Judy Simpson	• Athlete and Gladiators TV personality	Independent
John Sorrel	• Chair, Design Council	National public body
Martin Sorrell	• Chief Executive, WPP	Private business
Baroness Symons	• Parliamentary Under Secretary, FCO	Central government
Harriet Ware-Austin	• Amnesty International	Voluntary/charity

DEPARTMENT OF HEALTH (DH)

Name	Affiliation	Classification

1   Review of the Breast Screening Programme in Devon and the Implications for the Breast Cancer Screening Programme as a Whole.
To visit the Royal Devon & Exeter Hospital Trust to establish the facts surrounding the provision of breast services; to report these findings to the Secretary of State for Health; in the light of these findings to consider implications for breast services as a whole & to report to the Secretary of State for Health.

Dame Deidre Hine (Chair)	• Chief Medical Officer, Welsh Office, • Former Senior Lecturer in Geriatric Medicine, University of Wales College of Medicine	Central government
Dr M Brindle	• President of the Royal College of Radiologists	Professional association
J.R.C. Sainsbury	• Consultant Surgeon, Huddersfield Royal Infirmary	Health
G. Oliver	• Cancer Nursing Specialist, Liverpool	Health
P. Cunningham	• Chief Executive, Royal Marsden NHS Trust	Health
Polly Toynbee	• Social policy journalist	Independent

2   Independent Review of Proposals for the Transfer of Bulk Blood Processing and Testing from Liverpool to Manchester
To examine whether current proposals guarantee safety & reliability of blood components to hospitals on Merseyside and N. Wales and provide adequate support for high-quality clinical services in the Merseyside and N Wales areas.

Professor John Cash	• President, Royal College of Physicians of Edinburgh • Former Director, Blood Transfusion Service, Scotland	Professional association

3   Review of Cervical Screening Services at Kent and Canterbury Hospitals NHS Trust

Established in June 1999 to investigate all circumstances surrounding the failures of the cytology screening programme in Kent & Canterbury Hospital; identify the lessons to be learnt to ensure that the risks to patients are minimised and that public confidence is restored and maintained. Reported October 1997.

Sir William Wells (Chair)	• Chairman, South Thames regional office of the NHS Executive	Central government
Dr Sue Atkinson	• Director of Public Health, South Thames NHS Executive	Health
Bob Nicholls	• General Medical Council	National public body
Dr Peter Smith	• Consultant, Royal Liverpool University Hospital	Health

4   The Cervical Screening Action Group

Established in December 1997, following the report into cervical cancer screening at Kent and Canterbury NHS Trust, to monitor current action to improve the quality of and public confidence in the NHS Cervical Screening Programme and to consider staffing and any other issue   requiring further action.

Sir Kenneth Calman (Chair)	• Chief Medical Officer, Department of Health	Central government
Dr Mary Buchanan	• Women's Nationwide Cancer Control Campaign	Voluntary/charity
Dr Muir Gray	• National Screening Committee, Department of Health	Central government
Professor Rod Griffiths	• Director of Public Health, West Midlands Region, NHS Executive	Health
Professor Roddy McSween	• Royal College of Pathologists	Professional association
Julietta Patnick	• NHS Cervical Screening Programme	Health
Professor Denis Pereira Gray	• Royal College of General Practitioners	Professional association
Dr John Shepherd	• Royal College of Obstetricians and Gynaecologists	Professional association
Tera Younger	• South Thames Region, NHS Executive	Health

5   Review of Consent Provisions of the Human Fertilisation and Embryology Act, 1990

Established in 1997 to review the Act's consent aspect. Consultation paper issued in September 1997 for return of responses by December 1997.

Professor Sheila McLean (Chair)	• Professor of Law and Ethics in Medicine, University of Glasgow	Academic/research

6   Chronic Fatigue Syndrome Main Working Group

To help promote better understanding of Chronic Fatigue Syndrome.

Professor Allen Hutchinson (Chair)	• Director, Public Health, School of Health and Related Research, University of Sheffield	Academic/research
Naomi Wayne (Deputy Chair)	• Chief Executive, Action for ME	Voluntary/charity
Dr Trudi Chalder	• Senior Lecturer, Department of Psychological Medicine, King's College Hospital, London	Academic/research
Dr Anthony Cleare	• Senior Lecturer (Linbury Trust Fellow), Department of Psychological Medicine, King's College Hospital, London	Academic/research
Roma Gant	• Person with ME	Independent
Jonathan Hull	• Person with ME	Independent
Dr Nigel Hunt	• General Practitioner, Rivermead Gate Medical Centre, Chelmsford	Health
Simon Lawrence	• Person with ME • Co-ordinator, 25% ME Group	Voluntary/charity
Mavis Moore	• Chief Executive, ME Association	Voluntary/charity
Dr Derek Pheby	• Epidemiologist, University of West of England	Academic/research
Dr Alison Round	• Consultant, Public Health Medicine, North and East Devon Health Authority	Health
Dr Charles Shepherd	• General Practitioner • Medical Adviser, ME Association	Health
Patricia Smith	• Carer	Independent
Dr Peter White	• Consultant Psychiatrist, St. Bartholomew's Hospital	Health

7   Chronic Fatigue Syndrome Children's Group

Judith Waterman (Chair)	• Retired Speech and Language Therapist Officer • Clinical Advice Team, NHS Executive	Independent
Judy Acreman	• Senior Nurse Therapist, Child and Family Services, Ashurst Hospital, Southampton	Health
Jane Colby	• Child Services Development Officer, Action for ME	Voluntary/charity

Dr Alan Franklin	• Honorary Consultant Paediatrician, Mid Essex Health Authority • Paediatric Medical Adviser, ME Association and West Care • Chair, Children's Focus Group on ME/CFS, West Care	Health
Professor Elena Garalda	• Professor of Child and Adolescent Psychiatry, St Mary's Hospital Medical School, London	Academic/research
Anna Grace Lidstone	• Co-ordinator and Editor, TYMES	Voluntary/charity
Rachel Lynds	• Association of Youth with ME	Voluntary/charity
Dr Anne McIntyre	• Medical Adviser, ME Association	Voluntary/charity
Mavis Moore	• Chief Executive, ME Association	Voluntary/charity
Jill Moss	• Director, Association of Youth with ME	Voluntary/charity
Dr Nigel Speight	• Consultant Paediatrician, Family Service Directorate, Department of Paediatrics, Dryburn Hospital, London	Health

8   Chronic Fatigue Syndrome Reference Group

Maureen Carmody	• Clinical Nurse Specialist, Department of Psychiatry, Royal Southampton Hospital	Health
Dr Betty Dowsett	• Honorary Consultant Microbiologist, South Essex NHS Trust	Health
Dr Leslie Finley	• Consultant Neurologist, National ME Centre	Health
Tanya Harrision	• Blue Ribbon for the Awareness of ME	Voluntary/charity
Professor Tony Pinching	• Immunologist, St Bartholomew's Hospital, London	Health
Dr Chris Richards	• Case History Research on ME	Academic/research
Marie Simmons	• Senior Counsellor, West Care	Health
Kate Sweeney	• Senior Physiotherapist, Royal Free Hospital, London	Health
Professor Simon Wessely	• Professor of Epidemiological and Liaison Psychiatry and Director, Chronic Fatigue Syndrome Research Unit, King's College School of Medicine, London	Academic/research
Dr Adrian Winbow	• Consultant Psychiatrist, Hayes Grove Priory Hospital, Kent	Health
Dr Andrew Wright	• General Practitioner • National Medical Advisor, Action for ME	Health
11 patients and 4 carers	• *Representing ME patients and carers*	Independent

9   Strategic Review of Health Services in London
This review's report was accepted in full by the Government in February 1998, thus reversing both the Tomlinson Report's 1992 advice to close Bart's Hospital and Labour's 1997 election pledge to keep open emergency services at Guy's Hospital.

Sir Leslie Turnberg (Chair)	• Former President, Royal College of Physicians • Former Professor and Dean of Medicine, University of Manchester	Independent
Francine Bates	• Assistant, Director Carers National Association	Voluntary/charity
Professor Ian Cameron	• Provost and Vice-Chancellor, University of Wales College of Medicine	Academic/research
Professor Brian Jarman	• Professor of General Practice, Imperial College, London	Academic/research
Denise Platt	• Department of Health • Former Head of Social Services, Local Government Association	Central government

10   Review of the Latest Information Available on Inequalities in Health
To conduct an independent review identifying priority areas for future policy development and report to the Secretary of State for Health. A White Paper covering this topic was published in July 1999.

Sir Donald Acheson (Chair)	• Former Chief Medical Officer, Department of Health • Former Professor of Clinical Epidemiology, University of Southampton • Former Chair, SW Hants and Southampton District Health Authority	Independent
Professor David Barker	• Director, Medical Research Council Environmental Epidemiology Unit	Academic/research
Dr Jacky Chambers	• Director of Public Health, Birmingham Health Authority	Local public spending body
Professor Hilary Graham	• Director, Economic and Social Research Council health inequalities programme, University of Lancaster	Academic/research
Professor Michael Marmot	• Professor of Epidemiology and Public Health, University College London • Director, International Centre for Health and Society	Academic/research
Dr Margaret Whitehead	• Visiting Fellow, King's Fund, London (health study charity) • Author of The Health Divide	Academic/research

11 Review of the Mental Health Act
To carry out a thorough review of the 1983 Mental Health Act

Professor Genevra Richardson (Head)	• Professor of Public Law, Queen Mary and Westfield College, University of London • Formerly at Mental Health Act Commission	Academic/research
Ros Alstead	• Director, Nursing and Quality, South Birmingham Mental Health NHS Trust	Health
William Bingley	• Chief Executive, Mental Health Act Commission	National public body
Dr Anne Bird	• Consultant psychiatrist, Department of Psychiatry, Royal Free Hospital	Health
Jenny Goodall	• Head, Community Care, Royal Borough of Kensington and Chelsea	Local government
Rodney Lind	• Deputy Chief Constable, Wiltshire Constabulary	Police
Grainne McMorrow	• Legal Officer, SANE • Barrister specialising in mental health law • Former Mental Health Act Commissioner	Voluntary/charity
Dr Robert Mather	• General Practitioner, North Oxford Medical Centre	Health
Dr David Ndegwa	• Clinical Director, Forensic Services, Lambeth Healthcare NHS Trust	Health
Nigel Pleming QC	• Ex-vice chair, Mental Health Act Commission • Public law barrister	Independent
Dr David Shiers	• General Practitioner • Carer	Health

12 NHS Charter Advisory Group
To develop a new NHS Charter to mark the 50th anniversary of the NHS and as part of the Government's initiative to modernise the NHS.

Greg Dyke (Lead)	• Chairman and Chief Executive, Pearson TV • Former Chief Executive, London Weekend Television	Private business
Rodney Bickerstaffe	• General Secretary, Unison	Trade union
Prof. Nicholas Bosanquet	• Professor of Health Policy, LSE, University of London	Academic/research
Frank Burns	• Head of IM&T, NHS Executive	Central government
Ruth Evans	• Director, National Consumer Council	National public body
Christine Hancock	• General Secretary, Royal College of Nursing	Trade union
Sir Herman Ousley	• Chair, Commission for Racial Equality	National public body
Clare Rayner	• President, Patients' Association	Voluntary/charity

13 NHS Efficiency Task Force
To advise Ministers on more efficient and effective patient care across the NHS by considering good practice brought to the attention of the Task Force through ministerial correspondence and local networks and Audit Commission value-for-money studies.

David Fillingham	• St Helen's and Knowsley Health Authority, Merseyside	Local public spending body
John Flook	• Executive Director of Finance, County Durham Health Authority	Local public spending body
Peter Homa	• Chief Executive, Leicester Royal Infirmary NHS Trust	Local public spending body
Philip Hunt	• Chief Executive, Birmingham Research Park	Private business
Lionel Joyce	• Chief Executive, Newcastle City Health NHS Trust	Local public spending body
Peter D Lees	• Senior Lecturer, Wessex Neurological Centre, Southampton General Hospital	Academic/research
Mike Marchment	• Chief Executive, Warwickshire Health Authority	Local public spending body
Dr Ian Rutter	• Westcliffe Surgery, Shipley	Health

14 NHS Staff Involvement Task Force
To identify how front line health service staff can work with local managers to improve the way Britain's hospitals are run.

Hugh Taylor (Chair)	• Director, Human Resources, NHS Executive	Central government
Bob Abberley	• Head of Health, UNISON	Trade union
David Amos	• Human Resources Director, St. Mary's, Paddington	Health
Helen Bailey	• Clinical support nurse, Rochdale Health Care Trust	Health
Andrew Foster	• Chair, Wigan and Leigh Trust	Local public spending body
Clive Mason	• Porter, Princess Royal Hospital, Telford, Shropshire	Health
Pat Oakley	• Senior consultant, Practices Made Perfect Ltd	Private business
Karen Picking	• Head, organisational development, South Tees Acute Hospital	Health

Pam Smith	• Medical laboratory scientific officer, Royal Hampshire County Hospital, Winchester	Health
Dr Lynda Stewart	• Junior doctor, Lewisham Hospital	Health
Hugh Stirk	• National personnel manager, Unilever	Private business
Dr Paul Thorpe	• Junior doctor, Bristol Royal Infirmary	Health
Hilary Walsgrove	• Staff nurse, Royal Bournemouth General Hospital	Health

15 Review of the Evidence Relating to Silicon Breast Implants

To review the evidence relating to the possible health risks associated with silicone gel breast implants and examine the issues relating to pre-operative patient information.

Professor Roger Sturrock (Chair)	• Centre for Rheumatic Diseases, Royal Infirmary, Glasgow	Academic/research
Professor Roger Batchelor	• Former Professor of Immunology, Royal Postgraduate Medical School, Hammersmith Hospital	Academic/research
Professor David London	• Former Professor of Medicine, University of Birmingham • Registrar, Royal College of Physicians	Academic/research
Tim Milward	• Consultant Plastic Surgeon, Leicester Royal Infirmary	Health
Professor Alan Silman	• Professor of Epidemiology, Arthritis and Rheumatism Research Council	Academic/research
Professor John Sloane	• Professor of Histopathology, University of Liverpool • Chair, Cancer Services sub-committee, Royal College of Pathologists • Member, Department of Health Advisory Committee on Cancer Registration	Academic/research

16 Review of the Law Relating to Surrogacy

To consider: whether payments to surrogate mothers should continue to be allowed; the regulation of surrogacy arrangements through a recognised body; whether changes are needed to the Surrogacy Arrangements Act 1985 and/or Section 30 of the Human Fertilisation & Embryology Act 1990.

Professor Margaret Brazier (Chair)	• Professor of Law and Director, Institute of Medicine, Law and Bioethics, University of Manchester • Former member, Nuffield Council on Bioethics • Former Chair, Animal Procedures Committee, Home Office	Academic/research
Professor Alastair Campbell	• Professor of Ethics in Medicine, University of Bristol	Academic/research
Professor Susan Golombok	• Professor of Psychology and Director, Family and Child Psychology Research Centre, City University	Academic/research

17 Review of Thoracic Surgical Services at Plymouth Hospitals Trust

To review the investigation undertaken in 1998 by Plymouth Hospitals NHS Trust into thoracic surgery services, report to the Secretary of State and make the findings available to the General Medical Council.

Baroness Audrey Emerton (Chair)	• Chair, Brighton Health Care NHS Trust • Lay member, General Medical Council	Local public spending body
Dr Linda Patterson	• Medical Director, Burnley Health Care NHS Trust • Member, General Medical Council	Health
Deidre Watson	• Honorary Secretary, Society of Cardiothoracic Surgeons of Great Britain • Thoracic surgeon, Norfolk and Norwich NHS Trust	Professional association

18 Waiting List Action Team

To consider action to be taken to end people having to wait over 18 months for treatment.

Stephen Day (Chair)	• Regional Director, West Midlands , Department of Health	Central government
James Barbour	• Chief Executive, Central Manchester Healthcare • Chair, North West Waiting List Action Team Regional Task Force	Health
Alan Bedford	• Chief Executive, East Sussex, Brighton and Hove Health Authority • Chair, South Thames Waiting List Action Team Regional Task Force	Local public spending body
Ian Carruthers	• Chief Executive, Dorset Health Authority • Chair, South and West Waiting List Action Team Regional Task Force	Local public spending body
Ken Cunningham	• Chief Executive, Stoke Mandeville Hospital • Chair, Anglia and Oxford Waiting List Action Team Regional Task Force	Health
Clare Dodgson	• Chief Executive, Sunderland Health Authority • Chair, Northern and Yorkshire Waiting List Action Team Regional Task Force	Local public spending body
David Highton	• Chief Executive, Chelsea and Westminister Hospital • Chair, North Thames Waiting List Action Team Regional Task Force	Health
Christopher Howgrave-Graham	• Chief Executive, Coventry Health Authority • Chair, West Midlands Waiting List Action Team Regional Task Force	Local public spending body

| Graham Smith | • Chief Executive, Lincoln County Hospital
• Chair, Trent Waiting List Action Team Regional Task Force | Health |

Eight Regional Task Forces to support the Waiting List Action Team

To improve the organization of health services, emergency and continuing care services; identify national 'product champions'; and support the Chief Executive in accounting to ministers for the performance of the NHS in these areas.

19	**North West**	
James Barbour (Chair)	• Chief Executive, Central Manchester Healthcare • Member, Waiting List Action Team	Health

20	**South Thames**	
Alan Bedford (Chair)	• Chief Executive, East Sussex, Brighton and Hove Health Authority • Member, Waiting List Action Team	Local public spending body

21	**South and West**	
Ian Carruthers (Chair)	• Chief Executive, Dorset Health Authority • Member, Waiting List Action Team	Local public spending body

22	**Anglia and Oxford**	
Ken Cunningham (Chair)	• Chief Executive, Stoke Mandeville Hospital • Member, Waiting List Action Team	Health

23	**Northern and Yorkshire**	
Clare Dodgson (Chair)	• Chief Executive, Sunderland Health Authority • Member, Waiting List Action Team	Local public spending body

24	**North Thames**	
David Highton (Chair)	• Chief Executive, Chelsea and Westminster Hospital • Member, Waiting List Action Team	Health

25	**West Midlands**	
Christopher Howgrave-Graham (Chair)	• Chief Executive, Coventry Health Authority • Member, Waiting List Action Team	Local public spending body

26	**Trent**	
Graham Smith (Chair)	• Chief Executive, Lincoln County Hospital • Member, Waiting List Action Team	Health

Membership: 17 outside persons.

HOME OFFICE (HO)

Name	Affiliation	Classification

1   Community Fire Safety Task Force

To propose a community fire safety strategy and supporting action plans which will significantly reduce the number of fires and casualties over the next five years.

Fiona Driscoll	• Chief Executive, Driscoll Communications	Private business
Vicki Harris	• Head, Fire Safety Unit, Home Office	Central government
Malcolm Levi	• Marketing Director, Tesco plc	Private business
Graham Meldrum	• Chief Fire Officer, West Midlands Fire Service	Local government
Lynne Peacock	• Group Operations Director, Woolwich plc	Private business
Susan Young	• Managing Director, BRK Brands	Private business
Gareth Hills (support)	• Fire Safety Unit, Home Office	Central government

2   Review of Arrangements for Confiscation of Criminal Assets

To review the operation of the restraint, confiscation and money laundering statutory provisions; identify areas where change is a priority; determine which changes require primary legislation and which could be brought in by other means; make proposals on issues requiring urgent primary legislation.

Perry Nove	• Association of Chief Police Officers	Professional association
Roy Penrose	• Association of Chief Police Officers	Professional association
Janice Woolley	• Justices' Clerks Society	Professional association

3   **Review of the Provision of Court Welfare Services (joint with LCD, DH and WO)**
To identify the range of welfare services currently provided by the Probation Service, Guardian ad Litem and Reporting Officer Service and the children's work of the Official Solicitor's Department and other agencies in family proceedings, and to consider the scope for improvements to the effectiveness of their work through the creation of a new unified service.

Representatives from   • *Association of Chief Officers of Probation, Association of Directors of Social Services, Association of Guardian ad Litem and Reporting Officers Panel Managers, Central Probation Council, HM Inspectorate of Probation, Judiciary, Law Society, Local Government Association, National Association of Guardians Ad Litem and Reporting Officers*

4   **Working Party on Electoral Procedures**
To review changes resulting in more open and fair electoral procedures; registration of the homeless; access to polling stations for the disabled; absent voting arrangements; automated voting and counting; a rolling/continuous register; citizenship education. In July 1999 a final report recommended sweeping changes.   Membership has included the following:

Cllr Muriel Barker	• Local Government Association	Local government
Kay Barton	• Civil Law and Legal Aid Division, Scottish Office	Central government
Pat Bradley	• Chief Electoral Officer for Northern Ireland, Northern Ireland Office	Central government
Nick Easton	• Local Government Association	Local government
David Gardner	• Labour Party	Voluntary/charity
Peter Gilbert	• Rights and European Division, Northern Ireland Office	Central government
Paul Gribble	• Conservative Central Office	Voluntary/charity
Suzanne Hudson	• National Association of Local Councils	Local government
Richard Lester	• Association of Council Secretaries and Solicitors	Professional association
David Loxton	• Liberal Democrats	Voluntary/charity
David Monks	• Society of Local Authority Chief Executives	Professional association
Mike Penn	• National Constitutional Officer, Labour Party	Voluntary/charity
Chris Rennard	• Director of Campaigns and Elections, Liberal Democrats	Voluntary/charity
Janet Rutherford	• Local Government Association	Local government
Nigel Stewart	• Convention of Scottish Local Authorities	Local government
Gareth Thomas	• Devolution Unit, Welsh Office	Central government
John Turner	• Association of Electoral Administrators	Professional association
Robin Wendt	• National Association of Local Councils	Local government
Andrew Whetnall	• Local Government Sponsorship Unit, Department for the Environment, Transport and the Regions	Central government
Madeleine Williams	• Association of London Government	Local government

5   **Human Rights Task Force**
To maintain a dialogue between the Government and non-governmental organisations on the readiness of Departments, other public authorities and the legal profession for implementation of the Human Rights Act.

Lord Williams of Mostyn QC (Chair)	• Minister of State, Home Office	Central government
Ross Cranston MP	• Solicitor-General	Central government
Geoff Hoon MP	• Minister of State, Lord Chancellor's Department	Central government
Francesca Klug	• Human Rights Incorporation Project, King's College, London	Academic/research
Anne Owers	• Director, Justice	Voluntary/charity
Andrew Puddephatt	• Director, Article 19 • Former Director, Charter88 and Liberty	Voluntary/charity
Sarah Spencer	• Institute for Public Policy Research	Academic/research
Veena Vasista	• 1990 Trust	Voluntary/charity
John Wadham	• Director, Liberty	Voluntary/charity

6   **Misuse of Public Office Group (Review of Bribery and Corruption Law)**
This group advised on this topic within the internal review of bribery and corruption law conducted by some seventeen Home Office and other officials under an outside chair (Stephen Silber, QC: a member of the Law Commission) which also reviewed this branch of the law.

Rod Ainsworth	• Audit Commission	National public body
Richard Horsman	• Committee on Standards in Public Life (secretariat)	National public body
Bill Magee	• Accounts Commission for Scotland	National public body

Derrick Marks	• Commission for Local Administration (Scotland)	National public body
Elwyn Moseley	• Commission for Local Administration (Wales)	National public body
Edward Osmotherly	• Commissioner for Local Administration	National public body
John Rees	• Local Government Association	Local government

7 Older Volunteers Working Group
To look at ways in which the participation of older people in the community can be increased.

Janet Atfield	• Director, RSVP	Voluntary/charity
Chris Ball	• Voluntary Sector Secretary, Manufacturing, Science and Finance union	Trade union
Alan Brown	• Department of the Environment, Transport and the Regions	Central government
Charles Carter	• Director, Millennium Debate of the Age	Voluntary/charity
Carol Clinton	• Policy Officer, Local Government Association	Local government
Jean Cooper	• Assistant General Secretary, Civil Service Retirement Fellowship	Voluntary/charity
Gilliam Crosby	• Deputy Director, Centre for Policy on Ageing	Voluntary/charity
Justin Davis Smith	• Director, National Centre for Volunteering	Voluntary/charity
John Edmonds	• General Secretary, General and Municipal Boilermakers • Member, Skills Task Force (DfEE) • Member, Competitiveness Advisory Group (DTI) • Competitiveness Working Party; Enhancing Business Performance Through Developing Individuals (DTI)	Trade union
Sue Evans	• Director, REACH	Voluntary/charity
Rob Griffiths	• Assistant Director, Partnerships and Strategy, Anchor Trust	Voluntary/charity
Richard Gutch	• Chief Executive, Arthritis Care	Voluntary/charity
Monica Hartwell	• Director, Contact the Elderly	Voluntary/charity
Carol Hodson	• Director, Volunteering, Women's Royal Voluntary Service	Voluntary/charity
Diana Holland	• National Secretary, Transport and General Workers Union	Trade union
Brian Holmes	• Department for Education and Employment	Central government
Gordon Lishman	• Operations Director, Age Concern	Voluntary/charity
Mike Metcalf	• Director, Ford Motor Co. Ltd	Private business
Jan Nadolski	• Development Manager, Help the Aged	Voluntary/charity
David Obaze	• Director, NCBV	Voluntary/charity
Peri O'Connor	• Volunteer Coordinator, Royal National Institute for the Blind	Voluntary/charity
Helen Reeve	• Director, National Association of Volunteer Bureaux	Voluntary/charity
Paul Sellers	• Policy Officer, Trades Union Congress	Trade union
Joe Simpson	• Media and National Projects Director, The New Millenium Experience Co. Ltd	Private business
Christopher Spence	• National Centre for Volunteering	Voluntary/charity
Christine Stanley	• Director, Dark Horse Venture	Voluntary/charity
John Stanley	• Hammond Communications Ltd	Private business
Carolyn Sumberg	• Development Officer, Volunteers and Community, Jewish Care	Voluntary/charity
Chris Warren	• Employee Involvement Manager, BiTC	Private business
Ted Webb	• Department of Health	Central government
Angela Whitcher	• Head, Information and Public Affairs, Abbeyfield House	Voluntary/charity
Eileen Wimbury	• Chair, National Association of Volunteer Bureaux	Voluntary/charity
Richard Worsley	• Director, Carnegie Third Age Programme	Voluntary/charity

8 Advisory Group on the Strategic Review of National Police Training
This internal review reported in October 1998. The police authority and officer representatives forming this advisory group were as follows:

Carol Gustafson	• Association of Police Authorities	Local government
David Hayward	• Police Federation	Police
Robin Hobbs	• Police Federation	Police
Alan Moss	• Police Superintendents' Association	Police

David Palmer	• Police Superintendents' Association	Police
Bill Wilkinson	• Association of Police Authorities	Local government

9 Joint Working Party on Senior Police Staffing

Established in November 1998 to address the recruitment problem (notably the lack of financial management skills) among potential chief officers. The Home Secretary was reported to have ruled nothing out, even the unprecedented direct recruitment into those grades of outsiders from the public or private sectors.

Representatives: • *Home Office; Association of Police Authorities; Association of Chief Police Officers*

10 Working Group on the Review of the Long-Term Future of Prison Health Care (joint with Department of Health)

The group supported the internal review on this subject begun in October 1997 in response to reports by the Chief Inspector of Prisons and the Health Advisory Committee for the Prison Service. It subsumed the earlier review of prison nursing care and reported in late 1998.

Dr Alison Evans	• Wakefield Health Authority	Local public spending body
Dr John O'Grady	• Health Advisory Committee to the Prison Service	Health
Prof Denis Pereira-Gray	• Royal College of General Practitioners	Professional association

11 Race Relations Forum

To provide an opportunity for members to give ethnic minority communities a new and effective voice at the heart of government

Rt Hon Jack Straw MP (Chair)	• Home Secretary	Central government
Rumman Ahmed	• Community Relations Adviser, Kensington and Chelsea Council • Muslim Cultural Heritage Centre	Local government
Yasmin Alibhai-Brown	• Journalist and broadcaster • Research Fellow, Institute for Public Policy Research	Independent
Michael Boye-Anawomah	• Former official, National Association of Citizens' Advice Bureaux	Independent
Rachel Campbell	• Headteacher, Mount Stuart Primary School, Cardiff • Member, Commonwealth Institute Advisory Committee	Local public spending body
Thomas Chan	• Advocacy Services Manager, Camden and Islington Community Health Service NHS Trust • Member, Executive Committee, Redbridge London Borough Race Equality Council • Former member, Advisory Council on Race Relations	Local public spending body
Gobnait Ni Chrualaoi	• Community Development Officer, Birmingham Irish Community Forum	Local public spending body
Lincoln Crawford QC	• Chair, Race Relations Committee of the Bar Council • Chair, Independent Adoption Service • Chair, Prince's Trust (South London) Sports Committee	Professional association
Mohammed Dhalech	• Equality Officer, Rural Race Equality Project • Chair, South West Race Equality Network	Voluntary/charity
Lord Dholakia	• Vice Chairman, National Association for the Care and Resettlement of Offenders • Member, Police Complaints Authority	Voluntary/charity
Zerbanoo Gifford	• Director, The Asha Foundation • Former Director, Anti-Slavery International	Voluntary/charity
Bernie Grant MP	• Labour MP for Tottenham	Independent
Ros Howells	• Former Equal Opportunities Director, Greenwich Race Equality Council • Former member, Advisory Council on Race Relations	Local public spending body
Lee Jasper	• Director, 1990 Trust	Voluntary/charity
Makbool Javaid	• Assistant Solicitor, Dibb, Lupton, Alsop	Private business
Dr Gus John	• Consultant on community relations • Former Director of Education, London Borough of Hackney	Private business
Mukami McCrum	• Director, Central Scotland Racial Equality Council	Local public spending body
Norman McLean	• Director, National Mentoring Consortium, University of East London	Education
Dr Dwain Neil	• Recruitment Manager, Shell International • Former member, Advisory Council on Race Relations	Private business
Sir Herman Ouseley	• Chairman, Commission for Racial Equality	National public body
Adam Hafejee Patel	• Former President, Lancashire Council of Mosques	Voluntary/charity
Shushila Patel	• Independent consultant, NHS Executive Equal Opportunities Unit • Chair, Redbridge Refugee Forum, London • Former Deputy Director, NHS Ethnic Health Unit, Leeds Health Authority	Private business

Trevor Phillips	• Chair, London Arts Board • Producer, Factual Programmes, London Weekend Television • Former Chair, Runnymede Trust (ethnic relations research charity)	Local public spending body
Rachel Pickvance Opportunities Advisory Panel to Head of the Home Civil Service	• Vice President, Human Resources, Chase Manhattan Bank •	Member, Equal Private business
Iqbal Sacranie Council on Race Relations	• Joint Convenor, UK Action Committee on Islamic Affairs • Voluntary/charity	Former member, Advisory
Gurbux Singh	• Chief Executive, Haringey London Borough	Local government
Ranjit Sondhi Commission for Racial Equality • Authority	• Senior Lecturer, Community and Youth Studies, Westhill College, Birmingham • Academic/research	Former Deputy Chairman, Consultant to the Radio
Dr Richard Stone Racial Equality • the investigation of Stephen Lawrence's murder	• Treasurer, Maimonides Foundation • Member, Runnymede Trust's commission studying Islamophobia •	Chair, Jewish Council for Member, official inquiry into Voluntary/charity
Rt Rev Wilfred Wood Croydon, London • Corporation	• Chair, Martin Luther King Memorial Trust • Non-executive director, Mayday Healthcare NHS Trust • Voluntary/charity	Suffragan Bishop of Member, Housing

12 National Steering Group on High Profile Sex Offenders

Established in May 1998 to consider whether new machinery is necessary to handle sex offenders – the group has to identify high profile, difficult-to-place offenders in prison and assess their release plans, oversee their handling and consider any funding necessary to meet likely additional accommodation costs. The group combines policy advice and casework functions.

Hugh Marriage (Chair)	• Head, Criminal Policy Strategy Unit, HO	Central government
Brian Briscoe	• Chief Executive, Local Government Association	Local government
Penny Buller	• Association of Chief Officers of Probation	Professional association
Tony Butler Gloucestershire Constabulary	• Association of Chief Police Officers • Professional association	Chief Constable,
Don Groubin	• Royal College of Psychiatrists	Professional association
Gill Mackenzie	• Association of Chief Officers of Probation	Professional association

13 Review of the Tote Steering Group (joint with HM Treasury and the Tote)

To look at the possibility of broader partnership between the Horserace Totaliser Board (the Tote) and the private sector. Privatisation announced, May 1999.

Peter Jones (Chair)	• Chair, Tote	National public body
Home Office and HM Treasury officials government		Central

Review of the Tote Working Group

John Heaton	• Chief Executive, Tote	National public body
Tom Phillips	• Financial Director, Tote	National public body
Home Office and HM Treasury officials		Central government

14 Vehicle Crime Reduction Action Team

Established September 1998 to recommend on implementing a given 14-point action plan for achieving a 30% reduction over five years covering (inter alia) more secure vehicle licensing; vehicle identification, locking, car parking, insurance procedures, vehicle record-keeping and a Michigan scheme for funding anti-vehicle crime work from an insurance levy.

Mike Wear (Chair)	• Director, Fleet Operations, Ford Motor Company	Private business
Tony Baker	• Association of British Insurers	Trade association
John Dawson	• Group Public Policy Director, Automobile Association	Private business
John Ford	• Chief Executive, Driving and Vehicle Licensing Authority, DETR	Central government
Christopher MacGowan	• Chief Executive, Retail Motor Industry Federation	Trade association
Arthur Monk	• Superintendents Association • Merseyside Police	Police
John Plowman	• Director of Road and Vehicle Safety, DETR	Central government
John Rowell	• Head of Crime Reduction Unit, Scottish Office	Central government
Ernie Thompson	• Chief Executive, Society of Motor Manufacturers and Traders	Trade association
John Thompson	• Head of Crime Prevention Agency, Home Office	Central government
Ken Williams	• Chief Constable, Norfolk Constabulary	Police

15   Volunteering Forum

To consider ways to promote community volunteering, notably among younger people. A Home Office official has chaired the Forum.

Jenny Baker	• National Trust	Voluntary/charity
Elizabeth Crowther-Hunt	• Prince's Trust	Voluntary/charity
Peter Davies	• Business in the Community	Voluntary/charity
Vicky Daybell	• National Centre for Volunteering	Voluntary/charity
John Forster	•	Independent
Elisabeth Hoodless	• Community Service Volunteers	Voluntary/charity
Andrea Kelmanson	•	Independent
Martyn Lewis	• YouthNet	Voluntary/charity
Alison West	• Community Development Foundation	Voluntary/charity
Tom Wylie	• National Youth Agency	Voluntary/charity

16   Review of Vulnerable or Intimidated Witnesses Advisory Group (joint with the Lord Chancellor's Department)

To identify improvements in the criminal justice system's treatment of such witnesses, in support of the internal officials' review.

One representative from each of:

	• *Association of Chief Police Officers*	Professional association
	• *Local Government Association*	Local government
	• *Victim Support*	Voluntary/charity

17   Youth Justice Task Force

To drive forward the Government's proposed changes for young offenders; to provide advice on taking forward an action plan as agreed by the interdepartmental ministerial group on Youth Justice. A Youth Justice Board (a new NDPB or quango) followed on from this task force, with the chair and one or two members (e.g., Cedric Fullwood) in common. It launched pilot schemes under the new Crime and Disorder Act in September 1998 and saw reasonable progress on the new policies except the controversial child curfew orders and parenting orders (Home Office figures of August 1999).

Lord Warner (Chair)	• Senior Policy Adviser, Home Office, 1997-98 • Chair, Youth Justice Board 1998- • Former Director, Social Services, Kent County Council	Central government
William Atkinson	• Head, Phoenix High School, Shepherds Bush	Education
Jonathan Black	• Clerk to the Justices, Hampshire	Judiciary
Cathryn Bowker	• Youth Court prosecutor, Brighton	Judiciary
Tony Butler	• Chief Constable, Gloucestershire Constabulary	Police
Paul Cavadino	• Penal Affairs Consortium	Voluntary/charity
Anne Fuller	• Lay magistrate, outer London	Judiciary
Cedric Fullwood	• Former Chief Probation Officer, Greater Manchester	Independent
Ian Johnston	• Assistant Commissioner, Metropolitan Police	Police
Tom Luce	• Head of Social Care Policy, Department of Health	Central government
John Lyon	• Deputy Director, Criminal Policy, Home Office	Central government
David Norgrove	• Divisional Director, Marks and Spencer plc • Social Exclusion Unit Policy Action Team 16: Learning Lessons (CO)	Private business
Denise Platt	• Department of Health • Former Head of Social Services, Local Government Association	Central government
Teresa Reynolds	• Victim Support	Voluntary/charity
Jenny Rowe	• Criminal Policy Division, Lord Chancellor's Department	Central government
Joan Webster	• Chief Superintendent, Gwent Constabulary	Police
Geoffrey Wicks	• Stipendiary magistrate, Inner London	Judiciary
Andrew Williamson	• Director of Social Services, Devon County Council	Local government

DEPARTMENT FOR INTERNATIONAL DEVELOPMENT (DFID)

Name	Affiliation	Classification
1 Development Awareness Working Group		

Established in January 1998, following a commitment in the White Paper (Eliminating World Poverty: a Challenge for the 21st Century) of November 1997, to advise on promoting public awareness of development issues, through the education system and at large. Listed by DFID as an Advisory Public Body (ANDPB). It was always seen as a standing body, although its initial formal life was eighteen months. First report, of April 1999, is being considered.

Name	Affiliation	Classification
George Foulkes MP (Chair)	• Under-Secretary of State, DFID	Central government
Tany Alexander	• One World Week	Voluntary/charity
Gillian Beauchamp	• DfEE	Central government
Douglas Bourn	• Development Education Association • Member, Sustainable Development Education Panel (DETR)	Education
Professor Tim Brighouse	• Chief Education Officer, City of Birmingham • Vice-chair, Standards Task Force (DfEE)	Local government
Paddy Coulter	• Director, International Broadcasting Trust	Voluntary/charity
Liz Cumberbatch	• Workers Educational Association	Voluntary/charity
Bisi Adeleye Fayemi	• Akina Mama Wa Africa (African issues group)	Voluntary/charity
John Fisher	• Director, Research and Education, TGWU	Trade union
Jaya Graves	• Southern Voices	Voluntary/charity
Libby Grundy	• Council for Environmental Education • Member, Sustainable Development Education Panel (DETR)	Voluntary/charity
Judith Hemery	• Central Bureau (education visits and exchanges), British Council	National public body
Phil Hope MP	• MP (Labour) for Corby	Independent
Elenid Jones	• Development Education Council	Voluntary/charity
Robin Lloyd-Jones	• Cyfanwyd (Welsh development education)	Voluntary/charity
Stephen MacCloskey	• One World Centre, Belfast	Voluntary/charity
Jane Nelson	• Prince of Wales Business Leaders Forum	Voluntary/charity
Ashok Ohri	• Independent consultant	Private business
Dan Rees	• Volunteer Service Overseas	Voluntary/charity
Tony Robinson	• Actor: leader of Comic Relief	Voluntary/charity
Scott Sinclair	• Director, Development Education Centre	Voluntary/charity
Peter Smith	• Ofsted	Central government
Jon Snow	• Journalist and broadcaster, Channel 4 Television	Independent
John Sutton	• General Secretary, Secondary Heads Association	Education
Derek Walker	• Director, World Aware	Voluntary/charity
John Westaway	• Member, former School Curriculum and Assessment Authority • Member, Sustainable Development Education Panel (DETR)	Independent
Tom Wylie	• Director, National Youth Agency • Member, Sustainable Development Education Panel (DETR)	Voluntary/charity
Frances Burns (secretariat)	• Deputy Head, Information Department, DFID	Central government
Richard Calvert (secretariat)	• Head of Information, DFID	Central government

Three sub-groups of the Working Group's members have considered 'Themes and Partnerships', 'Formal/Informal Structures' and 'Learning from Others'.

LORD CHANCELLOR'S DEPARTMENT (LCD)

Name	Affiliation	Classification
1 Review of Civil Justice and Legal Aid		

To consider whether existing reform proposals would reduce cost, delay and complexity of civil litigation.

Name	Affiliation	Classification
Sir Peter Middleton	• Chair, Barclays de Zoete Wedd and Deputy Chair, Barclays Bank • Former Permanent Secretary, HM Treasury	Private business

2 Clinical Negligence Working Group

To provide a forum for the discussion of potential court procedures for clinical negligence cases.

Name	Affiliation	Classification
Janet Howe (Chair)	• Supreme Court Policy Branch, LCD	Central government
Professor Alan Aitkenhead	• Expert in clinical negligence	Academic/research
Jane Chapman	• Association of Litigation and Risk Managers	Trade association
Ian Foster	• Master, Queen's Bench Division, Royal Courts of Justice	Judiciary
John Grace QC	• Bar Council	Professional association
Liz Humphreys	• Supreme Court Policy Branch, LCD	Central government
Steve Humphreys	• Supreme Court Policy Branch, LCD	Central government
Paulette James	• Woolf Implementation Team, Court Service HQ, LCD	Central government
Russell Levy	• Association of Personal Injury Lawyers	Professional association
Liz Ryan	• NHS Executive	Health
Dr Isabel Sanderson	• Scheme Manager, Medical Protection Society (Clinical Negligence Scheme for Trusts)	Trade association
Arnold Simanowitz	• Action for Victims of Medical Accidents	Voluntary/charity
Colin Stutt	• Legal Aid Board	National public body
Robert Sumerling	• Le Brasseur J. Tickle	Private business
Dr Christine Tomkins	• The Medical Defence Union	Trade association
District Judge Walker	• Association of District Judges	Professional association
Steve Walker	• National Health Service Litigation Authority	National public body
Jacqueline Fincham (secretariat)	• Supreme Court Policy Branch, LCD	Central government

3   Review of Lord Chancellor's Department Funding for Marriage Support and Research Services
To advise the criteria the Department should adopt in responding to requests from a wide range of agencies for core grants or project funding.

Sir Graham Hart	• Chair, King's Fund (London health care charity) • Former Permanent Secretary, Department of Health	Voluntary/charity

4   Multi-Party Situations Working Group
To produce suitable court procedures for multi-party situations in court cases.

Janet Howe (Chair)	• Supreme Court Policy Branch, LCD	Central government
Daniel Brennan QC	• Chair, Bar Council	Professional association
James Burnett-Hitchcock	• Cameron McKenna Solicitors	Private business
Catherine Davidson	• Rule Drafting Division, LCD	Central government
David Hodge QC	• Bar Council	Professional association
Liz Humphreys	• Supreme Court Policy Branch, LCD	Central government
Paulette James	• Woolf Implementation Team, Court Service	Central government
Alison Macnair	• Legal Aid Division, LCD	Central government
Roger Pannone	• Pannone and Partners (solicitors)	Private business
Andrew Prynne QC	• Bar Council	Professional association
Colin Stutt	• Legal Aid Board	National public body
Marlene Winfield	• National Consumer Council	National public body
Michael Wrankmore (Secretary)	• Supreme Court Policy Branch, LCD	Central government

NORTHERN IRELAND OFFICE (NIO)

Name	Affiliation	Classification

1   Review of Services for Acutely Ill Children
To review current provision of services for the acutely ill child and the principles on which services should develop.

Dr H. Campbell (Chair)	• Chief Medical Officer, Northern Ireland DHSS	Central government
Dr C.K. Beattie	• Consultant in Public Health Medicine, Eastern Health & Social Services Board, Northern Ireland DHSS	Health
V.E. Boston	• Consultant Paediatric Surgeon, Royal Belfast Hospital for Sick Children	Health
Dr M. Boyle	• Senior Medical Officer, Northern Ireland DHSS	Central government

Dr A.T. Brown	• Consultant Paediatrician, Ulster, North Down & Ards Health and Social Services Trust	Health
Dr C.W.B. Corkey	• Consultant Paediatrician, Daisy Hill Hospital	Health
R. Coulter	• Paediatric Project Nurse, Ulster, North Down & Ards Health and Social Services Trust	Health
Professor J.A. Dodge	• Emeritus Professor of Child Health, Queen's University, Belfast	Academic/research
Dr J.S. Garvin	• General Practitioner, Armagh Health Centre	Health
Dr V.F.D. Gleadhill	• Consultant Paediatrician, Ulster, North Down & Ards Health and Social Services Trust	Health
Dr E.M. Hicks	• Consultant Paediatric Neurologist, Royal Belfast Hospital for Sick Children	Health
M. Hinds	• Nursing Officer, Northern Ireland DHSS	Central government
Dr E.M. Hutton	• Consultant Paediatrician, Foyle Health and Social Services Trust	Health
Dr J.G. Jenkins	• Consultant Paediatrician, Antrim Area Hospital	Health
Professor B.G. McClure	• Queen's University, Belfast	Academic/research
Dr Brian McCord	• Consultant Paediatrician, Altnagelvin Area Hospital	Health
Dr T. Ryan	• General Practitioner, Duncairn Gardens	Health
Dr M.C. Stewart	• Speciality Advisor in Paediatrics, NICPGMDE	Health
L. Surgenor	• Nursing Admininistrator, Royal Belfast Hospital for Sick Children	Health
Dr A.M. Telford	• Director of Public Health, Southern Health & Social Services Board	Health
Dr P. Woods	• Medical Officer, Northern Ireland DHSS	Central government

2 Regional Review of Adult Cardiology Services in Northern Ireland

To review the current provision of cardiology services in Northern Ireland.

Dr H. Campbell (Project Sponsor)	• Chief Medical Officer, Northern Ireland Department of Health and Social Services	Central government
Professor J.A. Adgey	• Cardiologist, RG Hospital	Health
Dr K. Balnave	• Cardiologist, Craigavon Area Hospital	Health
Dr N.C. Chaturvedi	• Physician with interest in Cardiology, Mid Ulster	Health
Dr G. Dalzell	• Cardiologist, RG Hospital	Health
Dr H. Dunn	• Cardiologist, Altnagelvin	Health
Dr O. Finnegan	• Physician with interest in Cardiology, Coleraine	Health
Dr B. Gaffney	• Health Promotion, Health Promotion Agency	National public body
Dr D. Higginson	• Cardiologist, Ulster Hospital D	Health
V. Hodgkinson	• Cardiology Technician, RG Hospital	Health
Dr F. Kee	• Public Health Physician, Northern Health and Social Services Board	Health
Dr P. Kilbane	• Chief Executive, Eastern Health and Social Services Board	Health
Sister H. Knight	• Cardiology Nursing Representative, RG Hospital	Health
Dr B. McClements	• Cardiologist, MI Hospital	Health
Dr B. McConnell	• Public Health Physician, Western Health and Social Services Board	Health
Dr G. Richardson	• Cardiologist, BC Hospital	Health
Dr C. Russell	• Physician with interest in Cardiology, Tyrone County	Health
Nuala Shannon	• Cardiology Nursing Representative, Mid Ulster	Health
Dr P. Sharkey	• GP	Health
Dr B. Sweeney	• GP	Health
G. Wells	• Cardiology Nursing Representative, BC Hospital	Health
Dr C. Wilson	• Cardiologist, Antrim	Health
M. Callaghan (Project Support)	• Northern Ireland Department of Health and Social Services	Central government
Dr D. Corrigan (Project Support)	• Southern Health and Social Services Board	Local public spending body
A. Graham (Project Support)	• Eastern Health and Social Services Board	Local public spending body

M. Hinds (Project Support)	• Northern Ireland Department of Health and Social Services	Central government
Dr M. McCarthy (Project Support)	• Northern Ireland Department of Health and Social Services	Central government
H. Reid (Project Co-ordinator)	• Eastern Health and Social Services Board	Local public spending body
Dr D. Stewart (Project Support)	• Eastern Health and Social Services Board	Local public spending body
Representatives	*Cardiac surgery and ambulance services*	Health
Professor A.R. Latimer (External Advisor)		Academic/research

3   Northern Ireland Strategy on Alcohol Misuse Quality Council
To evaluate the existing strategy by consulting with key stakeholders.

Desmond Bannon	• Down and Lisburn Health and Social Services Trust	Local public spending body
Mary Black	• Northern Health and Social Services Board (Health Promotion), Northern Ireland DHSS	Local public spending body
Paul Conliffe	• Health and Social Services Executive, Northern Ireland DHSS	Central government
Dr Philip Donaghy	• Eastern Health and Social Services Board, Northern Ireland DHSS	Local pubic spending body
Dr Brian Gaffney	• Northern Ireland Health Promotion Agency	National public body
Katrina Godfrey	• Health Promotion Branch, Northern Ireland DHSS	Central government
Dr J. Harbison	• Health and Social Policy Group, Northern Ireland Department of Health and Social Services	Central government
Judith Hill	• Nursing and Midwifery, Northern Ireland DHSS	Central government
Robert Hunniford	• Community Affairs Division, Royal Ulster Constabulary	Police
Alastair Hutchinson	• Northern Ireland Office	Central government
Paul Martin	• Social Services Inspectorate, Northern Ireland DHSS	Central government
Dr Glenda Mock	• Medical and Allied Services, Northern Ireland DHSS	Central government
Dr Diana Patterson	• Shaftesbury Square Hospital	Health

4   Northern Ireland Strategy on Alcohol Misuse Project Team

Martin Cardwell	• North Down and Ards Health and Social Services Trust	Local public spending body
Tony Fleck	• Northern Ireland Drinks Industry	Trade association
Joe Flynn	• Ex-service user	Independent
Dr Tom Gardiner	• Information and Analysis Unit, Northern Ireland DHSS	Central government
Hazel Gibson	• Down and Lisburn Health and Social Services Trust (Mental Health)	Local public spending body
Jim Gibson	• Health Promotion Branch, Northern Ireland DHSS	Central government
Nessa Greenaway	• Southern Health and Social Services Board (Health Promotion), Northern Ireland DHSS	Local public spending body
Nigel Grimshaw	• Community Affairs Division, Royal Ulster Constabulary	Police
Joe Hilman	• Nursing and Midwifery Advisory Group, Northern Ireland DHSS	Central government
Jack Houlahan	• Northlands	Local public spending body
Dr Denis McMahon	• Policy Development and Review Unit, Northern Ireland DHSS	Central government
Ivan McMaster	• Social Legislation, Northern Ireland DHSS	Central government
Tony O'Brien	• Information and Analysis Branch, Northern Ireland DHSS	Central government
John Park	• Social Services Inspectorate, Northern Ireland DHSS	Central government
Rob Phipps	• Northern Ireland Health Promotion Agency	National public body
Eddie Rooney	• Northern Ireland DHSS	Central government
Maeve Toland	• Western Health and Social Services Board, Northern Ireland DHSS	Local public spending body
Boyd Turner	• Mental Health Branch, Northern Ireland DHSS	Central government
Alan Urquhart	• Policy Development and Review Unit, Northern Ireland DHSS	Central government
Dr Gerry Waldron	• Northern Health and Social Services Board, Northern Ireland DHSS	Local public spending body
Carol Weir	• Northern Ireland Community Addiction Service	National public body

5 Review of the Northern Ireland Ambulance Service

To agree a common agenda for the future in the light of the DHSS's 'Regional Strategy For Health and Social Wellbeing' 1997-2002.

Tom Frawley (Chair)	• Area General Manger, Western Health and Social Services Board, Northern Ireland DHSS	Central government
Representatives	From the four Health and Social Services Boards, the Northern Ireland Ambulance Service Trust and clinicians with relevant experience of Accident and Emergency services including general medical practitioners.	

6 Northern Ireland Advisory Committee on Blood Safety

To provide advice to the Chief Medical Officer (NI) on all maters relating to the quality and safety of blood products and to ensure that appropriate guidance is put into practice and monitored. An initial period of three years was announced.

Dr D.H. Campbell	• Department of Health and Social Services (DHSS) Northern Ireland Office	Central government
P. Blair	• National Health Service Trust	Health
Dr C. Bharucha	• Northern Ireland Blood Transfusion Service	National public body
Dr D. Corrigan	• Health and Social Services Board	National public body
Dr P. Coyle	• National Health Service Trust	Health
Dr G. Lavery	• National Health Service Trust	Health
Dr E. Mayne	• National Health Service Trust	Health
Dr E. Mitchell	• DHSS, NIO	Central government
Dr C. Morris	• National Health Service Trust	Health
Dr B. McClelland	• Edinburgh Blood Transfusion Service	Health
Dr M. McClelland	• Northern Ireland Blood Transfusion Service	National public body
H. Robinson	• DHSS, NIO	Central government
Dr J. Watson	• Health and Social Services Board	National public body
Dr T. Wyatt	• DHSS, NIO	Central government
Dr A. Mairs	• DHSS, NIO	Central government

7 Review of the District Councils' Community Service Programme Advisory Group

To assess the extent to which the Community Services programme has clearly defined aims and objectives.

Joe Wright (Chair)	• Head of NI Voluntary Activity Unit's Community Development Branch	Voluntary/charity
Representatives	From the community and voluntary sector, from the independent advice sector and from District Councils (a Chief Executive and a Community Services Officer).	

8 Review of Criminal Injuries Compensation Arrangements in Northern Ireland

To advise on the fitness for purpose of criminal injuries compensation arrangements in Northern Ireland in the light of the experiences of the victims of terrorist crime.

Sir Kenneth Bloomfield	• Northern Ireland Victims Commissioner • Former Head, Northern Ireland Civil Service and Second Permanent Secretary, NIO	Independent
Marion Gibson	• Manager, Staff Care Services and Crisis Support Team, South and East Belfast Health and Social Services Trust	Local public spending body
Professor Desmond Greer	• Professor of Common Law, Queen's University Belfast	Academic/research

9 Review of Criminal Justice

To address the structure, management and resourcing of publicly funded elements of the criminal justice system.

Jim Daniell (Leader)	• Director of Criminal Justice, Northern Ireland Office	Central government
Ian Maye	• Criminal Justice Policy Division, Northern Ireland Office	Central government
David Seymour	• Legal Secretary to the Law Officers	Central government
Glenn Thompson	• Director, Northern Ireland Court Service	Central government
His Honour John Gower QC (Independent Assessor)	• Retired English Circuit Judge	Independent
Eugene Grant QC (Independent Assessor)	• Founder and secretary, Criminal Bar Association (Northern Ireland) • Former Chair, General Council of the Bar of Northern Ireland	Professional association
Professor John Jackson (Independent Assessor)	• Professor of Public Law and Head of the Law School, Queen's University, Belfast	Academic/research
Dr Bill Lockhart (Independent Assessor)	• Director, Extern organization working with released offenders • Director, Centre for Independent Research and Analysis of Crime	Voluntary/charity
Professor Joanna Shapland	• Professor of Criminal Justice, University of Sheffield	

| (Independent Assessor) | • Director of the Institute for the Study of the Legal Profession | Academic/research |

10   Fundamental Review of the Economic Development Strategy in Northern Ireland
To produce a new Economic Development Strategy for Northern Ireland up to the year 2010.

Gerry Loughran (Chair)	• Permanent Secretary, Department of Economic Development, Northern Ireland	Central government
Frank Bunting	• Chair, Northern Irish/Irish Congress of Trade Unions	Trade union
Chris Gibson	• Director, Golden Vale Ltd	Private business
David Gibson	• Under Secretary, Department of Economic Development, Northern Ireland	Central government
Alan Gillespie	• Chair, Industrial Development Board for Northern Ireland • Managing Director, Goldman Sachs	National public body
Patrick Haren	• Group Chief Executive, Viridian Group plc	Private business
Stephen Kingon	• Regional Partner, Pricewaterhouse Coopers	Private business
Aideen McGinley	• Chief Executive, Fermanagh District Council	Local government
John McGinnis	• Managing Director, The McGinnis Group	Private business
Roy McNulty	• Chair, Short Brothers Plc	Private business
Bruce Robinson	• Chief Executive, Industrial Development Board	National public body
Teresa Townsley	• Director, MTF Consulting Group	Private business

The following sector working groups have been established:
> food processing, textiles and apparel, software, health technologies, engineering, electronics, tourism, tradeable services, construction services, agriculture and telecommunications.

The following cross-sector working groups have been set up:
> culture, innovation and design, investment and finance, exports and marketing Northern Ireland, skills and education, infrastructure and energy.

11   Northern Ireland Strategy for Education Technology Strategic Management Group
To secure the implementation of the recommendations in the Northern Ireland Education Technology Strategy and to put in place the Northern   Ireland components of the National Grid for Learning.

Gordon Topping (Chair)	• Chief Executive, North Eastern Education and Library Board, Northern Ireland Department of Education	Central government
John Anderson	• Education and Training Inspectorate, Northern Ireland Department of Education	Central government
Roy Beattie	• Deputy Executive, Class project	Central government
Aidan Hamill	• Director, Northern Ireland Council for the Curriculum, Examinations and Assessment	Local public spending body
Owen Lynch	• Chief Executive, NCET (Education Technology)	Voluntary/charity
Eddie McArdle	• Deputy Director, Council for Catholic Maintained Schools (Northern Ireland)	Voluntary/charity
Sheila McCaul	• Senior Education Officer Western Education and Library Board	Local public spending body
Ted McGuigan	• Northern Ireland Department of Education	Central government
Tom McMullan	• Director, Class project	Central government
Beth Porter	• Chief Librarian, South Eastern Education and Library Board (Library Service)	Local public spending body
John Simpson	• Northern Ireland Growth Challenge	Voluntary/charity
John Wilkinson	• Principal, Dromore High School	Education
David Woods	• Northern Ireland Department of Education	Central government

12   Northern Ireland Strategy for Education Technology Teacher Education Group

Sheila McCaul (Chair)	• Senior Education Officer Western Education and Library Board	Local public spending body
John Anderson	• Education and Training Inspectorate, Northern Ireland Department of Education	Central government
Roger Austin	• Lecturer, University of Ulster	Academic/research
Jean Cogger	• Principal, Sydenham Primary School	Education
Peter Finn	• Director of European Office, St. Marys	Education
Tom Heskith	• Deputy Director, Regional Training Unit, Northern Ireland Department of Education	Central government
Danny Hillen	• Class project	Central government
John Magaud	• Information Technology Adviser, North Eastern Education and Library Board	Local public spending body
Marie Martin	• European Awareness Officer, Western Education and Library Board	Local public spending body
Beth Porter	• Chief Librarian, South Eastern Education and Library Board (Library Service)	Local public spending body
Mae Watson	• Senior Tutor, Stranmillis School	Education

13 Northern Ireland Strategy for Education Technology Curriculum and Assessment Group

John Anderson	• Education and Training Inspectorate, Northern Ireland Department of Education	Central government
Maureen Bennett	• Education and Training Inspectorate, Northern Ireland Department of Education	Central government
Pat Browne	• Librarian, Friends School	Education
Peter Garrett	• Principal, Ballyhenry High School	Education
Aidan Hamill	• Director, Northern Ireland Council for the Curriculum, Examinations and Assessment	Local public spending body
Paddy Mackey	• Senior Adviser, Western Education and Library Board	Local public spending body
Michael Montgomery	• Belfast Education and Library Board, Northern Ireland Department of Education	Central government
Una O'Kane	• Principal, St. Mary's Grammar School, M'Felt	Education
Ebhlin Tinneny	• Information Technology Advisory Officer, South Eastern Education and Library Board	Local public spending body
John Wilkinson	• Principal, Dromore High School	Education

14 Equality Commission Working Group
To make recommendations for the establishment of a new Equality Commission and merging of the four existing equality bodies.

Dr Joan Stringer	• Member, Equal Opportunities Commission (Great Britain) • Principal and Vice-Patron, Queen Margaret College, Edinburgh • Member, Consultative Steering Group on the Scottish Parliament (SO)	National public body
Sir Robert Cooper	• Chair, Fair Employment Commission for Northern Ireland	Local public spending body
Harry Goodman	• Chief Executive, Fair Employment Commission for Northern Ireland	Local public spending body
Joan Harbison	• Chair, Commission for Racial Equality for Northern Ireland	Local public spending body
Harry McConnell	• Chair, Northern Ireland Disability Council	Local public spending body
Sheila Rogers	• Chief Executive, Commission for Racial Equality for Northern Ireland	Local public spending body
Joan Smyth	• Chair and Chief Executive, Equal Opportunities Commission for Northern Ireland	Local public spending body

15 The Further Education Consultative Committee
Established in October 1998 to advise and recommend upon the strategic management and development of the FE section in Northern Ireland. Interested bodies were asked to provide representatives (numbers in brackets) as follows:

John McFall, MP (Chair)	• Parliamentary Secretary, NIO	Central government
	• Association of Chief Executives of Education and Library Boards (1)	Education
	• Association of Northern Ireland Colleges (4)	Education
	• Belfast Institute of Further and Higher Education (1)	Education
	• Department of Agriculture (NIO) (1)	Central government
	• National Union of Students/Union of Students in Ireland (1)	Voluntary/charity
	• Northern Ireland Committee, Irish Congress of Trade Unions (3)	Trade union
	• Northern Ireland Council for Adult Education (1)	Education
	• Northern Ireland Council for Voluntary Action (1)	Voluntary/charity
	• Northern Ireland Growth Challenge (7)	Voluntary/charity
	• Northern Ireland Higher Education Council (1)	National public body
	• Post-Primary Principals (2)	Education
	• Queen's University, Belfast (1)	Education
	• Training and Employment Agency (2)	Central government
	• University of Ulster (1)	Education

16 Working Group on Integrated Education
Established in June 1998, following the Belfast Agreement, to examine the present levels of integration within schools and to consider ways of promoting further development. The members also formed two sub-groups (on Transformation and Education for Mutual Understanding). A report, 'Towards a Culture of Tolerance: Integrating Education' went out for comment by interested bodies in Winter 1998 for responses by March 1999.

Don Hill (Chair)	• Deputy Secretary, Northern Ireland Department of Education	Central government
Dr Mark Browne	• School Policy and Planning, Northern Ireland Department of Education	Central government
David Clement	• HELM Corporation Ltd	Private business
Marie Cowan	• Principal, Oakgrove College	Education
Donal Flanagan	• Council for Catholic Maintained Schools (Northern Ireland)	Voluntary/charity

Dr Tony Gallagher	• School of Education, Queen's University, Belfast	Academic/research
Rev. Canon Houston • McKelvey	Transferor Representatives Council	Voluntary/charity
Dr Alan Smith	• Integrated Education Fund	Voluntary/charity
Geraldine Tigchelaar	• Principal, Fort Hill College	Education
Gordon Topping	• Education and Library Boards • Chair, Northern Ireland Strategy for Education Technology Strategic Management Group	Local public spending body
Michael Wardlow	• Northern Ireland Council for Integrated Education	Voluntary/charity

17 Millennium Volunteers Advisory Committee

Established in October 1997 to promote youth employment and education in Northern Ireland using community volunteers.

Gemma Brolly	• Volunteer Bureaux, Northern Ireland	Voluntary/charity
Paul Cavanagh	• North West Community Network	Voluntary/charity
Darren Curtis	• Northern Ireland Youth Forum	Voluntary/charity
Arthur Dempster	• Youth Council for Northern Ireland	Voluntary/charity
Nial Fitzduff	• Rural Community Network	Voluntary/charity
Leslie Frew	• Health and Social Service Management Executive, Northern Ireland Office	Central government
Esther Halsall	• The Prince's Trust Volunteers	Voluntary/charity
Ryan Hanvey	• Duke of Edinburgh Award Scheme • Youthnet	Voluntary/charity
Glen Jordan	• Youth Link Northern Ireland	Voluntary/charity
Geraldine Linford	• Youthnet	Voluntary/charity
Greg Martin	• Bryson House	Voluntary/charity
Angela Matthews	• Youth Council for Northern Ireland	Voluntary/charity
Helen McDonald	• Millennium Volunteer Chair	Voluntary/charity
Angela McGregor	• Young Citizens in Action	Voluntary/charity
Gerry McGuiness	• Belfast Education and Library Board • Association of Chief Executives of Education and Library Boards	Central government
Richard Millen	• The Prince's Trust Volunteers • Youthnet	Voluntary/charity
Dr Duncan Morrow	• Millennium Volunteer Chair	Voluntary/charity
Jack Palmer	• Community Relations Branch, Department of Education, Northern Ireland Office	Central government
Stephen Quigley	• Co-ordinator, Nucleus Project	Voluntary/charity
Vinod Tandon	• Institute of Directors	Trade association
Kieran Teague	• Personnel Manager, Disability Action	Voluntary/charity
Murray Watt	• Rathcoole Community Forum • Northern Ireland Environment Link	Voluntary/charity

18 Northern Ireland New Deal Task Force

To advise on implementing the New Deal programme in Northern Ireland.

Bill McGinnis (Chair)	• Chair, Sperrin Metal Products • Chair, Training and Employment Agency	Private business
Jason Caldwell	• Northern Ireland Youth Forum	Voluntary/charity
Paddy Doherty	• Derry Inner City Trust	Voluntary/charity
Mary Donelly	• Short Brothers plc	Private business
Rev Harold Good	• Northern Ireland Association for the Care and Rehabilitation of Offenders	Voluntary/charity
Karen Hargan	• Desmond and Sons Ltd	Private business
Howard Hastings	• Hastings Hotel Group	Private business
Peter Holmes	• Deputy Secretary, Department for Education and Employment, NIO	Central government
Mary McKee	• Northern Ireland Youth Council	Voluntary/charity
Jim McCusker	• Northern Ireland PSA	Local public spending body
Jim McKeown	• National Association of Teachers in Further and Higher Education	Trade union

Brendan McSherry	• Northern Ireland 2000	Voluntary/charity
Raymond Mullan	• Newry/Kilkeel Further Education College	Education
Quintin Oliver	• Northern Ireland Council of Voluntary Associations	Voluntary/charity
Ian Walters	• Chief Executive, Training and Employment Agency	Local public spending body
Alan Watt	• WISE Group	Voluntary/charity

19 Review of Paediatric Surgical Services in Northern Ireland

To consider available guidance on the provision of paediatric surgical services.

Dr B. Bell	• Consultant Paediatrician, Craigavon Area Hospital	Health
Dr C. Beattie	• Consultant in Public Health Medicine, Eastern Health and Social Services Board	Health
V. Boston	• Consultant Paediatric Surgeon, Royal Belfast Hospital for Sick Children	Health
Dr M. Boyle	• Medical Officer, Northern Ireland Department of Health and Social Services	Central government
Sister G. Hanna	• Theatre Department, Antrim Hospital	Health
W.G. Humphries	• Consultant Surgeon, Antrim Hospital	Health
Dr F. Kennedy	• Consultant in Public Health Medicine, Northern Health and Social Services Board	Health
Dr P. Loughran	• Consultant Anaesthetist, Daisy Hill Hospital	Health
E. McElkerney	• Directorate Manager, Woman and Child Health Directorate, Ulster Hospital	Health
Dr S. McGovern	• Consultant, Accident and Emergency Department, Craigavon Area Hospital	Health
Dr K. O'Kane	• Senior House Officer, Public Health Medicine, Southern Health and Social Services Board	Health
K.J.S. Panesar	• Consultant Surgeon, Altnagelvin Hospital	Health
Dr J.A. Phillips	• Consultant Paediatrician, Erne Hospital	Health
W.J.I. Stirling	• Consultant Surgeon, Craigavon Area Hospital	Health
Dr R. Taylor	• Consultant Paediatric Anaesthetist, Royal Belfast Hospital for Sick Children	Health
Dr A.M. Telford	• Director of Public Health, Southern Health and Social Services Board	Health

20 University for Industry Advisory Group for Northern Ireland

Established in Autumn 1998, to advise the Training and Employment Agency and the Department for Education (Northern Ireland) on the adaptations, if any, required to the UfI model to meet Northern Ireland's needs.

Brian Carlin (Chair)	• Northern Ireland Growth Challenge	Voluntary/charity
Karen Beckett	• Valpar Industrial Ltd	Private business
Pauline Buchanan	• Communication Workers Union	Trade union
Patricia Burns	• ICL Ltd	Private business
Professor Wallace Ewart	• University of Ulster	Education
Peter Gallagher	• NW Institute of Further and Higher Education	Education
Dr Patrick Haren	• Northern Ireland Electricity	Privatised business
Paul Hendon	• BT Northern Ireland	Privatised business
Eileen Kelly	• Educational Guidance Service for Adults	Voluntary/charity
Nuala O'Donnell	• INTO Serving Education	Voluntary/charity

21 Northern Ireland Victims Commission

A single commissioner to investigate the needs of victims of communal violence. His report, 'We Will Remember Them' (May 1998) was followed by a Victims Liaison Unit within the NIO to implement his recommendations.

Sir Kenneth Bloomfield (Commissioner)	• Former Head, Northern Ireland Civil Service and Second Permanent Secretary, NIO	Independent

22 Policy Review of the Youth Service: Northern Ireland

Established in June 1997 to prepare recommendations for a policy framework and 'action agenda' for the future development of the Youth Service. The review was conducted by a policy review group, a review steering group and five working groups (facilities and support services; human resources; involvement of young people; monitoring and evaluation; and volunteering and community involvement). Working group members were nominees of both NIO and voluntary bodies and drawn from both sources.

Stephen Turner (Chair)	• National Council of YMCAs of Ireland	Voluntary/charity
Joanne Cappa	• Northern Ireland Youth Forum	Voluntary/charity
Dr Michael Day	• Centre for Youth Work Studies, Brunel University, London	Academic/research
Mary Finnegan	• Corrymeela Community	Voluntary/charity

Avila Kilmurray	• Northern Ireland Voluntary Trust	Voluntary/charity
Ruth Leitch	• Queen's University, Belfast	Academic/research
Dr William McCarney	• Formerly St. Mary's Training College	Academic/research
Emmet Norris	• Northern Ireland Youth Forum	Voluntary/charity
Karen Simpson	• Premier Power	Private business
Ronnie Wilson	• Opportunity Youth	Voluntary/charity
Stephen Young (Secretariat)	• Department of Education, Northern Ireland Office	Central government

23 Review Steering Group

Ronnie Jordan (Chair)	• Department of Education, Northern Ireland Office	Central government
Gilbert Bell	• North-Eastern Education and Library Board	Local public spending body
John Birch	• Education and Training Inspectorate	Central government
Gregory Butler	• Southern Education and Library Board	Local public spending body
David Guilfoyle	• Youth Council for Northern Ireland	National public body
Hans Martin	• South-Eastern Education and Library Board	Local public spending body
Barry Mulholland	• Belfast Education and Library Board	Local public spending body
Walter Rader	• Youthnet	Voluntary/charity
Mo Sykes	• Northern Ireland Youth Forum	Voluntary/charity
Stephen Turner	• National Council of YMCAs of Ireland	Voluntary/charity
Jack Walls	• Western Education and Library Board	Local public spending body
Louisa Ward	• Northern Ireland Youth Forum	Voluntary/charity
Joe Reynolds (Secretary)	• Department of Education, Northern Ireland Office	Central government

24 Working Group on Facilities and Support Services

Oliver Magill (Chair)	• Belfast Education and Library Board	Local public spending body
David Brady	• Jordanstown Student Union	Voluntary/charity
Billy Burniston	• Education and Training Inspectorate	Central government
Glen Jordan	• YouthLink Northern Ireland	Voluntary/charity
Dawn Latimer	• Share Discovery '80' Ltd	Private business
Antoinette McKeown	• Playboard	Voluntary/charity
Mary McGarrigle	• Youth Council for Northern Ireland	Voluntary/charity
Hans Martin	• South-Eastern Education and Library Board	Local public spending body
Jack Walls	• Western Education and Library Board	Local public spending body
Gregory Butler (Secretary)	• Southern Education and Library Board	Local public spending body

25 Working Group on Human Resources

Roger Courtney (Chair)	• Simon Community	Voluntary/charity
Lesley Crothers	• Northern Ireland Youth Forum	Voluntary/charity
Gerry Devine	• North-Eastern Education and Library Board	Local public spending body
Bill Haugh	• Western Education and Library Board	Local public spending body
Richard Loudon	• University of Ulster	Academic/research
Russell McCaughey	• Education and Training Inspectorate	Central government
John McCormick	• Youth Council for Northern Ireland	National public body
Denis Palmer	• YouthAction	Voluntary/charity
Hilary West-Hurst	• Guide Association	Voluntary/charity
Paddy White	• YouthLink Northern Ireland	Voluntary/charity
Marie Young	• Voluntary Service Belfast	Voluntary/charity

26 Working Group on the Involvement of Young People

Mo Sykes (Chair)	• Northern Ireland Youth Forum	Voluntary/charity
Gilbert Bell	• North-Eastern Education and Library Board	Local public spending body

Acquin Crawford	• Belfast Education and Library Board	Local public spending body
Trevor Creighton	• Carrickfergus Youth Centre	Voluntary/charity
Mary Lyons	• Youth Council for Northern Ireland	National public body
Ciara McClusky	• Northern Ireland Youth Forum	Voluntary/charity
Heath McMaster	• Ruralis	Voluntary/charity
Paddy Mooney	• NIACRO	Voluntary/charity
Lynsey Taylor	• Voluntary Service Belfast	Voluntary/charity

27   Working Group on Monitoring and Evaluation

John Birch (Chair)	• Education and Training Inspectorate, NIO	Central government
Rita Burke	• Educationa nd Training Inspectorate, NIO	Central government
Hugh Campbell	• University of Ulster	Academic/research
Fred Davidson	• Education and Training Inspectoratte, NIO	Central government
Peter Graham	• YouthAction	Voluntary/charity
Austin Hewitt	• Education and Training Inspectorate	Central government
Pat Jordan	• Youth Council for Northern Ireland	National public body
Anne McCausland	• Western Education and Library Board	Local public spending body
Robin McRoberts	• South-Eastern Education and Library Board	Local public spending body
Margaret McTeggert	• NIACRO	Voluntary/charity
Sean Mullin	• Shantallow Youth Centre	Voluntary/charity
Nigel O'Connor	• National Union of Students/Union of Students of Ireland	Voluntary/charity
Maeve Young	• Belfast Education and Library Board	Local public spending body

28   Working Group on Volunteering and Community Involvement

Jim McDonald (Chair)	• YouthNet	Voluntary/charity
Trevor Boyle	• YouthNet	Voluntary/charity
Rita Burke	• Education and Training Inspectorate, NIO	Central government
Howard Crowe	• Western Education and Library Board	Local public spending body
Frances Forte	• Scout Foundation, Northern Ireland	Voluntary/charity
Lisa-Marie McDade	• Maiden City	Voluntary/charity
Bill Osborne	• Voluntary Service Belfast	Voluntary/charity
John Quinliven	• Youth Council for Northern Ireland	National public body
Angela Taylor	• Southern Education and Library Board	Local public spending body
Jim Thompson	• Belfast Education and Library Board	Local public spending body
Walter Rader (Secretary)	• YouthNet	Voluntary/charity

SCOTTISH OFFICE (SO)

Name	Affiliation	Classification

1   Review of Scotland's Bathing Waters
Established in March 1998 to advise on the criteria for choosing the list of bathing waters and to assess applications for listing from local authorities under a Scottish Office official as chair.

Representatives(number per body as shown):	• Convention of Scottish Local Authorities (1)	Local government
	• Keep Scotland Beautiful (1)	Voluntary/charity
	• Scottish Environment Protection Agency (1)	National public body
	• Scottish Tourist Board (2)	National public body
	• Scottish Water Authorities (1)	National public body
	• Scottish Wildlife and Countryside Link (3)	Voluntary/charity

2 Working Group to Promote Biodiversity in Agriculture

To promote biodiversity and sustainable development from within the agricultural community and to raise awareness in farming and crofting communities.

John Henderson (Chair)	• Agriculture, Environment and Fisheries Dept, Scottish Office	Central government
Representatives from:	the NFUS, Scottish Landowners' Federation, Scottish Crofters' Union, Crofters' Commission, Scottish Agriculture College, Farming Wildlife Advisory Group, Forestry Commission, Scottish Natural Heritage, COSLA, Scottish Farming and Countryside Education Trust & RSPB (representing the Scottish Wildlife & Countryside Link)	

3 GP Out-of-Hours Service Working Group

Established in Spring 1998 to review the arrangements for GP out-of-hours cover across Scotland, identify best practice and make recommendations on any priority actions to improve services. Reported October 1998.

Deirdre Hutton (Chair)	• Chair, Scottish Consumer Council • Vice Chair, National Consumer Council	National public body
Christine Campbell	• Argyll & Clyde Local Health Council	Health
Dr Mary Church	• Scottish General Medical Services Committee	Health
Rosslyn Crocket	• Ayrshire and Arran Community Trust	Voluntary/charity
Dr Colin Hunter	• Royal College of General Practitioners	Professional association
Thom Kirkwood	• Patients' Association	Voluntary/charity
Hayden Newton	• Scottish Ambulance Service	Health
Dr Charles Swainson	• Edinburgh Royal Infirmary	Health
Dr Hamish Wilson	• Grampian Health Board	Health
Secretariat:		
Gillian Baxendine	• NHS Management Executive, Scottish Office	Central government
John Hannah	• NHS Management Executive, Scottish Office	Central government
Pauline Scott	• NHS Management Executive, Scottish Office	Central government

4 Scottish Out-of-Hours Study Group

This group researched current practice for the Working Group, reporting In Summer, 1998

Professor John Bain	• Tayside Centre for General Practice, University of Dundee	Academic/research
Dr Neil Drummond	• Senior Research Fellow, Public Health Research Unit, University of Glasgow	Academic/research
David Heaney	• Research Fellow, Department of General Practice, University of Edinburgh	Academic/research
Dr Katrina Moffat	• General Practitioner, Department of General Practice, University of Glasgow	Health
Dr Catherine O'Donnell	• Research Fellow, Department of General Practice, University of Edinburgh	Academic/research
Dr Fiona Paxton	• Lecturer, Department of General Practice, University of Glasgow	Academic/research
Dr Susan Ross	• Clinical Trials Co-ordinator, Health Services Research Unit, University of Aberdeen	Academic/research
Tony Scott	• Health Economist, Health Economics Research Unit, University of Aberdeen	Academic/research

5 Expert Panel on Information Technology for the Scottish Parliament

To provide advice to the Scottish Office on how the Parliament might use IT to promote internal efficiency and innovative ways of working.

Alistair Brown (Chair)	• Director, Administrative Services, Scottish Office	Central government
Alistair Baker	• Scotland Regional Manager, Microsoft Corporation	Private business
Roger Beattie	• Chair, Edinburgh Telematics Partnership and Community Investment Co-ordinator Edinburgh, IBM UK (Scotland)	Private business
Peter Black	• Network Services Director, Scottish Telecom	Privatised business
Lesley Beddie	• Professor of Computing, Napier University	Academic/research
Peter Dixon	• Regional Director, Scotland, Oracle Corporation UK Ltd	Private business
Paul Grice	• Head of Legislation and Implementation Division, Constitution Group, Scottish Office	Central government
Nic Hopkins	• Technical Director, Central Computers and Telecommunications Agency (CCTA)	Central government
Ann Mathieson	• Keeper, National Library of Scotland	National public body
Dik McFarlane	• Office of the Director, British Telecom (Scotland)	Privatised business
Alan Nairn	• Director of Information Technology, Perth and Kinross Council • Secretary, Society of IT Managers (Scotland)	Local government
Matthew O'Connor	• Director of Business Services, Telewest Communications	Private business

| Jane Wainwright | • Director of Information Systems, House of Commons Library | Independent |
| Ann Weatherstone | • Head of Architecture and Change Programme, National Australia Group | Independent |

6 Land Reform Policy Group

Established in October 1997 to identify and assess proposals for land reform in rural Scotland, taking account of their cost, legislative and administrative implications and their likely impact on the social and economic development of rural communities and on the natural heritage. Consultation papers issued, February and July 1998. 'Road show' visits by the Group were open to all. Final report ('Recommendations for Action') January 1999. 'Core members' were as follows.

Lord Sewel (Chair)	• Parliamentary Under Secretary of State (Agriculture, Environment and Fisheries), Scottish Office	Central government
Isabelle Low (Deputy chair)	• Head, Land Use Division, Scottish Office	Central government
Professor John Bryden	• Arkleton Centre, University of Aberdeen	Academic/research
Murray Elder (now Lord Elder)	• Special Adviser to the Secretary of State for Scotland	Central government
Alan Fraser	• Enterprise and Tourism Division, Scottish Office	Central government
Douglas Greig	• Chief Economist, Agriculture, Environment and Fishers Department, Scottish Office	Central government
David Henderson-Howat	• Chief Conservator, Forestry Commission	Central government
Joyce Lugton	• Civil Law Division, Scottish Office	Central government
Hugh MacDiarmid	• Solicitor's Office, Scottish Office	Central government
John Randall	• Head, Countryside and Natural Heritage Unit, Scottish Office	Central government
Philip Rycroft	• Head, Agricultural Policy Co-ordination and Rural Development Division, Scottish Office	Central government

7 Commission on Local Government and Scottish Parliament

To consider how to build the most effective relations between local government and the Scottish Parliament and Scottish Executive.

Neil McIntosh (Chair)	• Former Chief Executive, Strathclyde Regional Council • Convenor, Scottish Council of Voluntary Organisations	Local government
Professor Alan Alexander	• Professor of Local and Public Management, University of Strathclyde • Founding Director, Scottish Local Authorities Management Centre	Academic/research
Andrew Cubie	• Senior Partner, Fyfe Ireland WS • Former Chairman, CBI Scotland • Member, Action Group on Standards in Scottish Schools • Chairman, Scotland's Health at Work	Private business
Graham Leicester	• Political consultant • Director, Scottish Council Foundation	Private business
Eileen Mackay	• Chair, Secretary of State for Transport's Standing Advisory Committee on Trunk Road Assessment • Former Principal Finance Officer, Scottish Office • Non-executive director, Royal Bank of Scotland Group plc	National public body
Cllr Margaret Millar	• Deputy Convenor, Fife Council • Former Provost, Dunfermline District Council • Lecturer, Lauder College • Director, Queen Margaret Hospital NHS Trust • Director, Kingdom FM Radio Ltd	Local government
Matt Smith	• Scottish Secretary, Unison • Treasurer, Scottish TUC • Member, Executive of the Scottish Council for Development and Industry • Director, John Wheatley Centre	Trade union
Maureen Watt	• Chair of community council • Scottish National Party spokesperson, consumer affairs and water policy • Former SNP Vice Convener, local government policy	Local government

8 Scottish Advisory Task Force on the New Deal 'To get young Scottish people back to work.'

Ian Robinson (Chair)	• Chief Executive, Scottish Power	Privatised business
Archie Bethell	• Managing Director, Motherwell Bridge Holdings Ltd	Private business
Anne Clark	• Executive Director, Highland Community Care Forum	Voluntary/charity
Avril Ross Dewar	• Chief Executive, Ross Campbell Consultants	Private business
John Gallacher	• Managing Director, Cruden Estates Ltd	Private business
Keith Geddes	• Leader, City of Edinburgh Council	Local government

Fred Goodwin	• Chief Executive, Clydesdale Bank plc	Private business
Hugh Henry	• Leader, Renfrewshire District Council	Local government
Michael Leech	• Principal, Stevenson College	Education
Carmen McAteer	• Regional Officer, Manufacturing, Science and Finance Union	Trade union
Bill Neish	• Manager, Marks and Spencer plc	Private business
John Rafferty	• Director, National Lottery Charities Board (Scotland)	National public body
Martin Sime	• Chief Executive, Scottish Council for Voluntary Organisations	Voluntary/charity
Alan Sinclair	• Chief Executive, The Wise Group	Private business
Jim Stretton	• Chief Executive, Standard Life Assurance	Private business
Raymond Young	• Director, Forward Scotland	Voluntary/charity

9 Prestwick Task Force To assist in the economic development of Prestwick in the light of recent job losses.

Brian Wilson (Chair)	• Minister of State for Education and Industry, Scottish Office	Central government
Barry Allan	• Chair, Enterprise Ayrshire	Local public spending body
Steve Callan	• Operations Manager, Rohr	Private business
Campbell Christie	• General Secretary, Scottish TUC	Trade union
Sir Richard Evans	• Chief Executive, British Aerospace	Privatised business
John Horsburgh	• General Manager, Human Resources, Greenwich Caledonian	Private business
Matthew Hudson	• Chair, Glasgow Prestwick Internatonal Airport Ltd	Private business
Charlie Johnston	• General Manager, Rohr (US aerospace company)	Private business
David Macdonald	• Chief Executive, Enterprise Ayrshire	Local public spending body
Tom Nicholson	• Deputy Managing Director, British Aerospace	Privatised business
Sandra Osborne MP	• MP (Labour) for Ayr	Independent
George Thorley	• Chief Executive, South Ayrshire Council	Local government
Martin Togneri	• Director, Locate in Scotland	Central government
Ian Welsh	• Leader, South Ayrshire Council	Local government
Tracey White	• Assistant Secretary, Scottish TUC	Trade union
Tom Williams	• General Manager, British Aerospace Aerostructures	Privatised business
Rt. Hon. Viscount Younger of Leckie	• Chair, Prestwick Aviation Holdings Ltd • Former Secretary of State for Scotland	Private business

10 Scottish Parliament All-Party Consultative Steering Group
To bring together views on and consider the operational needs and working methods of the Scottish Parliament.

Rt. Hon. Henry McLeish MP (Chair)	• Minister for Home Affairs, Devolution and Transport, Scottish Office	Central government
Professor Alice Brown	• Department of Politics, University of Edinburgh	Academic/research
Campbell Christie	• General Secretary, Scottish TUC	Trade union
Andrew Cubie	• Confederation of British Industry (Scotland)	Trade association
Paul Cullen QC	• Conservative Party in Scotland	Voluntary/charity
Keith Geddes	• Convention of Scottish Local Authorities	Local government
Deidre Hutton	• Scottish Consumer Council	National public body
Joyce McMillan	• Former Chair, Scottish Constitutional Commission	Voluntary/charity
Esther Robertson	• Scottish Constitutional Commission	Voluntary/charity
Alex Salmond MP	• Leader, Scottish National Party	Voluntary/charity
Dr Joan Stringer	• Principal, Queen Margaret's College	Education
Jim Wallace MP	• Spokesperson, Scots Affairs, Liberal Democrats	Voluntary/charity
Canon Kenyon Wright	• Scottish Constitutional Convention	Voluntary/charity

11 Advisory Committee on the Co-ordination and Provision of Education for Severe Low-Incidence Disabilities
Established in August 1998 to consider (inter alia) inter-authority payment for the education of children with SEN and the relationship between education authorities and the independent and grant-aided special schools sectors.

Professor Sheila Riddell (Chair)	• Professor of Social Policy (Disability Studies), University of Glasgow	Academic/research

Jane Ansell	• Director, Sleep Scotland	Voluntary/charity
Ann Auchterlonie	• Scottish Development Officer, AFASIC • Former Deputy Director of Education, Fife Regional Council	Voluntary/charity
Jane Baines	• Chair, Scottish Association for Pre-School Home Visiting Teachers for Children with Special Needs	Education
Moira Bissett	• Co-ordinator, Parent to Parent, Tayside • Board member, Children in Scotland	Voluntary/charity
Alison Closs	• Lecturer in Special Educational Needs, Moray House Institute of Education	Academic/research
George Gordon	• Chair, Board of Governors, Craighalbert Centre • Former HM Chief Inspector with responsibility for SEN	Education
Anne Grayshan	• Chair, Graysmill School Board	Education
Jimmy Hawthorn	• Group Manager (Children and Families), Borders Council Social Work Department	Local government
Margaret Orr	• Senior Education Officer, SEN, Glasgow City Council	Local government
Gordon Phillips	• Principal, National Autistic Society, Daldorch House School	Voluntary/charity
Dr Sheelagh Phillips	• Senior Clinical Medical Officer, Yorkhill NHS Trust	Health
Nicholas Watson	• Department of Nursing Studies, University of Edinburgh	Academic/research

12   Expert Panel on Sex Offending
To have a strategic role in implementing the recommendations of the Skinner Report: 'A Commitment to Protect'.

Hon Lady Cosgrove (Chair)	• High Court judge, Scotland • Former senior Sheriff of Lothian and Borders • Former Chair, Mental Welfare Commission for Scotland	Judiciary
Tim Davison	• Chief Executive, Greater Glasgow Community Health Care Trust	Local public spending body
Brian Fearon	• Director of Social Work and Housing, East Dunbartonshire Council	Local government
Jeane Freeman	• Deputy Chair, Parole Board for Scotland	National public body
Ilona Kruppa	• Consultant clinical psychologist, Integrated Service for Sex Offenders	Health
John Orr	• Chief Constable, Strathclyde Police	Police
Bill Rattray	• Governor, Peterhead Prison, Scottish Prison Service	Central government
Dr Anne Stafford	• Policy Officer, Children First	Voluntary/charity
Geraldine Watt	• Assistant Procurator Fiscal, Glasgow	Judiciary
Dr Tom White	• Consultant Psychiatrist, State Hospital, Carstairs	Health

13   Review of the Improvement of Skills and Employability for Young People with Special Needs

Robert Beattie (Chair)	• Community Investment Co-ordinator, IBM • Non-executive Director, Stevenson College • Edinburgh Health Care NHS Trust • Scottish Council for Voluntary Organisations • Member, Lothian Employers Network on Disabilities	Private business
Maggi Allan	• Director of Education, South Lanarkshire Council	Education
Alison Cox	• Lecturer in Special Needs, Stevenson College	Academic/research
Rosemary Davidson	• Chief Executive, Renfrewshire Careers Partnership	Local government
David Dimmock	• Education Liaison Manager, Standard Life Assurance	Private business
Caroline Farquhar	• Chair, Support Training Action Group (STAG)	Voluntary/charity
Brian Kirkaldy	• Principal Educational Psychologist, Fife County Council	Education
Baroness Linklater	• Executive Chairman, The New School, Butterstone	Education
George McSorley	• Chief Executive, Unity Enterprise	Voluntary/charity
Ian Miller	• Chair, Skill in Scotland	Voluntary/charity
Cllr Elaine Murray	• South Ayrshire Council	Local government
Frank Pignatelli	• Director, Scottish Business in the Community	Voluntary/charity
Malcolm Smith	• Director of Social Work, Western Isles	Local government
Eleanor Spalding	• Principal Officer, Special Needs Services, Renfrewshire	Local government
David Watt	• Socialist Education Association	Education

14 Ministerial Action Group on Standards in Scottish Schools

Established July 1997 as a standing body to advise on Scottish school education targets and progress towards them while also monitoring and reporting on target-setting in individual schools.

Brian Wilson, MP(Chair) (replaced by Helen Liddell, MP)	• Minister for Education and Industry, Scottish Office	Central government
Andrew Cubie	• Confederation of British Industry (Scotland)	Trade association
Anne Dean (resigned February 1998)	• Director, Human Resources, Royal Bank of Scotland	Private business
Joyce Ferguson	• Primary school Head teacher	Education
Alison Kirby	• Convenor, Scottish Parent Teacher Council	Voluntary/charity
Professor John MacBeath	• Director, Quality in Education, University of Strathclyde	Academic/research
Cllr. Elizabeth Maginnis	• Convenor, Edinburgh City Council	Local government
Bruce Malone	• Secondary school Head teacher, Glasgow	Education
Professor Andrew Miller	• Principal, University of Sterling	Education
David Miller	• Chair, Scottish Qualification Authority	National public body
Ann Reeve	• Primary school Senior teacher	Education
Iain Rose	• High school Principal teacher	Education
Ronnie Smith	• General Secretary, Education Institute of Scotland	Trade union
Bill Speirs	• Deputy General Secretary, Scottish Trades Union Congress	Trade union
John Travers	• Director of Education, North Lanarkshire Council	Local government
Professor John Ward	• Chair, Scottish Advisory Council on Education and Training Targets	National pubic body

15 University for Industry Scottish Advisory Group

Established October 1997 to advise on the design and implementation of this public/private partnership in Scotland, intended to strengthen competitiveness and improve employability; also to inform the DfEE's UFI Design and Implementation Advisory Group of Scottish experience (no common membership).

Professor Alastair Macarlane (Chair)	• Former Principal, Heriot Watt University	Independent
David Anderson	• Director, Skills and Development, Enterprise Ayrshire	Trade association
Professor John Cowan	• Former Director, Open University in Scotland	Independent
Robert Craig	• Director, Scottish Library Association •Director, Scottish Library and Information Council	Professional association
David Ennis	• Senior Director, Oki UK Ltd	Private business
Jack Kelly	• Managing Director, Scottish Power Learning	Private business
Evelyn McCann	• Director of Skills, Scottish Enterprise	National public body
Nigel Paine	• Director, Scottish Council for Educational Technology	Education
Mike Webster	• Principal, Perth College	Education

DEPARTMENT OF SOCIAL SECURITY (DSS)

Name	Affiliation	Classification

1 Ad-Hoc Group of External Stakeholders – Decision Making and Appeals

Representatives from:	Age Concern, Law Society, National Association of Citizens Advice Bureaux, Child Poverty Action Group, National Council for One-Parent Families,Local Government Association and an independent solicitor.

2 Disability Benefits Forum

To consider possible options for changes in benefits for long-term sick and disabled people and carers. Uniquely among all the advisory or executive groups listed here, this Forum 'exploded' in May 1999 when 12 members resigned as a collective protest at perceived government policy on this subject. Being only one meeting short of its intended period, the Forum was disbanded.

Baroness Hollis (Chair)	• Parliamentary Under Secretary, DSS	Central government
Peter Adeane	• National Association of Citizen Advices Bureaus	Voluntary/charity
David Behan	• Local Government Association	Local government
Ian Bruce	• Royal National Institute for the Blind • Co-chair, Disability Benefits Consortium	Voluntary/charity
Jane Campbell	• National Centre for Independent Living • Member, Disability Rights Task Force (DfEE)	Voluntary/charity

Alison Cobb	• Mind	Voluntary/charity
Nicole Davoud	• Independent disability consultant	Private business
Prof. Rodney Grahame	• Chair, Disability Living Allowance Advisory Board	National public body
Jill Harrison	• Carers National Association	Voluntary/charity
Marilyn Howard	• Independent Disability Consultant	Private business
Rachel Hurst	• Rights Now! • Member, Disability Rights Task Force (DfEE)	Voluntary/charity
Brian Lamb	• Scope • Member, Disability Rights Task Force (DfEE)	Voluntary/charity
Margaret Lavery	• RADAR	Voluntary/charity
Carol Lee	• People First	Voluntary/charity
Colin Low	• National Federation of the Blind of the UK • Member, Disability Rights Task Force (DfEE)	Voluntary/charity
Brian McGinnis	• Mencap	Voluntary/charity
Dr Lotte Newman	• Royal College of General Practitioners	Professional association
Lorna Reith	• Disability Alliance	Voluntary/charity
Roy Sainsbury	• Social Research Unit, University of York	Academic/research
James Strachan	• Chief Executive, Royal National Institute for the Deaf • Member, Disability Rights Task Force (DfEE)	Voluntary/charity
Pauline Thompson	• Disablement Income Group	Voluntary/charity
Richard Wood	• British Council of Organisations of Disabled People • Co-chair, Disability Benefits Consortium • Voluntary/charity	Member, Disability Rights Task Force (DfEE)

3   Pensions Education Working Group
To examine ways of educating people about pensions and retirement.

John Allen	• Qualifications and Curriculum Authority	National public body
Susan Anderson	• CBI	Trade association
Lorraine Fletcher	• Equal Opportunities Commission	National public body
Mike Hampton	• Association of British Insurers	Trade association
Professor David Knights	• Director, Financial Services Research Centre, University of Manchester Institute of Science and Technology	Academic/research
Sally McCombie	• Consumers Association	Voluntary/charity
Gill Nott	• Chair, Personal Finance Education Group • Chief Executive, ProShare	Private business
Victoria Nye	• Association of Unit Trusts and Investment Funds	Trade association
Rhoslyn Roberts	• National Association of Pension Funds	Trade association
Joanne Segars	• TUC	Trade union
Sue Skinner	• NatWest Group	Private business
Alison Tracy	• Financial Services Authority	National public body

4   Pension Provision Group
To provide independent analysis of pension provision.

Tom Ross (Chair)	• Vice President, National Association of Pension Funds • Director, Aon Consulting	Trade association
Ruth Hancock	• Senior Research Fellow, Age Concern Institute of Gerontology, King's College, London	Academic/research
Paul Johnson	• Deputy Director, Institute of Fiscal Studies	Academic/research
Stewart Ritchie	• Director (Pensions Development), Scottish Equitable plc	Private business
Joanne Segars	• Pensions Group, TUC	Trade union
Anne Wood	• Pensions fund manager, Storehouse plc	Private business
David Yeandle	• Head of Employment Affairs, Engineering Employers Federation	Trade association

5   **Pension Sharing Consultation Panel**
Established in November 1997 to help develop policy and procedures for sharing pensions on divorce.

Representatives from:

	Faculty of Actuaries	Professional association
	Institute of Actuaries	Professional association
	British Diplomatic Spouses Association	Voluntary/charity
	Association of British Insurers	Trade association
	Association of Consulting Actuaries	Professional association
	Fairshares	Voluntary/charity
	The Law Society	Professional association
	Law Society of Scotland	Professional association
	Lord Chancellor's Ancillary Relief Advisory Group	
	Joint Working Group on Occupational Pensions	
	Society of Pension Consultants	Trade association
	National Association of Pension Funds	Trade association
	Association of Pensions Lawyers	Professional association
	Association of Pensions Lawyers, Scotland	Professional association
	Pensions Management Institute	Trade association
	Association of Pension Trustees	Trade association
	Self-invested Personal Pensions Provider Group	Trade association
	Solicitors' Family Law Association	Professional association
	Women's National Commission	National public body
	Inland Revenue	Central government
	Lord Chancellor's Department	Central government
	Northern Ireland Office	Central government
	Scottish Office	Central government
	Department of Social Security	Central government
	HM Treasury	Central government

6   **War Pensions Hearing Loss Review**
To review the scientific evidence on noise-induced hearing loss and war pensions

Name	Affiliation	Classification
Sir Kenneth Calman (Chair)	• Chief Medical Officer, Department of Health	Central government
Professor Adrian Davis	• Institute of Hearing Research, Medical Research Council	Academic/research
Dr Guy Lightfoot	• Dept of Clinical Engineering, Royal Liverpool Hospital	Academic/research
Professor Mark Lutman	• Institute of Sound and Vibration Research	Academic/research
Professor Linda Luxon	• Institute of Laryngology and Otology, University College London Medical School	Academic/research

DEPARTMENT OF TRADE AND INDUSTRY (DTI)

Name	Affiliation	Classification

1   **Better Payment Practice Group**
To advise Ministers on how to achieve the government's policy of improving delays in commercial payments.

Sir Clive Thompson (Chair)	• President, Confederation of British Industry	Trade association
Representatives from:	• Association of British Insurers	Trade association
	• British Bankers Association	Trade association
	• British Chambers of Commerce	Trade association
	• Business Link Network Company	Trade association
	• Factors and Discounters Association	Trade association
	• Federation of Small Businesses	Trade association
	• Forum of Private Business	Trade association
	• Institute of Credit Management	Trade association

	• Institute of Directors	Trade association
	• National Farmers Union	Trade association
	• Union of Independent Companies	Trade association
	• DTI	Central government

2 Company Law Review Steering Group

To consider how core company law can be modernised in order to provide a simple, efficient and cost-effective framework for carrying on business.

Richard Rogers (Chair)	• Director, Company Law and Investigations, DTI	Central government
The Hon Mrs Justice Arden	• High Court Judge • Chair, Law Commission , Jan 1996 – Feb 1999 • Member, Company Law Committee and Financial Panel, the Law Society	Judiciary
Robert Bertram	• Former partner, Shepherd and Wedderburn (Scottish solicitors) • Member, Monopolies and Mergers Commission • Visiting Professor, Heriot Watt University, Edinburgh	Independent
Sir Stuart Hampson	• Chair, John Lewis Partnership plc • Former civil servant, Board of Trade and DTI • Founding member of London First	Private business
Professor John Kay	• Peter Moores Director of the Said Business School, University of Oxford • Director, London Economics (consultancy) • Former Director, Institute of Fiscal Studies	Academic/research
Profesor John Parkinson	• Department of Law, University of Bristol	Academic/research
Colin Perry	• Chair, Small and Medium Enterprises Council, CBI • Chair/Chief Executive/director of small companies	Private business
John Plender	• Chair, Pensions and Investment Research Consultants Ltd • Journalist and broadcaster • Former Financial Editor, The Economist	Private business
Rosemary Radcliffe	• Head of Economics, Pricewaterhouse Coopers • Member, Advisory Group on Competitiveness, DTI	Private business
Jonathan Rickford (Project Director of the Review)	• Consultant on UK and European regulation and commercial law • Former Solicitor to DTI and British Telecom	Private business
Bryan Sanderson	• Managing Director (Chemicals) BP plc • President, Board of CEFIC (European Chemical Industry Council) • Non-executive director of British Steel • Member, Advisory Group on Competitiveness, DTI	Private business
Richard Sykes QC	• Company lawyer • Council member, Voluntary Service Overseas	Private business

3 Company Law Review Consultative Committee

To provide a forum for discussion of issues pertinent to the Company Law Review, for the key interest groups involved and to enhance the public consultation on the review.

Brian Hilton (Chair)	• Director General, Corporate and Consumer Affairs, DTI	Central government
Andrew Baker	• CISCO	Trade association
Stuart Bell	• Research Director, Pensions and Investment Research Consultants Ltd	Private business
David Bennett	• Partner, Bennett & Robertson (solicitors)	Private business
Joan Bingley	• Institute of Chartered Secretaries and Administrators	Professional association
Mark Boleat	• Director General, Association of British Insurers	Trade association
Bill Callaghan	• Head of Economic and Social Affairs, TUC	Trade union
Chris Christou	• Partner, Leigh, Christou & Co (accountants)	Private business
Paul Geradine	• Head of Listing, London Stock Exchange	Private business
Peter Goldsmith QC	• Former Chair, Bar Council	Professional association
Nick Goulding	• Forum of Private Business	Private business
Mark Goyder	• Centre for Tomorrow's Company	Academic/research
Ronald A Henderson	• Finance Director, BICC plc	Private business
Tim Herrington	• Law Society	Professional association
Nick Janmohamed	• National Consumer Council	National public body
John Kingman	• HM Treasury	Central government

Tim Melville-Ross	• Director General, Institute of Directors	Trade association
Charles Monaghan	• Unilever plc • Member, Institute of Chartered Accountants of Scotland	Private business
Roger Myddleton	• *Representing the Committee of Inquiry: A New Vision for Business*	
Paul Myners	• Chief Executive, Natwest Wealth Management • Chairman, Gartmore Investment Management plc	Private business
Gill Nott	• Chief Executive, Proshare (UK) Ltd	Private business
Tom Preece	• Federation of Small Businesses	Trade association
Ann Robinson	• Director General, National Association of Pension Funds	Trade association
Ken Rushton	• CBI	Trade association
Clive Sherling	• Apex Partners	Private business
Chris Swinson	• President, Institute of Chartered Accountants in England and Wales	Professional association
Simon Williams	• Head of Corporate Affairs, Co-operative Bank plc	Private business

4   Competitiveness Advisory Group

To advise the Secretary of State on the needs of business when developing and implementing policies to improve UK competitiveness.

Rt Hon Margaret Beckett MP (Chair)	• Secretary of State for Trade and Industry (replaced by subsequent Secretaries of State since July 1998)	Central government
Sir Jeremy Beecham	• Chair, Local Government Association	Local government
C K Chow	• Chief Executive, GKN plc	Private business
Sir Terence Conran	• Chair, Conran Holdings Ltd	Private business
John Edmonds	• General Secretary, Union for General, Municipal, Boilermakers	Trade union
Dr Chris Evans	• Director, Merlin Scientific Services Ltd	Private business
Sir Richard Evans	• Chief Executive, British Aerospace, plc	Privatised business
Ian Gibson	• Managing Director and Chief Executive, Nissan Motor Manufacturing (UK) Ltd	Private business
Anthony Greener	• Chair, Guinness plc	Private business
Jan Hall	• European Chief Executive, GGT Group plc	Private business
Terry Leahy	• Chief Executive, Tesco plc	Private business
Judy Lever	• Director, Blooming Marvellous Ltd	Private business
Dr Tony Marchington	• Chief Executive, Oxford Molecular Group plc	Private business
John Monks	• General Secretary, Trades Union Congress	Trade union
Rosemary Radcliffe	• Head of Economics, Pricewaterhouse Coopers	Private business
Bryan Sanderson	• Managing Director, (Chemicals) British Petroleum plc	Private business
Cob Stenham	• Chair, Arjo Wiggins Appleton plc	Private business
Sir Richard Sykes	• Chair and Chief Executive, Glaxo Wellcome plc	Private business
Adair Turner	• Director General, CBI	Trade association
Perween Warsi	• Managing Director, S and A Foods Ltd	Private business

5   Competitiveness Working Party; Encouraging Innovation

To develop proposals to encourage more firms to be innovative in all aspects of their performance.

Bevan Braithwaite	• Chair, TWI	Private business
Dr Peter Doyle	• Director, Zeneca Group Ltd	Private business
John Golding	• Chair, Hewlett Packard Ltd	Private business
Anthony Greener	• Co-Chair, Diageo plc	Private business
John Hall	• Spencer Stuart and Associates Ltd	Private business
Dr Sue Ion	• Director, Technology and Operations, British Nuclear Fuels Ltd	National public body
Stephen Lusty	• Managing Director, Airmaster Engineering Ltd	Private business
Roy McNulty	• Chair, Short Brothers plc	Private business
Dr George Poste	• Chief Scientific and Technology Officer, SmithKline Beecham plc	Private business
Professor Sir Gareth Roberts	• Vice Chancellor, University of Sheffield	Academic/research
Jonathan Sands	• Managing Director, Elmwood Design Ltd	Private business

Dan Sequerra	• Chief Executive, Kirklees Metropolitan Borough Council	Local government
John Sorrell	• Chair, Design Council • Chair, Interbrand Newell and Sorrell	National public body

6 Competitiveness Working Party; Promoting the Best of Best Practice
To help develop proposals to maximise the potential of all firms through the adoption of best practice.

Alec Daley	• Anite Group plc, Manufacturing Council, Confederation of British Industry	Private business
James Dyson	• Dyson Applicances Ltd	Private business
Sir Tom Farmer	• Kwik Fit Holdings Ltd	Private business
Jackie Kernahan	• Forte UK Ltd	Private business
Tina Mason	• Dutton Engineering (Woodside) Ltd	Private business
Professor Colin New	• School of Management, Cranfield University	Academic/research
Amber Paul	• Caparo Industries plc	Private business
Rosemary Radcliffe	• Head of Economics, Pricewaterhouse Coopers	Private business
John Saunders	• Hereford and Worcester, Business Link	Private business
Fiona Skinner	• R F Brookes Ltd	Private business
Cob Stenham	• Arjo Wiggins Appleton plc	Private business
Lynn Williams	• Amalgamated Engineering and Electrical Union	Trade union

7 Competitiveness Working Party; Making the Most of the Information Age
To develop proposals to ensure that the new opportunities of the information age are fully exploited by business, particularly small firms and their employees.

Sir Jeremy Beecham	• Chair, Local Government Association	Local government
Alan Calder	• Business Link London City Business Partners	Private business
Julia Collins	• Pricewaterhouse Coopers	Private business
Sue Davidson	• BT Business Connections	Private business
Brian Davis	• Nationwide Building Society	Private business
Ron Dunn	• Ascada Ltd	Private business
Mike Fischer	• Research Machines Ltd	Private business
Balram Gidoomal	• Winning Communications Ltd	Private business
Nigel Hartnell	• ICL Services Ltd	Private business
James Hehir	• Ipswich Borough Council	Local government
Terry Leahy	• Tesco plc	Private business
William Sargent	• FrameStore	Private business
Professor Peter Swann	• Manchester Business School	Academic/research
Suzanna Taverne	• Pearson plc	Private business
Tony Young	• Communication Workers Union	Trade union

8 Competitiveness Working Party; Enhancing Business Performance Through Developing Individuals

Brendan Barber	• TUC	Trade union
Bruce Collings	• Ethicon Endo-Surgery Ltd	Private business
David Compston	• Allott and Lomax	Private business
Jeremy Crook	• Black Training and Enterprise Group	Private business
Jeannie Drake	• Communications Workers Union	Trade union
Anthony Dubbins	• Graphical, Paper and Media Union	Trade union
John Edmonds	• General Secretary, Union for General, Municipal, Boilermakers	Trade union
Professor Alan Gibbs	• Small Business Centre, Durham University Business School	Academic/research
Allan Johnston	• British Steel plc	Privatised business
Mike Kinski	• Scottish Power	Privatised business
Anne Minto	• Engineering Employers Federation	Trade/prof. Association
Tony Morgan	• Industrial Society	Voluntary/charity
Stephen Moss	• Springboard UK	Voluntary/charity

John Oliver	• Leyland Trucks Ltd	Private business
Bryan Sanderson	• BP International Ltd	Private business
Peter Smith	• Wigan Borough Council	Local government
Ann Toler	• Boots the Chemists Ltd	Private business
Perween Warsi	• S and A Foods Ltd	Private business
Cecilia Wells	• Human resources consultant	Private business
Gwenda Williams	• Human resources manager, Hyder plc	Private business

9 Competitiveness Working Party; Increasing Business Investment

Sir David Barnes	• Zeneca	Private business
Professor S K Bhattacharyya	• Warwick Manufacturing Group	Private business
Tony Bonner	• Contract Chemicals Ltd	Private business
Dr Chris Evans	• Merlin Scientific Services Ltd	Private business
Amelia Fawcett	• Morgan Stanley Group (Europe)	Private business
Robert Fleming	• Pace Micro Technology plc	Private business
Lord Hollick	• Chief Executive, United News Media plc • Government Special Adviser	Private business
Alan Hughes	• ESRC Centre for Business Research, Cambridge University	Academic/research
Judy Lever	• Blooming Marvellous Ltd	Private business
Roger Lyons	• Union for Manufactiuring, Science and Finance	Trade union
John Melbourn	• 3i Group plc	Private business
Magnus Mowat	• Allen plc	Private business
Helen Murlis	• Hay Management Consultants Ltd	Private business
Tom O'Neill	• Pilkington Optronics	Private business
John Rose	• Rolls Royce plc	Privatised business
Dominic Shorthouse	• E M Warburg, Pincus and Co International Ltd	Private business
Malcolm Taylor	• Bridgeport Machines Ltd	Private business
David Watson	• British Petroleum plc	Private business

10 Competitiveness Working Party; Maximising Competitiveness in Europe

Peter Agar	• Confederation of British Industry	Trade association
Keith Bogg	• Marks and Spencer plc	Private business
Sir John Carter	• Commercial Union plc	Private business
C K Chow	• GKN plc	Private business
Ian Evans	• Hyder plc	Private business
Donald Hepburn	• Unilever plc	Private business
Christopher King	• Avon Rubber, plc	Private business
John Langston	• TI Group plc	Private business
Peter Lehmann	• Centrica plc	Private business
Henry Manisty	• Reuters Ltd	Private business
Keith McCullagh	• British Biotech plc (when appointed)	Private business
John Mellon	• Reed Elsevier plc	Private business

Eight Regional Competitiveness Working Parties:

11 East Midlands

Fiona Skinner	• RF Brooks	Private business
Malcom Taylor	• Bridgeport Machines	Private business
Ann Toler	• Boots the Chemists	Private business
Perween Warsi	• S&A Foods Ltd	Private business

12 Eastern Region

Bevan Braithwaite	• TWI	Private business

James Hehir	• Ipswich Borough Council	Local government
Alan Hughes	• Centre for Business Research, University of Cambridge	Academic/research
Tina Mason	• Dutton Engineering	Private business
Prof. Colin New	• Cranfield University School of Management	Academic/research
Cecilia Wells	• Human resources consultant	Private business

13 North East

Sir Jeremy Beecham	• Chair, Local Government Association	Local government
Professor Alan Gibbs	• Small Business Centre, Durham University Business School	Academic/research

14 North West

Charles Allen	• Granada	Private business
Sir David Barnes	• Zeneca plc	Private business
Tony Bonner	• Contract Chemicals	Private business
David Compston	• Allan and Lomax	Private business
Dr Peter Doyle	• Zeneca plc	Private business
Ken Fox	• Allan Construction	Private business
Dr Sue Ion	• British Nuclear Fuels Ltd	National public body
Magnus Mowat	• Ryalux Ltd	Private business
John Oliver	• Leyland Trucks	Private business
Peter Smith	• Wigan Borough Council	Local government
Professor Peter Swann	• Manchester Business School	Academic/research

15 South East

Alec Daley	• Anite Group • CBI	Private business
Mike Fischer	• Research Machines	Private business
John Golding	• Hewlett Packard	Private business
Balram Gidoomal	• Winning Communications	Private business
Terry Leahy	• Tesco plc	Private business

16 South West

Brian Davies	• Nationwide Building Society	Private business
James Dyson	• Dyson Appliances	Private business

17 West Midlands

Prof. S.K. Bhattacharyya	• Professor of Manufacturing, University of Warwick	Academic/research
Amber Paul	• Caparo Industries	Private business
John Saunders	• Hereford and Worcester Business Links	Private business

18 Yorkshire and Humberside

Robert Fleming	• Pace Micro Technology	Private business
Denise Howard	• Whiterose Line	Private business
Stephen Lusty	• Airmaster Engineering	Private business
Prof. Sir Gareth Roberts	• Vice Chancellor, University of Sheffield	Education
Jonathan Sands	• Elmwood Design	Private business
Dan Sequerra	• Kirklees Metropolitan Borough Council	Local government

19 Database Market Strategy Group

Established November 1998 to study the implementation of the Copyright and Rights in Databases Regulations of 1997 in the publishing industry and education and library fields.

John Startup (Chair)	• Director, Copyright Division, DTI	Central government
Toby Bainton	• Standing Conference on National and University Libraries	Education
Clive Bradley	• Director, Confederation of Information Communication Industries	Trade association
Roger Broadie	• Chairman, Copyright and Designs Committee	Trade association

Professor Sir Roger Elliot	• The Royal Society	Professional association
Trevor Fenwick	• Directory & Databases Publishers Association	Trade association
Frank Harris	• Educational Copyright Users' Forum	Education
Anne Joseph	• Reed Elsevier (UK) (publishers)	Private business
Henry Manisty	• Reuters plc	Private business
Ross Shimmon	• Chief Executive, The Library Association	Professional association
Steve Sidaway	• Chadwyck-Healey (publishers)	Private business

20 Review of Electricity Trading Arrangements

Conducted for the DTI by the Director General of the Office of theElectricity Regulator with three independent assessors (added under pressure on the DTI from the electricity supply industry)

Prof. Stephen Littlechild	• Director General, Office of the Electricity Regulator	Central government
Prof. Lord Currie	• London Business School	Academic/research
Nicholas Duslacher	• Chair, Securities and Futures Authority • Stockbroker	Private business
Sir Peter Walter	• Company director	Private business

21 Export Forum

To carry out a full assessment of how well the UK's export programmes work (joint with Foreign and Commonwealth Office)

Tom Harris (Chair)	• Director General, Export Promotion, DTI	Central government
Sir Andrew Burns (Alternative Chair)	• Foreign and Commonwealth Office	Central government
Tony Bastock	• Chemical Industries Association	Trade association
Robert Beresford	• Overseas Project Board	National public body
Martin Briggs	• Government Office for the East Midlands	Central government
Richard Brown	• Aston Fittings Manufacturing Ltd	Private business
Ian Campbell	• Institute of Export	Trade association
Garry Campkin	• CBI	Trade association
Mark Conaty	• HM Treasury	Central government
Emmanuel Cotter	• North London Business Development Agency	Local public spending body
Ted Dilley	• Cable and Wireless	Privatised business
David Fawcett	• Department for Culture, Media and Sport	Central government
Peter Godwin	• British Overseas Trade Board	National public body
Glenys Goucher	• Business Link, North Derbyshire	Private business
Ken Jackson	• TUC	Trade union
Roy Leighton	• British Invisibles	Private business
Victor Lunn-Rockcliffe	• Export Credits Guarantee Department	Central government
Dorothy MacKenzie	• Dragon International Consulting	Private business
Hector Munro	• British Council	National public body
David Orchard	• MAFF	Central government
Ron Taylor	• British Chambers of Commerce	Trade association
Richard Wood	• DETR	Central government

22 Review of Structure of Export Promotion

To examine the arrangements for providing official support and promotion for exports (other than defence goods and services) and investment abroad.

Sir Richard Wilson (Chair)	• Cabinet Secretary, Cabinet Office	Central government
Harry Bush	• Enterprise and Growth Unit, Treasury	Central government
Sir Ronald Hampel	• Chair, ICI plc	Private business
Tom Harris	• Director General of Export Promotion, DTI	Central government
Martin Henry	• Chair, Lasotolite Ltd	Private business
David John	• Chair, British Oxygen Company plc	Private business
Eric Peacock	• Chief Executive, Herts Business Link	Private business

| John Shepherd | • Deputy Under Secretary of State, Foreign Office | Central government |

23 Low Pay Commission
To recommend to the Government the initial rate at which the minimum wage might be introduced and other matters referred to it by Ministers as a standing body (ANDPB).

Professor George Bain (Chair)	• Vice-Chancellor, Queen's University, Belfast • Former Principal, London Business School • Chair, former Commission on Public Policy and British Business	Academic/research
Professor William Brown	• Professor of Industrial Relations, University of Cambridge	Academic/research
Bill Callaghan	• Head, Trades Union Congress Economic and Social Affairs Dept	Trade union
John Cridland	• Director of Human Resources Policy, Confederation of British Industry	Trade association
Lawrence Dewar	• Chief Executive, Scottish Grocers' Federation	Trade association
Rita Donaghy	• Member, National Executive Council, Unison	Trade union
Paul Gates	• General Secretary, Knitwear, Footwear and Apparel Trades Union	Trade union
Professor David Metcalf	• Department of Economics, London School of Economics	Academic/research
Stephanie Monk	• Director of Human Resources, Granada Group	Private business

24 Oil and Gas Industry Task Force
Established in November 1998 to develop strategies for reducing the cost base of UK oil and gas operations and priortise initiatives aimed at improving the competitiveness of the industry in the face of continuing low international oil prices.

Rt. Hon. John Battle MP (Chair)	• Minister for Energy and Industry, DTI	Central government
Lord Macdonald (Vice-Chair)	• Minister for Business and Energy, Scottish Office	Central government
Mike Bowyer	• Managing Director, PES International	Private business
Malcolm Brinded	• Managing Director, Shell UK Exploration and Production	Private business
Syd Fudge	• Chair, Offshore Contractors Association • Chief Executive, Kvaerner Oil and Gas	Trade association
Francis Gugen	• Vice-President, UK Offshore Operators Association • Manging Director, Amerada Hess	Trade association
Mark Hope	• Honorary Secretary, UK Offshore Operators Association • Technical Director, Enterprise Oil	Trade association
Alan Jones	• Honorary Treasurer, UK Offshore Operators Association • Director and General Manager, BP Exploration	Trade association
James McCallum	• President, Global Marine-Europe • Chair, Stretch Performance Network	Private business
John Macdonald	• Managing Director, Texaco	Private business
Dinah Nichols	• Director General, Environmental Protection, DETR	Central government
Godfrey Robson	• Scottish Office	Central government
Steve Robson	• HM Treasury	Central government
Tom Smith	• Chair and Managing Director, Nessco Ltd	Private business
Anna Walker	• Director General, Energy, DTI	Central government
Sir Ian Wood	• Chair and Managing Director, John Wood Group • Chair, Scottish Enterprise	Private business
Julian Thomson (Industry Assessor)	• Group Manager, Marketing and Communications, Stolt Comex Seaway Ltd	Private business
Keith Mayo (Secretariat)	• DTI	Central government

25 Spectrum Management Advisory Group
Established in October 1998 to advise DTI and its Radiocommunications Agency on policy issues arising from the management of the radio wavelengths spectrum.

Dr John Forrest (Chair)	• Chair, Brewton Group	Private business
Dr Mark Armstrong	• Nuffield College, University of Oxford	Academic/research
Professor Sue Birley	• Imperial College Management School, University of London	Academic/research
Dr Kevin Bond	• Chair, Yorkshire Water Services plc	Privatised business
David Brown	• Chairman, Motorola	Private business
Keith Harlow	• BBC	National public body

Dr Mohamed Ibrahim	• Chairman, Mobile System International plc	Private business
Stephen Lowe	• Eurobell Holding plc	Private business
Michael Short	• Cellnet plc	Private business
Andrew Sleigh	• Ministry of Defence	Central government

26 TECH Stars Steering Group
To look at ways to help emerging technology based businesses to succeed.

Peter Agar	• CBI	Trade association
Professor Sue Birley	• Imperial College Management School, University of London	Academic/research
Ronald Cohen	• Apax Partners and Co	Private business
Hermann Hauser	• Amadeus Capital Partners Ltd	Private business
Alistair Keddie	• Innovation Unit, DTI	Central government
Craig Pickering	• HM Treasury	Central government
Adrian Piper	• Bank of England	National public body
John Thompson	• DTI	Central government

HM TREASURY (HMT)

Name	Affiliation	Classification

1 Review of Alcohol and Tobacco Fraud
To conduct a review of the effect on the Exchequer and on industry revenue of alcohol and tobacco fraud, smuggling and cross-border shopping, also looking at relevant health and law and order issues. Established July 1997. Reported July 1998.

Joint Working Party representatives:

	• Ministry of Agriculture, Fisheries and Food	Central government
	• Department of the Environment, Transport and the Regions	Central government
	• Department of Health	Central government
	• Industrial Policy Division, Scottish Office	Central government
	• Department of Trade and Industry	Central government
	• Bonded Warehouse Keepers Association	Trade association
	• Brewers and Licensed Retailers Association	Trade association
	• British International Freight Association	Trade association
	• British Vehicle Rental and Leasing Association	Trade association
	• Duty Free Confederation	Trade association
	• Federation of Wholesale Distributors	Trade association
	• Freight Transport Association	Trade association
	• Gin and Vodka Association of Great Britain	Trade association
	• Imported Tobacco Products Advisory Council	National public body
	• National Association of Cider Makers	Trade association
	• National Federation of Retail Newsagents	Trade association
	• Road Haulage Association	Trade association
	• Scotch Whiskey Association	Trade association
	• Scottish Licensed Trade Association	Trade association
	• Tobacco Manufacturers Association	Trade association
	• United Kingdom Warehouse Keepers Association	Trade association
	• Wine and Spirits Association of Great Britain and Northern Ireland	Trade association

2 Consultation Groups on the Review of Alcohol and Tobacco Fraud
Consultation Groups on the Review of Alcohol and Tobacco Fraud. To explore with the drinks and tobacco trades the costs to them of implementing the Review's recommendations. Established November 1998; consultation paper issued January 1999.

Representatives	• The trade associations listed above

3   Independent Review of the Banking Sector

To assess competition and its constraints, e.g., in clearing and credit card payment structures. At least one bank's resistance to revealing information was reported in August 1999.

Don Cruickshank (Chair)	• Chair, Action 2000 (the Government's Anti-Millenium Bug Campaign) • Former Director General, Oftel • Former Chief Executive, NHS in Scotland	Independent

4   Task Force on Banks' Assistance to Credit Unions

Announced July 1998; membership announced September 1998. This group's topic is linked to the two Policy Action Teams of the Cabinet Office's Social Exclusion Unit (out of 18 PATs) which are Treasury-led: 'Business' and 'Financial Services'. This task force arranged 'public discussions' in four cities outside London to serve its own and these two PATs' needs. Written comments were also invited from relevant organisations. Expected to report in summer 1999 on how banks and building societies could assist an expansion of credit union services.

Fred Goodwin (Chair)	• Deputy Group Chief Executive, Royal Bank of Scotland	Private business
Andrew Blessley	• NatWest Bank plc	Private business
Ray Donnelly	• Heriot-Watt University	Academic/research
Rose Dorman	• Dalmuir Credit Union	Voluntary/charity
Paul Duffin	• Halifax plc	Private business
Gillian Ford	• Clydesdale bank	Private business
Rosalind Gilmore	• Former Chief Registrar of Friendly Societies	Independent
Gerald Gregory	• Britannia Building Society	Private business
Roger Hollick	• Derbyshire Building Society	Private business
Geoff Rutland	• Midland Bank plc	Private business
Christopher Smith	• Cooperative Bank plc	Private business
Ralph Swoboda	• Association of British Credit Unions	Voluntary/charity

5   Business Advisory Group on European Monetary Union

To support a national programme of practical information, guidance and monitoring on the Euro's impact and the preparations for any decision by the UK to join.

Kate Barker	• Confederation of British Industry	Trade association
Adrian Coles	• Building Societies Association	Trade association
Robert Colvill	• British Retail Consortium	Trade association
Stephen Davies	• Institute of Directors	Trade association
Barry Goddard	• Council for Travel and Tourism	Trade association
Nicholas Goulding	• Forum of Private Business	Trade association
Chris Hurford	• Chartered Institute of Public Finance and Accountancy	Professional association
David Lea	• Trades Union Congress	Trade union
Michael Lewis	• Association for Payment Clearing Services	Trade association
Sheila McKechnie	• Consumers' Association	Voluntary/charity
Graham Mackenzie	• Engineering Employers Federation	Trade association
Donald Martin	• Federation of Small Businesses	Trade association
Christopher Pearce	• The Hundred Group of Finance Directors	Trade association
David Perry	• Institute of Chartered Accountants in England and Wales	Professional association
Dr Ian Peters	• British Chambers of Commerce	Trade association
Anthony Stern	• Association of Corporate Treasurers	Professional association
Tim Sweeney	• British Bankers' Association	Trade association
Janette Weir	• Association of British Insurers	Trade association
Rob Wirszycz	• Computing Services and Software Association	Trade association
Geoffrey Yeowart	• The Law Society	Professional association

6 **Task Force on Economic Instruments for Industrial and Commercial Use of Energy (joint with Customs and Excise, DETR and DTI)**

To examine the use of economic instruments to improve the industrial and commercial use of energy and to help reduce greenhouse gas emissions. Established March 1998; Consultation paper June 1998; report published November 1998 ('Economic Instruments and the Business use of Energy – a Report by Lord Marshall'). The decision to introduce a new tax in 2001 was criticised by the Trade and Industry select committee in July 1999.

Lord Marshall (Chair)	• Former President, Confederation of British Industry • Chair, British Airways	Trade association
John Gieve	• Director, Budget and Public Finances, HM Treasury	Central government
David Howard	• Commissioner, Excise and Central Policy, Customs and Excise	Central government
Dinah Nichols	• Director General, Environment Protection Group, DETR	Central government
Alastair MacDonald	• Director General, Industry, Department of Trade and Industry	Central government

7 **Financial Management Working Group**

Established in 1998 to promote better financial management criteria and quality standards in smaller companies. A Working Group, with the same chair and other members studied the implementation of the Financial Management Working Group's recommendations.

Andrew Godfrey (Chair)	• Grant Thornton	Private business
Representatives from:	• Association of Chartered Certified Accountants	Professional association
	• Association of Independent Businesses	Trade association
	• Bank of England	National public body
	• Barclays plc	Private business
	• British Bankers Association	Trade association
	• British Chamber of Commerce	Trade association
	• Chartered Institute of Management Accountants	Professional association
	• Confederation of British Industry	Trade association
	• University of Durham Business School	Academic/research
	• Federation of Small Businesses	Trade association
	• Forum of Private Businesses	Trade association
	• Institute of Chartered Accountants	Professional association
	• Institute of Directors	Trade association
	• Lloyds TSB	Private business
	• Midland Bank plc	Private business
	• NatWest Bank plc	Private business
	• Riverside Consultants	Private business
	• ROMTEC plc	Private business
	• Department of Trade and Industry	Central government
	• HM Treasury	Central government

8 **Working Group on the Financing of High Technology Business** (previously known as the McCullagh Group)

To look at ways of improving the UK's record of investment in research and development. Established November 1997; reported November 1998.

Dr Keith McCullagh (Original Chair) (resigned ; replaced by Dr Peter Williams) • Chief Executive, British Biotech plc (when appointed)		Private business
Dr Peter Williams (Chair)	• Executive Chair, Oxford Instruments Group plc	Private business
Peter Agar	• Deputy Director General, Confederation of British Industry	Trade association
Sir David Cooksey	• Chair, Advent Ltd	Private business
Dr Herman Hauser	• Director, Amadeus Capital Partners Ltd	Private business
Dr Derek Higgs	• Chief Executive, Prudential Portfolio Managers	Private business
Dr Alistair Keddie	• Director, Innovation Unit, Department of Trade and Industry	Central government
Geoff Lindey	• Head of UK Institutional Investment, JP Morgan	Private business
Peter Meinertzhagen	• Chair, ABN Abro Hoare Govett	Private business
Craig Pickering	• Head of Industry Team, Treasury	Central government
David Quysner	• Managing Director, Abingworth Management Ltd	Private business

Richard Regan	• Head of Investment Affairs, Association of British Insurers	Trade association
Mike Smith	• Head of Business Finance Division, Bank of England	National public body
Christine Soden	• Finance Director, Chiroscience plc	Private business
Hugh Stevenson	• Chairman, Mercury Asset Management	Private business

9 Private Finance Initiative Task Force

To advance the PFI and public/private Partnerships. Draft plans published for comment October 1998; consultation paper issued January 1999. A 'second review' of the PFI was established in November 1998 and reported internally in March 1999. By mid-1999 this Task Force had become a two-part executive unit under Adrian Montague as Chief Executive: the Policy Team (of Treasury officials) and the Projects Team (of private business secondees) responsible for promoting individual PFI deals, supported by a Projects Review Group, and with some one dozen Departments' PFI potential divided among them. £4.8B of PFI projects (at July 1999) was planned to become £12B during the current Parliament.

| Adrian Montague (Chief Executive) | • Former Co-Head, Global Projects Finance, Dresdner Kleinwort Benson Bank | Private business |

Policy Team

Tim Wilson (Head of Team	• HM Treasury	Central government
Ken Brazier	• HM Treasury	Central government
Alastair Campbell	• HM Treasury	Central government
Robin Morgan	• HM Treasury	Central government
Jackie Sear	• HM Treasury	Central government

Projects Team

Adrian Montague	• Former Co-Head, Global Projects Finance, Dresdner Kleinwort Benson Bank	Private business
Martin Buck	• Project Manager, formerly Nicholls Associates	Private business
Andrew Carty	•	Private business
Kate Cohen	• Management consultant • Former Assistant Director, Office of Passenger Rail Franchising	Private business
Helen Dell	• Economic consultant • Former World Bank and EU Commission	Private business
David Goldstone	• Chartered public sector accountant • Formerly Pricewaterhouse Coopers	Private business
David Lee Private business	• Project finance lawyer •	Formerly Allen and Overy
Fred Maroudas	• Project finance banker • Formerly Dresdner Kleinwort Benson	Private business
Richard Powell	• Facilities management specialist • Formerly Johnson Controls	Private business
Douglas Sutherland	• Owner/director, InterResource Ltd (software company)	Private business
Lindsay Watson	•	Private business
Kathryn Lewis (Task Force Secretary) (Projects Review Group Secretary)	•	Private business

10 Review of Private Finance Machinery

To consider the need for and appropriate role of a new public/private Private Finance Task Force; the roles and effectiveness of the Private Finance Panel and its Executive. Established May 1997; reported June 1997.

| Malcolm Bates (Reviewer) | • Chair, Pearl Group plc
• Chair, Premier Farnell plc
• Chair, Business in the Arts | Private business |

11 Smaller Quoted Companies Working Group

To consider problems of capital formation and taxation. Established August 1998; reported November 1998.

Derek Riches (Chair)	• Managing Director, Merrill Lynch Broker Services	Private business
Brian Basham	• Chair, Equity Development Ltd	Private business
Andrew Baker	• Partner, Wedlake Bell	Private business
Jamie Borwick	• Chief Executive, Manganese Bronze plc	Private business
William Dalton	• Chief Executive, Midland Bank plc	Private business
Clifford Hardcastle	• Chair, Denistron International plc	Private business
Christopher Higson	• London Business School	Academic/research

Richard Kilsby	• Executive Director, London Stock Exchange (when appointed)	Private business
George Metcalfe	• Chair, UMECO plc	Private business
Katie Morris	• Chief Executive, CISCO	Trade association
Edwin Moses	• Chief Executive, Oxford Asymmetry International	Private business
Craig Pickering	• Head of Industry Team, HM Treasury	Central government

12 Review of Tax and Benefits

To recommend the streamlining and modernisation of the tax and benefit systems so as to promote work incentives, reduce poverty and welfare dependency and strengthen community and family life.

Martin Taylor (Lead)	• Chief Executive, Barclays Bank (until 1999) • Chief Executive and Chair, Courtaulds Textiles plc	Private business

other members from HM Treasury, DfEE, DSS & Inland Revenue.

WELSH OFFICE (WO)

Name	Affiliation	Classification

1 All Wales Agri-Environment Scheme Working Group

To advise the Secretary of State on the technical details of a new Welsh Agri-environment scheme.

R. Nowell-Phillips	• Farmers Union of Wales	Trade association
J. Salmon	• Country Landowners Association	Trade association
M. Thomas	• National Farmers Union of Wales	Trade association
N. Thomas	• Royal Society for the Protection of Birds	Voluntary/charity

2 Education and Training Action Group

To help improve school performance to ensure all pupils reach satisfactory standards by the end of compulsory education.

Peter Hain MP (Chair)	• Parliamentary Under Secretary of State, Welsh Office	Central government
Brian Connolly	• Director, Gwent Training and Enterprise Council • Divisional Officer, ISTC	Local public spending body
Sandra Davies	• Head, Ogmore School • Former member, National Council for Educational Technology	Education
Cllr Jeff Jones	• Leader, Bridgend County Borough Council • Education spokesperson, Welsh Local Government Association	Local government
Trefor Jones	• Chief Executive, Pilkington Optronics • Board member, Welsh Development Agency • Vice Chair, CELTEC	Private business
Caroline Lewis	• Vice Principal, Cleg Menai • Member, Qualifications, Curriculum and Assessment Authority for Wales	Education
Dr John Llewellyn	• Chair, Careers Services Association, Wales • Chief Executive, Careers Company, North West Wales	Trade association
John McDowall	• Director, British Steel plc • Member, National Advisory Committee on Education and Training Targets	Privatised business
Dr Brynley Roberts	• Former Chief Executive/Librarian, National Library of Wales • Member, Higher Education Funding Council for Wales	Independent
Anne Robertson	• Former Assistant Director (Education and Training) CBI Wales • Chair of Governors Ysgol Gyfun Rhydfelin	Independent
John Stephenson	• Principal, Coleg Powys • Vice Chair, FFORWM	Education
Mary Thorley	• Head, Johnstown Primary School • Chair, Wales Primary School Association	Education
Dick Webster	• Director, Mid-Cast Engineering • Chair, Further Education Funding Council for Wales	Private business
Professor Adrian Webb	• Vice Chancellor, University of Glamorgan • Member, National Committee of Inquiry into Higher Education (Dearing Committee)	Education
Gwenda Williams	• Group Human Resources Manager, Hyder plc • Chair, Chwarae Teg • Member, Steering Group, Opportunity 2000	Private business

3 Review of Health Promotion Arrangements in Wales Steering Group

Dr Jean Blamire (Chair)	• Head of Public Health Division, Welsh Office	Central government

Lesley Chang-Kee	• Welsh Office	Central government
Dr William Clee	• Chair, Welsh Advisory Committee on Drug and Alcohol Misuse	National public body
Dr Edward Coyle	• Director of Public Health, Gwent Health Authority	Local public spending body
Jane Davidson	• Head of Social Affairs, Welsh Local Government Association	Local government
Tom Davies	• Director of Education, Cardiff County Council	Local government
Hugh Gardiner	• Director of Social Services, City and County of Swansea	Local government
Phillip Johnson	• Nursing Division, Welsh Office	Central government
Brian Lennox-Smith	• Vice-Chair, Association of Community Health Councils	Health
David Middleton	• Director, FPA Cymru (representing The Wales Council for Voluntary Action)	Voluntary/charity
Dr Geoffrey Morgan	• General Practitioner, Cardiff	Health
Graham Muir	• Personnel Manager, Hyder Industrial Ltd	Private business
Karin Phillips	• Social Services Policy Division, Welsh Office	Central government
Michael Ponton	• Chief Executive, Health Promotion Authority for Wales	National public body
Dr Glynne Roberts	• Health Promotion Manager, Gwynedd Community Health NHS Trust	Local public spending body
David Seal	• Director of Housing & Regulatory services, Pembrokeshire County Council	Local government
Richard Thomas	• Chief Executive, Morriston Hospital NHS Trust	Local public spending body
Dr Paul Tromans	• Health Professionals Group, Welsh Office	Central government

4   National Assembly Advisory Group

To assist the Secretary of State in the preparation of guidance to the Standing Orders Commission, to consider the Assembly's committee structure, conduct of members; conduct of business etc.

John Elfed Jones (Chair)	• Chair, International Greetings plc • Former Chair, Welsh Language Board • Former Chair, Welsh Water	Private business
Professor Nick Bourne	• Leader, 'Just Say No' campaign • Former Dean of Law, University of Swansea • Assistant Principal, Swansea Institute of Higher Education	Voluntary/charity
Ioan Bowen Rees	• President, Wales Association of Community and Town Councils • Former Chief Executive, Gwynedd County Council	Local government
Marjorie Dykins	• Chair, Wales Council for Voluntary Action • Chair, Wrexham Early Years Forum	Voluntary/charity
Ken Hopkins	• National Institute of Adult Continuing Education • Former chair, Labour Party Policy Commission which drew up Labour Party's proposals for a Welsh Assembly • Former Director of Education, Mid Glamorgan County Council	Education
Mari James	• Centre for Advanced Studies, University of Wales, Cardiff • Vice chair, 'Yes for Wales' campaign	Academic/research
Helen Mary Jones	• Equal Opportunities Commission	National public body
Howard Marshall	• Senior Regional Officer, (North Wales) Unison	Trade union
Eluned Morgan MEP	• MEP (Labour) for Mid and West Wales	Independent
Joyce Redfearn	• Chief Executive, Monmouthshire County Council	Local government
Colwyn Philipps, Viscount St Davids	• Former Conservative Government Whip and Spokesman on Welsh Affairs • Member, Milford Haven Port Authority • Governor, Welsh College of Music and Drama	Independent
Ray Singh	• Member, Commission for Racial Equality • Member, Welsh Advisory Committee on Drugs and Alcohol Misuse • Member, Bar Council Race Relations Council	National public body
Ian Spatling	• Vice Chair, CBI Wales • Chief Executive, Wolff Steel • Chair, Swansea Bay Partnership • Non Executive Director, West Wales Training and Enterprise Council	Trade association
Kirsty Williams	• Vice President, Welsh Liberal Democrats	

5   NHS Wales Trust Reconfiguration Steering Group

To improve the quality of hospital and community health care in Wales through the establishment of a more effective and efficient structure of NHS Trusts.

Peter Gregory (Chair)	• Director, Health Department, Welsh Office	Central government

Peter Bryant	• Wales Council for Voluntary Action	Voluntary/charity
Marion Bull	• Chief Nursing Officer, Welsh Office	Central government
John Button	• Chair, NHS Trust	Local public spending body
Dr Tony Calland	• General Medical Steering Committee (Wales) (British Medical Association)	Professional association
Prof. Ian Cameron	• University of Wales College of Medicine	Academic/research
Jane Davidson	• Welsh Local Government Association	Local government
Marion Evans	• Director of Patient Care, NHS Health Authority	Local public spending body
Derek Gregory	• TUC Wales	Trade union
Dr Ruth Hall	• Chief Medical Officer, Welsh Office	Central government
Liz Hewett	• Nursing Director, NHS Trust	Local public spending body
Dr Sharon Hopkins	• Director of Public Health, NHS Health Authority	Local public spending body
Bob Hudson	• Institute of Health Services Management	Professional association
Stuart Johnston	• General Dental Steering Committee (Wales) (British Dental Association)	Professional association
Gareth Jones	• Health Department, Welsh Office	Central government
Dr Arthur Kentrick	• Chair, Health Authority Chair	Local public spending body
David Lewis	• Director of Finance, NHS Trust	Local public spending body
Chris Mason	• Joint Consultants Committee of the British Medical Association	Professional association
Cllr. Dewi Pritchard	• Welsh Association of Community Health Councils	Health
Bernadine Rees	• Joint Committee for Nursing, Midwifery and Health Visiting (Wales)	Professional association
Peter Stansbie	• Chief Executive, Health Authority	Local public spending body
Martin Turner	• Trust Executive Advisory Group	Central government
Eifion Williams	• Director of Finance, NHS Health Authority	Local public spending body
Dr Jeff Williams	• Medical Director, NHS Trust	Local public spending body
Cllr David Murray	representing Chairs of Social Services Committees	Local government

6   Wales New Deal Advisory Task Force

To give advice to the Secretary of State on how the New Deal can be developed and implemented to meet the needs and circumstances of Wales; to promote the New Deal, particularly to the business, voluntary and environment sectors; to receive regular reports on progress in implementing the New Deal.

Graham Hawker (original Chair) • Group Chief Executive, Hyder plc		Private business
Paul Loveluck (Chair)	• Chief Executive, Hyder plc • Chief Executive, Countryside Council for Wales	Private business
Graham Benfield	• Director, Wales Council for Voluntary Action	Voluntary/charity
Leighton Carnell	• Corporate Director, Barclays Bank plc	Private business
Spencer Davies	• Managing Director, Spencer Davies Engineering Ltd	Private business
Sheila Drury	• Chief Executive, Kemitron Ltd	Private busines
Dr Haydn Edwards	• Coleg Menai, Bangor	Education
Margaret Evans	• Prince's Trust Volunteers	Voluntary/charity
Gareth George	• Wales Director, Barclays Cymru	Private business
Jane Hutt	• Chwarae Teg	Private business
David Jenkins	• General Secretary, Wales (TUC)	Trade union
Roger Jones	• Managing Director, Penn Pharmaceuticals	Private business
John Newton-Jones	• Farmworld	Private business
Anne Poole	• National Institute of Adult Continuing Education Cymru	Education
Adam Price	• Executive Manager, Menter a Busnes	Private business
Sue Price	• Executive Director, Groundwork Merthyr and Rhondda Cynon Taf	Private business
Gill Richards	• Partner, Atebion	Private business
Cherry Short	• Commission for Racial Equality	National public body
Huw Vaughan Thomas	• Chief Executive, Denbighshire County Council	Local government
The Rev. Kevin Watson	• Churches in Wales Together	Voluntary/charity

Alison Lea Wilson	• Partner, Anglesey Sea Zoo	Private business
Wendy Yates	• Director of Personnel, City and County of Swansea	Local government

7   Welsh Transport Advisory Group
To provide advice on the development and implementation of an integrated & sustainable transport policy for Wales.

Peter Hain MP (Chair)	• Parliamentary Under Secretary of State, Welsh Office	Central government
Brian Bigwood	• Member, Wales Wildlife and Countryside Link • Council for the Protection of Rural Wales	Voluntary/charity
Professor Stuart Cole	• University of North London	Academic/research
Frank Cook	• Regional Director, Freight Transport Association	Trade association
Neil Crumpton	• Friends of the Earth (transport campaigner)	Voluntary/charity
Brian Curtis	• Divisional Officer, TUC Wales • National Union of Rail, Maritime and Transport Workers	Trade union
Howard Davies	• Secretary General, British Air Transport Association	Trade association
Cllr Sue Essex	• Countryside Council for Wales • Planning Department, University of Wales, Cardiff	National public body
Bev Fowles	• Managing Director, Brewers Motor Services	Private business
Simon Halfacree	• Regional Technical Support Officer, Environment Agency	National public body
Ben Hamilton-Baillie	• Regional Manager, Sustrans	Private business
Michael Harper	• Vice Chair, Disability Wales	Voluntary/charity
Charles Hogg	• Chair, Rail Users' Consultative Committee for Wales	National public body
Richard Jarvis	• Welsh Local Government Association • Director of Planning, Flintshire County Council	Local government
James Maggs	• Local Organiser, National Federation of Bus Users	Voluntary/charity
Denys Morgan	• Welsh LGA • Director of Technical Services, Neath Port Talbot Borough Council	Local government
Robert Palmer	• CBI Wales • Managing Director, Economic Packaging Ltd	Trade association
Dr Sian Phipps	• The Pedestrians Association • Co-ordinator, Environment Wales for the Prince's Trust	Voluntary/charity
Jim Sheils	• Account Executive, Railtrack plc	Privatised business
Peter Tudball	• British Chamber of Shipping • Chair, Casu Investment Ltd	Trade association
David Weir	• Association of Train Operating Companies • Managing Director, Wales and West Railways	Trade association
David Worskett	• Director of Public Affairs, Royal Automobile Club	Private business

EXAMPLES OF FURTHER TASK FORCES, ADVISORY GROUPS ETC ESTABLISHED SINCE 1 JANUARY 1999

MINISTRY OF AGRICULTURE, FISHERIES AND FOOD (MAFF)

Food Chain Initiative

Task Force on Livestock Farming

CABINET OFFICE (CO)

Modernising Government Quality Schemes Task Force

DEPARTMENT FOR CULTURE, MEDIA AND SPORT (DCMS)

Steering Group on the Roles of the Proposed Architecture Commission

Design Group to Recommend on the Role of the New National Museums and Libraries Authority

Advisory Group to Consider and Recommend on Public Suggestions for a New Statue in Trafalgar Square, London

DEPARTMENT FOR EDUCATION AND EMPLOYMENT (DFEE)

Post-school Basic Skills Strategy Group (supported by a Technical Supplementation Group)

Independent Review Panel on Recent Mass Closures of Pre-School Playgroups

DEPARTMENT OF ENVIRONMENT, TRANSPORT AND THE REGIONS (DETR)

Commission for Integrated Transport (successor to the Fundamental Review of Transport Policy)

Lord Donaldson's Review of DETR's Proposed Reorganisation of the Maritime and Coastguard Agency's Coastal Stations. This retired senior judge's review was an agreed exercise between DETR and their trade union critics on the issue. His report was accepted in full by DETR in July 1999.

Road Haulage Forum

Forum on the Future of Social Housing

White-Headed Duck Task Force

HOME OFFICE (HO)

Forum on Animal Experiments (Vivisection)

LORD CHANCELLOR'S DEPARTMENT (LCD)

Community Legal Service Quality Task Force

Review of the Crown Office List (Judicial Review Processes)

NORTHERN IRELAND OFFICE (NIO)

Advisory Committee on Communicable Disease Control

Northern Ireland Science Park Foundation

Northern Ireland Skills Task Force

SCOTTISH OFFICE (SO)

Advisory Group on the Review of the Mental Health (Scotland) Act, 1984

DEPARTMENT OF TRADE AND INDUSTRY (DTI)

Kosovo (Reconstruction Contracts) Task Force

Task Force on Manufacturing Industry

WELSH OFFICE (WO)

European Structural Funds Task Force

INTERNAL GOVERNMENT REVIEWS OF POLICY AND ADMINISTRATIVE ISSUES

May 1997 to December 1999

MINISTRY OF AGRICULTURE, FISHERIES AND FOOD (MAFF)

Review of access provisions under the Agri-Environment Schemes

Report expected by end of 1999

Review of the UK legislation controlling the disposal of animal waste

Consultation on legislation following the review expected summer 1998. Consultation on the proposal to restrict disposal by landfill. First stage announced, October 1997; second state now in train, covering rendered and catering waste animal remains.

Review of Common Agricultural Policy payments systems

Announced February 1998. A consultancy of Coopers and Lybrand (now Pricewaterhouse Coopers) by MAFF and the Cabinet Office.

Review of Environmentally Sensitive Areas, Stage IV

Report expected June 1999

Review of the Hill Livestock Compensatory Allowance Scheme

Carried out by Agricultural Economics Unit of the University of Exeter and Drew Associates. Remit to examine the rationale for providing Government support to livestock farmers in the Less Favoured Areas of England; assess the effects of the HLCA Scheme in England against the stated objectives of maintaining the viability of livestock farming in the LFAs, maintaining populations in, and conserving the value of, those areas; to consider whether the Scheme represents value for money. Consultation exercise, 1998-9.

Review of the Milk Development Council

Review required under the Industrial Organization & Development Act 1947. Consultation document issued. Reported 29 October 1997.

Review of Nitrate Sensitive Areas

Report expected April 1999

Review of the rates and structure of aid to farmers under the Organic Aid Scheme

Reported to ministers December 1997 (published 2 April 1998) following consultation.

Official Group on Organophosphates

To review processes for sharing information and achieving co-ordination between Departments; to draw together scientific evidence and identify any gaps to be remedied; to examine those processes by which Ops are licensed, and to advise whether procedures should be changed. Report published 25 June 1998.

Mr Richard Carden (Chair) Head of Food Safety and Environment

Directorate, MAFF. Officials from Dept of Health, DETR, MoD, Scottish, Welsh, N.Ireland Offices, Veterinary Medicines Directorate, the Pesticides Safety Directorate (MAFF executive agencies), the Medicines Control Agency (DH executive agency), the Health and Safety Executive.

Review of raw cows' drinking milk policy

Options being considered following consultation exercises.

Review of the future funding of regulatory arrangements for pesticides

Report due December 1998.

Review of pesticides

To review 24 pesticide compounds; with regard to public safety & environmental protection as part of the Government's regular annual checks on products approved for use. Review results to be considered by the independent Advisory Committee on Pesticides (membership of which is made up medical and environmental expertise claimed to be independent of Government & the agrochemical industry)

Review of arrangements for enforcing the rules on the welfare of animals exported live to the continent

To consider the arrangements for ensuring that animals are rested, fed, watered and cleared as fit prior to export in accordance with the law. Reported 27 September 1997 following consultation.

CABINET OFFICE (CO)

Review of the Code of Practice on Access to Government Information

Conducted by officials. Reported July 1997

Review of the effectiveness of the centre of Government

Announced by the Prime Minister January 1998. Conducted by the Cabinet Secretary (Sir Richard Wilson). Consultation with staff on his report. Changes took effect July 1998.

Review of the Charter Programme

Ministers (David Clark MP and Peter Kilfoyle MP) led this review by officials. Consultation paper published September 1997. Reported 30 July 1998.

Review of the existing Drugs Strategy

Chaired by Keith Halliwell, Anti Drugs Co-ordinator, Central Drugs Co-ordination Unit, Privy Council Office.

Chir recruited from public advert. White Paper 'Tackling Drugs to Build a Better Britain'. A new national strategy, with funding, announced in May 1999.

Review of the Government Information Service

Led by Robin Mountfield (Cabinet Office). Working Group reported November 1997.

Review of ministerial accountability

(incorporated within preparation of the 'Modernising Government' White Paper of 30 March 1999 (Cm4310).

Review of public appointments procedures

Implementing recommendations of the Committee on Standards in Public Life ('Nolan') (incorporated within preparation of the 'Modernising Government' White Paper of 30 March 1999 (Cm4310).

Review of quangos

Officials conducted the review 'with a view to reducing their number' (Prime Minister, 26.6.1997). Consultation Paper: 'Opening Up Quangos'. Reported 29 June 1998. White Paper on Modernising Government, (published 30 March 1999).

Review of the Women's National Commission
(begun in the Department of Social Security)

To examine the objectives, membership and the funding of the WNC in the light of the Government's need to ensure that there is an effective, efficient, independent channel of communication between women's organisations and Government. Reported Autumn 1998. (Transferred from the DSS on the appointment of Baroness Jay (Lord Privy Seal) as Minister for Women in July 1998). Reported January 1999.

DEPARTMENT FOR CULTURE, MEDIA AND SPORT (DCMS)

Review of policy on admission charging by national museums

Established Autumn 1997; consultation document 24 July 1998. Free admission for children announced, March 1999.

Review of arrangements for celebrating the Millennium

Commenced May 1997. Report published June 1997

Review of the National Lottery

Review carried out by officials. Submissions by outside bodies invited. White Paper published 21 June 1997.

MINISTRY OF DEFENCE (MOD)

Review of the arrangements for compensating Service personnel (or their dependants) and for the payment of death and invaliding benefit

To examine the arrangements for paying compensation and pensions for death, injury or illness, which arise as a result of military service. Announced 8 December 1997. Officials from within the MoD and DSS worked together to devise the new compensation arrangements. Publication of the outcome not yet determined.

Strategic Defence Review (joint with the Foreign and Commonwealth Office)

Launched on 28 May 1997 to determine the future direction of British defence policy. A major internal review which attempted expert and public consultation. Reported 8 July 1998

Review of pay deductions from British officer POWs and protected personnel in the European theatre in World War II

This was a further review, following Conservative ministers having reviewed the matter. Both reviews confirmed the existing rules and practice. Reported 24 July 1997.

DEPARTMENT FOR EDUCATION AND EMPLOYMENT (DFEE)

Review of the National Curriculum for the Year 2000

Commissioned from the Qualifications and Curriculum Authority: public consultation now in train.

Review of the qualifications appeal systems

Reported to ministers July 1998.

Review of the threshold exempting employers with fewer than 20 employees from the employment provisions of the Disability Discrimination Act 1995

Announced December 1997. Public consultation (142 responses) included ministers meeting representatives of small employers and the disabled. Liaison with DTI's Small Firms Minister and officials. Reported 12 June 1998. Threshold reduced to 15 on 1 December 1998.

DEPARTMENT OF THE ENVIRONMENT, TRANSPORT AND THE REGIONS (DETR)

(i)   Internal Reviews on Environment issues

(ii) Internal Reviews on Transport issues

(i)   Environment issues

Review of the National Air Quality Strategy

The National Air Quality Strategy was published, March 1997 and was endorsed by the new administration in July 1997. Terms of reference: 'to expand and refine the scientific, economic and technical basis for decision-making on air quality policy; to consider the case for changes to the scope and content of the Strategy and the legal framework for air quality policy; to make recommendations for further policy measures for the improvement of air quality'.

Review of sustainable production and use of chemicals (Formerly the Review of policy on chemicals in the environment)

Consultation document published 27 July 1998

Review of Compulsory Competitive Tendering regulations and guidance

Guidance issued 3 December 1997. Reported on 25 July 1997.

Review of the statutory framework for contaminated land issues

Concluded work, December 1997, contributing to the Comprehensive Spending Review.

Review of energy efficiency aspects of the Building Regulations

Announced February 198, contributing to the UK target on CO_2 levels.

Review of the Environmental Action Fund

Reported to ministers. 22 July 1998

Review of the Environmental Technology Best Practice Programme [joint with DTI].

Review of legislation relating to integration within the Environment Agency and Scottish Environment Protection Agency

Report due in 1999

Review of home buying and selling process (previously known as: 'Review of the conveyancing process') Reports to the Ministerial Task Group on the Home Buying Process)

Pilot: January 1998. Full study Autumn 1998. Report published 1999.

Inter-departmental review of fuel poverty policy including the

Home Energy Efficiency Scheme (formerly the Review of the HEES)

Reported late 1998

Review of local authorities' statutory recycling plans

Review of local government finance

Announced 25 July 1997. To balance between central direction and local discretion. Intended to collaborate with local government through the Central Local Partnership and with business and others with an interest in local government finance.

Review of opencast coal and planning policy

Initial consultation document published July 1997. Further consultation document published October 1998.

Review of planning controls over onshore oil, gas and coalbed methane extraction in England

Review of the need for planning permission to extend gardens

Review of political restrictions on local government officers

Review of the detail of the regulations governing politically restricted local government posts, especially the level and number of officers covered by the rules and the language of the rules.

Became incorporated into the Consultation Paper on *Modernising Local Government: a new Ethical Framework* (published 7 April 1998) and the Local Government White Paper.

Review of the Producer Responsibility Obligations (Packaging Waste) Regulations 1997

(Reported January 1999.)

Review of risk assessment and management within environmental protection policies. [Joint with the Environment Agency]

Reported 1998.

Review of UK sustainable development strategy

Review of Government policy on timber procurement

Consultation on walkers' access to uncultivated open private land in England and Wales ('The right to roam')

A consultation paper of February 1998 required responses by June 1998. Government action to extend access was announced in Spring 1999.

Review of the water charging system and the water abstraction licensing system (with Welsh Office & Office of Water Services)

To ensure a fair and sustainable system of charging for water and sewerage services, covering charges for measured and unmeasured systems and principles underpinning charges, enforcing payment, commercial and industrial customers, debt recovery arrangements.

Review of waste strategy for England and Wales

Final strategy to be published before the end of 1999

Review of standards of modern zoo practice

(ii) Transport issues

Technical audit of the new en-route Air Traffic Control Centre at Swanick

Technical report published November 1998 in response to a critical Select Committee report on Swanick.

Bus review

Announced 25 June 1997. Part of the development of an integrated transport policy. Bus priority measures, traffic restraint, passenger information, ticketing, regulatory measures to improve the quality of bus services, financial issues.

Review of the Pilotage Act 1987

Reported to Ministers 26 March 1998 and published 28 July 1998

Terms of reference: to review the way functions conferred by the Pilotage Act are discharged by competent harbour authorities and to make recommendations to Ministers on their response to that report and generally. DETR's Ports Division led the review, working with the Marine Safety Agency, the 3 port associations (BPA, UKMPG and UKIPA), the UK Harbour Masters' Association, the Chamber of Shipping, the Nautical Institute, NUMAST, T&GWU and the UK Pilots Association.

Review of railway safety standards arrangements

Comprehensive roads review

Announced 19 June 1997. To determine the role roads should play in an integrated transport policy and to establish a forward investment programme for the trunk road network. Wide consultation.

Review of road safety strategy and targets

Review of the safety regulation of London's minicabs

Review of speed policy

Launched in October 1998 in the context of integrated transport and road safety policies. Consultation of 'informed opinion' will precede publication in Autumn 1999.

Review of door to door transport for disabled Londoners

To identify options for improving the quality of service possibly within the framework of the Greater London Authority. Review contractor: Cranfield University.

Review of arrangements for transport safety

Review of Trust Ports

Report 8 August 1997. Second report, August 1998

Review of Vehicle Excise Duty for Lorries

Initial report expected Autumn 1999.

Review of voluntary transport provision

Announced 17 July 1997; covered the scale and scope of voluntary sector transport provision in rural and urban areas. Also contributed towards an integrated transport policy. Contractor: Steer Davies Gleave.

FOREIGN AND COMMONWEALTH OFFICE (FCO)

Review of the criteria used in considering licence applications for the export of conventional arms

To ensure that the risk of defence equipment exported and used for internal repression is fully taken into account, alongside all other relevant factors, in the assessment of all licence applications for the export of conventional arms. This review was taken forward by officials from the FCO, MoD, DTI, DFID, Customs and Excise and HM Treasury. Reported 28 July 1997. One outcome is an annual report on licenses granted, although the first (for May-December 1997) did not appear until March, 1999.

Review of policy towards the remaining UK Overseas Territories

Reported Autumn 1998: White Paper. FCO officials, with a minister in the chair.

Consultation: with governments, with Opposition leaders, with the Governors and with other bodies (eg environmental groups) on related topics.

DEPARTMENT OF HEALTH

Childrens Safeguards Review: Ministerial Task Force on the Government's response to the Utting Report (on children in care)

Established November 1997; Government policy statement September 1998, following this review across eleven of the seventeen ministerial Departments. A nationally controlled foster care service will be one outcome.

Review of general anaesthesia and sedation with dental treatment

Review of the NHS cash distribution system

Announced 10 November 1998. A wide ranging review of the formula used to make cash allocations to Health authorities and Primary Care Groups.

Review of proposed NHS Private Finance Initiative schemes

The ongoing review took account of Malcolm Bates' review of PFI at large for HM Treasury of May-June 1997.

Review of the suspensions procedures for doctors

Announced 27 October 1998.

Review of the wheelchair voucher scheme and the provision of electrical and indoor wheelchairs

Announced 30 June 1998. Included a survey of all health authorities to obtain details of the implementation of their voucher schemes and to estimate numbers of disabled people taking them up. Due to be completed 'Spring 1999'.

HOME OFFICE (HO)

Ministerial Group on Alcopops

To consider what measures are needed to prevent or inhibit the promotion of alcoholic carbonates and other alcoholic drinks in ways likely to attract young people under 18; the sale or supply of such drinks to them; and the public order consequences of obtaining them. These measures should embrace self-regulation by the industry, possible administrative & legislative action by Govt and monitoring the results. Chair & members: ministers. Home Office officials acted as assessors. Green Paper published. Series of consultation meetings with interest groups, July 1997: statement by Ministerial Group on Alcopops outlining immediate actions and further work planned. Considerable cooperation by industry groups was reported.

Measures to deal with anti-social behaviour

Outcomes were considered for the Crime and Disorder Bill. Consultation paper issued September 1997.

Review of the law relating to bribery and corruption

Chaired by Stephen Silber QC (member of the Law Commission). Members are 17 Home Office and other officials and outside persons.

Review of community safety

Contributing to the Crime and Disorder Bill.

Review to consider permanent UK-wide counter terrorism legislation (joint with the Northern Ireland Office)

Consultation document 1998. Lord Lloyd had conducted an independent review for the Conservative government of proposals to replace the current Acts with permanent UK-wide counter terrorism legislation.

Review of delay in the criminal justice system

Consultation exercise on report, 1997.

Ad hoc ministerial group on the family

To examine the effectiveness & coherence of existing policies in supporting families. Chair: Jack Straw, Home Sec. Members: Alun Michael (later replaced) (Home Office); Solicitor General; Dawn Primarolo (Treasury); Paul Boateng (Health); Alan Howarth (DfEE); Barbara Roche (later replaced) (DTI); Geoff Hoon (Lord Chancellor's Department);

Nick Raynsford (DETR). Consultation: Ministerial seminar, on 'Promoting successful parenting' involving outside experts, November 1997. No distinct reports produced. Consultation paper 'Supporting

Families', November 1998 and public responses. A national research institute on families' needs was announced in May 1999.

Review of financial regulation and legislation in Jersey, Guernsey and the Isle of Man

Announced January 1998. Andrew Edwards (chair) with officials and the financial authorities in the islands.

Review of the Fire Precautions (Workplace) Regulations 1997

To address concerns over the UK's implementation of the general fire safety provisions of the European Framework Directive.

Consultation document published, August 1998, for replies by November 1998.

Review of the regulation of the football pools industry

This entailed Government proposals, under its Deregulation Initiative, to permit purchases at 16 years and broadcast advertising. No consultation paper but public views were requested.

Review of immigration and asylum appeals

Interdepartmental review between the Home Office and the Lord Chancellor's Department produced a consultation paper on 13 July 1998.

Review of immigration detention policy

Review of UK's position under various international human rights instruments

Announced 3 July 1997. Home Office led. No formal membership, principally conducted in inter-departmental correspondence. Consultation: no Green Paper etc published; some NGOs have submitted papers. To review the UK's position under various international human rights instruments including the question of accession to the ECHR, and the International Covenant on Civil and Political Rights, and acceptance of the rights of individual petition under other UN human rights treaties and whether any of the UK's reservation to human rights treaties can be withdrawn.

Review of the liquor licensing laws

Announced 5 May 1998. To review all aspects of the process, various types and substance of liquor licensing laws and their enforcement, 'recognising a need for better regulation to allow leisure and tourism industries to develop in a way that reflects today's society'. Proposals for change will be offered for a 'full public consultation'. Process will continue into 2000.

Strategic review of national police training

(Reported October 1998). An advisory group of police authority and officer representatives was appointed (see the list of external groups, above).

Review on the interdepartmental working group on preventing unsuitable people from working with children

Review of the future role and funding of local civil protection in England and Wales

Working document 'The Future Role and Funding of Local Civil Protection in England and Wales' published November 1997. Reported February 1998 (submitted to ministers January 1998). Outcomes announced in the Chancellor of the Exchequer's statement 14 July 1998.

Extensive consultation with all local authorities in England and Wales, professional emergency planning organisations and representative bodies (LGA, SOLACE, ACPO, CACFOA) – 287 questionnaire replies and 205 written responses received.

Ministers, Home Office and other officials and outside persons were involved.

Prisons-probation review

To identify and assess options for closer and more integrated work between the Prison Service and the Probation Service of England & Wales.

Paid outside consultants used. Consultation Paper. Final report issued internally April 98. The Association of Chief Officers of Probation provided an external adviser (Jenny Roberts).

Review of Prison Service drugs strategy

Chair and members: Home Office officials. Paid outside assessors/ consultants also used. Consultation at conferences and by post. Reported March 1998, public report 12 May 1998. Subsumed into the Review of the long term future of prison health care.

Review of Prison Service investigation strategy

No terms of reference – it developed from an operational need to review all serious incidents, complaints from prisoners and the public and discipline cases. Chair & members: Home Office officials. A draft Prison Service Order was circulated to the trade unions and senior managers. Reported Autumn 1998. New procedure to be implemented in 1999, under a Prison Service Order.

Review of the Prison Service Quantum Project

Set up August 1998. Reported 1999. Technical exercise to enable the Prison Service to meet its business objectives through more efficient use of IT.

Review of the operation of release of prisoners on Temporary Licence

To review the arrangements for release on temporary licence. Home Office officials as Chair and members. Consultation with prison governors, and other interested agencies such as the Probation Service (no public consultation). More than one report. Reported to ministers in June. Outcome announced 22 July 1998. (Speech to the Prison Reform Trust).

Review of secure accommodation for young offenders and other young persons

Announced November 1997 following the Chief Inspector of Prisons' published report, 'Thematic Review of Young Prisoners'.

Review of sex offences

Led to the new Sex Offender Orders in the Crime and Disorder Act, 1998. A further 'review of the law on sex offenders' was begun in early 1999.

Review of possibly reviewable prison sentences for sex-offenders

Review of the control of unscrupulous immigration advisors (joint with the Lord Chancellor's Department)

This was a manifesto commitment so the consultation exercise was not strictly speaking part of a normal review. Membership: ministers and officials. Consultation paper published 22 January 1998. Reported 1998.

Review of the venue for trial in either-way offences

A consultation paper of July 1998 offered options for changing defendants' current right to elect for jury trial (following the Narey Review of Delay in the Criminal Justice System) and requested responses by September 1998.

Ministerial task force on relations between Government and the voluntary, volunteering and community sectors

To oversee and monitor the implementation of the 'Compact' between the Government and the voluntary sectors.

Review of vulnerable or intimidated witnesses (joint with the Lord Chancellor's Department)

To identify measures at all stages of the criminal justice process which will improve the treatment of vulnerable witnesses including those likely to be subject to intimidation. An officials' steering group was joined by three external members (from the police (ACPO) Local Government Association and Victim Support). Reported internally June 1998.

Review of Government proposals for youth justice

To set out for consultation the Government's proposals for reform of the youth justice system in England and Wales. Outcomes were implemented in the Crime and Disorder Bill. Part of the White Paper 'No More Excuses – A new approach to tackling youth crime in England and Wales' (Nov 1997).

DEPARTMENT FOR INTERNATIONAL DEVELOPMENT (DFID)

Review of DIFD's relationships with civil society organisations including NGOs

Widespread consultation on paper published Summer 1998.

Review of international development policy

Report published 5 November 1997. White Paper *Eliminating World Poverty: a challenge for the 21st century*. No specific group membership. Widespread consultation during June-Sept 1997.

LORD CHANCELLOR'S DEPARTMENT (LCD)

Review of enforcement of civil court judgments

To address public concern about the effectiveness of the present arrangements in enabling plaintiffs to enforce civil court judgments. Several consultation papers were published from May 1998 for responses by 1 September 1999. The review consulted experts in the field such as solicitors and barristers.

Review of civil court procedures

(i)   A working paper (Judicial Case Management) of July 1997 proposed twin tracks for case management, and reviewed certain other reforms arising from the Woolf Review – for responses by September 1997.

(ii)   A consultation paper of June 1998 summarised options on pre-trial and trial costs and their control – for responses by August.

Review of pre-trial procedures in serious fraud cases

The review (announced in May 1998) has assessed current compliance with existing rules and considered changes. No consultation paper offered.

Review of procedures consequent on the decision to transfer or commit fraud trials

To evaluate the existing procedures which follow a decision to commit or transfer for trial in serious fraud cases. Reported to ministers, October 1998.

A review of specialist jurisdictions of the High Court

Procedures covering allocation of work to Chancery, Commercial, Patents and Official Referees' courts to be reviewed. No consultation paper.

Study and evaluation of current tax appeals systems

To consider the current tax appeals system, taking account of the current and necessary structures & organization of the VAT & Duties Tribunals & the General & Special Commissioners of Income Tax, in the light of the changing role of the tribunals, and developments in administrative justice and tribunals generally. Reported to ministers September 1998

NORTHERN IRELAND OFFICE (NIO)

Criminal injuries compensation review

Northern Ireland drugs strategy review

Announced 24 March 1998. Undertaken by the Central Co-ordinating Group for Action Against Drugs, an interdepartmental group, in association with the NI Drugs Campaign.

Implementation of the EU Directive on the Internal Market in Electricity

Review of the industrial development support services: Northern Ireland

Reported March 1998

Review of information services in the Northern Ireland Office

Many Departments conducted such a review within the context of the Cabinet Office's overall review of the Government Information Service.

Review of street trading in Northern Ireland

Announced 2 September 1998. The consultation paper contained 'many new proposals' for a field still relying on an Act of 1929.

Review of training centres and further education colleges in Northern Ireland

Joint with DfEE and the Training & Employment Agency. To examine the demand and provision for vocational education and training in the further education system and Training and Employment Agency training centres. Reported to ministers May 1998. Report and consultation paper published.

Review of Northern Ireland Transport Holding Company

NITHC is a public corporation established under the Transport Act (NI) 1967. To review the structure for delivering public transport services; consultants commissioned (PricewaterhouseCoopers).

Review of Trust Ports in Northern Ireland

Announced to Parliament 12 May 1998. An extension of the GB Review of Trust Ports with special reference to NI. Comments were invited by public advertisement. Outside consultants were part of the review process. To review the role and status of Trust Ports in Northern Ireland, with particular reference to their strategic importance to the Northern Ireland economy.

Review of the 1993 strategy for the support of the voluntary sector and for community development in Northern Ireland

Announced 20 June 1997.

SCOTTISH OFFICE (SO)

Review of Community Disposals and the use of custody for women offenders in Scotland

Reported to ministers in April 1998 (*A Safer Way*). Results announced May 1998

Review of community education

Reported 1998

Review of the law and practice of compulsory purchase and land compensation

Reported on phase 1 Spring 1999

Review of countryside access legislation in Scotland

Reported winter 1998

Review of domestic violence by Scottish Partnership

Interim report in April 1999

Comprehensive review of the food related scientific services in Scotland

Reported 1998

Review of Gaelic broadcasting

Conducted by an individual academic consultant. Reported to ministers in June 1998, published for consultation June 1998.

National review of health resource allocation

Report expected June 1999.

HIV health promotion review group

Report expected Spring 1999.

Review of the system of land ownership and management in Scotland

Extensive public consultation on the Scottish Office's discussion document.

Learning disability review

Review to identify areas of Scotland appropriate for designation as National Parks

Reported to ministers in November 1997 and to Parliament on 16 December 1997

Review of opencast coal planning policy in Scotland

To follow up the plan for opencasting, published in April 1997. Reported 1998, following consultation.

Review of the public health function

Report expected during 1999.

Review of public health legislation

Report expected Summer 1999.

Review of the Scottish roads programme

Reported winter 1998-99

Review of the rural water and sewerage grant scheme

Reported 1998

Review of the School Placing Request system in Scotland

Reported 1998

Review of the Scottish Awards Agency for Scotland

Announcement to Parliament 12 May 1998

Scottish Enterprise strategy review

Scottish Enterprise, in consultation with the Scottish Office, to examine their objectives with a view to improving the effectiveness, responsiveness and accountability of the enterprise network in Scotland. Reported to ministers.

Review of Scottish Homes support for owner occupation

Reported to ministers in December 1997: Results announced in July 1998

Review of Scottish Homes support for rented housing

Reported to ministers in March 1998: Results announced in July 1998

Review of arrangements for the supervision of sex offenders in Scotland

Announced on 16 December 1997

Review of Sites of Special Scientific Interest (SSSIs) in Scotland

Review of Skye Bridge tolls

Outcome announced by the Secretary of State on 4 July 1998.

Review of transport policy in Scotland

To enable decisions to be taken on the future roads programme which complement the Government's overall approach on transport policy. White Paper published 22 July 1998.

Scottish interdepartmental review of the treatment of vulnerable and intimidated witnesses

Reported 1998

Review of the Scottish water industry

To consider the steps to be taken to strengthen local democratic control of the three Scottish water authorities. A Steering group of SO officials included one external member (a director of Standard Life Assurance). Reported to ministers in November 1997, published 16 December 1997.

DEPARTMENT OF SOCIAL SECURITY (DSS)

Review of benefit fraud and error

Green Paper published 13 July 1998.

Review of Child Support

Green Paper published 6 July 1998 for comments by 30 November 1998. A simpler parental support policy and other changes were announced in Spring 1999.

Housing Benefit simplication and improvement project

Review of pensions

Announced July 1997. Consultation documents published November 1997 and December 1998. Two independent groups on pensions provision and education fed into it. Nearly 600 responses to the 1998 consultation. Government announcement on the new stakeholder pension, April 1999 and a consultation paper (Stakeholder Pensions: Minimum Standards – the Government Proposals) was published in June, with more papers promised. A further policy review was announced in July 1999 following criticism from Labour MPs and party members.

Review of the major components of the social security system

A continuing exercise: no timetable or reports. A further policy review was announced in July 1999 following criticism from Labour MPs and party members.

DEPARTMENT OF TRADE AND INDUSTRY (DTI)

Review of the Assisted Areas map

Consultation paper issued July 1998.

Review of the framework for overseeing developments in biotechnology (joint with Cabinet Office and the Office of Science and Technology)

Announced 17 December 1998. To look at the range of committees established to provide the Government with expert advice.

Review of clean coal technology

Review undertaken by officials in consultation with the industry and university researchers. Reported 8 October 1998.

Review of company rescue mechanisms (joint with HM Treasury)

Interdepartmental task force on competitiveness in Europe

To advise on the implementation of the Government's manifesto objectives to complete the Single Market and promote flexible labour markets across the EU. Reported to ministers 6 April 1998

Chair: Lord Simon (Minister for Trade and Competitiveness in Europe) DTI.

Members: Ministers and officials from DTI, FCO, DfEE, MAFF, Treasury, MoD, Home Office, Scottish Office, Cabinet Office, DETR.

Review on Government consents for power stations

Announced December 1997. Review of how security of supply issues, including fuel diversity, should be taken into account when the Government is considering applications for consent for power station developments.

Review of new and renewable energy

To examine the status and prospects for renewables including examination of what would be necessary and practical to achieve 10% (from 2% now) electricity from renewables by 2010 and what contribution renewables could make to reducing greenhouse gas emissions.

Consultation document, early 1999.

Review of energy sources for power regeneration

To look at the medium and longer term scenarios for the development of generating capacity and sources of fuel supply for generation, and consider the implications of high levels of dependence on any particular fuel, source of supply, transport route or technology.

Public consultation from December 1997 to 16 February 1998.

Preliminary conclusions published on 25 June 1998. Further consultation on specific proposals between 25 June and 20 July. Conclusions set out in October 1998 White Paper

Audit of the Foresight Programme

Audit initiated by the President of the Board of Trade in a letter to the Deputy Prime Minister, May 1997. To review progress reports from the Whitehall Foresight Group and consider other issues relating to the development and presentation of Foresight as and when necessary. Chair: John Battle MP (DTI minister). Members: officials from HM Treasury, DETR, DfEE, Department of Health, Northern Ireland Office, Scottish Office, Welsh Office. Reported to Ministers 22 October 1997.

Franco-British taskforce to tackle jobs and growth

To examine and compare UK and French policies with regard to taxation policy, access to capital, regulatory structures and development of jobs in new enterprises

Review of the effect of insolvency law on enterprise

Report published in June 1999 suggesting variable sanctions or impediments on bankrupts.

Review of metrication

Review of the Code of Practice on Newspaper Supply

To review the terms for supplying new retailers of newspapers. Reported September 1997. No alterations to the code were suggested.

Review of the Post Office

Announced May 1997. To review options for implementing the Government's election manifesto pledge to grant the Post Office greater commercial freedom to make the most of new opportunities.

Consultation with Post Office senior management, Post Office unions, the Post Office Users' National Council and other major users' groups, and other interested parties. Outcome of review announced to Parliament on 7 December 1998.

Review of purchasers in good faith of goods from someone other than the true owner

No consultation paper issued.

Review of the Small Firms Loan Guarantee Scheme

Intended to promote more applications from smaller technology-based firms.

Review of strategic export controls

Consultation from July-September 1998. Publication of White Paper.

Review of the Technical Help for Exporters Scheme

Review of UK weights and measures

Review of utilities regulation

Led by DTI, but reported to an inter-departmental ministerial committee. To consider whether changes are required to the system of regulation of the utility industries in order to ensure open and predictable regulation, whilst providing sufficient incentives to managers to innovate, raise standards and improve efficiency. Green Paper, 'A Fair Deal for Consumers' published March 1998. Reported 27 July 1998.

HM TREASURY

Review of aggregates tax

Report date was for some time under review. A consultation paper was published, June 1998.

Review of the general Anti-Avoidance Rule

A consultation paper was issued in October 1998.

Review of average earnings figures

Established October 1998; reported March 1999.

Review of the Bank of England's financial arrangements

The Bank's finances have been reviewed to ensure that they are in line with the Bank's new responsibilities and best practice of transparency and accountability.

Review of Capital Gains Taxation of companies

Announced in 17 March 1998 Budget. To consult industry widely on the reform of capital gains tax. No formal terms of reference. A further review includes a Working Group with representative bodies.

Review of charities' taxation

To explore the options for a simpler, more coherent system of tax reliefs which is better suited to the way charities work today and to inform the Government's negotiating position in the forthcoming EC review of VAT social reliefs. Charities, umbrella bodies, accountants, small businesses, etc., were asked to send initial views by 1 Dec 1997 which were worked into the consultation paper. These parties were invited to comment again once the Charities' Taxation Review consultation document was published in March 1999. Steering group members: officials from the Inland Revenue, Treasury, Home Office, Charity Commission, DETR & Cabinet Office.

Review of government civil procurement

Established December 1998; reported April 1999.

Review of company car taxation

Review announced and views invited March 1999. Terms of reference have altered since March 1998 as a result of the consultation process and the Government is now concentrating efforts on considering how the regime might be altered to send better environmental signals. No formal review body. The review is being taken forward by the Personal Tax Division of the Inland Revenue in conjunction with Treasury officials. No reports published. The outcome of this continuing review may depend upon further public consultation (informally or via a written consultation document).

Comprehensive Spending Review (all Departments: Treasury-led)

To ensure that public spending decisions reflect the Government's long-term priorities and meet the country's long-term needs. The conclusions will inform public spending plans for the rest of this Parliament. Established May 1997. Reported 14 July 1998. (Some 24 main departmental and six interdepartmental reviews were conducted by the Treasury and Departments also consulted outside bodies.

Review of company double tax relief

A review of the functioning and fairness of the existing system, while having regard to the overall cost of the relief. Report date under review. A consultative document discussed the purpose of double taxation relief; international comparisons and the credit and the exemption methods of relieving double taxation. Since March 1998 consultation has taken place with business representatives.

Review of employee share ownership

A consultation paper issued December 1998 and technical notes in March 1999.

Review on the revenue effect of a reduced rate of VAT for energy efficient materials and alternative options for targeted relief to help those on low incomes to save energy

Section 111 of the Finance Act 1997 commits the Treasury to report by March 1998 on the consequences to the Exchequer of a reduced rate of VAT for energy-saving materials. This review broadens the scope of that study so that it also looked at the best way of giving help where it is needed. Established July 1997. Report published November 1997. Discussions held with representative bodies.

Review of graduated Vehicle Excise Duty for cars

Consultation document issued 16 June 1998.

Review of Landfill Tax

Announced in the July 1997 budget. To review the operation and level of the landfill tax. Review carried out by Customs and Excise in close consultation with other Government departments with an interest in waste policy. Representations were sought from the waste management industry, waste producers, local authorities, environmental groups and other interested parties. 530 representations received. Report published Budget day, 18 March 1998.

Review of leakage and avoidance of direct taxes

To identify situations in which significant amounts of tax are, or are at risk of, leaking from the Exchequer and to consider how the Inland Revenue approaches the defeat and deterrence of tax avoidance schemes. An outcome of the rolling review is expected to be proposed for legislation to counter tax leakage in future Finance Bills. Rolling review (initial results announced in 17 March 1998 Budget statement) – work is ongoing.

Review of the North Sea fiscal regime

To ensure that an appropriate share of North Sea profits are being taxed while continuing to maintain a high level of oil industry interest in the future development of the UK's oil and gas reserves. The outcome (in September 1998) was to maintain the status quo in view of low oil prices.

Review of management recruitment incentives for high tech small and medium enterprises

Established March 1998; reported March 1999: a technical note was published.

Review of research and development (joint with the DTI)

Consultation document published 17 March 1998; initial report published January 1999; no set report date – ongoing consultation

Review of public/private partnership options for the Royal Mint

All major stakeholders were invited to contribute. Reported 1998. The decision to grant greater commercial freedom within public ownership was announced in July 1999.

Review of VAT group treatment

Consultation paper issued 9 June 1998, followed by meetings with business interests.

Review of VAT registration limits

Consultation paper issued 10 July 1998, followed by a meeting with business interests.

Review of the Venture Capital Trust scheme and Enterprise Investment scheme

To take views from interested parties on the exclusion of arrangements where a substantial part of the return to investors is guaranteed, or which are backed by property, from the Venture Capital Trust scheme and Enterprise Investment scheme. A number of representative bodies and companies were consulted, principally the British Venture Capital Association and the Enterprise Investment and Business Expansion Scheme Association. Results announced in Budget statement 17 March 1998.

WELSH OFFICE

Welsh childcare strategy working group

To review existing resources in the Welsh Office linked to childcare and to identify a scheme to promote the provision of childcare services.

Review of economic regeneration in Wales

To establish the priorities for developing a more productive, high quality, high value, competitive world class economy.

Proposals for modernising local government

To examine and consult on options for modernising local government in Wales. Reported 31 July 1998

Review of the National Curriculum in Wales

To advise the Secretary of State on a range of options for slimming down the National Curriculum within primary schools in Wales. Report to ministers, 1998.

Review of opencast coal planning policy

To consider how effectively the Government's planning policies for opencast mining deal with the issues raised and to undertake a full review of *Minerals Policy Guidance 3*. Reported winter 1998-99.

Strategic review of the Welsh trunk road programme

To consider the relative priority of particular routes and schemes within the programme; the scope for altering those priorities; the need to manage the network more effectively and the scope to promote alternative transport modes wherever appropriate. Reported 28 July 1998.

Review of the role of the Welsh Language Board in Welsh education

Reported 1999

EXAMPLES OF INTERNAL GOVERNMENT REVIEWS ESTABLISHED SINCE 1 JANUARY 1999

May 1997 to December 1999

DEPARTMENT FOR EDUCATION AND EMPLOYMENT (DFEE)

Analytical Review of Adult Learning

Review of Adventure Activities Licensing Scheme.

HOME OFFICE (HO)

Working group on the PM's announcement of a task force on the active community.

Inter-departmental working group (including a member of the Law Commission) on the Commission's report (No. 237) recommending a new offence of corporate killing within involuntary manslaughter.

Steering group on the Home Secretary's action plan on the recommendations of the Macpherson Report on the Stephen Lawrence murder investigation.

Review of the law on sex offenders.

DEPARTMENT OF TRADE AND INDUSTRY (DTI)

Review of the Export Credit Guarantee Department's remit and commercial guidelines

HM TREASURY

Inquiry into lower rate ring-fenced tonnage-based tax and enhanced training incentives. Established in March 1999.

A-Z of 'OUTSIDER' MEMBERS

David Brown Chair, University for Industry Design and Implementation Advisory Group (DfEE)

Gilroy Brown Advisory Group on Raising Ethnic Minority Pupil Achievement (DfEE)

Harper Brown Social Exclusion Unit Policy Action Team 4: Neighbourhood Management (CO)

Professor Margaret Brown Numeracy Task Force (DfEE)

Richard Brown Export Forum (DTI)

Simon Brown Cleaner Vehicles Task Force Main Working Group (DETR); Cleaner Vehicles Task Force Information and Labelling Subgroup (DETR); Cleaner Vehicles Task Force Technology and Testing Subgroup (DETR)

Tim Brown Cleaner Vehicles Task Force Main Working Group (DETR); Cleaner Vehicles Task Force Alternative Fuels Subgroup (DETR)

Professor William Brown Low Pay Commission (DTI)

Colin Browne Tourism Forum Communications Strategy Working Group (DCMS)

Pat Browne Northern Ireland Strategy for Education Curriculum and Assessment Group (NIO)

Richard Browne Observer (from November 1997), Numeracy Task Force (DfEE)

David Bruce Review of Film Policy Action Committee (DCMS)

Ian Bruce Disability Benefits Forum (DSS)

Michael Brunson Advisory Group on Education for Citizenship and Democracy (DfEE)

Peter Bryant NHS Wales Trust Reconfiguration Steering Group (WO)

Martin Buck Private Finance Task Force (HMT)

Peter Buckingham Review of Film Policy Broadening the Audience Sub-Group (DCMS)

Sir Alan Budd Review of Future Funding of the BBC (DCMS)

Gordon Bull National Advisory Group on Special Educational Needs (DfEE)

Penny Buller Release of Dangerous Offenders Working Group (HO)

Frank Bunting Fundamental Review of the Economic Development Strategy in Northern Ireland (NIO)

Tania Burchardt Social Exclusion Unit Policy Action Team 14: Financial Services (CO)

Richard Burdett Urban Task Force (DETR)

Professor David Burghes Numeracy Task Force (DfEE)

Suzanne Burn Clinical Negligence Working Group (LCD); Multi-Party Situations Working Group (LCD)

James Burnett-Hitchcock Multi-Party Situations Working Group (LCD)

Brendan Burns Tourism Forum (DCMS); Tourism Forum Domestic Tourism Working Group (DCMS); Chair, Tourism Forum Domestic Tourism Working Group: Distribution Sub-Group (DCMS)

Timothy Burrill Review of Film Policy Training and Education Sub-Group (DCMS)

Alastair Burt Review of the List of Nationally Important Sporting Events Which Must Be Made Available on Free-to-Air Terrestrial TV Channels (DCMS)

Tony Burton Urban Task Force (DETR)

Tony Butler Youth Justice Task Force (HO); Release of Dangerous Offenders Working Group (HO)

David Butler Social Exclusion Unit Policy Action Team 7: Unpopular Housing (CO)

John Button NHS Wales Trust Reconfiguration Steering Group (WO)

Professor John Bynner Social Exclusion Unit Policy Action Team 12: Young People (CO); Effective Post-School Basic Skills Provision Working Group (DfEE)

C

Gill Cable Social Exclusion Unit Policy Action Team 8: Anti-Social Behaviour (CO)

Dinah Caine Review of Film Policy Review Group (DCMS); Review of Film Policy Action Committee (DCMS); Review of Film Policy Training and Education Sub-Group (DCMS)

Alan Calder Competitiveness Working Party; Making the Most of the Information Age (DTI)

Jason Caldwell Northern Ireland New Deal Task Force (NIO)

Bill Callaghan Low Pay Commission (DTI); Company Law Review Consultative Committee (DTI)

Steve Callan Prestwick Task Force (SO)

Dr Tony Calland NHS Wales Trust Reconfiguration Steering Group (WO)

Geoff Callow Cleaner Vehicles Task Force Alternative Fuels Subgroup (DETR)

Professor Ian Cameron Strategic Review of Health Services in London (DH); NHS Wales Trust Reconfiguration Steering Group (WO)

Professor Alastair Campbell Review of the Law Relating to Surrogacy (DH)

Ian Campbell Export Forum (DTI)

Jane Campbell Disability Rights Task Force (DfEE); Disability Benefits Forum (DSS)

Rachel Campbell Race Relations Forum (HO)

Garry Campkin Export Forum (DTI)

Bridged Canavan Social Exclusion Unit Policy Action Team 8: Anti-Social Behaviour (CO)

Tony Cann Review of the Bureaucratic Burden on Teachers (DfEE)

Joanne Cappa Policy Review of the Youth Service, Northern Ireland (NIO)

Sue Cara Further Education Student Support Advisory Group (DfEE)

Martin Cardwell Northern Ireland Strategy on Alcohol Misuse Project Team (NIO)

Peter Carey Gifted and Talented Children Advisory Group (DfEE)

Christine Carling New Deal Task Force Advisory Group (DfEE)

Maureen Carmody Chronic Fatigue Syndrome Reference Group (DH)

Mike Carnaby Effective Post-School Basic Skills Provision Working Group (DfEE)

Leighton Carnell Wales New Deal Advisory Task Force (WO)

Ian Carruthers Waiting List Action Team (DH); Chair, South and West Regional Task Force to support the Waiting List Action Team (DH)

Charles Carter Older Volunteers Working Group (HO)

Sir John Carter Competitiveness Working Party; Maximising Competitiveness in Europe (DTI)

Hilary Carty Independent Review of the Future of the Royal Opera House Companies and the English National Opera (DCMS)

Professor John Cash Chair, Independent Review of proposals for the transfer of Bulk Blood Processing and Testing from Liverpool to Manchester (DH)

Paul Cavadino Youth Justice Task Force (HO)

Dr Trudi Chalder Chronic Fatigue Syndrome Main Working Group (DH)

Baroness Chalker Panel 2000 Advisory Group (FCO)

Tony Challinor Social Exclusion Unit Policy Action Team 14: Financial Services (CO)

Dr Neil Chalmers Sustainable Development Education Panel (DETR)

Dr Jacky Chambers Review of the Latest Information Available on Inequalities in Health (DH)

Anne Chan Special Educational Needs Working Group on the future role and training of Educational Psychologists (DfEE)

Thomas Chan Race Relations Forum (HO)

Jane Chapman Clinical Negligence Working Group (LCD)

Simon Chapman Air Quality Forum (DETR)

Peter Chappelow Tourism Forum (DCMS); Tourism Forum Domestic Tourism Working Group: Distribution Sub-Group (DCMS)

Allan Charlesworth Better Regulation Task Force (CO)

Jack Charlton Review of the List of Nationally Important Sporting Events Which Must Be Made Available on Free-to-Air Terrestrial TV Channels (DCMS)

Balbir Chatrik Social Exclusion Unit Policy Action Team 12: Young People (CO)

Dr N.C. Chaturvedi Regional Review of Adult Cardiology Services in Northern Ireland (NIO)

Alan Cherry Urban Task Force (DETR)

Pat Chick Special Educational Needs Working Group on the future role and training of Educational Psychologists (DfEE)

Bob Chilton Social Exclusion Unit Policy Action Team 16: Learning Lessons (CO)

Steve Chinn Advisory Group on Independent/State School Partnerships (DfEE)

Sir Trevor Chinn Cleaner Vehicles Task Force (DETR)

Val Chinn Social Exclusion Unit Policy Action Team 1: Jobs (CO)

C K Chow Competitiveness Advisory Group (DTI); Competitiveness Working Party; Maximising Competitiveness in Europe (DTI)

Campbell Christie Prestwick Task Force (SO); Scottish Parliament all-party Consultative Steering Group (SO)

Chris Christou Company Law Review Consultative Committee (DTI)

Gobnait N Chrualao Race Relations Forum (HO)

Anne Clark Scottish Advisory Task Force on the New Deal (SO)

Colin Clark Tourism Forum Whitehall Issues Working Group (DCMS)

Alastair Clarke Gifted and Talented Children Advisory Group (DfEE)

Dr Andrew Clarke Airborne Particles Expert Group (DETR)

Margaret Clarke Tourism Forum (DCMS); Tourism Forum Domestic Tourism Working Group: Sustainability Sub-Group (DCMS)

Dr Anthony Cleare Chronic Fatigue Syndrome Main Working Group (DH)

Dr William Clee Review of Health Promotion Arrangements in Wales Steering Group (WO)

David Clement Working Group on Integrated Education (NIO)

Barry Cleverdon Tourism Forum Business Tourism Working Group (DCMS)

Carol Clinton Older Volunteers Working Group (HO)

Alison Cobb Disability Benefits Forum (DSS)

Ellen Cockburn Social Exclusion Unit Policy Action Team 2: Skills (CO)

Jean Cogger Northern Ireland Strategy for Education Technology Teacher Education Group (NIO)

Kate Cohen Private Finance Task Force (HMT)

Ronald Cohen TECH Stars Steering Group (DTI)

Jane Colby Chronic Fatigue Syndrome Children's Group (DH)

Professor Stuart Cole Welsh Transport Advisory Group (WO)

Neale Coleman Social Exclusion Unit Policy Action Team 4: Neighbourhood Management (CO)

Adrian Coles Business Advisory Group on European Monetary Union (DTI)

Chris Collier Tourism Forum Domestic Tourism Working Group: Sustainability Sub-Group (DCMS)

Michael Collier Review of the Bureaucratic Burden on Teachers (DfEE)

Bruce Collings Competitiveness Working Party; Enhancing Business Performance Through Developing Individuals (DTI)

Julia Collins Competitiveness Working Party; Making the Most of the Information Age (DTI)

Chris Collison Coalfields Task Force (DETR)

Robert Colvill Business Advisory Group on European Monetary Union (DTI)

David Compston Competitiveness Working Party; Enhancing Business Performance Through Developing Individuals (DTI); North West Regional Competitiveness Working Party (DTI)

Command and Control (DETR)

Mary Donelly Northern Ireland New Deal Task Force (NIO)

Dr Christl Donnelly Deputy Chair, Review of Bovine TB in Cattle and Badgers (MAFF)

Alison Dougan Development Awareness Formal/Informal Structures Sub-Group (DFID)

Peter Downes Sustainable Development Education Panel (DETR)

Tony Downes Cleaner Vehicles Task Force Main Working Group (DETR); Convenor, Cleaner Vehicles Task Force Technology and Testing Subgroup (DETR)

Dr Betty Dowsett Chronic Fatigue Syndrome Reference Group (DH)

Colin Doyle Tourism Forum Domestic Tourism Working Group: Distribution Sub-Group (DCMS)

Dr Peter Doyle Competitiveness Working Party; Encouraging Innovation (DTI); North West Regional Competitiveness Working Party (DTI)

Jeannie Drake Competitiveness Working Party; Enhancing Business Performance Through Developing Individuals (DTI)

Chris Drew Social Exclusion Unit Policy Action Team 15: Information Technology (CO)

Sheila Drew-Smith Social Exclusion Unit Policy Action Team 16: Learning Lessons (CO)

David Drewry Panel 2000 Advisory Group (FCO)

Fiona Driscoll Community Fire Safety Task Force (HO)

Kay Driver Advisory Group on Raising Ethnic Minority Pupil Achievement (DfEE)

Martin Drury Tourism Forum (DCMS); Tourism Forum Presentation of Heritage Working Group (DCMS)

Sheila Drury Wales New Deal Advisory Task Force (WO)

Anthony Dubbins Competitiveness Working Party; Enhancing Business Performance Through Developing Individuals (DTI); Skills Task Force (DfEE)

Keith Dugmore Social Exclusion Unit Policy Action Team 18: Better Information (CO)

Graham Duncan Social Exclusion Unit Policy Action Team 16: Learning Lessons (CO)

Dr H. Dunn Regional Review of Adult Cardiology Services in Northern Ireland (NIO)

Janet Dunn Special Educational Needs Working Group on Provision of Speech and Language Therapy Services (DfEE)

Ron Dunn Competitiveness Working Party; Making the Most of the Information Age (DTI)

Anthony Dunnett Urban Task Force (DETR)

Nicholas Duslacher Review of electricity trading arrangements (DTI)

Clive Dutton Urban Task Force Working Group Two (DETR)

Dr Chris Dye Review of the Current Rules on Quarantine of Imported Pet Animals (MAFF)

Greg Dyke Lead, NHS Charter Advisory Group (DH)

Marjorie Dykins National Assembly Advisory Group (WO)

Professor Alan Dyson National Advisory Group on Special Educational Needs (DfEE)

James Dyson Competitiveness Working Party; Promoting the Best of Best Practice (DTI); South West Region Regional Competitiveness Working Party (DTI)

E

David Eade New Deal Task Force Advisory Group (DfEE)

Robbie Earle Football Task Force Working Group (DCMS)

Nick Easton Working Party on Electoral Procedures (HO)

Lord Eatwell Agricultural Advisory Group (MAFF)

John Edmonds Skills Task Force (DfEE); Older Volunteers Working Group (HO); Competitiveness Advisory Group (DTI); Competitiveness Working Party; Enhancing Business Performance Through Developing Individuals (DTI)

Dr Haydn Edwards Wales New Deal Advisory Task Force (WO)

Helen Edwards Social Exclusion Unit Policy Action Team 8: Anti-Social Behaviour (CO); New Deal Task Force (DfEE)

John Edwards Coalfields Task Force (DETR)

Michael Edwards Tourism Forum Business Tourism Working Group (DCMS)

Philip Edwards Social Exclusion Unit Policy Action Team 18: Better Information (CO)

Quentin Edwards Advisory Group on Independent/State School Partnerships (DfEE)

Sir John Egan Chair, Construction Task Force (DETR); Tourism Forum Business Tourism Working Group (DCMS)

Naomi Eisenstadt Social Exclusion Unit Policy Action Team 8: Anti-Social Behaviour (CO)

Mark Elder Independent Review of the Future of the Royal Opera House Companies and the English National Opera (DCMS)

John Elfed Jones Chair, National Assembly Advisory Group (WO)

Michael Elliot Tourism Forum (DCMS); Tourism Forum Strategic Planning Working Group (DCMS)

Harvey Elliott Tourism Forum Communications Strategy Working Group (DCMS)

Michael Ellis Assessor, Lord Donaldson's Review of Salvage and Intervention and Their Command and Control (DETR)

David Elstein Review of Film Policy Action Committee (DCMS)

Baronness Audrey Emerton Review of thoracic surgical services at Plymouth Hospitals Trust (DH)

Paul Ennals Social Exclusion Unit Policy Action Team 11: Schools Plus (CO); Vice-Chair, National Advisory Group on Special Educational Needs (DfEE)

Cllr Sue Essex Welsh Transport Advisory Group (WO)

Derek Etherington Task Force on Alternatives to Tobacco Sponsorship (DCMS)

Stuart Etherington Interchange Steering Council (CO); New Deal Task Force Advisory Group (DfEE)

Treva Etienne Review of Film Policy Action Committee (DCMS)

Dr Alison Evans Review of the long-term future of Prison Health Care (HO)

Carole Evans Standards Task Force (DfEE)

Dr Chris Evans Competitiveness Advisory Group (DTI); Competitiveness Working Party; Increasing Business Investment (DTI)

Gwenlian Evans Review of the Bureaucratic Burden on Teachers (DfEE)

Ian Evans Competitiveness Working Party; Maximising Competitiveness in Europe (DTI)

Margaret Evans Wales New Deal Advisory Task Force (WO)

Ms Marion Evans NHS Wales Trust Reconfiguration Steering Group (WO)

Matthew Evans Independent Review of the Future of the Royal Opera House Companies and the English National Opera (DCMS)

Richard Evans Social Exclusion Unit Policy Action Team 8: Anti-Social Behaviour (CO)

Sir Richard Evans Competitiveness Advisory Group (DTI); Prestwick Task Force (SO)

Robert Evans Cleaner Vehicles Task Force Technology and Testing Subgroup (DETR)

Ruth Evans Review of Future Funding of the BBC (DCMS); Sustainable Development Education Panel (DETR); NHS Charter Advisory Group (DH)

Sue Evans Older Volunteers Working Group (HO)

Mick Everett Social Exclusion Unit Policy Action Team 10: Arts and Sport (CO)

Paul Everitt Cleaner Vehicles Task Force Main Working Group (DETR)

Tim Exell National Advisory Group on Special Educational Needs (DfEE)

Dr Deborah Eyre Gifted and Talented Children Advisory Group (DfEE)

Sir Richard Eyre Chair, Independent Review of the Future of the Royal Opera House Companies and the English National Opera (DCMS)

F

Ade Fabunmi-Stone Social Exclusion Unit Policy Action Team 1: Jobs (CO)

Peter Fanning Social Exclusion Unit Policy Action Team 17: Joining It Up Locally (CO)

Sir Tom Farmer Competitiveness Working Party; Promoting the Best of Best Practice (DTI)

Richard Farnell Social Exclusion Unit Policy Action Team 9: Community Self-Help (CO)

Imtiaz Farookhi Urban Task Force Working Group Two (DETR)

Caroline Farquhar Review of the Improvement of Skills and Employability for Young People with Special Needs (SO)

Matthew Farrow Tourism Forum Human Resources Working Group (DCMS)

Richard Faulkner Vice Chair, Football Task Force (DCMS); Football Task Force Working Group (DCMS)

Amelia Fawcett Competitiveness Working Party; Increasing Business Investment (DTI)

Dr. P. Fawcett Independent Panel on Gulf Veterans' Illnesses Interactions Research (MoD)

R. Fawcett National Advisory Group on New Start (DfEE)

Lesley Feakes Special Educational Needs Working Group on Provision of Speech and Language Therapy Services (DfEE)

Brian Fearon Expert Panel on Sex Offending (SO)

Eric Fellner Review of Film Policy Broadening the Audience Sub-Group (DCMS)

Gary Ferguson Review of Film Policy Action Committee (DCMS); Review of Film Policy Achieving 20% Market Share Sub-Group (DCMS)

Richard Ferre Review of the Role of TECs (DfEE)

Tom Fidell Cleaner Vehicles Task Force Alternative Fuels Subgroup (DETR)

Hugh Field Better Regulation TaskForce (CO)

John Field Cleaner Vehicles Task Force Main Working Group (DETR)

Richard Fielden Urban Task Force Working Group One (DETR)

Denise Fielding Careers Service Special Needs Task Force (DfEE)

David Fillingham NHS Efficiency Task Force (DH)

Dr Leslie Finley Chronic Fatigue Syndrome Reference Group (DH)

Dan Finn Social Exclusion Unit Policy Action Team 1: Jobs (CO); New Deal Task Force Advisory Group (DfEE)

Peter Finn Northern Ireland Strategy for Education Technology Teacher Education Group (NIO)

Mary Finnegan Policy Review of the Youth Service, Northern Ireland (NIO)

Dr O. Finnegan Regional Review of Adult Cardiology Services in Northern Ireland (NIO)

Sandy Finnigan Advisory Group on Raising Ethnic Minority Pupil Achievement (DfEE)

Mike Fischer Competitiveness Working Party; Making the Most of the Information Age (DTI); South East Region Regional Competitiveness Working Party (DTI)

Professor Bernard Fisher Airborne Particles Expert Group (DETR)

John Fisher Development Awareness Working Group (DFID); Development Awareness Themes and Partnerships Sub-Group (DFID)

Donal Flanagan Working Group on Integrated Education (NIO)

Tony Fleck Northern Ireland Strategy on Alcohol Misuse Project Team (NIO)

Robert Fleming Competitiveness Working Party; Increasing Business

Cleaner Vehicles Task Force Information and Labelling Subgroup (DETR)

Nigel Green Review of Film Policy Action Committee (DCMS); Review of Film Policy Achieving 20% Market Share Sub-Group (DCMS)

Nessa Greenaway Northern Ireland Strategy on Alcohol Misuse Project Team (NIO)

Graham Greene Tourism Forum Presentation of Heritage Working Group (DCMS)

Anthony Greener Competitiveness Advisory Group (DTI)

Anthony Greener Competitiveness Working Party; Encouraging Innovation (DTI)

Adrian Greenwood Social Exclusion Unit Policy Action Team 8: Anti-Social Behaviour (CO)

Celia Greenwood Social Exclusion Unit Policy Action Team 10: Arts and Sport (CO)

Prof. Desmond Greer Review of Criminal Injuries Compensation Arrangements in Northern Ireland (NIO)

Derek Gregory NHS Wales Trust Reconfiguration Steering Group (WO)

Prof. Edward Gregson Music Industry Forum (DCMS)

Paul Gribble Working Party on Electoral Procedures (HO)

Rob Griffiths Older Volunteers Working Group (HO)

Andy Grimm Cleaner Vehicles Task Force Information and Labelling Subgroup (DETR)

Nigel Grimshaw Northern Ireland Strategy on Alcohol Misuse Project Team (NIO)

Prof. A. Grossman Independent Panel on Gulf Veterans' Illnesses Interactions Research (MoD)

Don Groubin Release of Dangerous Offenders Working Group (HO)

Nigel de Gruchy Review of the Bureaucratic Burden on Teachers (DfEE)

Libby Grundy Sustainable Development Education Panel (DETR); Development Awareness Working Group (DFID); Development Awareness Formal/Informal Structures Sub-Group (DFID)

Francis Gugen Oil and Gas Industry Task Force (DTI)

Richard Gutch Older Volunteers Working Group (HO)

Richard Guy Review of the Role of TECs (DfEE)

Michael Gwilt Cleaner Vehicles Task Force (DETR)

Michael Gwilym Housing Sounding Board (DETR)

David Gye Construction Task Force (DETR)

H

Roger de Haan Tourism Forum Widening Access to Tourism Working Group (DCMS)

David Hackett Tourism Forum Business Tourism Working Group (DCMS)

Nigel Haigh Cleaner Vehicles Task Force (DETR)

Simon Halfacree Welsh Transport Advisory Group (WO)

Denise Hall Skills Task Force (DfEE)

Geoff Hall Further Education Student Support Advisory Group (DfEE)

Graham Hall Social Exclusion Unit Policy Action Team 15: Information Technology (CO)

Jan Hall Competitiveness Advisory Group (DTI)

John Hall Competitiveness Working Party; Encouraging Innovation (DTI)

Sir Peter Hall Urban Task Force (DETR)

Steven Hall Working Party on Legal Deposit (DCMS)

Aidan Hamill Northern Ireland Strategy for Education Technology Strategic Management Group (NIO); Northern Ireland Strategy for Education Curriculum and Assessment Group (NIO)

Ben Hamilton-Baillie Welsh Transport Advisory Group (WO)

Sir Ronald Hampel Review of Structure of Export Promotion (DTI)

Albert Hampson Tourism Forum Business Tourism Working Group (DCMS)

Peter Hampson Social Exclusion Unit Policy Action Team 6: Neighbourhood Wardens (CO)

Peter Hampson Tourism Forum (DCMS); Tourism Forum Whitehall Issues Working Group (DCMS); Tourism Forum Domestic Tourism Working Group (DCMS); Tourism Forum Domestic Tourism Working Group: Quality Sub-Group (DCMS)

Sir Stuart Hampson Company Law Review Steering Group (DTI)

Mike Hampton Pensions Education Working Group (DSS)

Christine Hancock NHS Charter Advisory Group (DH)

Ruth Hancock Pension Provision Group (DSS)

Brian Handley Tourism Forum Whitehall Issues Working Group (DCMS); Tourism Forum Visitor Attractions Working Group (DCMS)

Sister G. Hanna Review of Paediatric Surgical Services in Northern Ireland (NIO)

Joan Harbison Equality Commission Working Group (NIO)

David Harbourne Tourism Forum (DCMS); Tourism Forum Communications Strategy Working Group (DCMS); Tourism Forum Human Resources Working Group (DCMS)

Patrick Haren Fundamental Review of the Economic Development Strategy in Northern Ireland (NIO)

Karen Hargan Northern Ireland New Deal Task Force (NIO)

Professor David Hargreaves Standards Task Force (DfEE)

Anne Harley Sustainable Development Education Panel (DETR)

Sir John Harman New Deal Task Force (DfEE)

Michael Harper Welsh Transport Advisory Group (WO)

Craig Harris Social Exclusion Unit Policy Action Team 2: Skills (CO)

Kevin Harris Social Exclusion Unit Policy Action Team 15: Information Technology (CO)

Jill Harrison Disability Benefits Forum (DSS)

Professor Roy Harrison Air Quality Forum (DETR)

Tanya Harrison Chronic Fatigue Syndrome Reference Group (DH)

Sir Graham Hart Review of Lord Chancellor's Department Funding for Marriage Support and Research Services (Lord Chancellor's Dept)

Romaine Hart Review of Film Policy Broadening the Audience Sub-Group (DCMS)

Sally Hart Social Exclusion Unit Policy Action Team 10: Arts and Sport (CO)

Nigel Hartnell Competitiveness Working Party; Making the Most of the Information Age (DTI)

Monica Hartwell Older Volunteers Working Group (HO)

Lord Haskins Chair, Better Regulation TaskForce (CO); New Deal Task Force; Interchange Steering Council (CO)

Caroline Hassan Social Exclusion Unit Policy Action Team 12: Young People (CO)

Professor Carmen Hass-Klau Fundamental Review of Transport Policy (DETR)

Walter Hasselkus Cleaner Vehicles Task Force (DETR)

Howard Hastings Northern Ireland New Deal Task Force (NIO)

Dr Herman Hauser Working Group on the Financing of High Technology Business (previously, the McCullagh Group) (HMT); TECH Stars Steering Group (DTI)

Graham Hawker Chair, Wales New Deal Advisory Task Force (WO)

Steve Hawkes Cleaner Vehicles Task Force Fleet Purchasing Guidance Subgroup (DETR)

Dr Maurice Hayes Independent Commission on Policing Northern Ireland (NIO)

Carolyn Hayman New Deal Task Force Advisory Group (DfEE)

Paula Hay-Plumb Chair, Coalfields Task Force (DETR)

Nicola Hayward Tourism Forum (DCMS); Tourism Forum Human Resources Working Group (DCMS); Tourism Forum Domestic Tourism Working Group: Quality Sub-Group (DCMS)

Richard Headicar Urban Task Force Working Group One (DETR)

Andy Heath Music Industry Forum (DCMS)

John Heaton Review of the Tote Working Group (HO)

James Hehir Competitiveness Working Party; Making the Most of the Information Age (DTI); Eastern Region Regional Competitiveness Working Party (DTI)

Cllr Chris Heinitz Football Task Force (DCMS)

Samantha Hellawell Social Exclusion Unit Policy Action Team 15: Information Technology (CO)

Judith Hemery Development Awareness Working Group (DFID); Development Awareness Formal/Informal Structures Sub-Group (DFID); Joint Chair, Development Awareness Learning from Others Sub-Group (DFID)

Christine Hemming Air Quality Forum (DETR)

Sir Denys Henderson Tourism Forum (DCMS)

Gavin Henderson Independent Review of the Future of the Royal Opera House Companies and the English National Opera (DCMS)

Ronald A Henderson Company Law Review Consultative Committee (DTI)

Dr Keith Hendry Review of Salmon and Freshwater Fisheries (MAFF)

Steve Heneghan Football Task Force (DCMS)

Hugh Henry Scottish Advisory Task Force on the New Deal (SO)

Martin Henry Review of Structure of Export Promotion (DTI)

Nick Henwood Effective Post-School Basic Skills Provision Working Group (DfEE)

Donald Hepburn Competitiveness Working Party; Maximising Competitiveness in Europe (DTI)

Professor Stephen Heppell Standards Task Force (DfEE)

Tim Herrington Company Law Review Consultative Committee (DTI)

Philip Heseltine Cleaner Vehicles Task Force Alternative Fuels Subgroup (DETR)

Derek Heselton Review of Salmon and Freshwater Fisheries (MAFF)

Julie Hesketh Air Quality Forum (DETR)

Liz Hewett NHS Wales Trust Reconfiguration Steering Group (WO)

Peter Hewitt Review of Film Policy Action Committee (DCMS)

Michelle Heyworth People's Panel Advisory Group (CO)

John Hickman Airborne Particles Expert Group (DETR)

Dr E.M. Hicks Review of Services for Acutely Ill Children (NIO)

Dr D. Higginson Regional Review of Adult Cardiology Services in Northern Ireland (NIO)

Dr Derek Higgs Working Group on the Financing of High Technology Business (previously, the McCullagh Group) (HMT)

David Highton Waiting List Action Team (DH); Chair, North Thames Regional Task Force to support the Waiting List Action Team (DH)

Roger Higman Cleaner Vehicles Task Force Main Working Group (DETR); Convenor, Cleaner Vehicles Task Force Information and Labelling Subgroup (DETR); Housing Sounding Board (DETR)

Greg Hill Review of the Bureaucratic Burden on Teachers (DfEE)

Stephen Hill Social Exclusion Unit Policy Action Team 17: Joining It Up Locally (CO)

John Hills Social Exclusion Unit Policy Action Team 1: Jobs (CO)

Billy Hinshelwood Review of Film Policy Film Finance Sub-Group (DCMS)

Michael Hirst Tourism Forum (DCMS); Tourism Forum Whitehall Issues Working Group (DCMS); Chair, Tourism Forum Business Tourism Working Group (DCMS); Tourism Forum Strategic Planning Working Group (DCMS)

Graham Hitchen Social Exclusion Unit Policy Action Team 10: Arts and Sport

Roger Jones Wales New Deal Advisory Task Force (WO)
Trefor Jones Education and Training Action Group (WO)
Amanda Jordan New Deal Task Force Advisory Group (DfEE)
Stephen Joseph Fundamental Review of Transport Policy (DETR)
Lionel Joyce NHS Efficiency Task Force (DH)
Graham Jukes Air Quality Forum (DETR)
DeAnne Julius Skills Task Force (DfEE)

K

John Kay Company Law Review Steering Group (DTI)
Christine Keates Advisory Group on Raising Ethnic Minority Pupil Achievement (DfEE)
Dr F. Kee Regional Review of Adult Cardiology Services in Northern Ireland (NIO)
Sara Keene Review of Film Policy Broadening the Audience Sub-Group (DCMS)
Brian Kelly Air Quality Forum (DETR)
Jim Kelly Review of Film Policy Broadening the Audience Sub-Group (DCMS)
Ray Kelly Tourism Forum Communications Strategy Working Group (DCMS)
Elaine Kempson Social Exclusion Unit Policy Action Team 14: Financial Services (CO)
Angus Kennedy Social Exclusion Unit Policy Action Team 4: Neighbourhood Management (CO)
Dr F. Kennedy Review of Paediatric Surgical Services in Northern Ireland (NIO)
Professor Ian Kennedy Chair, Review of the Current Rules on Quarantine of Imported Pet Animals (MAFF)
Sir Anthony Kenny Chair, Working Party on Legal Deposit (DCMS)
Dr Arthur Kentrick NHS Wales Trust Reconfiguration Steering Group (WO)
Duncan Kenworthy Review of Film Policy Review Group (DCMS); Review of Film Policy Action Committee (DCMS); Review of Film Policy Achieving 20% Market Share Sub-Group (DCMS)
Jackie Kernahan Competitiveness Working Party; Promoting the Best of Best Practice (DTI)
David Kerr Advisory Group on Education for Citizenship and Democracy (DfEE)
Tony Kershaw Football Task Force (DCMS)
John Kettlewell Social Exclusion Unit Policy Action Team 5: Housing Management (CO)
C. Kiddle Advisory Group on Raising Ethnic Minority Pupil Achievement (DfEE)
Jill Kieran Standards Task Force (DfEE)
Dr P. Kilbane Regional Review of Adult Cardiology Services in Northern Ireland (NIO)
Alan Kilburn Housing Sounding Board (DETR)
Avila Kilmurray Policy Review of the Youth Service, Northern Ireland (NIO)
Christopher King Competitiveness Working Party; Maximising Competitiveness in Europe (DTI)
Kanya King Music Industry Forum (DCMS)
Neil Kinghan Social Exclusion Unit Policy Action Team 17: Joining It Up Locally (CO)
Stephen Kingon Fundamental Review of the Economic Development Strategy in Northern Ireland (NIO)
Kevin Kinsella Review of Film Policy Action Committee (DCMS)
Mike Kinski Competitiveness Working Party; Enhancing Business Performance Through Developing Individuals (DTI)
Phil Kirby Urban Task Force (DETR)
Brian Kirkaldy Review of the Improvement of Skills and Employability for Young People with Special Needs (SO)
Francesca Klug Human Rights Task Force (HO)
Michael Knapp Sustainable Development Education Panel (DETR)
Alan Knight Sustainable Development Education Panel (DETR)
Sister H. Knight Regional Review of Adult Cardiology Services in Northern Ireland (NIO)
John Knight Social Exclusion Unit Policy Action Team 4: Neighbourhood Management (CO)
Professor David Knights Pensions Education Working Group (DSS)
Ilona Kruppa Expert Panel on Sex Offending (SO)
Zarina Kurtz Social Exclusion Unit Policy Action Team 18: Better Information (CO)

L

Dr Mike Ladle Review of Salmon and Freshwater Fisheries (MAFF)
Brian Lamb Disability Rights Task Force (DfEE); Disability Benefits Forum (DSS)
J. Landeryou National Advisory Group on New Start (DfEE)
Cllr Graham Lane Chair, Further Education Student Support Advisory Group (DfEE)
Tim Lang Social Exclusion Unit Policy Action Team 13: Shops (CO)
James Langley Cleaner Vehicles Task Force Main Working Group (DETR); Cleaner Vehicles Task Force Fleet Purchasing Guidance Subgroup (DETR)
John Langston Competitiveness Working Party; Maximising Competitiveness in Europe (DTI)
Conrad Lashley Tourism Forum (DCMS); Tourism Forum Human Resources Working Group (DCMS)
Prof. A.R. Latimer External Advisor, Regional Review of Adult Cardiology Services in Northern Ireland (NIO)
Diane Laurillard University for Industry Design and Implementation Advisory Group (DfEE)

Paul Lautman Social Exclusion Unit Policy Action Team 5: Housing Management (CO)
Lyn Lavers Tourism Forum Communications Strategy Working Group (DCMS)
Margaret Lavery Disability Benefits Forum (DSS)
James Law Special Educational Needs Working Group on Provision of Speech and Language Therapy Services (DfEE)
Cllr Peter Lawrence Further Education Student Support Advisory Group (DfEE)
Simon Lawrence Chronic Fatigue Syndrome Main Working Group (DH)
Sir William Lawrence Tourism Forum Widening Access to Tourism Working Group (DCMS)
Professor Richard Layard New Deal Task Force Advisory Group (DfEE); Effective Post-School Basic Skills Provision Working Group (DfEE)
David Lea Cleaner Vehicles Task Force (DETR); Cleaner Vehicles Task Force Main Working Group (DETR); Business Advisory Group on European Monetary Union (DTI)
Alison Lea Wilson Wales New Deal Advisory Task Force (WO)
Charles Leadbeater Social Exclusion Unit Policy Action Team 16: Learning Lessons (CO)
Nicholas Leahy Cleaner Vehicles Task Force Main Working Group (DETR)
Terry Leahy Competitiveness Advisory Group (DTI); Competitiveness Working Party; Making the Most of the Information Age (DTI); South East Region Regional Competitiveness Working Party (DTI)
Adrian Leather Social Exclusion Unit Policy Action Team 12: Young People (CO)
Peter Leaver QC Football Task Force (DCMS); Football Task Force Working Group (DCMS)
Carol Lee Disability Benefits Forum (DSS)
David Lee Private Finance Task Force (HMT)
John Lee Tourism Forum (DCMS); Tourism Forum Whitehall Issues Working Group (DCMS); Chair, Tourism Forum Visitor Attractions Working Group (DCMS); Tourism Forum Strategic Planning Working Group (DCMS)
Peter Lee Football Task Force Working Group (DCMS)
Professor Simon Lee Standards Task Force (DfEE)
Michael Leech Scottish Advisory Task Force on the New Deal (SO)
Peter D Lees NHS Efficiency Task Force (DH)
Peter Lehmann Competitiveness Working Party; Maximising Competitiveness in Europe (DTI)
David Leibling Cleaner Vehicles Task Force Main Working Group (DETR); Cleaner Vehicles Task Force Fleet Purchasing Guidance Subgroup (DETR)
Graham Leicester Commission on Local Government and Scottish Parliament (SO)
Torsten Leidiger Cleaner Vehicles Task Force Fleet Purchasing Guidance Subgroup (DETR)
Roy Leighton Export Forum (DTI)
Gerard Lemos Social Exclusion Unit Policy Action Team 9: Community Self-Help (CO)
Brian Lennox-Smith Review of Health Promotion Arrangements in Wales Steering Group (WO)
Mark Leonard Panel 2000 Advisory Group (FCO)
Richard Lester Working Party on Electoral Procedures (HO)
Colin Leventhal Review of Film Policy Review Group (DCMS); Review of Film Policy Action Committee (DCMS); Review of Film Policy Film Finance Sub-Group (DCMS)
Judy Lever Competitiveness Advisory Group (DTI); Competitiveness Working Party; Increasing Business Investment (DTI)
Roger Levett Urban Task Force Working Group One (DETR)
Malcolm Levi Community Fire Safety Task Force (HO)
Lord Levy Panel 2000 Advisory Group (FCO)
Russell Levy Clinical Negligence Working Group (LCD)
Caroline Lewis Education and Training Action Group (WO)
David Lewis NHS Wales Trust Reconfiguration Steering Group (WO)
Michael Lewis Business Advisory Group on European Monetary Union (DTI)
Claudia Lewis-Moore Social Exclusion Unit Policy Action Team 8: Anti-Social Behaviour (CO)
Anna Grace Lidstone Chronic Fatigue Syndrome Children's Group (DH)
Dr Guy Lightfoot War Pensions Hearing Loss Review (DSS)
Prof. S. Lightman Independent Panel on Gulf Veterans' Illnesses Interactions Research (MoD)
Sir Donald Limon Advisory Group on Education for Citizenship and Democracy (DfEE)
Paul Lincoln National Advisory Group on Special Educational Needs (DfEE)
Rodney Lind Review of the Mental Health Act (DH)
Geoff Lindey Working Group on the Financing of High Technology Business (previously, the McCullagh Group) (HMT)
Maurice Lindsay Task Force on Alternatives to Tobacco Sponsorship (DCMS)
Baroness Linklater Review of the Improvement of Skills and Employability for Young People with Special Needs (SO)
Geoffrey Lipman Tourism Forum (DCMS); Tourism Forum Strategic Planning Working Group (DCMS); Tourism Forum Domestic Tourism Working Group (DCMS); Chair, Tourism Forum Domestic Tourism Working Group: Sustainability Sub-Group (DCMS)
John Lippe Cleaner Vehicles Task Force Information and Labelling Subgroup (DETR)
David Lipsey Review of Future Funding of the BBC (DCMS)
Stuart Lipton Urban Task Force (DETR)

Janet Major Standards Task Force (DfEE)

Ken Male Tourism Forum (DCMS); Tourism Forum Domestic Tourism Working Group: Distribution Sub-Group (DCMS)

Naseem Malik Social Exclusion Unit Policy Action Team 8: Anti-Social Behaviour (CO)

Shahid Malik Social Exclusion Unit Policy Action Team 1: Jobs (CO)

Robina Mallett National Advisory Group on Special Educational Needs (DfEE)

Tracey-Jane Malthouse Disability Rights Task Force (DfEE)

Joyce Mamode Fundamental Review of Transport Policy (DETR)

Henry Manisty Competitiveness Working Party; Maximising Competitiveness in Europe (DTI)

Joe Mann Disability Rights Task Force (DfEE)

Fred Manson Urban Task Force Working Group One (DETR)

Dr Tony Marchington Competitiveness Advisory Group (DTI)

Mike Marchment NHS Efficiency Task Force (DH)

David Mark Airborne Particles Expert Group (DETR)

Stephen Marks Cleaner Vehicles Task Force Main Working Group (DETR)

Professor Michael Marmot Review of the Latest Information Available on Inequalities in Health (DH)

Fred Maroudas Private Finance Task Force (HMT)

Professor John Marsh Agricultural Advisory Group (MAFF)

Bob Marshall Social Exclusion Unit Policy Action Team 1: Jobs (CO)

Lord Marshall Chair, Task Force on Economic Instruments for Industrial and Commercial Use of Energy (HMT, DETR and DTI); Chair, Interchange Steering Council (CO); Panel 2000 Advisory Group (FCO)

Howard Marshall National Assembly Advisory Group (WO)

Jerry Marston Social Exclusion Unit Policy Action Team 9: Community Self-Help (CO)

David Martin Cleaner Vehicles Task Force Main Working Group (DETR)

Donald Martin Business Advisory Group on European Monetary Union (DTI)

Sir George Martin Music Industry Forum (DCMS)

Marie Martin Northern Ireland Strategy for Education Technology Teacher Education Group (NIO)

Peter Martin Sustainable Development Education Panel (DETR)

Steven Martin Social Exclusion Unit Policy Action Team 1: Jobs (CO)

Dr. C. Martyn Independent Panel on Gulf Veterans' Illnesses Interactions Research (MoD)

Chris Mason NHS Wales Trust Reconfiguration Steering Group (WO)

Clive Mason NHS Staff Involvement Task Force (DH)

Tim Mason Tourism Forum (DCMS) ; Tourism Forum Presentation of Heritage Working Group (DCMS); Tourism Forum Widening Access to Tourism Working Group (DCMS)

Tim Mason Community Fire Safety Task Force (HO)

Tina Mason Competitiveness Working Party; Promoting the Best of Best Practice (DTI); Eastern Region Regional Competitiveness Working Party (DTI)

Bert Massie Disability Rights Task Force (DfEE); New Deal Task Force Advisory Group (DfEE)

Francois Matarasso Social Exclusion Unit Policy Action Team 10: Arts and Sport (CO)

Bill Mather Social Exclusion Unit Policy Action Team 10: Arts and Sport (CO)

Dr Robert Mather Review of the Mental Health Act (DH)

Ann Mathieson Expert Panel on Information Technology for the Scottish Parliament (SO)

Anthony Mayer Urban Task Force (DETR); Construction Task Force (DETR)

Ed Mayo Social Exclusion Unit Policy Action Team 3: Business (CO)

Pamela Meadows Better Regulation TaskForce (CO)

Andrea Mearing Effective Post-School Basic Skills Provision Working Group (DfEE)

Peter Meinertzhagen Working Group on the Financing of High Technology Business (previously, the McCullagh Group) (HMT)

John Melbourn Competitiveness Working Party; Increasing Business Investment (DTI)

Graham Meldrum Community Fire Safety Task Force (HO)

John Mellon Competitiveness Working Party; Maximising Competitiveness in Europe (DTI)

Rt Hon David Mellor QC Chair, Football Task Force (DCMS); Chair, Football Task Force Working Group (DCMS)

Tim Melville-Ross Company Law Review Consultative Committee (DTI)

Andrew Mercer Cleaner Vehicles Task Force Technology and Testing Subgroup (DETR)

Peter Mercer Advisory Group on Raising Ethnic Minority Pupil Achievement (DfEE)

Geoff Merchant Social Exclusion Unit Policy Action Team 16: Learning Lessons (CO)

Professor David Metcalf Low Pay Commission (DTI)

Mike Metcalf Older Volunteers Working Group (HO)

David Middleton Review of Health Promotion Arrangements in Wales Steering Group (WO)

Sir Peter Middleton Review of Civil Justice and Legal Aid (Lord Chancellor's Dept); Tourism Forum Domestic Tourism Working Group (DCMS); Tourism Forum Domestic Tourism Working Group: Sustainability Sub-Group (DCMS)

Rt. Hon. Bruce Millan Chair, Review of Mental Health (Scotland) Act 1984 (SO)

Cllr Margaret Millar Commission on Local Government and Scottish Parliament (SO)

Andy Miller Social Exclusion Unit Policy Action Team 11: Schools Plus (CO)

Dr E. Miller Independent Panel on Gulf Veterans' Illnesses Interactions Research (MoD)

Ian Miller Review of improvement of Skills and Employability for Young People with Special Needs (SO)

Anthea Millett Advisory Group on Raising Ethnic Minority Pupil Achievement (DfEE)

Tony Millns Review of the Bureaucratic Burden on Teachers (DfEE)

Martin Mills Music Industry Forum (DCMS)

Stephen Mills Tourism Forum Widening Access to Tourism Working Group (DCMS); Tourism Forum Domestic Tourism Working Group: Sustainability Sub-Group (DCMS)

Dr Alison Millward New Deal Task Force (DfEE)

Tim Milward Review of the Evidence relating to Silicon Breast Implants (DH)

Anne Minto Competitiveness Working Party; Enhancing Business Performance Through Developing Individuals (DTI)

Dr Heidi Safia Mirza Social Exclusion Unit Policy Action Team 11: Schools Plus (CO); Standards Task Force (DfEE)

Ashwin Mistry Skills Task Force (DfEE)

Sir Nigel Mobbs Construction Task Force (DETR)

Sir Brian Moffatt Construction Task Force (DETR)

Fiona Moir Careers Service Special Needs Task Force (DfEE)

Charles Monaghan Company Law Review Consultative Committee (DTI)

Michael Monaghan Cleaner Vehicles Task Force Main Working Group (DETR)

Stephanie Monk New Deal Task Force (DfEE); Low Pay Commission (DTI)

David Monks Working Party on Electoral Procedures (HO)

John Monks Competitiveness Advisory Group (DTI)

Jack Monro Tourism Forum Business Tourism Working Group (DCMS)

Adrian Montague Urban Task Force Working Group Three (DETR); Chair, Private Finance Task Force (HMT)

Prof. Diane Montgomery Gifted and Talented Children Advisory Group (DfEE)

Michael Montgomery Northern Ireland Strategy for Education Curriculum and Assessment Group (NIO)

Ronnie Moodley Social Exclusion Unit Policy Action Team 9: Community Self-Help (CO)

David Moore Review of Salmon and Freshwater Fisheries (MAFF)

Mavis Moore Chronic Fatigue Syndrome Main Working Group (DH); Chronic Fatigue Syndrome Children's Group (DH)

Peter Moore Tourism Forum (DCMS); Chair, Tourism Forum Human Resources Working Group (DCMS); Tourism Forum Strategic Planning Working Group (DCMS)

Denys Morgan Welsh Transport Advisory Group (WO)

Elenid Morgan Development Awareness Working Group (DFID)

Eluned Morgan MEP National Assembly Advisory Group (WO)

Dr Geoffrey Morgan Review of Health Promotion Arrangements in Wales Steering Group (WO)

Huw Morgan Air Quality Forum (DETR)

Tony Morgan Competitiveness Working Party; Enhancing Business Performance Through Developing Individuals (DTI)

Nalin Morjaria Social Exclusion Unit Policy Action Team 16: Learning Lessons (CO)

L. Morphy National Advisory Group on New Start (DfEE)

Bill Morris New Deal Task Force (DfEE)

Sue Morris Special Educational Needs Working Group on the future role and training of Educational Psychologists (DfEE)

Professor Ivan Morrison Review of Bovine TB in Cattle and Badgers (MAFF)

Stephen Morrison Review of Film Policy Action Committee (DCMS)

Sir Claus Moser Chair, Effective Post-School Basic Skills Provision Working Group (DfEE)

Jill Moss Chronic Fatigue Syndrome Children's Group (DH)

Stephen Moss Tourism Forum (DCMS); Tourism Forum Human Resources Working Group (DCMS); Competitiveness Working Party; Enhancing Business Performance Through Developing Individuals (DTI)

Mervyn Mountjoy Review of Salmon and Freshwater Fisheries (MAFF)

Magnus Mowat Competitiveness Working Party; Increasing Business Investment (DTI); North West Regional Competitiveness Working Party (DTI)

Daniel Muijs Observer, Numeracy Task Force (DfEE)

David Muir Social Exclusion Unit Policy Action Team 11: Schools Plus (CO)

David Muir Cleaner Vehicles Task Force Technology and Testing Subgroup (DETR)

Graham Muir Review of Health Promotion Arrangements in Wales Steering Group (WO)

Raymond Mullan Northern Ireland New Deal Task Force (NIO)

Michael Mulquin Social Exclusion Unit Policy Action Team 15: Information Technology (CO)

Shaun Mundy Social Exclusion Unit Policy Action Team 14: Financial Services (CO)

Hector Munro Export Forum (DTI)

Helen Murlis Competitiveness Working Party; Increasing Business Investment (DTI)

Cllr David Murray NHS Wales Trust Reconfiguration Steering Group (WO)

Cllr Elaine Murray Review of improvement of Skills and Employability for Young People with Special Needs (SO)

Jonathon Murray Cleaner Vehicles Task Force Main Working Group (DETR); Convenor, Cleaner Vehicles Task Force Alternative Fuels Subgroup (DETR)

Dr J.A. Phillips Review of Paediatric Surgical Services in Northern Ireland (NIO)

Tom Phillips Review of the Tote Working Group (HO)

Trevor Phillips Independent Review of the Future of the Royal Opera House Companies and the English National Opera (DCMS); Race Relations Forum (HO)

Rob Phipps Northern Ireland Strategy on Alcohol Misuse Project Team (NIO)

Dr Sian Phipps Welsh Transport Advisory Group (WO)

Rachel Pickavance Race Relations Forum (HO)

Karen Picking NHS Staff Involvement Task Force (DH)

Frank Pignatelli Review of the Improvement of Skills and Employability for Young People with Special Needs (SO)

Alison Pilling Football Task Force (DCMS)

Professor Tony Pinching Chronic Fatigue Syndrome Reference Group (DH)

Adrian Piper TECH Stars Steering Group (DTI)

Bill Pitt Social Exclusion Unit Policy Action Team 8: Anti-Social Behaviour (CO)

David Pitt-Watson Literacy Task Force (DfEE)

Sue Plant Personal Social and Health Education Advisory Group (DfEE)

Denise Platt Social Exclusion Unit Policy Action Team 12: Young People (CO) Disability Rights task Force (DfEE) Strategic review of Health Sevices in London (DH) Youth Justice Task Force (HO)

Mike Platt Tourism Forum Business Tourism Working Group (DCMS)

Nigel Pleming QC Review of the Mental Health Act (DH)

John Plender Company Law Review Steering Group (DTI)

David Pocklington Cleaner Vehicles Task Force Forecourt Emissions Testing Subgroup (DETR)

Stephen Pocklington Air Quality Forum (DETR)

Eve Pollard Tourism Forum (DCMS); Tourism Forum Communications Strategy Working Group (DCMS)

Brian Pomeroy Disability Rights Task Force (DfEE)

Michael Ponton Review of Health Promotion Arrangements in Wales Steering Group (WO)

Anne Poole Wales New Deal Advisory Task Force (WO)

Professor Frederick Pooley Airborne Particles Expert Group (DETR)

Jonathon Porrit Agricultural Advisory Group (MAFF); Tourism Forum Domestic Tourism Working Group: Sustainability Sub-Group (DCMS)

Beth Porter Northern Ireland Strategy for Education Technology Strategic Management Group (NIO); Northern Ireland Strategy for Education Technology Teacher Education Group (NIO)

Dr Alex Porter Advisory Group on Education for Citizenship and Democracy (DfEE)

Dr George Poste Competitiveness Working Party; Encouraging Innovation (DTI)

David Potter Review of Film Policy Film Finance Sub-Group (DCMS)

Liz Potter Social Exclusion Unit Policy Action Team 5: Housing Management (CO)

Don Potts Cleaner Vehicles Task Force Main Working Group (DETR); Cleaner Vehicles Task Force Fleet Purchasing Guidance Subgroup (DETR); Cleaner Vehicles Task Force Information and Labelling Subgroup (DETR)

Dr Anne Powell Review of Salmon and Freshwater Fisheries (MAFF)

Nik Powell Review of Film Policy Export Sub-Group (DCMS)

Richard Powell Private Finance Task Force (HMT)

Professor Anne Power Social Exclusion Unit Policy Action Team 7: Unpopular Housing (CO); Housing Sounding Board (DETR); Urban Task Force (DETR)

Usha Prashar Advisory Group on Education for Citizenship and Democracy (DfEE)

Tom Preece Company Law Review Consultative Committee (DTI)

Vivienne Press Air Quality Forum (DETR)

Adam Price Wales New Deal Advisory Task Force (WO)

Cllr John Price Tourism Forum (DCMS); Tourism Forum Strategic Planning Working Group (DCMS); Chair, Tourism Forum Domestic Tourism Working Group (DCMS)

Sue Price Wales New Deal Advisory Task Force (WO)

Frank Price Air Quality Forum (DETR)

Cllr. Dewi Pritchard NHS Wales Trust Reconfiguration Steering Group (WO)

Andrew Prynne QC Multi-Party Situations Working Group (LCD)

Andrew Puddephatt Human Rights Task Force (HO)

Robert Purry Better Regulation TaskForce (CO)

Lord Puttnam Creative Industries Task Force (DCMS); Standards Task Force (DfEE)

Q

David Quarmby Tourism Forum (DCMS); Chair, Tourism Forum Presentation of Heritage Working Group (DCMS); Tourism Forum Strategic Planning Working Group (DCMS); Panel 2000 Advisory Group (FCO)

David Quysner Working Group on the Financing of High Technology Business (previously, the McCullagh Group) (HMT)

R

Heather Rabbatts Review of Future Funding of the BBC (DCMS); Housing Sounding Board (DETR)

Rosemary Radcliffe Competitiveness Advisory Group (DTI); Competitiveness Working Party; Promoting the Best of Best Practice (DTI); Company Law Review Steering Group (DTI)

John Rafferty Scottish Advisory Task Force on the New Deal (SO)

Peter Rainbird Skills Task Force (DfEE)

Peter Rand Tourism Forum Business Tourism Working Group (DCMS)

Michael Ratcliffe Independent Review of the Future of the Royal Opera House Companies and the English National Opera (DCMS)

Angela Rawson Careers Service Special Needs Task Force (DfEE)

Dr. D. Ray Independent Panel on Gulf Veterans' Illnesses Interactions Research (MoD)

Mike Raycraft Construction Task Force (DETR)

Clare Rayner NHS Charter Advisory Group (DH)

Maria Reader Social Exclusion Unit Policy Action Team 10: Arts and Sport (CO)

Gail Rebuck Creative Industries Task Force (DCMS)

Joyce Redfearn National Assembly Advisory Group (WO)

Karl Redmond Policy Review of the Youth Service, Northern Ireland (NIO)

Bernadine Rees NHS Wales Trust Reconfiguration Steering Group (WO)

Dan Rees Development Awareness Working Group (DFID); Development Awareness Learning from Others Sub-Group (DFID)

John Rees Misuse of Public Office Subgroup (HO)

Helen Reeve Older Volunteers Working Group (HO)

Mike Reeves Careers Service Special Needs Task Force (DfEE)

Richard Regan Working Group on the Financing of High Technology Business (previously, the McCullagh Group) (HMT)

Peter Reichardt Music Industry Forum (DCMS)

Ann Reid Air Quality Forum (DETR)

H. Reid Regional Review of Adult Cardiology Services in Northern Ireland (NIO)

Keith Reid Cleaner Vehicles Task Force Alternative Fuels Subgroup (DETR)

Brian Reilly Review of Film Policy Training and Education Sub-Group (DCMS)

C. Reindorp National Advisory Group on New Start (DfEE)

Lorna Reith Disability Benefits Forum (DSS)

Uriah Rennie Football Task Force Working Group (DCMS)

Professor David Reynolds Literacy Task Force (DfEE); Chair, Numeracy Task Force (DfEE)

Mike Reynolds Task Force on Alternatives to Tobacco Sponsorship (DCMS)

Teresa Reynolds Youth Justice Task Force (HO)

Rupert Rhymes Tourism Forum (DCMS)

Dr Chris Richards Chronic Fatigue Syndrome Reference Group (DH)

Charles Rice Fundamental Review of Transport Policy (DETR)

Susan Rice Social Exclusion Unit Policy Action Team 14: Financial Services (CO)

Sir Tim Rice Music Industry Forum (DCMS)

Gill Richards Wales New Deal Advisory Task Force (WO)

Professor Roy Richards Airborne Particles Expert Group (DETR)

Sam Richards Urban Task Force Working Group Two (DETR)

Dr G. Richardson Regional Review of Adult Cardiology Services in Northern Ireland (NIO)

Prof. Genevra Richardson Head, Review of the Mental Health Act (DH)

Prof. Sheila Riddell Chair, Advisory Committee on the Co-ordination and Provision of Education for Severe Low Incidence Disabilities (SO)

Tony Ridley Urban Task Force Working Group One (DETR)

Richard Rieser National Advisory Group on Special Educational Needs (DfEE)

Kate Ripley Special Educational Needs Working Group on Provision of Speech and Language Therapy Services (DfEE)

Stewart Ritchie Pension Provision Group (DSS)

Caroline Roaf Special Educational Needs Working Group on the future role and training of Educational Psychologists (DfEE)

Graham Robb Advisory Group on Education for Citizenship and Democracy (DfEE)

Dr Brynley Roberts Education and Training Action Group (WO)

Professor Sir Gareth Roberts Competitiveness Working Party; Encouraging Innovation (DTI); Yorkshire and Humberside Regional Competitiveness Working Party (DTI)

Dr Glynne Roberts Review of Health Promotion Arrangements in Wales Steering Group (WO)

Hugh Roberts Cleaner Vehicles Task Force Main Working Group (DETR)

John Roberts New Deal Task Force (DfEE)

Michael Roberts Fundamental Review of Transport Policy (DETR)

Rhoslyn Roberts Pensions Education Working Group (DSS)

Anne Robertson Education and Training Action Group (WO)

Esther Robertson Scottish Parliament all-party Consultative Steering Group (SO)

Andrew Robinson Social Exclusion Unit Policy Action Team 3: Business (CO)

Ann Robinson Company Law Review Consultative Committee (DTI)

Bruce Robinson Fundamental Review of the Economic Development Strategy in Northern Ireland (NIO)

Carol Robinson Numeracy Task Force (DfEE)

Dickon Robinson Urban Task Force Working Group Two (DETR)

Ian Robinson Chair, Scottish Advisory Task Force on the New Deal (SO)

Ken Robinson Tourism Forum (DCMS); Chair, Tourism Forum Whitehall Issues Working Group (DCMS); Tourism Forum Visitor Attractions Working Group (DCMS); Tourism Forum Strategic Planning Working Group (DCMS)

Prof. Kenneth Robinson Chair, Creative and Cultural Education National Advisory Committee (DfEE)

Tony Robinson Development Awareness Working Group (DFID)

Prof. Brian Robson Urban Task Force Working Group Three (DETR)

Professor Christopher Robson Numeracy Task Force (DfEE)

Jennifer Robson Tourism Forum (DCMS)

Lord Rogers Chair, Urban Task Force (DETR)

Sheila Rogers Equality Commission Working Group (NIO)

Tony Rogers Tourism Forum Business Tourism Working Group (DCMS)

Jim Rose Advisory Group on Raising Ethnic Minority Pupil Achievement (DfEE)

John Rose Competitiveness Working Party; Increasing Business Investment (DTI)

Avril Ross Dewar Scottish Advisory Task Force on the New Deal (SO)

Tom Ross Chair, Pension Provision Group (DSS); Chair, Review of Pensions (DSS)

Sue Roulstone Special Educational Needs Working Group on Provision of Speech and Language Therapy Services (DfEE)

Dr Alison Round Chronic Fatigue Syndrome Main Working Group (DH)

John Routledge Housing Sounding Board (DETR)

Rosalind Rowe Urban Task Force Working Group Three (DETR)

Iain Roxburgh New Deal Task Force Advisory Group (DfEE); Skills Task Force (DfEE)

Ken Rushton Company Law Review Consultative Committee (DTI)

Dr C. Russell Regional Review of Adult Cardiology Services in Northern Ireland (NIO)

Janet Russell Better Regulation Task Force (CO)

Norman Russell Working Party on Legal Deposit (DCMS)

Dr Philippa Russell Disability Rights Task Force (DfEE); National Advisory Group on Special Educational Needs (DfEE)

Judith Rutherford New Deal Task Force Advisory Group (DfEE)

Dr Ian Rutter NHS Efficiency Task Force (DH)

Jonathan Rutter Review of Film Policy Export Sub-Group (DCMS)

Liz Ryan Clinical Negligence Working Group (LCD)

Dr T. Ryan Review of Services for Acutely Ill Children (NIO)

S

Haroon Saad Social Exclusion Unit Policy Action Team 2: Skills (CO)

John Sacher Interchange Steering Council (CO)

Iqbal Sacranie Race Relations Forum (HO)

Shahwar Sadeque Panel 2000 Advisory Group (FCO)

Roy Sainsbury Disability Benefits Forum (DSS)

Valerie Saint Review of the Public Analyst Arrangements Service in England and Wales (MAFF)

Eric Salama Creative Industries Task Force (DCMS)

J Salmon All Wales Agri-Environment Scheme Working Group (WO)

Margaret Salmon University for Industry Design and Implementation Advisory Group (DfEE)

Steven Salmon Air Quality Forum (DETR)

Alex Salmond MP Scottish Parliament all-party Consultative Steering Group (SO)

Peter Salsbury Better Regulation Task Force (CO)

Tessa Sambrook Special Educational Needs Working Group on Provision of Speech and Language Therapy Services (DfEE)

Georges Sampeur Tourism Forum Business Tourism Working Group (DCMS)

Marc Samuelson Review of Film Policy Action Committee (DCMS); Review of Film Policy Training and Education Sub-Group (DCMS)

Sir Sydney Samuelson Review of Film Policy Inward Investment Sub-Group (DCMS)

Martin Sandbach Tourism Forum Visitor Attractions Working Group (DCMS); Tourism Forum Domestic Tourism Working Group: Distribution Sub-Group (DCMS)

Bryan Sanderson Competitiveness Advisory Group (DTI); Competitiveness Working Party; Enhancing Business Performance Through Developing Individuals (DTI); Company Law Review Steering Group (DTI) Clinical Negligence Working Group (LCD)

Jonathan Sands Competitiveness Working Party; Encouraging Innovation (DTI); Yorkshire and Humberside Regional Competitiveness Working Party (DTI)

William Sargent Competitiveness Working Party; Making the Most of the Information Age (DTI)

John Saunders Competitiveness Working Party; Promoting the Best of Best Practice (DTI); West Midlands Regional Competitiveness Working Party (DTI)

Liz Sayce Disability Rights Task Force (DfEE)

Dennis Scard Music Industry Forum (DCMS)

Dr. G. Schild Independent Panel on Gulf Veterans' Illnesses Interactions Research (MoD)

Tom Schuller Social Exclusion Unit Policy Action Team 2: Skills (CO)

Ann Scott Tourism Forum Communications Strategy Working Group (DCMS)

Ridley Scott Review of Film Policy Review Group (DCMS); Review of Film Policy Action Committee (DCMS); Review of Film Policy Inward Investment Sub-Group (DCMS)

Sharon Scott Social Exclusion Unit Policy Action Team 9: Community Self-Help (CO)

Susan Scott-Parker Disability Rights Task Force (DfEE)

Valerie Scoular New Deal Task Force (DfEE)

David Seal Review of Health Promotion Arrangements in Wales Steering Group (WO)

Harry Seaton Social Exclusion Unit Policy Action Team 7: Unpopular Housing (CO)

Prof. Sedgwick Independent Panel on Gulf Veterans' Illnesses Interactions Research (MoD)

Richard Segal Review of Film Policy Review Group (DCMS); Review of Film Policy Action Committee (DCMS); Review of Film Policy Achieving 20% Market Share Sub-Group (DCMS)

Joanne Segars Pension Provision Group (DSS); Pensions Education Working Group (DSS)

Anthony Sell Tourism Forum (DCMS); Tourism Forum Business Tourism Working Group (DCMS); Tourism Forum Presentation of Heritage Working Group (DCMS)

Paul Sellers Older Volunteers Working Group (HO)

Ric Senat Review of Film Policy Action Committee (DCMS); Review of Film Policy Inward Investment Sub-Group (DCMS)

John Senior Gifted and Talented Children Advisory Group (DfEE)

Dan Sequerra Competitiveness Working Party; Encouraging Innovation (DTI); Yorkshire and Humberside Regional Competitiveness Working Party (DTI)

Professor Herbert Sewell Review of the Current Rules on Quarantine of Imported Pet Animals (MAFF)

Jenny Shackleton New Deal Task Force (DfEE)

Caroline Shah Social Exclusion Unit Policy Action Team 3: Business (CO)

Nuala Shannon Regional Review of Adult Cardiology Services in Northern Ireland (NIO)

Professor Joanna Shapland Independent Assessor, Review of Criminal Justice (NIO)

Dr P. Sharkey Regional Review of Adult Cardiology Services in Northern Ireland (NIO)

Sawtantar Sharma Review of Film Policy Film Finance Sub-Group (DCMS)

J. Sharman National Advisory Group on New Start (DfEE)

Rowie Shaw Advisory Group on Raising Ethnic Minority Pupil Achievement (DfEE); Review of the Bureaucratic Burden on Teachers (DfEE)

Professor Clifford Shearing Independent Commission on Policing Northern Ireland (NIO)

Tom Shebbeare New Deal Task Force (DfEE)

David Sheepshanks Football Task Force (DCMS)

Jim Sheils Welsh Transport Advisory Group (WO)

David Shelton Coalfields Task Force (DETR)

Dr Charles Shepherd Chronic Fatigue Syndrome Main Working Group (DH)

Clive Sherling Review of the List of Nationally Important Sporting Events Which Must Be Made Available on Free-to-Air Terrestrial TV Channels (DCMS); Company Law Review Consultative Committee (DTI)

Dr David Shiers Review of the Mental Health Act (DH)

Cherry Short Wales New Deal Advisory Task Force (WO)

Dominic Shorthouse Competitiveness Working Party; Increasing Business Investment (DTI)

Helena Shovelton Better Regulation TaskForce (CO)

Professor Alan Silman Review of the Evidence relating to Silicon Breast Implants (DH); Independent Panel on Gulf Veterans' Illnesses Interactions Research (MoD)

Arnold Simanowitz Clinical Negligence Working Group (LCD)

Martin Sime Scottish Advisory Task Force on the New Deal (SO)

Howard Simmons Social Exclusion Unit Policy Action Team 9: Community Self-Help (CO)

Marie Simmons Chronic Fatigue Syndrome Reference Group (DH)

Joanna Simons Social Exclusion Unit Policy Action Team 6: Neighbourhood Wardens (CO)

Joe Simpson Older Volunteers Working Group (HO)

John Simpson Northern Ireland Strategy for Education Technology Strategic Management Group (NIO)

Judy Simpson Panel 2000 Advisory Group (FCO)

Karen Simpson Policy Review of the Youth Service, Northern Ireland (NIO)

Lindsey Simpson Review of the Role of TECs (DfEE)

Nicola Simpson People's Panel Advisory Group (CO)

Dr Anne Sims Further Education Student Support Advisory Group (DfEE)

Alan Sinclair New Deal Task Force Advisory Group (DfEE); Scottish Advisory Task Force on the New Deal (SO)

Peter Sinclair Interchange Steering Council (CO)

Scott Sinclair Development Awareness Working Group (DFID); Development Awareness Formal/Informal Structures Sub-Group (DFID)

Jon Singer Cleaner Vehicles Task Force Alternative Fuels Subgroup (DETR)

Anil Singh Social Exclusion Unit Policy Action Team 5: Housing Management (CO)

Gurbux Singh Race Relations Forum (HO)

Ray Singh National Assembly Advisory Group (WO)

Michael Skapinker Tourism Forum Business Tourism Working Group (DCMS)

Fiona Skinner Competitiveness Working Party; Promoting the Best of Best Practice (DTI); East Midlands Regional Competitiveness Working Party (DTI)

Sue Skinner Pensions Education Working Group (DSS)

Brian Slater Special Educational Needs Working Group on Provision of Speech and Language Therapy Services (DfEE)

Sue Slipman Better Regulation Task Force (CO)

Professor John Sloane Review of the Evidence relating to Silicon Breast Implants (DH)

Teresa Smallbone Cleaner Vehicles Task Force Main Working Group (DETR); Cleaner Vehicles Task Force Information and Labelling Subgroup (DETR)

Dr Alan Smith Working Group on Integrated Education (NIO)

Baroness Smith Review of Film Policy Achieving 20% Market Share Sub-Group (DCMS)

Dela Smith National Advisory Group on Special Educational Needs (DfEE)
Geoff Smith Working Party on Legal Deposit (DCMS)
Graham Smith Waiting List Action Team (DH); Chair, Trent Regional Task Force to support the Waiting List Action Team (DH)
Sir John Smith Football Task Force Working Group (DCMS); Independent Commission on Policing Northern Ireland (NIO)
Jon Smith Task Force on Alternatives to Tobacco Sponsorship (DCMS)
Sir Joseph Smith Review of the Current Rules on Quarantine of Imported Pet Animals (MAFF)
Kevin Smith Smart Procurement Partnerships Group (MoD)
Kingsley Smith Coalfields Task Force (DETR)
Malcolm Smith Review of the Improvement of Skills and Employability for Young People with Special Needs (SO)
Matt Smith Commission on Local Government and Scottish Parliament (SO)
Dr Michael Smith Careers Service Special Needs Task Force (DfEE)
Mike Smith Working Group on the Financing of High Technology Business (previously, the McCullagh Group) (HMT)
Pam Smith NHS Staff Involvement Task Force (DH)
Patricia Smith Chronic Fatigue Syndrome Main Working Group (DH)
Paul Smith Creative Industries Task Force (DCMS)
Peter Smith Advisory Group on Raising Ethnic Minority Pupil Achievement (DfEE); Development Awareness Working Group (DFID) ?
Peter Smith Competitiveness Working Party; Enhancing Business Performance Through Developing Individuals (DTI); North West Regional Competitiveness Working Party (DTI)
Peter Smith QC Independent Commission on Policing Northern Ireland (NIO)
Sir Roland Smith Football Task Force Working Group (DCMS)
Tom Smith Oil and Gas Industry Task Force (DTI)
Joan Smyth Equality Commission Working Group (NIO)
J. Snaith National Advisory Group on New Start (DfEE)
Jon Snow Development Awareness Working Group (DFID); Development Awareness Themes and Partnerships Sub-Group (DFID)
Christine Soden Working Group on the Financing of High Technology Business (previously, the McCullagh Group) (HMT)
Anne Sofer Advisory Group on Raising Ethnic Minority Pupil Achievement (DfEE)
Ranjit Sondhi Disability Rights Task Force (DfEE); Race Relations Forum (HO)
John Sorrel Panel 2000 Advisory Group (FCO)
John Sorrell Competitiveness Working Party; Encouraging Innovation (DTI)
Martin Sorrell Panel 2000 Advisory Group (FCO)
Hugh South Advisory Group on Raising Ethnic Minority Pupil Achievement (DfEE)
Eleanor Spalding Review of the Improvement of Skills and Employability for Young People with Special Needs (SO)
Les Sparks Urban Task Force Working Group Two (DETR)
Ian Spatling National Assembly Advisory Group (WO)
Dr Nigel Speight Chronic Fatigue Syndrome Children's Group (DH)
Christopher Spence Older Volunteers Working Group (HO)
James Spencer Tourism Forum (DCMS); Tourism Forum Whitehall Issues Working Group (DCMS); Tourism Forum Domestic Tourism Working Group: Quality Sub-Group (DCMS)
Sarah Spencer Human Rights Task Force (HO)
Susan Spencer Social Exclusion Unit Policy Action Team 14: Financial Services (CO)
Dr Anne Stafford Expert Panel on Sex Offending (SO)
Christine Stanley Older Volunteers Working Group (HO)
John Stanley Older Volunteers Working Group (HO)
Peter Stansbie NHS Wales Trust Reconfiguration Steering Group (WO)
Tabitha Stebbings Air Quality Forum (DETR)
John Stedman Airborne Particles Expert Group (DETR)
Geoff Steeley Social Exclusion Unit Policy Action Team 13: Shops (CO)
Max Steinberg Social Exclusion Unit Policy Action Team 7: Unpopular Housing (CO)
Cob Stenham University for Industry Design and Implementation Advisory Group (DfEE); Competitiveness Advisory Group (DTI); Competitiveness Working Party; Promoting the Best of Best Practice (DTI)
John Stephenson Education and Training Action Group (WO)
M. Stephenson National Advisory Group on New Start (DfEE)
Paul Sterling Cleaner Vehicles Task Force Alternative Fuels Subgroup (DETR)
Anthony Stern Business Advisory Group on European Monetary Union (DTI)
Alan Stevens Chair, Information Technology Skills Group
Sir Jocelyn Stevens Tourism Forum Presentation of Heritage Working Group (DCMS)
John Stevens Social Exclusion Unit Policy Action Team 17: Joining It Up Locally (CO)
Hugh Stevenson Working Group on the Financing of High Technology Business (previously, the McCullagh Group) (HMT)
Wilf Stevenson Review of Film Policy Review Group (DCMS); Review of Film Policy Action Committee (DCMS); Review of Film Policy Broadening the Audience Sub-Group (DCMS); University for Industry Design and Implementation Advisory Group (DfEE)
Dr D. Stewart Regional Review of Adult Cardiology Services in Northern Ireland (NIO)
Dr Lynda Stewart NHS Staff Involvement Task Force (DH)
Dr M.C. Stewart Review of Services for Acutely Ill Children (NIO)

Murray Stewart Social Exclusion Unit Policy Action Team 17: Joining It Up Locally (CO)
Nigel Stewart Working Party on Electoral Procedures (HO)
Hugh Stirk NHS Staff Involvement Task Force (DH)
W.J.I Stirling Review of Paediatric Surgical Services in Northern Ireland (NIO)
Rob Stoker Special Educational Needs Working Group on the future role and training of Educational Psychologists (DfEE)
Dr Richard Stone Race Relations Forum (HO)
F. Stoner National Advisory Group on New Start (DfEE)
Dr Michael Stopper Gifted and Talented Children Advisory Group (DfEE)
James Strachan Disability Rights Task Force (DfEE); Disability Benefits Forum (DSS)
Anita Straker Numeracy Task Force (DfEE)
Phil Street Social Exclusion Unit Policy Action Team 11: Schools Plus (CO)
Richard Street Social Exclusion Unit Policy Action Team 3: Business (CO)
Jim Stretton Scottish Advisory Task Force on the New Deal (SO)
Dr Joan Stringer Chair, Equality Commission Working Group (NIO); Scottish Parliament all-party Consultative Steering Group (SO)
Tony Struthers Urban Task Force Working Group Two (DETR)
John Stubbs Cleaner Vehicles Task Force Technology and Testing Subgroup (DETR)
Sukhvinder Stubbs Social Exclusion Unit Policy Action Team 17: Joining It Up Locally (CO); Deputy-Chair, Advisory Group on Raising Ethnic Minority Pupil Achievement (DfEE)
Sharon Studer Skills Task Force (DfEE)
Professor Roger Sturrock Chair, Review of the Evidence relating to Silicon Breast Implants (DH)
Colin Stutt Clinical Negligence Working Group (LCD); Multi-Party Situations Working Group (LCD)
Carolyn Sumberg Older Volunteers Working Group (HO)
Robert Sumerling Clinical Negligence Working Group (LCD)
Diane Summers Tourism Forum Communications Strategy Working Group (DCMS)
L. Surgenor Review of Services for Acutely Ill Children (NIO)
Douglas Sutherland Private Finance Task Force (HMT)
John Sutton Development Awareness Formal/Informal Structures Sub-Group (DFID)
Phillip Swan Tourism Forum (DCMS)
Professor Peter Swann Competitiveness Working Party; Making the Most of the Information Age (DTI); North West Regional Competitiveness Working Party (DTI)
Dr B. Sweeney Regional Review of Adult Cardiology Services in Northern Ireland (NIO)
Ed Sweeney Better Regulation TaskForce (CO)
Kate Sweeney Chronic Fatigue Syndrome Reference Group (DH)
Tim Sweeney Business Advisory Group on European Monetary Union (DTI)
Chris Swinson Company Law Review Consultative Committee (DTI)
Sir Richard Sykes QC Competitiveness Advisory Group (DTI); Company Law Review Steering Group (DTI)
Roger Sykes Social Exclusion Unit Policy Action Team 18: Better Information (CO)
Lindy Syson Careers Service Special Needs Task Force (DfEE)

T

Simon Taggart Air Quality Forum (DETR)
Museji Takolia Social Exclusion Unit Policy Action Team 3: Business (CO)
Marianne Talbot Advisory Group on Education for Citizenship and Democracy (DfEE)
Dr Nick Tate Standards Task Force (DfEE)
Suzanna Taverner Competitiveness Working Party; Making the Most of the Information Age (DTI)
Andy Taylor Social Exclusion Unit Policy Action Team 18: Better Information (CO)
Bob Taylor Tourism Forum (DCMS)
Gordon Taylor Football Task Force (DCMS)
Hugh Taylor Chair, NHS Staff Involvement Task Force (DH)
Keith Taylor Cleaner Vehicles Task Force (DETR)
Malcolm Taylor Competitiveness Working Party; Increasing Business Investment (DTI); East Midlands Regional Competitiveness Working Party (DTI)
Margaret Taylor Review of Film Policy Broadening the Audience Sub-Group (DCMS)
Marilyn Taylor Social Exclusion Unit Policy Action Team 13: Shops (CO)
Martin Taylor Lead, Review of Tax and Benefits (HMT)
Michael Taylor Tourism Forum Presentation of Heritage Working Group (DCMS)
Pamela Taylor Football Task Force Working Group (DCMS)
Peter Taylor Tourism Forum Widening Access to Tourism Working Group (DCMS)
Dr R. Taylor Review of Paediatric Surgical Services in Northern Ireland (NIO)
Rogan Taylor Football Task Force (DCMS)
Ron Taylor Export Forum (DTI)
Barry Tears Gifted and Talented Children Advisory Group (DfEE)
Dr A.M. Telford Review of Services for Acutely Ill Children (NIO); Review of Paediatric Surgical Services in Northern Ireland (NIO)
David Thomas Tourism Forum (DCMS)

Janette Weir Business Advisory Group on European Monetary Union (DTI)

Peter Welch University for Industry Design and Implementation Advisory Group (DfEE)

Sharon Welch Social Exclusion Unit Policy Action Team 1: Jobs (CO)

Cecilia Wells Competitiveness Working Party; Enhancing Business Performance Through Developing Individuals (DTI); Eastern Region Regional Competitiveness Working Party (DTI)

G. Wells Regional Review of Adult Cardiology Services in Northern Ireland (NIO)

Howard Wells Tourism Forum (DCMS)

Pauline Wells Tourism Forum Human Resources Working Group (DCMS)

Ian Welsh Prestwick Task Force (SO)

Keith Welton Disability Rights Task Force (DfEE)

Michael Wemms New Deal Task Force (DfEE)

Professor Simon Wessely Chronic Fatigue Syndrome Reference Group (DH)

Will Wesson Social Exclusion Unit Policy Action Team 4: Neighbourhood Management (CO)

Alison West Social Exclusion Unit Policy Action Team 9: Community Self-Help (CO)

John Westaway Sustainable Development Education Panel (DETR); Development Awareness Working Group (DFID)

Rose Wheeler Social Exclusion Unit Policy Action Team 17: Joining It Up Locally (CO)

Angela Whitcher Older Volunteers Working Group (HO)

Dr Peter White Chronic Fatigue Syndrome Main Working Group (DH)

Phil White Tourism Forum Widening Access to Tourism Working Group (DCMS)

Tracey White Prestwick Task Force (SO)

Dr Tom White Expert Panel on Sex Offending (SO)

Dr Margaret Whitehead Review of the Latest Information Available on Inequalities in Health (DH)

Tim Whitehead Tourism Forum Domestic Tourism Working Group: Sustainability Sub-Group (DCMS)

Damien Whitmore Tourism Forum Presentation of Heritage Working Group (DCMS)

Julian Whybra Gifted and Talented Children Advisory Group (DfEE)

Stuart Whyte Social Exclusion Unit Policy Action Team 6: Neighbourhood Wardens (CO)

Geoffrey Wicks Youth Justice Task Force (HO)

Angela Wigley Cleaner Vehicles Task Force Alternative Fuels Subgroup (DETR)

Steve Wilcox Housing Sounding Board (DETR)

Paul Wiles Social Exclusion Unit Policy Action Team 11: Schools Plus (CO)

John Wilkinson Northern Ireland Strategy for Education Technology Strategic Management Group (NIO); Northern Ireland Strategy for Education Curriculum and Assessment Group (NIO)

Eifion Williams NHS Wales Trust Reconfiguration Steering Group (WO)

Gwenda Williams Education and Training Action Group (WO); Competitiveness Working Party; Enhancing Business Performance Through Developing Individuals (DTI)

Howard Williams New Deal Task Force Advisory Group (DfEE)

Dr Jeff Williams NHS Wales Trust Reconfiguration Steering Group (WO)

John Williams Review of Salmon and Freshwater Fisheries (MAFF)

Kirsty Williams National Assembly Advisory Group (WO)

Lynn Williams Competitiveness Working Party; Promoting the Best of Best Practice (DTI)

Madeleine Williams Working Party on Electoral Procedures (HO)

Dr Peter Williams Working Group on the Financing of High Technology Business (previously, the McCullagh Group) (HMT)

Simon Williams Company Law Review Consultative Committee (DTI)

T. Williams National Advisory Group on New Start (DfEE)

Tom Williams Prestwick Task Force (SO)

Andrew Williamson Youth Justice Task Force (HO)

Howard Williamson Social Exclusion Unit Policy Action Team 12: Young People (CO)

Tim Williamson Air Quality Forum (DETR)

Dr C. Wilson Regional Review of Adult Cardiology Services in Northern Ireland (NIO)

Des Wilson Tourism Forum (DCMS)

Mike Wilson Special Educational Needs Working Group on the future role and training of Educational Psychologists (DfEE)

Miles Wilson Sustainable Development Education Panel (DETR)

Monica Wilson Disability Rights Task Force (DfEE)

Peter Wilson Social Exclusion Unit Policy Action Team 12: Young People (CO)

Eileen Wimbury Older Volunteers Working Group (HO)

Dr Adrian Winbow Chronic Fatigue Syndrome Reference Group (DH)

Marlene Winfield Multi-Party Situations Working Group (LCD)

Dr David Winkley Advisory Group on Independent/State School Partnerships (DfEE); Standards Task Force (DfEE); Gifted and Talented Children Advisory Group (DfEE)

Rob Wirszycz Business Advisory Group on European Monetary Union (DTI)

Keith Wiseman Football Task Force (DCMS)

Vanessa Wiseman Social Exclusion Unit Policy Action Team 11: Schools Plus (CO); National Advisory Group on Special Educational Needs (DfEE); Special Educational Needs Working Group on Provision of Speech and Language Therapy Services (DfEE)

Anne Wood Pension Provision Group (DSS)

Charles Wood Social Exclusion Unit Policy Action Team 9: Community Self-Help (CO)

David Wood Tourism Forum (DCMS); Tourism Forum Human Resources Working Group (DCMS)

Sir Ian Wood Oil and Gas Industry Task Force (DTI)

Richard Wood Disability Rights Task Force (DfEE); Disability Benefits Forum (DSS)

Rt Rev Wilfred Wood Race Relations Forum (HO)

Chris Woodcock New Deal Task Force Advisory Group (DfEE)

Dr Rosie Woodroffe Review of Bovine TB in Cattle and Badgers (MAFF)

Lucy Woods Independent Commission on Policing Northern Ireland (NIO)

John Woodward Review of Film Policy Action Committee (DCMS); Review of Film Policy Inward Investment Sub-Group (DCMS)

Shelagh Wooliscroft New Deal Task Force Advisory Group (DfEE)

Janice Woolley Review of Arrangements for Confiscation of Criminal Assets (HO)

David Worskett Welsh Transport Advisory Group (WO)

Richard Worsley Older Volunteers Working Group (HO)

Andy Worthington Social Exclusion Unit Policy Action Team 10: Arts and Sport (CO)

Jenny Wostrack Social Exclusion Unit Policy Action Team 10: Arts and Sport (CO)

Dr Andrew Wright Chronic Fatigue Syndrome Reference Group (DH)

Diane Wright Literacy Task Force (DfEE)

Joe Wright Chair, Review of the District Councils' Community Service Programme Advisory Group (NIO)

Canon Kenyon Wright Scottish Parliament all-party Consultative Steering Group (SO)

Tom Wylie National Advisory Group on New Start (DfEE); Sustainable Development Education Panel (DETR); Development Awareness Working Group (DFID)

XYZ

Patricia Yates Tourism Forum (DCMS); Tourism Forum Visitor Attractions Working Group (DCMS); Tourism Forum Domestic Tourism Working Group: Quality Sub-Group (DCMS)

Wendy Yates Wales New Deal Advisory Task Force (WO)

David Yeandle Pension Provision Group (DSS)

Geoffrey Yeowart Business Advisory Group on European Monetary Union (DTI)

Alex Youel Tourism Forum Domestic Tourism Working Group: Sustainability Sub-Group (DCMS)

Baroness Young of Old Scone Agricultural Advisory Group (MAFF)

Raymond Young Scottish Advisory Task Force on the New Deal (SO)

Susan Young Community Fire Safety Task Force (HO)

Tony Young Competitiveness Working Party; Making the Most of the Information Age (DTI)

Viscount Younger Prestwick Task Force (SO)

Jeanette York Social Exclusion Unit Policy Action Team 8: Anti-Social Behaviour (CO)

Sue Yoxall Social Exclusion Unit Policy Action Team 6: Neighbourhood Wardens (CO)

Annette Zera Effective Post-School Basic Skills Provision Working Group (DfEE); Further Education Student Support Advisory Group (DfEE)

Tricia Zipfel Social Exclusion Unit Policy Action Team 4: Neighbourhood Management (CO)

Roger Zogolovitch Urban Task Force Working Group One (DETR)

Sir Jack Zunz Urban Task Force Working Group One (DETR)

TASK FORCES, POLICY REVIEWS AND OTHER ADVISORY BODIES

This index contains all listed external task forces and other policy groups, their sub-groups and internal policy reviews.   Entries appear in alphabetical order under the full official name for each body. Some sub-groups should be looked up under the title of their main group.

RULING BY TASK FORCE